In the Collected Studies Series;

DOROTHY WHITELOCK
From Bede to Alfred

RAYMONDE FOREVILLE
Thomas Becket dans la tradition historique et hagiographique

RAYMONDE FOREVILLE
Gouvernement et vie de l'Eglise au Moyen-Age

PAUL MEYVAERT
Benedict, Gregory, Bede and Others

W. H. C. FREND
Town and Country in the Early Christian Centuries

W. H. C. FREND
Religion Popular and Unpopular in the Early Christian Centuries

KARL FERDINAND WERNER
Structures politiques du monde franc (VIe-XIIe siècles)

PHILIP GRIERSON
Dark Age Numismatics

PHILIP GRIERSON
Later Medieval Numismatics (11th-16th Centuries)

ARCHIBALD R. LEWIS
The Sea and Medieval Civilizations

JEAN GAUDEMET
La société ecclésiastique dans l'Occident médiéval

GILES CONSTABLE
Religious Life and Thought (11th-12th Centuries)

BRIAN TIERNEY
Church Law and Constitutional Thought in the Middle Ages

WALTER ULLMANN
Scholarship and Politics in the Middle Ages

WALTER ULLMANN
The Church and the Law in the Earlier Middle Ages

WALTER ULLMANN
The Papacy and Political Ideas in the Middle Ages

History, Law and Literature in 10th-11th Century England

B. Gaye

Professor Dorothy Whitelock

Dorothy Whitelock

History, Law and Literature in 10th-11th Century England

VARIORUM REPRINTS
London 1981

British Library CIP data

Whitelock, Dorothy
History, law and literature in 10th-11th century England. – (Collected studies series; CS128).
1. Great Britain – History – Anglo-Saxon period, 449-1066
2. Great Britain – History – Norman period, 1066-1154
I. Title II. Series
942.01 DA152

ISBN 0-86078-074-0

Published in Great Britain by Variorum Reprints
20 Pembridge Mews London W11 3EQ

Printed in Great Britain by Galliard (Printers) Ltd,
Great Yarmouth, Norfolk

VARIORUM REPRINT CS128

CONTENTS

This volume contains a total of 368 pages

FOREWORD

Apart from the first two items, which concern the Anglo-Saxon period as a whole, the contents of this volume of my collected papers deal with the post-Alfredian period, Nos. III to VI being mainly historical studies, VII to XVI studies on the authors after the Benedictine revival, and XVII a linguistic study with historical implications. As in the previous volume, *From Bede to Alfred. Studies in Early Anglo-Saxon Literature and History*, the items are reproduced as first published, except for some Addenda on later developments. My thanks are due to the editors and publishers named on the list of contents for the permission to reproduce these works, willingly granted and often with good wishes for the success of the volume, and also to Variorum Reprints for including it in their series.

DOROTHY WHITELOCK

Cambridge
August 1980

I

CHANGING CURRENTS IN ANGLO-SAXON STUDIES

THIS Chair was founded in 1878 for the promotion of the study of the Anglo-Saxon language and the languages cognate therewith, together with the antiquities and history of the Anglo-Saxons, by the will of the Rev. Dr Joseph Bosworth, Rawlinson Professor of Anglo-Saxon in the University of Oxford. I have had three distinguished predecessors and in no small measure do I owe my presence here to two of them: to Professor Chadwick, who trained me and aroused in me what has proved a lifelong interest in these studies; to Professor Dickins, who has given me help and inspiration for over a quarter of a century. I am conscious that my range is narrower than theirs, and than that of WalterSkeat, the great pioneer who was the first holder of this Chair. Wide though the objects of this Chair are, all my predecessors have produced expert work in other fields, whereas I must confine myself to Anglo-Saxon studies.

In Joseph Bosworth's will, first place is given to the study of the Anglo-Saxon language—naturally so, since this is the gateway to the appreciation of an extensive and interesting literature, and is also essential to the correct interpretation of important historical sources, and to an understanding of the later history of the English language. But it is clear that Bosworth did not wish to found a Chair of linguistics alone, but rather one of Anglo-Saxon civilisation. In following him, I am in effect repeating what Professor Chadwick impressed on many generations of his pupils. Hence it seems fitting to attempt in this lecture a survey of the outstanding developments in my time over the whole range of Anglo-Saxon studies, a survey which will illustrate their interdependence. This is a temerarious undertaking, since, with the great increase of specialisation in the last thirty years or so, there are inevitably large areas in which I am not an active participant in the work, but merely an interested spectator. Great developments have occurred on all fronts, and in the time at my disposal I shall be able to refer expressly to only a fraction of the contributions which have advanced knowledge. As I considered these in their hundreds during the last few weeks, I could not help recalling with a somewhat wry amusement how, when Professor Chadwick suggested that I should undertake research, I was afraid that before I could get going there would be nothing left to do.

The developments have been mainly in one direction: towards a fuller appreciation of the greatness of Anglo-Saxon civilisation, a realisation of its influence abroad, and an increased knowledge of the extent of its survival beyond the Norman Conquest.

Round about 1930, it was not uncommon to read in general histories remarks of the following kind: 'Saxon civilisation...deserved and was bound to fall. A universal and slovenly individualism, without restraint, without discipline, without education, and without effectual contact with Continental civilisation, was not even capable of self defence.'[1] One may contrast this with a statement in a history, intended for the general public, of 1949: 'It was a people rich in intellectual achievement, firm in faith, and very closely assimilated to the Latin Christian culture of western Europe, which came under Norman rule at the Battle of Hastings.'[2]

There were, of course, admirers of the Anglo-Saxons from the earliest days of historical study, and similar opposing views to those I have quoted could be collected from writers long before the period I am concerned with today,[3] the adverse view being particularly common in relation to the last age of pre-Conquest England. Apart from irrational prejudices on both sides, the adverse view is ultimately based on the statements of Norman and Anglo-Norman writers, or, for earlier periods of Saxon history, on the complaints of Anglo-Saxon ecclesiastics; the favourable view depends mainly on the concrete evidence of surviving records and objects. The striking thing is how in the present generation the detailed studies of historians, archaeologists, students of art and literature, palaeographers, students of charters and coins, have converged in bringing together an ever-increasing mass of evidence which has placed the favourable view beyond the reach of controversy.

Before proceeding to consider the outstanding results of work in various branches, I wish to mention a few important works of a general nature, which can justly be said to indicate changing currents in Anglo-Saxon studies. In 1932 R. W. Chambers powerfully attacked the myth of Saxon decadence in *On the Continuity of English Prose from Alfred to More and his School*,[4] and showed that the Norman Conquest caused no break in the development of English prose. In 1933 S. J. Crawford's *Anglo-Saxon Influence on Western Christendom*, published posthumously, made clear the far-reaching effect of the Anglo-Saxon mission on the relations between the Frankish rulers and the Papacy, and the strength of the Anglo-Saxon influence on learning and art on the Continent in the eighth century, as well as the role played by the Anglo-Saxons in preserving and transmitting classical culture. Further evidence in the same direction was supplied by W. Levison in *England and the Continent in the Eighth Century* in 1946, and additions continue to be made.

In 1936 there appeared Professor Darlington's article 'Ecclesiastical Reform in the Late Old English period'.[5] Its importance is clearly seen if we note that as great a scholar as Zachary Brooke could pronounce in 1931: 'The bishops were mostly uneducated and secularised, the lower clergy hopelessly ignorant; ecclesiastical synods and ecclesiastical law had fallen into disuse...simony, clerical marriage, and other abuses attacked by the reformers went on as a matter of course.'[6] But since Professor Darlington assembled the evidence relating to the late Anglo-Saxon Church, sweeping condemnations of this kind have ceased to be made in informed quarters. In fact, it is the pro-Norman party which is on the defensive; last year there appeared an article in which Professor Douglas claims that something can be said in defence of the pre-1066 bishops of the duchy of Normandy.[7] The wheel has come full circle.

The year 1943 was a great one for Anglo-Saxon scholarship, for in it Sir Frank Stenton's *Anglo-Saxon England* appeared.[8] In this Sir Frank brought together the results of his many earlier contributions to Anglo-Saxon history, together with much that was new; and, by the complete, balanced and convincing picture of Anglo-Saxon society which he provided, he surely gave the death-blow to accusations of sloth, stupidity, incompetence and barbarity levelled at the Anglo-Saxons. It is to this book that one must attribute the almost universal acceptance nowadays of an appreciative view of Anglo-Saxon civilisation. It rendered many other services, too many to enumerate. Of outstanding importance is its treatment of the Scandinavian element in English society.

Sir Frank was singularly well equipped to pronounce on this topic, by his early studies on the Domesday Survey of the Danelaw counties, by his unrivalled knowledge of the post-Conquest charters of this area, and as a leading place-name scholar. He would agree with me that it is the new material provided by the study of place-names, especially of field-names, which has been the main factor in a revolutionary reassessment of the density and nature of the Scandinavian settlement, proving that it 'had the dimensions of a migration'. The evidence of personal names supports this view, as will become clearer when more use is made of numismatic material and of unpublished records. The *Liber Vitae* of Thorney Abbey, for example, includes a large number of Scandinavian names.[9] Doubts have recently been expressed regarding the strength of Scandinavian influence in East Anglia, and no final decision can be made until the place-name material has been published and the personal names further studied. But the linguistic evidence should also be reckoned with. When, in spite of the general use of the West Saxon literary *koine* in the tenth and eleventh centuries, East Anglian documents not only use Scandinavian words,[10] but retain the Old Norse distinction between a singular *ære* (O.N. *eyrir*) and a plural *ore* (O.N. *aurar*),[11] one must postulate more than a slight and fleeting influence from this quarter. The fact that the thegn Thurstan gave property in Norfolk to his wife *to mund and to maldage*,[12] a phrase which occurs in Scandinavian law-codes, gives strong support to those twelfth-century writers who include East Anglia in the area under Danish law.

This conception of the density of the Danish settlement has provided the proper background for studying the Scandinavian influence on laws and institutions, especially since my re-dating of the so-called 'Laws of Edward and Guthrum' has removed one difficulty by allowing time for the development.[13] It has also explained much in the political history of the tenth and eleventh centuries, including King Edgar's attitude to the Danelaw. The greater importance now attached to the Scandinavian element in Anglo-Saxon art, which we owe largely to the work of Sir Thomas Kendrick,[14] is in agreement with this view of the nature of the settlement.

Place-name studies have supplied important material on many other matters. It is pleasant to note how big a share in these studies has been borne by Cambridge. Walter Skeat, the first holder of this Chair, was a leading pioneer; Sir Allen Mawer, who founded the English Place-Name Society, and was its Director for many years, was a pupil of Professor Chadwick; while Professor Dickins rendered the Society inestimable services long before he became its Director. Under his direction it issued some of its most distinguished volumes. Moreover, the late Dr Anna Paues, a distinguished linguistic scholar of Newnham College, to whose teaching I owe an enormous debt, was a helpful member of its first council.

There is no need for me to enlarge on the historical value of place-name evidence in relation to the problems of the English invasion, to Anglo-Saxon paganism, to social conditions, since it was abundantly demonstrated in Sir Frank Stenton's presidential addresses to the Royal Historical Society, 1939–43.[15] Material from this source is important for linguistic studies also. In regard to these, I am concerned only with those that serve a practical purpose, by the help they afford in the interpretation, dating and localisation of the written remains, and in the identification of place-names and personal names. An important trend of late years has been the re-examination of the basis for dating certain Anglo-Saxon developments, necessitated in part by advances in palaeography, and best represented by the careful and exact notes scattered through the works of Dr K. Sisam. A more reliable localisation of dialect features is being made possible by place-name evidence and by an improved knowledge of Middle English dialects. Numismatic evidence, at present little utilised, may help both with dating and localisation, and more use could be made of charters. More work is needed on personal names. What these can teach us was shown in 1937 by Dr von Feilitzen's excellent work on *The Pre-Conquest Personal Names of Domesday Book*.

When one turns from linguistics to literary studies, it is of course impossible to list all the improved editions, or the numerous studies which have deepened our appreciation. One change of direction has been towards scepticism as to the value of statistical tests in dating Anglo-Saxon poetry.

Another—which we owe to the common sense of Dr Sisam—is the abandonment of some unprofitable lines of speculation, such as on the identity of the poet Cynewulf or of the person who took the Vercelli Codex abroad.[16] The same scholar has taught what may be learnt by properly scrutinising a manuscript (e.g. the Exeter Book, the *Beowulf* MS., the MSS. of Ælfric's *Catholic Homilies*), and how an apparently hopeless tangle like that of the royal genealogies can be unravelled by patient investigation.[17] An important development is the shift of interest away from attempts to find pagan and heroic poetry behind some extant poems to an appreciative study of these in their own right. The heroic element was given its full mead of appreciation by W. P. Ker[18] and Professor Chadwick, whose *Heroic Age*[19] remains the classic work on the subject. It is now the turn of the religious element.

The older viewpoint, represented, for example, by Henry Bradley, who regarded the Christian passages in *Beowulf* as interpolations and 'poetically of no value',[20] was strongly opposed by Chambers in 1921,[21] while Professor Tolkien's British Academy lecture in 1936, '*Beowulf*: the Monsters and the Critics', has been influential in encouraging investigation in a new direction. Nor should one forget the work of distinguished foreign scholars like F. Klaeber,[22] L. L. Schücking[23] and A. Bonjour.[24] A similar drift away from a belief in a 'monkish scribe' who added a veneer of conventional Christianity to older poetry is apparent in a number of studies of *The Wanderer* and *The Seafarer*.[25] In my opinion, the assimilation of Christian ideas into a Germanic context, and their clothing in the traditional poetic diction, is one of the most moving features of Old English poetry. *Beowulf*, for example, would to me not be nearly so great and effective a poem if the poet had not chosen to introduce the song of Creation near the beginning, and to remind us, by constant and surely deliberate references later on, that the universe is God's, that the sun, 'clothed [like God in Ps. ciii. 2] in light', is 'the bright beacon of God', that it is God 'who loosens the bonds of the frost', God 'who has control of times and seasons'; in short, that behind the terrors of the monsters, born of the seed of Cain, who inhabit lone places, there is a divinely created and stable universe. To combat primitive fears of the natural universe seems to me a main theme among the many skilfully woven together in this many-stranded poem. The plot of the poem is not, as Chambers said it was in 1912,[26] 'a childish story'.

In regard to prose literature, most advance is with the later prose, whose variety and high quality were demonstrated by Chambers in 'On the Continuity of English Prose' in 1932. Articles by Dr Sisam in 1931–3 shed great light on the aims and methods of Ælfric.[27] More work is needed on this author, and much is already in progress, including an edition of unpublished homilies and one of the oldest manuscripts of his *Catholic Homilies*. Work is being done also on anonymous unpublished homilies. But the chief contribution of recent times in Anglo-Saxon prose studies is the virtual creation of the figure of Archbishop Wulfstan of York. From being regarded mainly as the author of a gloomy jeremiad, to whose name a number of spurious writings had happened to be attached, he is now seen as a scholar learned in continental ecclesiastical writings, a prolific author, a great stylist, and an outstanding political personage, to whom, before all others, we may reasonably give the credit for turning the young Cnut into a Christian monarch, and thus preventing the Danish Conquest of the eleventh century from being a sheer disaster to Anglo-Saxon civilisation. The series of studies which established Wulfstan's reputation began in 1923, when Karl Jost recognised his style in parts of the Anglo-Saxon Chronicle;[28] but this attracted little attention, and it was not until the 30's and 40's of this century that work by Jost, Dr Bethurum and myself won for Wulfstan his proper place.[29] Now, with Jost's important *Wulfstanstudien* of 1950, Dr Bethurum's edition of the genuine homilies,[30] and J. M. Ure's edition of the *Benedictine Office*,[31] both of which appeared in 1957, the only big desideratum is the edition of the *Institutes of Polity*, on which Jost has long been engaged. This emergence of Wulfstan from comparative obscurity is a remarkable example of the interrelation of Anglo-Saxon studies, for literary considerations, using stylistic criteria, have given to historians an important figure only dimly glimpsed in historical records.

Work on Wulfstan is responsible for the main advance in relation to the Anglo-Saxon laws, involving the re-dating of some codes, for his influence can be seen in the drafting of most of Ethelred's codes and of those of Cnut. Apart from this, and from Dr Sisam's demolition of the theory that Lambarde used a lost manuscript,[32] Liebermann's great edition of the laws stands uncontested. Wulfstan has invaded Chronicle studies also, for the detection of his style in the northern recension supports other evidence for York as the probable home of this. Charles Plummer's edition of the Anglo-Saxon Chronicle remains the basis of all later work, and many of his conclusions are still valid. But it suffers from the limitations that beset the work of a pioneer, even as great a pioneer as Plummer. He missed the importance of the Latin chronicler Æthelweard, which was demonstrated by Sir Frank Stenton in 1925.[33] Of wider significance is Plummer's failure to pay due attention to the minutiae of textual criticism. Hence his scheme of manuscript relationship takes no account of certain minor agreements between manuscripts C and D. If this clue is followed up, it seems to me to remove the necessity of postulating an early split of the northern recension into two versions; and with this, the evidence that a manuscript of the Chronicle reached the North in, or soon after, Alfred's reign vanishes, and the evidence for an official circulation of continuations at intervals in the tenth century becomes very slender.[34] There are some features of the transmission of the Chronicle in the eleventh century which remain obscure, but I hope they may be unravelled by further study.

An example of the converging of evidence of various types occurred when Mr Neil Ker recognised that many marginal entries, glosses and other additions to works which we were assigning to Wulfstan on stylistic grounds, and in manuscripts whose contents led us to connect them with him, were all written in the same handwriting, presumably that of Wulfstan himself, or of a secretary in close connexion with him.[35] This is only one of the innumerable services rendered to literary and historical studies by palaeographers, in notes, articles and introductions to editions. I must confine myself here to mentioning the wonderful corpus produced last year by Mr Ker, his *Catalogue of Manuscripts containing Anglo-Saxon*, which describes and dates all manuscripts which have any Anglo-Saxon, even a mere scrap or gloss. It affords impressive evidence of the sheer bulk of Anglo-Saxon writings. Particular attention should be given to the evidence it contains for the continued writing of Anglo-Saxon and use of pre-Conquest manuscripts long after the Norman Conquest, and for the movement of manuscripts across the Channel in both directions, which helps to discredit old views that Anglo-Saxon England was cut off from the intellectual life of Europe. The imported manuscripts, and many of those written in England, contain Latin works. Many manuscripts, whether produced at home or abroad, lie outside the scope of Mr Ker's catalogue, because they contain no Anglo-Saxon at all. A full list of these would be of great interest for the history of Latin scholarship in Anglo-Saxon times, especially if it were combined with a list of works known to Anglo-Saxon authors, a list which is increasing as more work is done on sources.[36] Such a work would be especially valuable for the later Saxon period. We know more about this aspect of the earlier period, where we have the help of E. A. Lowe's *Codices Latini antiquiores*.[37] which lists manuscripts prior to the ninth century, and of J. D. A. Ogilvy's *Books known to Anglo-Latin Writers from Aldhelm to Alcuin (670–804)*.[38] The knowledge of Latin works revealed by Anglo-Saxon poets should not be neglected.

From palaeography one naturally passes to manuscript illumination, for studies in this field, by continental and English scholars, similarly show the movement of manuscripts into and out of Anglo-Saxon England. They show also that there was a give and take in styles of illumination. The great influence of the insular style on the Continent as a result of the missionary activities of the seventh and eighth centuries has long been realised, and further examples keep coming to light. An appreciation of the strength of Anglo-Saxon influence abroad in the later Saxon period is of more recent origin, as is a recognition of the extent to which this style survived the Norman Conquest of England. Special mention must be made of three works by Professor Wormald: 'Decorated Initials in English MSS. from A.D. 900 to 1100', read to the Society of Antiquaries in 1941, 'The Survival of Anglo-Saxon Illumination after the Norman Conquest', read to the British Academy in 1944, and *English Drawings of the Tenth and Eleventh Centuries*, published in 1952. These works establish beyond doubt the continuance right on into the early twelfth century of the Anglo-Saxon style in initial ornament and outline drawing. Dr O. Pächt has shown that the Anglo-Saxon features in some of the Carilef manuscripts at Durham cannot be adduced in support of this continuance, since there is evidence for their production on the Continent.[39] But this means that they provide examples of the influence of Anglo-Saxon art across the Channel. Professor Wormald has demonstrated that this influence is clear in some centres, such as St Bertin's at St Omer and St Vaast at Arras, already by the end of the tenth century, while its strength in Norman houses in the second half of the eleventh century is being increasingly realised, as is shown, for example, in the work of Dr Dodwell.[40] The progress that has been made in establishing this influence is perhaps best shown by Professor Wormald's quiet little remark in the photographic reproduction of the Bayeux Tapestry published last year: '...the identification of its place of origin is much handicapped by the fact that both English and Norman MSS. of the second half of the eleventh century were deeply indebted to the great Anglo-Saxon school of illumination which had flourished in the second half of the tenth and in the first half of the eleventh centuries.'[41] This magnificent reproduction of the Bayeux Tapestry, which includes a definitive chapter on 'Style and Design' by Professor Wormald, is among the outstanding contributions of this generation to Saxon studies. It has been a great period for facsimiles also, with the Caedmon MS. in 1927, the Exeter Book in 1933, the Parker Chronicle and Laws in 1941, and the Lindisfarne Gospels in 1956; while under the general editorship of Dr Colgrave the series of *Early English Manuscripts in Facsimile*, which is being produced in Copenhagen, has lived up to its promise and issued a facsimile of an important manuscript each year from 1951 to 1957.[42]

The outstanding work on architecture in this period is Sir Alfred Clapham's *English Romanesque Architecture before the Norman Conquest*, which appeared in 1930, and gave a fuller picture than had previously been presented. Among other things, it produced evidence for a connexion with the Rhineland in the late Saxon period, and it showed how much could be gathered from literary sources about the larger churches of this age, not one of which has survived. It included a cogent defence of the then controversial dating of the great sculptured crosses of the North in the seventh and eighth centuries. This dating, supported by later writers, such as Dr Saxl in his illuminating article on the iconography of the Ruthwell cross,[43] is now accepted. But a proper appraisal of the southern school of sculpture of the tenth and eleventh centuries is hampered by the disagreement among experts as to the date of several fine specimens, e.g. the Barnack Majesty, the Daglingworth slabs, the Langford and Romsey roods, the York Madonna. With Sir Alfred Clapham,[44] Mr S. Casson[45] and Mr Talbot Rice[46] in favour of a pre-Conquest date, and Sir Thomas Kendrick[47] claiming all and Dr Saxl[48] some of them for the twelfth century, a layman may well hesitate to express an opinion. Yet has any effective answer been made to Sir Alfred Clapham's arguments for the earlier dating which were largely based on the architectural history of the pieces concerned? As regards the much fought over Chichester panels, the twelfth-century side seems, with Mr Zarnecki's study of them in 1952,[49] to be winning.

When one turns to archaeology certain spectacular discoveries leap to one's mind. Sutton Hoo made us revise our conceptions of the wealth of a seventh-century royal family, and vindicated the *Beowulf* poet from any charge of exaggeration in his references to treasure. Since it can be dated, as Mr Grierson has convincingly shown, between 650 and 660,[50] it has raised in an acute form the whole question of the relationship between Christianity and paganism in mid-seventh-century England. Of equal interest to *Beowulf* scholars is the excavation at Yeavering, since it provides the first archaeological evidence of impressive halls in which life could be lived nobly, as in the poem. Thirdly, there is what has been called 'a classic piece of field work', Sir Cyril Fox's survey of Offa's Dyke. His results, published year by year between 1926 and 1934, were embodied in 1955 in a handsome volume issued by the British Academy. This survey proved the Dyke to have been the concept of a single mind, and its construction possible only to a nation with great economic resources as well as previous experience of building large earthworks, governed by a ruler in unquestioned control of the Midlands. The Dyke thus became one of the factors which enabled Sir Frank Stenton to demonstrate the full significance of the 'bretwaldaship' and the greatness of Mercia, especially under Offa, the other factors being the evidence from coins and charters.

Though less impressive than these discoveries, the excavation of newly discovered cemeteries and of village sites, together with studies on the objects in our museums, such as those of Dr Leeds on brooches,[51] Dr Harden on glass,[52] and Dr Myres on pottery,[53] are bringing together a mass of evidence to bear on the problems of the English invasion, and on the intercourse with the Continent or between various parts of England in heathen times. Yet, in view of the inevitable lack of precision of typological dating, historians must not expect an exact picture from archaeological evidence alone. One development, largely owing to Mr T. C. Lethbridge's excavations at Burwell and Shudy Camps,[54] is the realisation that the conversion to Christianity did not instantly stop the burial of goods with the dead. Dr Myres's detailed comparison of the decorated pottery in England with that found on the Continent allows some firm conclusions as to the area from which the invaders came. What is more important is its confirmation of other evidence that there was a mass settlement of the Anglo-Saxons in the southern and eastern parts of Britain. The Romano-British influence is so slight that Dr Myres speaks of it as 'a faint and flickering continuance'. Thus the ceramic evidence supports Bede's statement that the homeland of the Angles was left deserted, a statement presumably approved by King Ceolwulf, to whose criticism Bede submitted his book, and confirmed also by the archaeology of this part of Denmark.[55] It is difficult to envisage the settlers as a small military caste, ruling a large population of subject Britons. A mass immigration of the English into Britain allows an unforced explanation of the rarity of British loanwords in Anglo-Saxon, even relating to activities which would be the domain of a subject population, and accounts also for the purely Teutonic nature of Anglo-Saxon institutions. The whole question of the nature and extent of pre-English influence on the Anglo-Saxons was examined with great thoroughness and sound sense by Mr R. Lennard in 1938,[56] and in my opinion nothing has since come to light to invalidate his conclusions that this influence was slight. In some quarters nowadays the pendulum seems to have swung too far from the discredited belief in the total extermination of the Britons in the south and east to an exaggerated view of their survival in large numbers. Though a slight British strain in the personal names, especially in Northumbria, is evidence for a certain amount of intermarriage, its importance can be overstressed. Caedmon bore a name of British extraction, but he composed poetry in the old Germanic style, as presumably did his comrades, ordinary peasant folk, at the gatherings he attended.

Knowledge of Christian antiquities advances steadily. The town sites of *Hamwih* and Thetford are being excavated,[57] and the latter place is now known to have carried on industries on a considerable scale, in iron and bronze work, and especially in pottery. The existence of glazed pottery of Anglo-Saxon date was unsuspected until comparatively recently.[58] More objects of the Christian period are being discovered, or are being recognised among the material in our museums, and on the Continent as well. Objects taken over by the Anglo-Saxon missionaries exerted so strong an influence that Dr Haseloff in his study of the Tassilo cup has recently claimed: 'Wide spheres of continental art-development must be regarded as an insular province of art in the eighth century.'[59] All that is in dispute in the long controversy over this magnificent chalice is whether it was made in England, or is a product of English influence on the Continent. Dr Haseloff takes the latter view, and has conveniently collected examples of English influence in the Rhineland, Bavaria, Frisia, Middle Germany and Scandinavia.

Among works on the Christian antiquities, mention must be made of the definitive study of the relics of St Cuthbert, a co-operative performance by a panel of experts,[60] and of Mr Bruce-Mitford's article on the late Saxon disc-brooches, which has added a fine specimen to the list of Anglo-Saxon works of art by his defence of the Fuller brooch.[61] It is a great advantage that objects of the Christian period are sometimes found in hoards which can be dated by coin evidence, such as the important Trewhiddle hoard. In an interesting paper on this hoard, read last November by Mr C. E. Blunt and Mr D. M. Wilson to the Society of Antiquaries, the desirability of a corpus of objects of the Christian period was stressed. This would be welcome, and would include many lovely things;[62] yet it would give an incomplete idea of the artistic richness of this age. The chances of survival of objects in precious metal are poor, and a corpus would need to be supplemented by the evidence of written records before anything like a true picture could be given.

The great value of numismatic evidence was realised by Professor Chadwick. Since his time, much new material has come to light. Particularly important for the early period is the work of Mr P. Grierson, which will necessitate a reconsideration of the wergild system, and for the later period the examination which Mr R. H. M. Dolley is making of the enormous number of Anglo-Saxon coins in Swedish museums. As for new finds, the greatest discovery for over a century was made only a month ago, near Norwich, and by the kindness of Mr Dolley I can touch briefly on its historical significance. It can be dated 924/925, and it shows that Edward the Elder established a mint, presumably at Norwich, very soon after his recovery of East Anglia from the Danes in 917, and thus it supplies additional evidence of the speed with which that amazingly competent king worked. The sixteen coins of York issues between about 900 and 915 indicate intercourse between the East Anglian Danes and those of South Northumbria, but the absence of any later Northumbrian coin suggests that the intercourse was broken by the capture of the kingdom of York by the Norsemen from Ireland about 919.

Numismatic evidence has vindicated the chronology established by Murray L. R. Beaven for the tenth-century kings of York,[63] and it has proved that Roger of Wendover had access to reliable material when he attributed a reform of the coinage to Edgar.[64] Moreover, it illustrates Anglo-Saxon influence on the Continent, for English coins were widely copied in Scandinavia, and recent evidence shows that they were sometimes imitated by the papal coinage, and in Switzerland, South Italy, Bohemia and Poland.[65] Much material has never yet been brought into any general survey of the Old English coinage. Many points of detail are still to be ascertained. But it can already be seen that the Anglo-Saxons of the age before the Conquest possessed a managed currency, which, if all other evidence were lacking, would prove the administrative efficiency of the late Old English government. The Norman kings continued the existing system.

In 1955 the British Academy set up a committee with Sir Frank Stenton as its Chairman for the systematic publication of the coins of the British Isles, and the first volume of its sylloge, dealing with the Ancient British and Anglo-Saxon coins in the Fitzwilliam Museum, edited by Mr Grierson, is now in press.

The respect now accorded Anglo-Saxon administration does not depend on numismatic evidence alone. Sir Frank Stenton has written of the system of taxation which the Norman kings took over from their Saxon predecessors, that 'as a piece of large-scale financial organization, it has no parallel in the Dark Ages'.[66] Much administrative skill was required for the tenth-century reorganisation of the Midlands into shires and hundreds, when the kings of Wessex had become rulers of all England and were faced with the problem of enforcing some measure of uniformity. The system of local government which they created survived the Norman Conquest. In the same century one can glimpse a political experiment, a search for stable frontiers and friendly relations with Celtic neighbours. Thus Edgar ceded Lothian to Kenneth of the Scots; and on the borders of Wales, where Offa had built a dyke and the Normans were to build their castles, the tenth-century code known as the *Dunsæte* survives as a witness to an attempt to ensure peaceful terms with one's neighbours by more civilised means. Edgar's permitting of local autonomy to the Northern Danelaw is another instance of enlightened and humane rule. We know less of the tenth-century kings than we know of King Alfred, but there is enough to suggest that some of his descendants inherited a good share of his qualities as a ruler.

The fertility of the Anglo-Saxon mind in inventing practical expedients in government was brought home to us by the appearance in 1952 of Dr Florence Harmer's excellent edition of *Anglo-Saxon Writs*. The importance of the writ was summed up by Sir Frank Stenton in 1955: 'It is one of the ironies of English history that the Anglo-Saxons, who have continually been blamed for their ineffectiveness in practical administration, should have devised the most efficient means of publishing the ruler's will which western Europe had so far known.'[67]

With the publication of Dr Harmer's writs, most of the vernacular documents are now available in modern editions, a circumstance largely owing to the vision of Professor Chadwick, who set his pupils to this work. The position is different with regard to the Latin charters, and a plea for a new corpus to replace Kemble's *Codex Diplomaticus Aevi Saxonici* has frequently been raised. No one will question its desirability, but no one who has read Sir Frank Stenton's illuminating study on *The Latin Charters of the Anglo-Saxon Period* will underestimate the formidable nature of such an undertaking. The documents need to be studied in their local background, but much is to be gained also from a study of them cartulary by cartulary. When a new Kemble eventually appears, it will have profited by a delay which allows use to be made of the local studies which are being produced.[68] The delay has had less serious consequences for English history than it would have had if Sir Frank Stenton's *Anglo-Saxon England* had not been based on an exhaustive knowledge of these documents; and now, in his book on the *Latin Charters*, he has given his general conclusions, based on a lifetime's study, and has written, as it were, an advance introduction to the 'Kemble' of the future. Yet the lack of such a work is a handicap to workers in many fields. It will require a co-operative effort to fill this gap, for it demands historical, linguistic, diplomatic and palaeographical knowledge, in all cases reaching beyond the Anglo-Saxon period, and the services of local historians and of historical geographers will be needed.

Anglo-Saxon studies are very much alive today;

and the Anglo-Saxons are worth study. They produced a vernacular literature centuries before most modern races of Europe. Their civilisation is of more than local interest. They carried Christianity to the Germans and Scandinavians, and, as we have seen, this was by no means their only contribution to European civilisation. Evidence that much of their civilisation survived the Norman Conquest is steadily being accumulated. Yet I do not wish to imply that nothing of importance happened in 1066. The Anglo-Saxon achievement will stand in its own right without any belittling of that of the Normans. It may be as well to end a lecture in praise of the Anglo-Saxons by quoting a recent comment in praise of the Normans. Professor Knowles used these words in 1954: 'Alike in the political, the economic and the religious spheres the Normans effected a revolution unique in English history, and yet at the same time they preserved, used and developed much that was native to England. They showed, indeed, a genius for strong and intelligent rule, devoid of any overruling policy of racial aggrandisement, which must be almost unique in Western history.'[69] That the Normans are now being commended as much for what they kept as for what they brought may perhaps be the main result of a generation of Anglo-Saxon studies.

NOTES

1. E. Wingfield-Stratford, *The History of British Civilisation* (2nd ed. London, 1930), p. 118.

2. Douglas Jerrold, *An Introduction to the History of England from the Earliest Times to 1204* (London, 1949), p. 352.

3. See D. C. Douglas, *The Norman Conquest and British Historians* (David Murray Foundation Lecture, Glasgow, 1946).

4. Introduction to *Nicholas Harpsfield's Life of Sir Thomas More*, ed. E. V. Hitchcock and R. W. Chambers (E.E.T.S., 1932); also issued separately.

5. *English Historical Review*, LI, 385–428.

6. *The English Church and the Papacy from the Conquest to the Reign of John* (Cambridge, 1931), pp. 47 f.

7. 'The Norman Episcopate before the Norman Conquest', *Cambridge Historical Journal*, XIII (1957), 101–15.

8. *The Oxford History of England*, vol. II (1943; 2nd ed. 1947).

9. 'Scandinavian Personal Names in the *Liber Vitae* of Thorney Abbey', *Saga-Book of the Viking Society*, XII (1940), 127–53.

10. E.g. *toft*, *Anglo-Saxon Wills*, ed. D. Whitelock, p. 68, ll. 4, 6, etc., *tuft*, p. 80, l. 8, p. 82, l. 14, *felage*, p. 80, l. 27, *turfgret*, p. 86, l. 19, *lisingar*, p. 92, l. 11; *sceppe*, *Anglo-Saxon Charters*, ed. A. J. Robertson, p. 192, ll. 15, 18, *scora*, p. 196, ll. 15, 17. Most interesting is the document printed from a Bury manuscript, *ibid.* p. 252, which, besides retaining the Old Norse declension of 'ore', gives directions for the celebration of the testator's *fyrræ ærflæ*, 'first funeral feast', in which *fyrræ* represents Old Norse *fyrre*, and *ærflæ* Old Norse *erfi-öl*, and also of his *hoþær hærflæ*, 'second funeral feast'. It should be noted also how the Bury registers about 1300 turn the Anglo-Saxon *circe* of their exemplars into *kirke*.

11. E.g. Robertson, *op. cit.* p. 252, l. 3 *twa ore* and *an ære*. See previous note.

12. Whitelock, *op. cit.* p. 82, l. 6.

13. 'Wulfstan and the so-called Laws of Edward and Guthrum', *English Historical Review*, LVI (1941), 1–21.

14. *Late Saxon and Viking Art* (London, 1949).

15. *Transactions of the Royal Historical Society*, 4th series, xxi–xxv.

16. *Studies in the History of Old English Literature* (Oxford, 1953).

17. 'Anglo-Saxon Royal Genealogies', *Proceedings of the British Academy*, XXXIX (1953), 287–348.

18. *Epic and Romance* (London, 1897).

19. Cambridge, 1912.

20. *Encyclopædia Britannica* (11th ed. 1910–11), III, 760.

21. *Beowulf: An Introduction* (1st ed. Cambridge, 1921).

22. *Beowulf and the Fight at Finnsburg* (1st ed. Boston, 1922), pp. xlviii–lii.

23. 'Wann enstand der Beowulf? Glossen, Zweifel und Fragen', *Beiträge zur Geschichte der deutschen Sprache und Literatur*, XLII (1917), 347–410.

24. *The Digressions in* Beowulf (Medium Ævum Monographs V, Oxford, 1950).

25. E.g. O. S. Anderson, *The Seafarer: An Interpretation* (K. Humanistiska Vetenskapssamfundets i Lund Årsberättelse, 1937–8); B. F. Huppé, '*The Wanderer*: Theme and Structure', *Journal of English and Germanic Philology*, XLII (1943), 516–38; R. M. Lumiansky, 'The Dramatic Structure of the Old English *Wanderer*', *Neophilogus*, XXXIV (1950), 104–12; D. Whitelock, 'The Interpretation of *The Seafarer*', *The Early Cultures of North-West Europe* (H. M. Chadwick Memorial Studies, Cambridge, 1950), pp. 259–72; S. B. Greenfield, '*The Wanderer*: A Reconsideration of Theme and Structure', *Journal of English and Germanic Philology*, L (1951), 451–65; I. L. Gordon, 'Traditional Themes in *The Wanderer* and *The Seafarer*', *Review of English Studies*, new series, V (1954), 1–13; S. B. Greenfield, 'Attitudes and Values in *The Seafarer*', *Studies in Philology*, LI (1954), 15–20; E. G. Stanley, 'Old English Poetic Diction and the Interpretation of *The Wanderer, The Seafarer* and *The Penitent's Prayer*', *Anglia*, LXXIII (1955), 413–66; J. E. Cross, '"Ubi sunt" Passages in Old English —Sources and Relationships', *Vetenskaps-Societetens i Lund Årsbok* (1956), 25–41.

26. *Widsith*, ed. R. W. Chambers (Cambridge, 1912), p. 181.

27. *Review of English Studies*, VII–IX, reissued in *Studies in the History of Old English Literature* (1953), pp. 148–98.

28. 'Wulfstan und die angelsächsische Chronik', *Anglia*, XLVII, 105–23.

29. See bibliography on pp. 56–8 of *Sermo Lupi ad Anglos*, ed. D. Whitelock (2nd ed. London, 1952).

30. *The Homilies of Wulfstan* (Oxford, 1957).

31. *The Benedictine Office: An Old English Text* (Edinburgh, 1957).

32. *Modern Language Review*, XVIII (1923), 100 ff.; XX (1925), 253 ff., reissued in *Studies in the History of Old English Literature*, pp. 232–58.

33. 'The South-Western Element in the Old English Chronicle', *Essays in Medieval History presented to T. F. Tout*, pp. 15–24. A modern edition of Æthelweard is being prepared by Mr A. Campbell.

34. See *The Peterborough Chronicle*, ed. D. Whitelock (Early English Manuscripts in Facsimile, IV, Copenhagen, 1954), pp. 28 f.

35. 'Hemming's Cartulary', *Studies in Medieval History presented to F. M. Powicke* (Oxford, 1948), pp. 70 f.

36. Note, for example, the number of Latin works used by Frithegod and Wulfstan the Precentor, as revealed in the edition by A. Campbell, *Frithegodi Monachi Breuiloquium Vitæ Beati Wilfredi et Wulfstani Cantoris Narratio Metrica de Sancto Swithuno* (Zürich, 1950).

37. Oxford, 1934–56. Seven parts have already appeared.

38. Cambridge, Mass., 1936. See also M. L. W. Laistner, 'The Library of the Venerable Bede', *Bede: his Life, Times, and Writings*, ed. A. Hamilton Thompson (Oxford, 1935), pp. 237–66, and W. Levison, 'Bede as Historian', *ibid.* pp. 111–51; B. Colgrave, *Felix's Life of Saint Guthlac* (Cambridge, 1956), pp. 16–18.

39. *Bodleian Library Record*, III (1950), 96–103.

40. *The Canterbury School of Illumination, 1066–1200* (1954); 'Un manuscrit enluminé de Jumièges au British Museum', *Jumièges: Congrès scientifique du XIIIe Centenaire, Rouen, 10–12 Juin, 1954* (Rouen, 1955), II, 737–41.

41. *The Bayeux Tapestry* (Phaidon Press, London, 1957), p. 30.

42. The volumes which have appeared are: I, *The Thorkelin Transcripts of Beowulf*, ed. by Kemp Malone; II, *The Leningrad Bede*, ed. by O. Arngart; III, *The Tollemache Orosius*, ed. by A. Campbell; IV, *The Peterborough Chronicle*, ed. by D. Whitelock: V, *Bald's Leechbook*, ed. by C. E. Wright; VI, *The Pastoral Care*, ed. by N. R. Ker; VII, *Textus Roffensis*, part I, ed. by P. Sawyer.

43. *Journal of the Warburg and Courtauld Institutes*, VI (1943), 1–19.

44. 'The York Virgin and its Date', *Archaeological Journal*, CV (1950), 6–13; 'Some Disputed Examples of Pre-Conquest Sculpture', *Antiquity*, XXV (1951), 191–5.

45. 'Byzantinism', *Burlington Magazine*, LIX (1931), 208–13; 'Byzantium and Anglo-Saxon Sculpture', *ibid.* LXI (1932), 265–74, LXII (1933), 26–36.

46. *English Art, 871–1100* (Oxford, 1952), pp. 7, 25, 100 f., 104, 114–21.

47. *Late Saxon and Viking Art* (London, 1949), pp. 48–52, 146.

48. F. Saxl and R. Wittkower, *British Art and the Mediterranean* (O.U.P. 1948), p. 27 (York Madonna and Langford Rood); F. Saxl, *English Sculptures of the Twelfth Century*, ed. by Hanns Swarzenski (London, 1954), pp. 23–32, 70 (York Madonna).

49. 'The Chichester Reliefs', *Archaeological Journal*, CX (1954), 106–19, a paper read in 1952.

50. 'The Dating of the Sutton Hoo Coins', *Antiquity*, XXVI (1952), 83–6.

51. 'The Distribution of the Angles and Saxons Archaeologically Considered', *Archaeologia*, XCI (1945), 1–106; *A Corpus of Early Anglo-Saxon Great Square-Headed Brooches* (Oxford, 1949).

52. 'Glass Vessels in Britain and Ireland, A.D. 400–1000', *Dark Age Britain* (Studies presented to E. T. Leeds, London, 1956), pp. 132–67.

53. 'Three Styles of Decoration on Anglo-Saxon Pottery', *Antiquaries Journal*, XVII (1937), 424–37; 'Some Anglo-Saxon Potters', *Antiquity*, XI (1937), 389–99; 'The Anglo-Saxon Pottery of Norfolk', *Norfolk Archaeology*, XXVII (1941), 185–214;

'Some English Parallels to the Anglo-Saxon Pottery of Holland and Belgium in the Migration Period', *L'Antiquité classique*, XVII (1948), 453–72; 'The Anglo-Saxon Pottery from Elkington', *Archaeological Journal*, CVIII (1952), 60–4; 'The Anglo-Saxon Pottery of Lincolnshire', *ibid.* 65–99; 'Romano-Saxon Pottery', *Dark Age Britain*, 16–39.

54. 'The Anglo-Saxon Cemetery, Burwell, Cambs.', *Proceedings of the Cambridge Antiquarian Society*, XXVII (1926), 72–9; XXVIII (1927), 116–23; XXIX (1928), 84–94; XXX (1929), 97–109; 'Recent Excavations in Anglo-Saxon Cemeteries in Cambridgeshire and Suffolk', *Cambridge Antiquarian Society Quarto Publications*, new series III (1931); 'A Cemetery at Shudy Camps, Cambs.', *ibid.* new series V (1936).

55. E. T. Leeds, 'Denmark and Early England', *Antiquaries Journal*, XXVI (1946), 29 f.; H. Jankuhn, 'The Continental Home of the English', *Antiquity*, XXVI (1952), 14–24.

56. 'From Roman Britain to Anglo-Saxon England', *Wirtschaft und Kultur: Festschrift zum 70 Geburtstag von Alfons Dopsch* (Leipzig, 1938), pp. 34–73.

57. For *Hamwih* see M. R. M. Muller and D. M. Waterhouse, in *Archaeological News Letter*, II (1949), 13 f., 50, 142; III (1950), 36 f., 134 f.; IV (1951), 62. For Thetford, see G. M. Knocker and R. G. Hughes, *ibid.* II, 117–22; III, 41–6; G. C. Dunning, *Archaeological Journal*, CVI (1951), 72 f.

58. T. C. Lethbridge and G. C. Dunning, 'Anglo-Saxon Glazed Pottery', *Archaeological News Letter*, II (1949), 26, 42. On late pottery see G. C. Dunning, 'Dating Medieval Pottery', *ibid.* I, no. 10, pp. 1–3, no. 12, pp. 1–3; II, 4–6.

59. G. Haseloff, *Der Tassilokelch* (Münchner Beiträge zur Vor- und Frühgeschichte, I, 1951), p. 67.

60. *The Relics of Saint Cuthbert*, ed. C. F. Battiscombe (O.U.P. 1956).

61. *Dark Age Britain*, pp. 171–201.

62. See, e.g., Hanns Swarzenski, *Monuments of Romanesque Art* (London, 1954), figs. 128, 135, 138 f., 142–51.

63. 'King Edmund I and the Danes of York', *English Historical Review*, XXXIII (1918), 1–9.

64. *English Historical Documents c. 500–1042*, ed. D. Whitelock (London, 1955), p. 258.

65. See E. Majkowski, 'Coins struck by Boleslav the Mighty, Duke of Poland (992–1025), with bust and name of Aethelred II of England', *Numismatic Chronicle*, 5th series, XIV (1934), 168–82; C. E. Blunt, 'On a coin of the "Temple" type, bearing the name of Aethelred, king of England', *ibid.* 6th series, III (1943), 101 f.; C. E. Blunt, 'Four Italian coins imitating Anglo-Saxon types', *British Numismatic Journal*, XXV (1947), 282–5. Evidence for the imitation of Anglo-Saxon coins in Switzerland will shortly be published by G. Hatz and R. H. M. Dolley, and for imitation in South Italy by J. P. C. Kent.

66. *Anglo-Saxon England*, p. 640.

67. *The Latin Charters of the Anglo-Saxon Period* (Oxford, 1955), p. 90.

68. See bibliography in *English Historical Documents c. 500–1042*, pp. 352 f. and add Cyril Hart, *The Early Charters of Essex: The Saxon Period* (Occasional Papers of the Department of English Local History, no. 10, Leicester, 1957).

69. 'Les relations monastiques entre la Normandie et l'Angleterre', *Jumièges: Congrès scientifique du XIIIe Centenaire*, I, 262.

II

SOME ANGLO-SAXON BISHOPS OF LONDON[1]

IN HISTORIES OF THE ANGLO-SAXON CHURCH THE SEE OF London does not figure prominently. This is not necessarily because it was unimportant; it may be merely because evidence relating to this see has not survived in quantity. Unfortunately, very little concerning this period has survived from the archives of St Paul's. This lecture is an attempt to see whether conclusions can be drawn about the men who held this see, by supplementing the meagre information from St Paul's with what can be assembled from other sources.

Most texts which claim to date from this period in the post-Conquest registers of St Paul's are spurious. But there survived into the seventeenth century an ancient roll from which Richard James, librarian to Sir Robert Cotton, transcribed a few extracts,[2] enough to show that it included genuine documents,[3] some as early as the eighth century, but only enough to whet our appetite.

One monastic house in the diocese, Barking, supplies some genuine early material, which has been fully studied by Dr Hart.[4] So also does Westminster, along with a lot of spurious matter.[5] Chertsey, which had early connections with St Paul's, was much given to forgery, but its cartulary preserves one important early document.[6] Most of my material is drawn from outside the diocese of London.

When William of Malmesbury composed his *Gesta Pontificum* about 1125, he failed to discover much about the bishops of London. Of those after Eorcenwald he says: 'The others lie so under the cloud

[1] I am indebted to Mr Kenneth Harrison and Dr N. R. Ker for advice on some points in this article.

[2] Printed by Gibbs, pp. 1–8. She discusses this *Rotulus Antiquus Ecclesie Sancti Pauli* on pp. vii–x. See also *Anglo-Saxon Writs*, ed. F. E. Harmer (Manchester, 1952), pp. 235–7.

[3] One must therefore reckon with the possibility that some lost genuine material was available to the post-Conquest forgers.

[4] Hart, pp. 117–45.

[5] See Harmer, op. cit., pp. 286–339; J. Armitage Robinson, *Flete's History of Westminster Abbey* (Cambridge, 1909), pp. 2–18.

[6] See pp. 5f. below.

of obscurity that their tombs are not known'.[1] He merely copies the names from an episcopal list, with the exception of Bishop Theodred.

The first mention of a bishop of London, after the Roman period, is in the letter which Gregory the Great sent along with the pallium to Augustine in 601.[2] By 'bishop of London' Gregory means Augustine, and he intended London to be the seat of the southern archbishop.[3] But by 604 this idea appears to have been abandoned, for Mellitus was made bishop of London, while Augustine remained at Canterbury.

What we know of the early history of the see comes mainly from Bede,[4] and I shall pass over it quickly. London was then the chief city of the East Saxons, whose kingdom included Middlesex and part of Hertfordshire, and, judging by its name, which means 'south region', Surrey as well. It was the overlord, King Ethelbert of Kent, who built and endowed St Paul's.[5]

In 616 or 617 the East Saxons reverted to paganism and ejected Bishop Mellitus. The re-conversion began about 654, by the Celtic-trained bishop, Cedd, sent by Oswiu of Northumbria at the request of Sigeberht of Essex. He worked from monastic centres at *Ythancaestir* (Bradwell-on-Sea) and Tilbury. London is not mentioned, though this does not outrule the possibility that he recovered St Paul's and some of its lands. During the plague of 664, in which

[1] GP p. 144.

[2] Bede, HE i. 29.

[3] I agree with Dr Hunter Blair (*The World of Bede*, London, 1970, pp. 61-3) that the letter implies that Augustine was then in London or was planning to go there. This matter will be fully investigated by Mrs S. M. Young in a dissertation on early Kent.

[4] HE ii. 3-7; iii. 7, 22, 23 and 30; iv. 6 and 11.

[5] St Paul's tradition attributed to him the gift of Tillingham, and BCS 8 is a forged charter to this effect. Dr Hart suggests that this estate included the Roman *Othona* (*Ythancaestir*, i.e. Bradwell-on-Sea) from which Bishop Cedd worked. See 'The St Paul's Estates in Essex' (*The Early Charters of Essex: The Norman Period*, Leicester University Press, 1957), Appendix B, pp. 29-30. Post-Conquest sources also claimed that King Ethelbert had granted 24 hides near the city wall; see *Regesta Regum Anglo-Normannorum 1066-1154*, ed. H. W. C. Davis (Oxford, 1913), i, nos. 246 and 274.

One can dismiss as fiction the Westminster claim that this house was founded in the time of Mellitus. On the legend of its miraculous consecration by St Peter, see J. Armitage Robinson, op. cit., pp. 2-11. Flete says that the tomb of King Sæberht's wife, whom he calls Ethelgoda, was discovered when a new cloister was being built in the reign of Henry III.

Cedd died at his monastery of Lastingham, Yorkshire, part of the East Saxons went back to the heathen faith, but were reclaimed by another Celtic-trained bishop, Jaroman of the Mercians, sent by King Wulfhere of Mercia. He returned to Mercia a year or two later, and then Wulfhere, who was overlord of the East Saxon kings, gave the see of London to Wini, an Englishman consecrated in Gaul, who had held the see of Winchester, but had been driven out by King Cenwealh of Wessex. Bede says that Wini bought the see of London, and this may be why the pre-Conquest lists of bishops of London omit his name. He was appointed during a vacancy at Canterbury, and it is possible that Archbishop Theodore did not acknowledge him. He did not attend Theodore's synod at Hertford in 672, and a charter issued for Chertsey in 672-4[1] is attested only by a bishop of Lichfield, asked to do so by the abbot, Eorcenwald. One would have expected the bishop of London to have been a witness. Bede says Wini held the see until his death.[2]

It was in his episcopate, though not by his initiative, that the monasteries of Chertsey and Barking were founded, by Eorcenwald, before he became bishop of London in 675.[3] When he founded Chertsey, Surrey was apparently under King Egbert of Kent (664-73).[4] It is probable that Eorcenwald was a member of the Kentish royal house, for it is only in this that the Frankish name-element *Eorcen* is met with.[5] But by the time when a sub-king of Surrey, Frithuwald, made a large grant to increase the monastery,[6] Wulfhere of Mercia was overlord of Surrey, as well as of Essex. It is likely to have been with his support that Eorcenwald founded the double monastery of Barking, for his sister Æthelburg. Soon

[1] See note 6, below. The only appearence of Wini as bishop of London is in the forged accounts of the foundation of Peterborough, in ASC 656E and BCS 22.

[2] One must therefore reject the story in the Winchester writer Thomas of Rudborne (*Anglia Sacra*, i, 192) that Wini resigned three years before his death and did penance for his simony as a monk at Winchester, and died and was buried there.

[3] Bede, HE iv. 6.

[4] This is stated in Frithuwald's charter.

[5] Post-Conquest Lives of Eorcenwald and of his sister Æthelburg claim royal descent, but from a King Offa, variously assigned to the East Saxons or East Angles. It is, however, a commonplace of hagiographical writers to claim royal origin for saints. Offa of Essex is chronologically impossible, and no King Offa of East Anglia is known to have existed.

[6] BCS 34; EHD no. 54.

afterwards he was made bishop of London by Archbishop Theodore.[1]

Eorcenwald is in one way the most famous of the bishops of London. His fame rests on his posthumous miracles. Bede, who would obtain his information from Nothhelm, priest of London,[2] says that Eorcenwald lived so holy a life that miracles bear witness to it. His is the only name entered for London in 'The Resting-Places of the English Saints' in its oldest version,[3] and he is entered under 30 April in pre-Conquest calendars from Winchester, Canterbury, Sherborne, Evesham, Worcester, Bury St Edmunds and Crowland.[4] His cult was greatly fostered in the mid-twelfth century and later,[5] and Lives of him were produced which are completely worthless for the historian.[6]

Bede does not enlarge on the qualities which caused contemporaries to regard Eorcenwald as a saint. But from documents it can be seen that he must greatly have impressed the rulers of his time, for he could persuade them to make large donations of land for religious purposes. Frithuwald, sub-king of Surrey, who placed his son in Eorcenwald's monastery at Chertsey, gave no less than 300 hides of land. A list of what Eorcenwald obtained for Barking is given in a charter alleged to have been issued by him.[7] There are difficulties in accepting it as it stands; among other things, it claims that he went to Rome 10 years previously in 677, which it calls the first indiction, and obtained there a privilege from Pope Agatho. 677 is the fifth indiction, the first being 673 or 688, and Agatho was pope only

[1] Bede, HE iv. 6.

[2] See p. 12.

[3] F. Liebermann, *Die Heiligen Englands* (Hanover, 1889), p. 13.

[4] *English Kalendars before A.D. 1100*. ed. F. Wormald (Henry Bradshaw Society, lxxii, 1934). The earliest is a West Country calendar, in Salisbury MS. 150, *c.* 969-78. A West Saxon eleventh-century calendar in Cotton Nero A. ii has him entered on 7 July as well as 30 April.

[5] W. Dugdale, *The History of Saint Paul's Cathedral* (with continuation by Henry Ellis, London, 1818), pp. 15-16, 215.

[6] See T. D. Hardy, *Materials relating to the History of Great Britain and Ireland* (RS 1862), i. Part I, 293-5. A twelfth-century Life is printed in Dugdale, op. cit., p. 289, and is mainly concerned with the alleged battle for his body between Chertsey and London. It makes him a pupil of Mellitus, who died 624. Capgrave's Life is given in *Acta Sanctorum*, April, III (Paris and Rome, 1866), 790-6.

[7] BCS 87; Hart, pp. 122-7. Unfortunately it survives only in a transcript made by Joscelyn (Cotton Vespasian A. ix, fos. 112-13) and in later copies of this.

from 678-81.[1] All the same, I believe that the list of grants for Barking is based on genuine material; two of them, one of 75 hides in Essex given by Œthelræd, a kinsman of King Sebbi of Essex,[2] and one of 70 hides in Battersea, Surrey, given by King Ceadwalla of Wessex,[3] have extant documents in their support. The list mentions also 40 hides at Barking and *Beddanhaam*[4] given by King 'Suidfrid',[5] which it places first, another grant, of 10 hides, from Œthelræd, 53 hides at Isleworth, Middlesex, and 40 at Erith and Swanscombe, Kent, from King Ethelred of Mercia, a hide near London from King Wulfhere of Mercia, and 10 hides above London from a woman called Quoenguyda.[6] I now think that Œthelræd's charter granting 75 hides[7] should be dated 686-8, when Ceadwalla of Wessex had control in Kent and almost certainly in Essex as well; but in any case, it was from Ceadwalla that Eorcenwald obtained Battersea for Barking,[8] and Eorcenwald attests the grant of Hoo, Kent, which

[1] One could suggest that Joscelyn misread a *vi* in the original as *i*, which he wrote as *prima*. The sixth indication would be 678, when Agatho was pope, and the date of Eorcenwald's charter would then be 688. But the story of the visit to Rome may be invented; two St Paul's forgeries (BCS 736, of which BCS 735 is a translation, and BCS 737) in the name of King Athelstan, speak of Eorcenwald's journey to Rome. They do not mention Agatho, but both St Paul's and Chertsey, in collusion, produced spurious privileges of Agatho (BCS 55 and 56), as also did Peterborough (BCS 48) and St Augustine's, Canterbury (BCS 38). The forgers would no doubt know from Bede (HE iv. 16 (18)), that Agatho gave a privilege for Wearmouth. The signatories of Eorcenwald's charter may have been copied from Œthelræd's charter.

[2] See note 7, below.

[3] See note 8, below.

[4] In Œthelræd's charter Æthelburg's monastery is called *Beddanhaam*, but this name was ousted by Barking.

[5] Probably an error for Swæfred, son of King Sebbi, perhaps by confusion with a mid-eighth-century king, Swithred.

[6] Joscelyn's transcript gives part only of her husband's name (. . . *aldi*), filled in as *Ædilbaldi* in his second copy. She is unknown; see D. Whitelock, EHR, lxxxiv (1969), 114f.

[7] BCS 81; EHD no. 60; Hart, pp. 127-35. The attestations of the West Saxon bishop, Hæddi, Abbot Hagona, probably a West Saxon, and Ecgbald, likely to be abbot of Hoo (see note 1, p. 8), are more easily explicable in Ceadwalla's time, as is the absence of any reference to permission from a Mercian overlord.

[8] BCS 82; Hart, pp. 135-41. This survives in an eleventh-century copy from Westminister, which obtained the estate from William I. It was tampered with there, but Dr Hart has established its original readings. In it Eorcenwald gives to the monastery of St Mary (Barking) 68 hides at Battersea which he has received from Ceadwalla, and has had confirmed by King Ethelred of Mercia. The charter is dated 13 June 693, but

Ceadwalla made to Abbot Ecgbald.[1] Then there is a charter, preserved in a Winchester cartulary, by which Ceadwalla gave 60 hides at Farnham, Surrey, to three men, to found a monastery. It is witnessed, as is Œthelræd's grant for Barking, by Bishops Eorcenwald, Wilfrid (of Northumbria, staying with Ceadwalla) and Hæddi of Winchester.[2] In his Life of Wilfrid, Eddi claims that Wilfrid had great influence with Ceadwalla,[3] but we should allow some also to Eorcenwald. The Farnham charter has diplomatic links with Frithuwald's charter for Chertsey and Œthelræd's for Barking,[4] and Eorcenwald, the only common denominator between all three, no doubt had a hand in the drafting. It can justifiably be claimed that Eorcenwald was effective in securing property for the church in Surrey, which was probably in his own diocese, and which was an area in which heathenism had been strong.[5] At the time when Ceadwalla made these grants he had not yet been baptised, but this was not out of hostility to the Christian faith, but because he wished his baptism to take place in Rome. He gave to Wilfrid a quarter of the Isle of Wight and of the booty he won in conquering it.[6]

its list of witnesses is a conflation of those of Ceadwalla's grant (which includes the same three bishops, Abbot Hagona and Hooc, as in Œthelræd's charter, plus the West Saxon Abbot Wynberht and some others) with those of Ethelred's confirmation.

[1] BCS 89.

[2] BCS 72; EHD no. 58. Farnham later belonged to Winchester Cathedral. The charter is dated 688, which does not agree with the date given by Eddi for Wilfrid's return to Northumbria, the second year of King Aldfrith, i.e. 686-7. See *The Life of Bishop Wilfrid by Eddius Stephanus*, ed. B. Colgrave (Cambridge, 1927), p. 90. Wilfrid may have paid Ceadwalla another visit in 688.

[3] Ed. Colgrave, p. 85.

[4] See EHD pp. 445, 447.

[5] The Farnham charter contains two names referring to heathen sanctuaries, *Cusanweoh* and *Besingahearh*. Two other monasteries in Surrey, Bermondsey and Woking, were probably founded when Ethelred of Mercia was overlord, for between 708 and 715 Pope Constantine granted a privilege for them to an Abbot Hædda, who is probably to be identified with Hedda, a priest of Peterborough who became abbot of Breedon-on-the-Hill, Leics., when it was founded by Friduric, a *princeps* of King Ethelred. See F. M. Stenton, 'Medeshamstede and its Colonies', *Essays in Honour of James Tait*, 1933, pp. 313-26, reprinted in *Preparatory to Anglo-Saxon England*, ed. D. M. Stenton, Oxford, 1970, pp. 179-92. M. Gibbs queries this identification in *Speculum*, xlviii (1973), 228, note 59, but I still prefer Stenton's interpretation of the facts.

[6] Bede, HE iv. 14(16). Eddi, perhaps deliberately, omits the incidents which show Ceadwalla, Wilfrid's friend, as a cruel ruler, but similar acts can be laid to the charge of Christian kings such as Ethelred of Mercia.

The list of lands which Eorcenwald obtained for Barking showed that he was able to obtain lands from East Saxon royalty, and from the Mercian overlords, Wulfhere and Ethelred. Was he equally successful in securing endowment for St Paul's? Here we have no early evidence. In later times St Paul's attributed to him and King Sebbi of Essex the grant of lands and a privilege.[1] They may have had evidence since lost, or it could have been a surmise. Tillingham may have been restored to Cedd,[2] and we do not know how much land Wini obtained when he bought the see.

Under Eorcenwald any Celtic features surviving from the missionary work of Cedd and Jaroman would tend to disappear. We hear nothing more of monasteries at *Ythancaestir* and Tilbury.[3] Eorcenwald was on good terms with Archbishop Theodore. Eddi's Life of Wilfrid says that Theodore invited Eorcenwald to the meeting he arranged in London with Wilfrid when attempting a reconciliation.[4]

More important is the mention of Eorcenwald, along with Bishop Hæddi of Winchester, as giving advice and instruction to Ine of Wessex when he issued his laws.[5] Ine calls Eorcenwald 'my

[1] BCS 735-737, forgeries in the name of King Athelstan. St Paul's also claimed that he was active in adding to their buildings; see W. Dugdale, op. cit., p. 74.

[2] See note 5, p. 4.

[3] They must have been weakened by the departure of some thirty of Cedd's followers to Lastingham to be near his body (HE iii. 23). But *Ythancaestir* was apparently still functioning when the name Southminster was given to a place in the *regio* of Dengie, to distinguish it from some more northern minster, presumably *Ythancaestir*. See P. H. Reaney, *The Place-Names of Essex*, p. 225.

[4] Ed. Colgrave, p. 87. It is likely that by Theodore's time, if not before, archbishops of Canterbury would possess a house in London. Theodore consecrated Hæddi as bishop of Winchester in London in 676 (HE iv. 12). Hertford and Hatfield, where he held councils, were probably in the diocese of London. We do not know the location of *Clofesho*, where synods were sometimes held up to 825, but from 785 Chelsea was also favoured (ASC 785 (*recte* 787); BCS 247-8, 254-7, 267, 302, 358, apart from BCS 60, which mentions a synod there in 671, but which is dubious). Synods met at London itself in 811 (BCS 335), 812 (BCS 340) and 845 (BCS 448). We rarely know where episcopal consecrations took place, but the choice of London for those of Helmstan, bishop of Winchester, in 838-9 (BCS 424) and Æthelbald, archbishop of York, in 900 (*Chronicle of Æthelweard*, ed. A. Campbell, p. 52) suggests that archbishops found it a convenient centre.

[5] F. Liebermann, *Die Gesetze der Angelsachsen*, i, 88. On the great importance of this code, 'the work of a responsible statesman', see F. M. Stenton, *Anglo-Saxon England* (3rd edn., Oxford, 1971), pp. 71f.

bishop', which may merely be in respect of Surrey.[1] The code puts first of all the command 'that the servants of God duly observe their proper rule'; it includes injunctions which put the church in a strong position. Heavy penalties are imposed for breach of its rules regarding the baptism of children, Sunday observance, and payment of churchscot; also for giving false witness in the bishop's presence. It refers to rights of sanctuary, attaches a higher value to the oath of a communicant, allows to a diocesan bishop the same compensation as that due to the king for forcible entry into his house, and acknowledges the rights of godparents to compensation if their godchild is killed. In Eorcenwald, London possessed an influential bishop at a period of great importance for consolidating the position of the English church.

Eorcenwald's successor, Waldhere, was not negligible. Bede refers to him only as spiritual advisor to King Sebbi,[2] but a letter which he wrote *c.* 704 to Archbishop Berhtwald was preserved in the Canterbury archives,[3] probably because of the strong expressions of loyalty and deference to the archbishop of Canterbury which it contains. It implies that Waldhere was much respected by the secular authorities, for it mentions a meeting at Brentford which had been planned to settle the discord between the West Saxons and Waldhere's own people, and states that both sides had agreed in advance to accept whatever terms might be agreed on by Waldhere and the West Saxon bishop. Waldhere is in a quandary, because a synod of the previous year had forbidden intercourse with the West

[1] If Ine retained any authority in Essex, like Ceadwalla, it was not for long. As we saw (note 8, p. 7), Eorcenwald obtained a confirmation of the grant of Battersea in 693 from Ethelred of Mercia.

[2] HE iv. 11.

[3] BCS 115; EHD no. 164. It is Cotton Augustus ii. 18, facsimiled in *British Museum Facsimiles*, i, pl. 6, and in A. Bruckner and R. Marichal, *Chartae Latinae Antiquiores*, iii (Olton and Lausanne, 1963), no. 185. Bruckner dates it late eighth century. So fine a parchment would hardly have been sacrificed for a mere copy, unless the document was of special importance; a letter from a bishop of London, expressing such subservience to the archbishop, describing him as 'ruling the government of all Britain', would be valued at Canterbury after the creation of the archbishopric of Lichfield, and especially when in 797-8 Cenwulf of Mercia was trying to remove the primacy to London. See p. 14. But, as N. P. Brooks, in *The Pre-Conquest Charters of Christ Church, Canterbury* (Oxford University dissertation, 1968), p. 5, note 2, points out, we have no Anglo-Saxon minuscule of the early eighth century for comparison with Waldhere's letter, and this may be contemporary.

Saxons until they obeyed the archbishop's decree about ordaining bishops, so he asks the archbishop for advice.[1] The West Saxon see was divided in 705, and I suspect that the planned meeting did take place, and that one result was the detachment of Surrey from the kingdom of Essex and the diocese of London. Between 708 and 715 Pope Constantine describes Bermondsey and Woking as being in the province of the West Saxons,[2] and between 732 and 745 a monk whose reference to 'our father Eorcenwald' shows to have belonged to Chertsey, writing to St Boniface, refers to Daniel of Winchester as 'my bishop'.[3]

Both Waldhere and his successor Ingwald were able to increase the lands of their see. A grant of 30 hides at Twickenham to Waldhere by King Swæfred of Essex and a *comes* Pæogthath has come down in a copy of the late eighth or early ninth century, probably made and preserved at Christ Church, Canterbury, which then held the estate.[4] The extracts made by James from the *rotula*[5] show us Waldhere receiving 10 hides at Ealing from King Ethelred of Mercia, to augment the monastery in the city of London, and some land in the *pagus* of Hemel Hempstead, from King Offa of Essex, and buying 50 hides at Fulham from Tyrhtil, bishop of Hereford;[6] and they show Bishop Ingwald receiving 70 hides in the *regio* of Dengie from King Swæfred and a grant of freedom from toll on a ship at London from King Æthelbald of Mercia, and buying land at an unnamed place for thirty *cannae* of silver.

In these bishops' time the church of London possessed a distinguished priest, who was later, in 735, to become archbishop of

[1] Though summoned to a meeting by Cenred of Mercia, Waldhere had not gone, not knowing the archbishop's wishes. This meeting was held 'about the reconciliation of Ælfthryth', and we do not know what this implies.

[2] See note 5, p. 8.

[3] M. Tangl, *Die Briefe des Heiligen Bonifatius und Lullus*, no. 36.

[4] Cotton Augustus ii. 82, facsimiled in *British Museum Facsimiles*, i. pl. 3; BCS 111. It is dated 13 June 704, and Cenred of Mercia heads the list of signatories; a confirmation made by Ceolred of Mercia at Ercall follows. A charter in which Offa of Mercia includes 30 hides at Twickenham in a grant to Christ Church (BCS 265) has peculiar features, but Christ Church did possess this estate in the early part of the ninth century (BCS 402). It may have been alienated from St Paul's by sale or exchange.

[5] Gibbs, pp. 3–7.

[6] One wonders why a bishop of Hereford should have a large estate in Middlesex for sale, but Tyrhtil may have been a man of this area.

Canterbury. This was Nothhelm, who twice visited Bede and brought to him documents for his history, including some which he had himself searched for in the papal archives at Rome.[1] It is less widely realised that he was a biblical scholar, for whom Bede wrote two of his exegetical works.[2] It would be he who brought to Bede a Life of St Æthelburg,[3] presumably written at Barking, where Æthelburg's successor was the Hildelith to whom, along with her nuns, Aldhelm dedicated his *De Virginitate*,[4] and who corresponded with Boniface.[5] The church in the diocese of London was not behind others in scholarship.

Bishop Ingwald helped to consecrate Tatwine archbishop of Canterbury in 731.[6] He attended a synod held by Archbishop Nothhelm in 736 or 737.[7] His death in 745 is recorded by annalists.[8] Of his successors, up to Theodred, we know little more than William of Malmesbury did, but we have charters from various archives which have their attestations. These do not show, as has been claimed, that London was almost the least important of sees;[9] they do show that bishops of London did not attend the courts of the

[1] HE Preface.

[2] *In Regum Librum XXX Quaestiones*, ed. D. Hurst (Corpus Christianorum Series Latina, CXIX, Bedae Opera, Pars II. 2, 289–322); *De VIII Questionibus*, Migne, PL xciii, 455–78, on which see P. Lehmann, *Sitzungsberichte der bayerischen Akademie der Wissenschaften*, Philos.-philol. und hist. Klasse (Munich, 1919), Abhandlung 4.

[3] Bede, HE iv. 10.

[4] *Aldhelmi Opera*, ed. R. Ehwald, pp. 228–9. Nine nuns are named; they include Cuthburg, perhaps the sister of Ine of Wessex, who left her husband, Aldfrith of Northumbria, and founded Wimborne. William of Malmesbury (GR i. 35, note 1) says she first became a nun under Hildelith at Barking.

[5] Tangl, op, cit., no. 10. It was from her that Boniface learnt of the vision of the monk of Wenlock.

[6] Bede, HE v. 23.

[7] BCS 156.

[8] *Historia Regum*, attributed to Symeon of Durham, and *Continuatio Bedae*.

[9] Stubbs (*Councils*, iii, 51) claimed this because Kemble (*Codex Diplomaticus*, i, xciv) gives a list of precedence of the sees with London at the bottom, except for Selsey. Little support is given in charters to this order. There is no consistency, but sometimes the arrangement is by kingdoms, and during the Mercian supremacy the Mercian sees of Lichfield. Leicester, Hereford, Worcester and Lindsey may precede the others. London is not normally placed with these, but it is not usually near the bottom. In the Legatine synod of 786, for example, Eadberht of London precedes seven bishops, and in an original of 798 (BCS 289) Heathoberht of London is fourth after the archbishops, with five bishops following him.

Mercian overlords except in special circumstances,[1] though they are present when the Mercian king is presiding over a synod of the whole southern church. At the synod of the southern province in which Offa of Mercia met the papal legates in 786,[2] London was represented by Bishop Eadberht. An underlying reason for the legates' visit was Offa's wish to create a separate archbishopric for Mercia, with its centre at Lichfield. This was partly because he was on bad terms with Archbishop Jænberht and the people of Kent,[3] but he may well have felt it incompatible with the dignity of his Mercian kingdom that it must obey an outside authority in ecclesiastical concerns. He carried his scheme through in 787 at what the Anglo-Saxon Chronicle calls 'the contentious synod'[4] at Chelsea. Bishop Eadberht may have been present. Some of Offa's coins have on the reverse the name Eadberht followed by a symbol which has been read as a monogram of E and P and interpreted as *episcopus*.[5] This is not usually accepted as evidence for coining rights for the bishop of London, since there is no other trace of any, and London was not allowed an episcopal moneyer in Athelstan's laws.[6] Yet it is not impossible that Offa granted an unprecedented right at a time when he was anxious to secure support for his policy of dividing the southern province.

When Lichfield became an archbishopric, London was left with Canterbury, according to William of Malmesbury.[7] Bishop Ead-

[1] E.g. BCS 171, 177 and 188, which all concern freedom from toll in London; BCS 177 was issued at London. In another grant of toll in London (BCS 149), issued at Willenhall, Staffs. or Warwicks., no bishop of London appears. There are a number of charters, attested by Mercian bishops alone, with no bishop of London. Waldhere's letter shows that a Mercian king might summon the bishop of London to a council, but apparently he was not a regular attendant.

[2] *Councils*, iii, 447–62; E. Dümmler, *Monumenta Germaniae Historica: Epistolae Karol. Aevi*, ii, no. 3; EHD no. 191.

[3] See Cenwulf's letter to Pope Leo III (*Councils*, iii, 521–3, BCS 287; EHD no. 204); but Leo's reply (*Councils*, iii, 523–5, BCS 288; EHD no. 205) says that Offa testified that it was 'the united wish and unanimous petition of you all, both on account of the vast size of your lands and the extension of your kingdom, and also for many more reasons and advantages.'

[4] *geflitfullic senoþ*.

[5] See C. E. Blunt, in *Anglo-Saxon Coins*, ed. R. H. M. Dolley (London, 1961), pp. 43–4.

[6] II Athelstan 14.2.

[7] GR i 85, GP p. 16.

berht was followed in rapid succession by Edgar, Cenwalh and, not before 793, by Eadbald, who attests no charters. The Anglo-Saxon Chronicle has an intriguing entry for 794 (*recte* 796), the year of Offa's death. It says that Eadbald, along with a bishop of Lindsey, 'left the country'. One would like to know why they left the country, and why the chronicler, usually uninterested in bishops, thought it worth recording. Eadbald's successor first appears in 798, so the see may have been vacant during the two crucial years, 796-8, when Kent was in revolt against Mercia, Archbishop Æthelheard, a Mercian, in flight from Canterbury, and Cenwulf of Mercia, when negotiating for the abolition of the archbishopric of Lichfield, trying to get papal permission to transfer the primacy from Canterbury to London.[1] I suspect that if Leo III had agreed to this, Cenwulf would have put Archbishop Æthelheard into the see of London, conveniently vacant. But in 798 Leo flatly refused, and in this year Cenwulf recovered control of Kent, Archbishop Æthelheard could go back to Canterbury, and we meet Heathoberht as bishop of London.[2] Thus for a second time London missed becoming the chief see of southern England.[3]

The formalities of suppressing the archbishopric of Lichfield took a long time. In 799 (BCS 293) its archbishop, Hygeberht, attests before his colleague of Canterbury, but by 801 he seems to have retired, for he witnesses BCS 302 merely as bishop, along with his successor Aldwulf. The papal letter to Æthelheard authorising the suppression is dated 18 January 802,[4] yet the final abolition was not completed until the synod of *Clofesho* on 12 October 803.[5] This long delay may suggest that there was more opposition to the abolition than our sources tell us. Hygebyrht attended the synod, as abbot.

[1] See the letters cited in note 3, p. 13, and for the whole question of the abolition of the archbishopric of Lichfield, see Stenton, *Anglo-Saxon England* (3rd. edn., 1971), pp. 215-8, 225-8.

[2] BCS 289. His death in 801, and a great fire in London soon after it, are recorded in the *Historia Regum* attributed to Symeon of Durham.

[3] A result of the temporary division of the province of Canterbury was that it became customary to enroll at Christ Church the professions of bishops to the archbishops of Canterbury, but that of Heathoberht is not included. The only surviving professions of bishops of London are from three successive bishops, Æthelnoth, about 805-11 (BCS 333), Ceolberht, 816-24 (BCS 376) and Deorwulf, 845-60 (BCS 498).

[4] *Councils*, iii, 536-7, BCS 305; EHD no. 209.

[5] *Councils*, iii, 542-4, BCS 310; EHD no. 210.

Bishop Osmund of London came to this synod with Heahstan, priest and abbot, three other priests and one person without title. Dümmler[1] suggested that Heahstan is the priest of this name to whom Alcuin wrote a few years earlier. But this is uncertain: Alcuin is writing to a former pupil, and though one of the two persons to whom he sends greetings bears the name of a person present at the synod, Beagnoth, he is one of the Rochester contingent. Heahstan is a common name.

When in 825 the East Saxons submitted to Egbert of Wessex, the bishops of London were left serving two masters. Bishop Ceolberht in 838[2] and Bishop Deorwulf in 860[3] attest charters of West Saxon kings, and in a grant preserved in garbled form at St Paul's[4] Ethelred of Wessex gives Navestock, Essex, to St Paul's monastery at Bishop Deorwulf's request. But the West Saxon kings did not control Middlesex or Hertfordshire or London itself,[5] except for the one year, 829 to 830, when Egbert obtained all Mercia and celebrated his triumph by minting coins in London.[6] One of the extracts made by James is a grant of 10 hides at Braughing, Hertfordshire, by Bishop Ceolberht and the brethren of St Paul's to a thegn of Wiglaf of Mercia, who came to the throne in 827. The only witness whom James chose to mention is a king of Essex.[7] Ceolberht attests a charter of Wiglaf of 836,[8] issued at Croft, Leicestershire, but as it was also attended by the non-Mercian bishops of Sherborne, Rochester and Selsey, the earlier practice by which synods of the southern province met under Mercian kings seems to be continuing. It is the

[1] Op. cit., no. 37.

[2] BCS 418.

[3] BCS 502.

[4] BCS 1210; Gibbs, pp. 2–3. The king's name, Ethelred, has been replaced by that of Edgar. It is dated 867.

[5] The appendix to FW (i, 264), and William of Malmesbury (GR i, 99) say that after the submission of the East Saxons to Egbert, London with the surrounding lands obeyed the Mercian kings as long as they reigned. Wiglaf deals with land in Middlesex in 831 (BCS 400) and Burgred of Mercia gives land in London to a bishop of Worcester in 857 (BCS 492). Wiglaf seems to have revived the London mint. On the issue of coins at London, see C. E. Blunt, C. S. S. Lyon and B. H. I. H. Stewart, 'The Coinage of Southern England, 796–840', *British Numismatic Journal*, xxxii (1963), 1–74, especially 6–8, 30–43.

[6] Ibid., p. 34.

[7] Gibbs, pp. 7–8.

[8] BCS 416; EHD no. 85.

last instance of this. It may be significant that no king is named as present at the synod which met *æt Astran* in 839,[1] nor at that at London in 845,[2] both of which were attended by Ceolberht of London. It was fortunate for him and other bishops of London, with their diocese divided between two overlords, that there were friendly relations between Wessex and Mercia, at least from the time of King Æthelwulf, as is shown by documentary and coin evidence.[3]

London suffered in the viking invasions. It was stormed in 842 and 851; the Danes spent 871-2 there. It was probably in Danish hands from 878 until Alfred won it back in 886.[4] After Deorwulf, who last appears in 867, the episcopal list gives Swithulf, of whom nothing is known, and then Heahstan, whose death in 897 is recorded in the Chronicle. The see was perhaps not continuously occupied; with Danes in London and Essex its bishops would have few lands to support them. No bishop of London is mentioned in a charter dealing with Walden, Hertfordshire, in 888 nor in one concerning London in 889.[5] Pope Formosus, writing to the bishops of England between 891 and 896, complains that there have been delays in filling sees.[6]

Heahstan became bishop in time to receive a copy of Alfred's translation of Gregory's *Pastoral Care*,[7] in the early 890s. I would like to attribute to St Paul's a single sheet with extracts from the Old

[1] BCS 421. The place cannot be identified, but as the synod is dated by the regnal year of Æthelwulf of Wessex and the two West Saxon bishops head the list, it must have been in West Saxon territory.

[2] BCS 448. This deals with land in Middlesex. Archbishop Ceolnoth and nine bishops were present. The absentees are those of Hereford, Winchester and Sherborne, but Ealhstan of Sherborne was with the army in that year.

[3] See ASC 853, 868; *Asser's Life of King Alfred*, ed. W. H. Stevenson, ch. 29; F. M. Stenton, *The Early History of the Abbey of Abingdon*, pp. 25-7; C. E. Blunt, 'Anglo-Saxon Coinage and the Historian', *Medieval Archaeology*, iv (1960), 6-7; and H. E. Pagan, 'Coinage in the Age of Burgred', *British Numismatic Journal*, xxxiv (1965), 11-27.

[4] Pagan (op. cit., p. 27) says we have only 'an embroidery by Florence of Worcester' to indicate the viking possession of London between the death of Ceolwulf II and Alfred's seizure of the city; but he ignores the evidence of Asser (ch. 83) that Alfred's occupation of London was preceded by fighting.

[5] BCS 557 and BCS 561. Neither is quite free from suspicion, but at least they have genuine material behind them.

[6] BCS 573; EHD no. 227.

[7] See p. 30.

English translation of Bede, and, if this is so, it implies that a manuscript of that work was available there.[1] London does not lie outside the range of Alfred's educational reforms.

When Formosus wrote the letter mentioned above, he rebuked the English bishops for their failure to preach against 'the abominable rites of the heathen'; but he had recently heard that they had now begun to do so. Possibly the appointment of Plegmund to Canterbury about 890 had contributed to new activity, and Heahstan of London may also have played a part. Almost all Essex was still in Danish control, and was not recovered until the campaigns of 912–17, and if missionary work was carried out there, it would be hampered by the Danish operations of 892–6. One of the most obscure matters of Anglo-Saxon history concerns the ecclesiastical administration of the Danish areas and the conversion of their settlers. Though we know so little of how this was effected, we must not forget that it was effected, and that much of the energy of the church would be absorbed in it. We have no means of knowing what part Heahstan and his successors Wulfsige, Æthelweard and Leofstan[2] took, but there is no doubt of the importance of Bishop Theodred.

He may have been bishop a few years before his first attestation in 926.[3] He was an important figure in the reign of King Athelstan. William of Malmesbury says he was with the king in his campaign against Anlaf in 937.[4] It was Theodred who brought to the arch-

[1] Cotton Domitian ix, fo. 11, printed by J. Zupitza, *Zeitschrift für deutsches Altertum*, xxx (1886), 185. The third extract (the beginning of Book II. ch. 3) has been altered to read 'Augustine . . . consecrated Mellitus first among the English people' instead of 'Augustine . . . consecrated two bishops; the one was called Mellitus, the other Justus', as if the writer was interested only in the see of London.

[2] See M. A. O'Donovan, 'An interim revision of episcopal dates for the province of Canterbury, 850–950', *Anglo-Saxon England*, ii, 97–8. Wulfsige attests charters from 900–909, many of them dubious. During his time, Æthelbald was consecrated archbishop of York in London in 900 (see note 4, p. 9). On the variations between the lists of bishops of London at this time see R. I. Page, 'Anglo-Saxon Episcopal Lists', *Nottingham Medieval Studies*, ix (1965), 91. I give the order as in CCCC 140.

[3] Except for BCS 632, a misdated Mercian charter (*recte* 915), there is a complete dearth from 909 to 925, when there survives a charter, issued by Athelstan on the day of his consecration (BCS 641). If this were not a late copy, one might argue that the absence of a bishop of London points to a vacancy in that see; but as the bishops of Winchester, Ramsbury, Hereford and Rochester are missing also, the list cannot be complete.

[4] GP p. 144.

bishop after the council of Whittlesbury Athelstan's message that he thought it cruel to put to death for theft such young persons as was the practice.[1] Theodred was one of those responsible[2] for drawing up the ordinance which gives this information, that of the 'peace-guild' of London, whose importance in relation to Athelstan's efforts to improve the peace of his land has recently been demonstrated by Professor Loyn.[3] It is possible that when the canons of St Paul's claimed that King Athelstan had granted them privileges at Theodred's request[4] they had evidence for this.

The late-tenth-century *Passio Sancti Eadmundi* by Abbo of Fleury says that Theodred was devoted to the shrine of St Edmund, and that he condemned to death eight thieves captured while trying to rob the shrine. Later, after reading the canons, he repented of this judgement and did penance for the rest of his life.[5]

But our main knowledge of him comes from his will, preserved in a cartulary of Bury St Edmund's.[6] From this we see why it fell to him to pass judgement on thieves caught at Bury. It shows that he held along with the see of London the diocese of Suffolk, possibly of all East Anglia. The East Anglian sees of Elmham and Dunwich lapsed at the Danish settlement, and we hear of no bishop of East Anglia until 955, two or three years after Theodred's death. The see henceforward took its title from Elmham, but an eleventh-century will and Domesday Book show that it had a Suffolk centre at Hoxne.[7]

Theodred makes bequests to and arrangements for his bishopric at Hoxne and his bishopric at London. To both he leaves money to

[1] VI Athelstan 12.1-12.3.

[2] Namely 'the bishops and reeves who belong to London'. The ordinance seems to apply to an area round the city, and other bishops concerned would be those of Dorchester, Winchester and Rochester, for areas in Bucks., Surrey and Kent; perhaps also the archbishop of Canterbury and the bishop of Worcester, with holdings in the city.

[3] H. R. Loyn, 'The Hundred in England in the Tenth and Early Eleventh Centuries', *British Government and Administration. Studies presented to S. B. Chrimes*, ed. H. Hearder and H. R. Loyn (Cardiff, 1974), pp. 4-6.

[4] BCS 737. This is spurious. James quotes a small portion of what may have been a genuine charter of Athelstan of 935 (Gibbs, p. 5), but one cannot tell whether it was a grant to St Paul's or to some other grantee.

[5] *Memorials of St. Edmund's Abbey*, ed. T. Arnold, i, 20-2.

[6] AS Wills, no. I, EHD, no. 106.

[7] AS Wills, no. XXVI; Domesday Book, ii, fo. 379.

be distributed for his soul, and he disposes of the stock which he has added to the episcopal estates at Hoxne and London, at Wimbledon, Sheen, Dengie and Fulham, usually leaving half to the church and half for his soul, and freeing all the men. To the church at Hoxne he gives two estates in Suffolk, and to St Paul's an estate at Southery, Norfolk, which he had received from the king, and three estates in Essex, *Chich* (St Osyth's), Dunmowe and Tillingham. We saw above that Tillingham was claimed to be part of the original foundation of St Paul's.[1] It may have been alienated in the troubled intervening times, and recovered by Theodred.[2] He leaves to St Paul's vestments, a chalice, his best mass-book and his best relics. He leaves four Suffolk estates to St Edmund's and two to the church at Mendham. These were probably small communities of secular priests.[3]

The name Theodred is almost certainly German,[4] and Theodred leaves ecclesiastical vestments to men with German names, Gundwine, Odgar and Theodred, and he had inherited a chasuble from a man with the German name of Gosebriht. It is not very rare to find men with German names in English churches at this time,[5] but Theodred has a remarkably strong German element in his clergy,

[1] See note 5, p. 4.

[2] But Hart, 'The St Paul's Estates in Essex', p. 34, thinks that when Theodred mentions these four estates he is merely acknowledging existing rights of the canons in them. If so, he must have made over to them his estate at Southery given him by the king.

[3] Other communities in this diocese, Stoke-by-Nayland, Suffolk, Mersea and Barking, Essex, are mentioned in the will of Ælfgar, ealdorman of Essex (AS Wills, no. II). Ælfgar says that Theodred brought him the king's permission to make his will. He leaves an annual food-rent from Heybridge to St Paul's.

[4] The element *þeod* is uncommon in English names, and Theodred is a very rare name. A Theodred became bishop of Elmham between 970 and 974, attesting BCS 1303 in 974, BCS 1314 in 975 and BCS 1201, which should be dated 973-5. It is probably the same bishop who occurs in a few charters between 982 and 995, for though the list of bishops of Elmham, preserved in the post-Conquest writers Florence of Worcester, William of Malmesbury and the *Textus Roffensis*, has two consecutive bishops of this rare name, this is probably an error. It is possible that Theodred of Elmham is the legatee Theodred in Bishop Theodred's will. It is not an insuperable objection to the suggestion that Theodred of London was of German origin that his sister's sons, Osgot and Offa, and his kinsman Osgot, Eadulf's son, have not got German names, for his sister may have married in England. Osgot, Eadulf's son, could have been his brother-in-law.

[5] AS Charters, no. XXXII, mentions a deacon *Freðegod* at Christ Church, Canterbury (perhaps the author of the verse Life of Wilfrid), and priests *Roðin* and *Bærhtram* at St Augustine's. There was a priest Godescalc at Abingdon in 931 (Stenton, *The Early*

and he mentions in this connection no men with English names. A bishop in charge of two dioceses only recently recovered from Danish possession may have welcomed reinforcements from Germany. There may have been a shortage of English clergy. It is possible that the visit of Bishop Coenwald of Worcester to all the German monasteries in 929[1] was in part a recruiting tour.

One cannot but wonder how Theodred had acquired such a large holding in Suffolk. Apart from estates in Essex and Norfolk left to St Paul's, and two estates in Cambridgeshire and one in Norfolk left to the king, all his lands lie in Suffolk, eight estates given to religious houses and twelve to his kin and other laymen. It is possible that he had been placed in charge of Suffolk before he was made bishop of London, perhaps not long after East Anglia surrendered to Edward the Elder in 917, and had become well established there. But in the complete absence of charters we can only guess.

Theodred leaves five pounds for his soul to every bishop's see. He makes a personal bequest of five mancuses of gold to the archbishop (Oda of Canterbury), an early exponent of monastic reform. The only religious house outside his own dioceses to receive anything is Dunstan's reformed monastery at Glastonbury. Fifty mancuses of gold are left to the Queen-Mother, Eadgifu, another supporter of the monastic movement. We ought therefore perhaps to add Theodred to that small group of ecclesiastics known to have favoured this movement in its early days, Archbishop Oda, Bishop Ælfheah I of Winchester and Bishop Coenwald of Worcester. Theodred's German contacts may have brought him into touch with the reform movements on the Continent. He had himself been abroad, at least once, for he bought a chasuble at Pavia, presumably when on a visit to Rome.

We may conclude that London had a very effective bishop at an important period of church history.[2] If we had to depend on records

History of the Abbey of Abingdon, p. 38). It may have been in this period that a manuscript of the Old Saxon poems *Heliand* and *Genesis* was brought to England. See B. J. Timmer, *The Later Genesis* (Oxford, 1948), pp. 16–18.

[1] See J. Armitage Robinson, *The Saxon Bishops of Wells* (British Academy Supplemental Papers, IV, 1918), pp. 60–2.

[2] From 940 on Theodred invariably heads the episcopal signatures, probably because of his seniority. About 935 a new diplomatic practice had begun, by which lists were

from St Paul's, he would be only a name. This is odd, for they had his body; one version of 'The Resting-Places of the English Saints' says St Theodred the bishop rests in London,[1] and William of Malmesbury, who says he was called 'the Good', speaks of his tomb by a window in the crypt, at a height conspicuous to passers-by.[2] Yet there is no trace of a cult of him at St Paul's. It looks like a lost opportunity.

Elsewhere, I have tried to distinguish Theodred's successor, Brihthelm, who succeeded him between 951 and 953, from two, or even three, contemporary namesakes.[3] At first he attests in the fifth or sixth place in charters, but in 956 it again becomes customary to place Winchester and London first. We know nothing about Brihthelm, except that he received 10 hides in Orsett, Essex, from King Eadwig in 957.[4] Later in that year, the kingdom was divided between Eadwig and Edgar, and the diocese of London was in Edgar's part. He recalled Dunstan from exile and made him bishop of Worcester. Soon after, in 958 or 959, he gave him the see of London, to hold in plurality. Dunstan witnesses a charter in 959, issued by Edgar before he became king of all England, as *Lundoniensis æcclesiæ præsul*.[5] His appointment to London is mentioned also by his biographers. Yet his name is omitted from the pre-Conquest episcopal lists for London. Moreover, both Ælfric and Wulfstan Cantor in their Lives of St Æthelwold mention only Dunstan's appointment to Worcester and to Canterbury, ignoring London.[6] It is possible that by their time the feeling against holding in plurality had hardened in some quarters. Dunstan may have relinquished London soon after becoming archbishop of Canterbury in 960, but one cannot be certain that the Ælfstan who attests from 961 is Dunstan's successor, for he could be Ælfstan of Rochester, and it is not until 964 that both appear together.

begun with the bishops of Winchester and London, and their sees were named, when others were usually left unnamed.

[1] *The Chronicle of Hugh Candidus*, ed. W. T. Mellows, p. 59.

[2] GP p. 144.

[3] 'The Appointment of Dunstan as Archbishop of Canterbury', *Otium et Negotium*, ed. F. Sandgren (Stockholm, 1973), pp. 233–6.

[4] Gibbs, p. 6.

[5] BCS 1052.

[6] Both Lives are edited by M. Winterbottom, *Three Lives of English Saints* (Toronto, 1972); see pp. 21, 38 and 42. For Ælfric's Life, see EHD no. 235, p. 834.

SOME ANGLO-SAXON BISHOPS OF LONDON

Post-Conquest Westminster documents and William of Malmesbury assign the re-foundation of the monastery at Westminster to Dunstan while he was bishop of London, and William says that he placed Wulfsige as abbot over a band of twelve monks.[1] Goscelin, in his Life of Wulfsige says that Wulfsige was born in London and placed in the church of Westminster at an early age, and, becoming an outstanding member in the monastic profession, was placed in charge of the monastery by King Edgar by Dunstan's advice.[2] It is probable that Dunstan kept the monastery under his own control for some years, before appointing an abbot.[3] Westminster was for long an unimportant house, and its abbots rarely attest charters. Wulfsige does not appear on a genuine charter until 988.[4] Goscelin is probably correct in saying that he continued to hold the abbey after he became bishop of Sherborne (in 993). He may have held it until 997, when his successor Ælfwig appears.[5] The date 971 sometimes given for Dunstan's re-foundation of Westminster has no firm basis.[6] Dunstan's concern with this house is seen in his granting it Sunbury, Middlesex, which he had brought in 968 for 200 mancuses of gold.[7] Other lands are said to have been his gifts[8].

The episcopate of his successor Ælfstan lasted until 995, right through the period of intensive monastic reform and of the reaction which followed it. The nunnery of Barking was probably reformed

[1] GP p. 178.

[2] Ed. C. H. Talbot, *Revue Bénédictine*, lxix (1959), 68–85. Goscelin then contradicts himself by ascribing the placing of monks in Westminster to Wulfsige after he became abbot. On the value of this Life, see M. A. O'Donovan, *Studies in the History of the Diocese of Sherborne* (Cambridge University dissertation, 1972), pp. 333–45.

[3] Bishop Oswald of Worcester appointed no abbot to his foundation of Ramsey.

[4] KCD 664. He attests also KCD 712 and 713, which belong to 990–1. BCS 1178 and 1179, which have him as abbot in 966, are Crowland forgeries.

[5] Apart from KCD 684, where Ælfwig's name is a later addition to a charter of 993.

[6] It is based on W. H. Stevenson's view (*Crawford Charters*, p. 90) that BCS 1048, which refers to this foundation, is genuine, and that its impossible date 951 is an error for 971. This charter has no witnesses. BCS 1351, a forgery based on it, has a list which could belong to 971, but also to any date from 963 to 972.

[7] See the discussion of this transaction by Korhammer in the article cited in note 1, p. 31.

[8] Hendon and *Lohðereslea*, Middlesex (BCS 1263, 1290). Dunstan presumably gave to Westminster the estate at *Cealuadune* given to him by King Edgar in 967 (BCS 1198), for the charter is preserved there.

in his time[1] and Westminster began to attract the generosity of donors.[2] Ælfstan may have held the abbey of Evesham from 991 until his death.[3] There is no hint that any attempt was made to introduce monks into St Paul's, though Ælfstan may have been a monk,[4] as his successors Wulfstan and Ælfhun were. We hear of two clerics of St Paul's who left to become monks elsewhere: Eadric joined Æthelwold when he founded Abingdon about 955[5] and Thurcytel, a kinsman of Archbishop Oscytel of York, who had bought himself a place in the priesthood of St Paul's, had become abbot of Bedford by 971.[6] He was expelled from there, before 978, presumably during the anti-monastic reaction, and he asked Bishop Ælfstan and the

[1] Nothing is known of the nature of the foundation there existing in Bishop Theodred's time (see note 3, p. 19). A nun called Eawynn to whom King Eadred gave Shopland, Essex, in 946 (Gibbs, p. 6) is unlikely to have been at Barking, since the charter was preserved at St Paul's. An Abbess Wulfhild was buried at Barking, according to the version of 'The Resting Places of the English Saints' used by Hugo Candidus (ed. Mellows, p. 63) and Goscelin wrote a Life of her (ed. M. Esposito, *Analecta Bollandiana*, xxxii (1913), 10–26), which says she was a nun of Wilton, who resisted the unwelcome attentions of King Edgar, and who was later made abbess of Barking. She was expelled by Queen Ælfthryth for twenty years, which she spent at Horton, Dorset. Some element of truth seems to underlie this tale, for an Abbess Wulfhild of Horton is mentioned in the *Liber Vitae* of Newminster (ed. Birch, p. 57), and Ælfthryth is shown to have had some connection with Barking by the bequest to her in Ælfflæd's will (AS Wills, no. XV) of a life-interest in Woodham, Essex, which ought by the terms of Ælfflæd's sister's will to have gone direct to Barking. In his Life of St Edith (ed. A. Wilmart, *Analecta Bollandiana*, lvi (1938), 76–7) Goscelin says that St Æthelwold made Edith abbess of Barking, as well as of *Nunnaminster*, Winchester, and an unnamed nunnery.

[2] Brickendon, Herts., in the will of Ælfhelm (AS Wills, no. XIII), and Kelvedon, Essex, and *Mearcyncgseollan* in the will of Leofwine (*Crawford Charters*, no. IX).

[3] *Chronicon Abbatiæ de Evesham* (ed. W. D. Macray, RS 1863, p. 80) says King Ethelred gave the abbey to Bishop Æthelsige (of Sherborne), who not long after incurred the king's wrath, and crossed the sea and never returned. This is no doubt a misunderstanding, for this bishop crossed the sea in 991 on an embassy from Ethelred to Richard of Normandy (*Memorials of St Dunstan*, ed. W. Stubbs, pp. 397–8; EHD no. 230); he is not mentioned again. Ethelred is then said to have given Evesham to Bishop Æthelstan, which must be an error for Ælfstan, either of London or of Rochester. It seems more likely that this Mercian house should be given to a bishop of London than to a Kentish bishop. Both Ælfstans died about the same time, 995. No abbot of Evesham occurs in the long list of abbots in KCD 684, dated 993.

[4] Both Edgar and Dunstan would wish to appoint a monk as Dunstan's successor.

[5] EHD no. 235, p. 833; Winterbottom, op. cit., pp. 20, 41.

[6] At some stage he founded the abbey of Crowland. On his career, see D. Whitelock, in *Saga-Book of the Viking Society*, xii, Part III (1941), 174–5. There is no need to suppose

clergy of St Paul's to admit him to communion and a share in their monastery. This was refused at first, until he gave an estate at Milton, Cambridgeshire, which they later exchanged with Ely, with the result that this whole transaction is entered in the *Liber Eliensis*.[1]

In Ælfstan's time St Paul's was burnt down in 962, but rebuilt in the same year. London was burnt in 982. In 992, when a great English fleet was assembled at London, a Bishop Ælfstan was put in charge of it, along with Ealdorman Ælfric, Earl Thored and Æscwig, bishop of Dorchester; Plummer suggests that Ælfstan is an error for Ælfric, bishop of Ramsbury (later archbishop), who left warships to the king and to certain counties in his will. Certainly, if active service with the fleet was required, both Ælfstans were rather old for it, but a bishop of London might have had duties in regard to its assembling and provisioning. Owing to the ealdorman's treachery, it was a great fiasco. In 994 London was attacked by Swegn and Olaf Tryggvason, and though they were repelled, they did great damage, raiding, burning and slaughtering in Essex and elsewhere.

The will of Æthelric, preserved at Christ Church, leaves land west of Rayne, Essex, to St Paul's, for the bishop to provide lights and to communicate Christianity to God's people there; and woods and open lands to Bishop Ælfstan for Copford, and an enclosure at Glazenwood. The bishop is asked to protect the widow and secure the validity of the will, but when this was called in question, owing to suspicions of Æthelric's complicity in a plot to make Swegn king, it was the archbishop of Canterbury and a layman who acted on the widow's behalf. No bishop of London is mentioned, and it is likely that the suit occurred during a vacancy in the see, 995–6.[2] Between about 975 and 991, Ealdorman Ælfgar's daughter Æthelflæd in her will left the reversion of Hadham, Hertfordshire, to St Paul's as an episcopal estate; this grant is mentioned in the will of her sister, Ælfflæd, which also leaves Heybridge, Essex, for the use of the community at St Paul's.

that he was an unsatisfactory character. Orderic Vitalis calls him a friend of Dunstan, Æthelwold and Oswold, The reluctance of the canons of St Paul's to receive him may have been because they did not wish to burden themselves with more members than their endowment could easily support.

[1] Book II, ch. 31.

[2] AS Wills, nos. XVI (1) and (2).

Wulfstan, who succeeded Ælfstan in 996, is one of the most outstanding of Anglo-Saxon ecclesiastics. He became archbishop of York and bishop of Worcester in 1002, and was an important advisor of kings Ethelred and Cnut, a drafter of their laws, a reformer of all orders of clergy, a prolific author of treatises and homilies, a scholar whose works and materials fill several manuscripts. Most of his career lies outside my present theme,[1] but there are a few aspects of his London period which have not been adequately considered.

If only we had records from St Paul's they might have shed light on his education and origin.[2] The *Liber Eliensis*[3] says he was a monk, then an abbot. Florence of Worcester wrongly calls him abbot in 1002; if he was an abbot in 996, it was not at an important house, for there is no room for him at any of them, and he signs no charters as abbot. But he had probably already given signs of his quality. From the first, he never drops below second place in the lists of episcopal signatories.[4] A letter to him from an unnamed *famulus supplex* is a refusal to undertake some translation at his request, because the writer cannot match Wulfstan's attainments.[5] The flowery terms in which these are described may be the reason why Wulfstan had the letter entered into one of his manuscripts. Its address is interesting: 'To the most illustrious lord, most full of divine doctrines and works, the most worthy of bishops of the metropolitan church of London.' Here 'metropolitan' seems merely to mean 'belonging to a metropolis', though to my knowledge the collocation 'metropolitan church' is used otherwise at this period only of the archiepiscopal churches of Canterbury and York. Yet it is not uncommon to find London spoken of in rather grandiloquent

[1] See the introductions to D. Bethurum, *The Homilies of Wulfstan* (Oxford, 1957) and D. Whitelock, *Sermo Lupi ad Anglos* (3rd. edn., London, 1963); also D. Bethurum, in *Continuations and Beginnings*, ed. E. G. Stanley (London, 1966), pp. 210–46.

[2] Like Dunstan, Wulfstan does not occur in episcopal lists of London until after the Conquest, but there is only one before this which does not stop with his predecessor, Ælfstan. This is CCCC 140, which has one name after Ælfstan, *Ealhun* (for Ælfhun), Wulfstan's successor.

[3] Book II, ch. 87. His interest in this monastery, where he chose to be buried, and in that of Peterborough, suggest some early connection with the fenland area.

[4] In contrast, the position of his successor varies greatly; usually he comes low down, e.g. eighth, ninth or tenth.

[5] Bethurum, *The Homilies of Wulfstan*, pp. 376–7.

terms, most strikingly by a bishop of Winchester in 838–9, who calls it 'the famous place constructed by the skill of the ancient Romans, commonly called throughout the space of the world the great city of London.'[1] The 'humble servant' who calls London a metropolitan church need not belong to London, or be remembering that Gregory the Great had intended London to be a metropolitan church.

As bishop of London, Wulfstan, using the *nom-de-plume* found in the rubrics to some of his homilies, issued three penitential letters, for men doing penance for slaying a kinsman.[2] In later life, he made a small collection of such letters,[3] and they are the only ones of this kind to survive from before the Conquest, except for two issued by Wulfsige, bishop of Sherborne, entered in a Sherborne manuscript.[4] One of these two is a letter to an unnamed pope, from *W. Scyreburnensis ęcclesie*, and it is identical with one in Wulfstan's collection, except that that is from *W. Anglorum archiepiscopus*. Jost, who could not envisage Wulfstan adopting without alteration a letter written by somebody else, wished to regard the letter in the Sherborne manuscript as a late entry, altered to make the *W* refer to a former bishop of Sherborne.[5] But, as we saw above,[6] Wulfsige may have retained the abbey of Westminster until 997, and thus be a near neighbour of Wulfstan when he became bishop of London. It would be easy for one of them to pass on to the other this penitential letter, and it would be fully in accord with Wulfstan's normal practice if he re-used it when a similar situation arose after he had become archbishop. Wulfsige may also have passed on to Wulfstan the pastoral letter which Ælfric had written for him.[7] Wulfstan uses

[1] BCS 424: 'in loco præclaro antiquorum Romanorum arte constructa vulgoque per tulluris [*sic*] spatio vocitato civitas Lundonia magna.'

[2] Bethurum, op. cit., pp. 374–5.

[3] Printed from CCCC 265 by Mary Bateson, EHR, x (1895), 728–30. It survives also in Copenhagen, Kongelike Bibl. Gl. kgl. S. 1595, and Bodleian MS. Barlow 37. Letters by or to Wulfstan are in Bethurum, op. cit., pp. 374–6.

[4] Paris, Bibl. Nat. Lat. 943. The two letters are printed as if one by Stubbs, *Memorials of St Dunstan*, pp. 408–9.

[5] *Wulfstanstudien* (Berne, 1950), p. 21. Palaeographical evidence does not support his view.

[6] See p. 22.

[7] B. Fehr, *Die Hirtenbriefe Ælfrics* (Hamburg, 1914, reprinted with supplement to the introduction by P. Clemoes, Darmstadt, 1966), pp. 1–34.

this in his 'Canons of Edgar', an early work.[1] He was himself in correspondence with Ælfric soon after 1002, and Ælfric wrote pastoral letters for him in 1005 and 1006.[2] In his London years Wulfstan would come much into contact with Archbishop Ælfric of Canterbury, who made him his executor in his will, leaving him a pectoral cross, a ring and a psalter.[3] He is a likely source for certain Canterbury documents which Wulfstan included in his own collections, such as the 'Constitutions of Oda' and letters written to tenth-century archbishops of Canterbury.[4]

This seems the place to consider the *Regula Sancti Pauli*, entered in the thirteenth-century St Paul's register *Liber L* and incorporated as chapters 14-16 in part III of Baldock's register.[5] It is regarded as pre-Conquest. Professor Brooke[6] has noted that this rule has not, as used to be thought, used the enlarged rule of Chrodegang of Metz, but the *De regula canonicorum* issued at the council of Aachen of 816, and usually ascribed to Amalarius of Metz.[7] The 'Rule of St Paul' consists of a longish extract from chapter 94, and almost the whole of chapters 99, 100, 124, 131 and 132. It has been provided with an introduction warning the canons of St Paul's to be content with their stipends, and to obey their bishop; to behave with due attention in chapter; to honour their patron St Paul and follow his precepts; and, though they cannot withdraw themselves entirely from the things of this world, to keep their minds on heavenly things.

There must have been available at St Paul's a manuscript of at least a large portion of this work. It does not seem to have been very widely known in pre-Conquest England. The *Regularis Con-*

[1] See Jost, *Anglia*, lxvi (1932), 265-315.

[2] On this dating see Clemoes in Fehr, op. cit., p. cxlv. Ælfric had received a letter from Wulfstan after he became archbishop, and his reply (Fehr, pp. 222-7) is not later than 1005.

[3] AS Wills, no. XVIII.

[4] Preserved in Cotton Vespasian A. xiv, a manuscript compiled for Wulfstan.

[5] See W. S. Simpson, *Registrum statutorum et consuetudinum ecclesie cathedralis sancti Pauli Londoniensis* (London, 1873), pp. 38-43. See Gibbs, p. xviii note 1.

[6] C. N. L. Brooke, in *A History of St Paul's Cathedral*, ed. W. R. Matthews and W. M. Atkins (London, 1957), pp. 11-15.

[7] *Monumenta Germaniae Historica*, Legum Sectio III, *Concilia*, II, Pars I, ed. A. Werminghoff, pp. 307-421.

cordia quotes it once and may have used its prologue.[1] Fehr was uncertain whether Ælfric in his pastoral letters used it, or its sources, mainly Isidor.[2]

Archbishop Wulfstan did know this work ascribed to Amalarius. The greater part of the last chapter, 145, which is a summary of the work, is found in two manuscripts of a collection of his materials which we call his 'Commonplace Book',[3] in both of them entered twice. Moreover, Wulfstan translated his selection from this chapter into Old English, under the rubric *De regula canonicorum*, and it survives in Junius MS. 121 of his works.[4] Jost has shown that he did this early in his literary career, for four other of his writings must be placed between it and a code issued in 1008.[5] It is possible, though not certain, that Wulfstan made this translation while he was at London. It seems natural to link his knowledge of Amalarius's work with the presence at London of the manuscript used by the 'Rule of St Paul'.

It is tempting to connect the presence of this manuscript there with Bishop Theodred's German contacts, but it could have been acquired by other means, for several Frankish canonical works reached England in the tenth century. Dunstan could have brought it, for he spent his exile in Ghent. It could even have been brought to London by Wulfstan himself, for he was well informed on canonical writings, at any rate later on.

He was much given to providing sets of injunctions for various orders of the clergy: his 'Canons of Edgar'[6] was mainly for parish

[1] Ed. Dom Thomas Symons (London, 1953), p. xlix.

[2] Fehr, op. cit., p. cxvii.

[3] See D. Bethurum, 'Archbishop Wulfstan's Commonplace Book', PMLA, lvii (1942), 916-29. CCCC 265 and the Copenhagen MS. contain this chapter. CCCC 265, and CCCC 190 (another manuscript of the 'Commonplace Book'), have precisely the same selection from Isidor's *Sententiae* which we find in chapters 20, 29 and 30 of Amalarius, and share with chapter 20 the reading *numisma* (*nomisma*) against Isidor's *numismata*. But they agree with Isidor in adding to chapter 29 *quod est vita* after *sacrum ministerium*, and in reading *plebes subiectas transfertur* when chapter 30 of Amalarius has *plebes subditas transit*, at least in the manuscripts used by Werminghoff.

[4] Ed. by Bethurum, no. Xa, and by Jost, *Die 'Institutes of Polity, Civil and Ecclesiastical'* (Berne, 1959), pp. 248-55.

[5] *Anglia*, lvi, 304.

[6] Ed. Jost, '*Institutes of Polity . . .*', pp. 178-209 and R. Fowler (EETS, 1972).

priests; he wrote sets of injunctions on how bishops should behave;[1] and he is almost certainly the author of the Law of the Northumbrian Priests, for his diocese of York.[2] It would be in character if he had provided his canons at St Paul's with a rule, if they had not one already. Yet the 'Rule of St Paul' may have been in existence when he arrived, or it may have been drawn up after his time. It is a different type of work from those of Wulfstan which I have mentioned; it consists of lengthy discussion, with much scriptural quotation, of a limited number of topics—the etymology of *clericus* and its implications, the avoidance of the society of women, simplicity of dress and humility of bearing, and, most particularly, care and reverence in performing the services in church, arguing for the presence of angels at them. It includes some repetition, where Amalarius was drawing on different sources. By contrast, the final chapter of Amalarius, which Wulfstan copied and translated, is straightforward and simple, and is intended to be memorised. Wulfstan compresses it, gets rid of repetition, and omits a few injunctions; even so, his version is much more comprehensive than the 'Rule of St Paul', including, for example, an insistence that the canons must sleep in one dormitory and eat in one refectory, and never be longer away from the minster than their master has given permission; the learned are not to look down on the less learned, the noble-born are not to despise those of baser birth.

Somehow, I do not think Wulfstan is responsible for the 'Rule of St Paul', though the matter might repay further study. If this rule was there when he arrived, he might still have extracted from Amalarius chapter 145, as a simpler rule, and translated it. Yet he need not have done this for St Paul's at all. It may be significant that a sentence referring to obedience to a bishop is omitted.[3] By the time he composed the code of 1008, it is assumed that at least the larger communities of canons will possess a rule: 'And canons, where there is property such that they can have a refectory and a dormitory, are to hold their minster with right observance and chastity, as their

[1] Jost, op. cit., pp. 59–61, 67–9, 75–7, 211–6 and 262–7.

[2] EHD no. 53.

[3] 'proprio episcopo in omnibus secundum canonicam institutionem obtemperent'. Wulfstan's rule may not be primarily intended for bodies of cathedral canons.

rule directs.'[1] The rule here mentioned could be that of Chrodegang of Metz;[2] yet Wulfstan may have translated the last chapter of Amalarius for houses in his dioceses which did not possess this rather long work. I cannot at present see that one can choose between various possibilities.

However, at the time when the 'Rule of St Paul' was composed, we may assume that the canons had no small degree of Latin education, if they were to understand it. The fact that we have little evidence of intellectual activities at St Paul's is not proof that there were none. In 1953 Dr Sisam wrote: 'Strangely enough, no book surviving from pre-Conquest times has been assigned to the principal city, though it must have used and produced many books, and at least one manuscript, Otho B. ii, derives from the copy of the Pastoral Care that Alfred sent to Heahstan, bishop of London.'[3] One book which we now know that it used was this work of Amalarius, and as for production, Mrs Horgan has recently said that the linguistic features of Otho B. ii are compatible with a London origin.[4] There are of course many pre-Conquest manuscripts whose provenance is unknown. Dr Sisam wrote the words quoted above when tentatively suggesting that the *Beowulf* manuscript might have been written at London, as this was the kind of place where Mercian and West Saxon met and south-eastern *io* forms were possible. This attractive hypothesis, however, stops far short of proof. As for the religious houses in the diocese of London, there comes from Barking a copy of the Gospels, with outline drawings, written about 1000,[5] and it is possible that a late-tenth-century copy of Aldhelm's *De virginitate*, belonging to Waltham Abbey in the Middle Ages, also came from Barking.[6] Westminster has recently been shown to be

[1] V Ethelred 7.

[2] This was translated about this time; see A. S. Napier, *The Old English version of the enlarged rule of Chrodegang* (EETS, 1916). Chapter 83 is entered in the CCCC 190 manuscript of the 'Commonplace Book'. An early-tenth-century English manuscript of the Latin text is in Brussels, Bibl. Royale, 8558-63.

[3] *Studies in the History of Old English Literature* (Oxford, 1953), p. 95.

[4] *Anglia*, xci (1973), 165.

[5] Bodley MS. 155. See N. R. Ker, *Catalogue of Manuscripts containing Anglo-Saxon*, No. 303; F. Wormald, *English Drawings of the Tenth and Eleventh Centuries* (London, 1952), p. 75.

[6] Lambeth Palace Library, MS. 200; see Wormald, op. cit., p. 73.

a possible place of origin for the Bosworth Psalter, for its main hand has been identified with that of a charter, preserved at Westminster, relating to the estate at Sunbury which was given by Dunstan, presumably with its title-deeds, to Westminster in or after 968; but it is possible that the surviving copy of the charter was made at Christ Church, Canterbury, before the transfer.[1]

To return to Wulfstan. Since we know that he took an interest in the estates of his sees of Worcester and York, we may guess that he had a hand in the re-organisation of the St Paul's lands for the purpose of the contribution of seamen for the manning of ships. The document which sets this out[2] is dated 995-8 by Dr Hart, and it is one of the few texts relating to pre-Conquest affairs which survived at St Paul's. A reference to Wulfstan as bishop occurs in a will preserved at Westminster,[3] in which a certain Leofwine leaves Barling, Essex, to his lord, Bishop Wulfstan.

Charters show Wulfstan in regular attendance at meetings of the witan. At some of these, weighty decisions would have to be taken, such as the raising of a naval and land force in 999, the purchase of a treaty from the Danes for £24,000, the outlawry of Ealdorman Leofsige of Essex for killing the king's high-reeve, and the marriage of Ethelred with Emma of Normandy, all in 1002. That he was influential can only be guessed from the choice of him for the combined sees of Worcester and York. The latter certainly required a man of character.

Wulfstan's successor Ælfhun is probably the abbot who attests charters from 975 to 995, and who is called abbot of Middleton in 993.[4] He took Ethelred's two youngest sons to safety in Normandy in 1013, and may have died there, for his successor was consecrated at York on 16 February 1014, only a fortnight after Swegn's death. Florence of Worcester calls him the boys' tutor; it is likely enough

[1] See P. M. Korhammer, 'The origin of the Bosworth Psalter', *Anglo-Saxon England*, ii (1973), 173-87.

[2] Robertson, AS Charters, no. LXXII. It is fully discussed by Hart, 'The St Paul's Estates in Essex'. It was copied into CCCC 383, a collection of Anglo-Saxon laws written in the first half of the twelfth century. There is no evidence that this collection was at St Paul's before the Conquest.

[3] *Crawford Charters*, no. IX.

[4] But an Abbot Ælfhun occurs in a Kentish transaction about 995 (AS Charters, no. LXIX); it is possible that there were two abbots of this name, though it is not common.

that London was one of the safer places for their upbringing. Hermann, in his *De miraculis sancti Eadmundi*,[1] accuses him of trying to steal the body of St Edmund when it had been brought to St Gregory's church in London for safety, from 1009–12. In 1012 St Paul's received legitimately a wonder-working saint, when the body of the martyred Archbishop Ælfheah was brought to London, and received by Bishop Ælfhun and Bishop Eadnoth of Dorchester. It was buried in St Paul's, and was working miracles at the time the chronicler was writing.

When King Ethelred died in London on 23 April, 1016, and was buried in St Paul's, 'the councillors who were in London' elected his son Edmund to succeed him. It is likely that Bishop Ælfwig[2] was present, and it looks as if this brought him into disfavour with Cnut, who was elected by a much larger gathering of the witan at Southampton.[3] Ælfwig's attestation is strangely missing from all but three of the genuine charters of Cnut, and it was in his time that Cnut took away from St Paul's the thirty-hide manor of Southminster, as we learn from Domesday Book.[4] In 1023 St Paul's lost its wonder-working saint when the body of St Ælfheah was translated with great pomp from London to Canterbury.

Bishop Ælfweard, appointed by Cnut in 1035, was on the contrary *persona grata* with that king, and is said to have been his kinsman. If true, this implies that he was of Danish descent on one side, and his grant of Hemington, Northamptonshire, and Horseheath, Cambridgeshire, to Ramsey suggests that he came from this area of the Danelaw. He became a monk at Ramsey, and was made abbot of Evesham about 1014–6, holding this in plurality with the see of London, which he is said to have accepted with reluctance. The chroniclers of both these monasteries[5] tell us a lot about him, especially about his benefits to them. It was Evesham, not London,

[1] Ed. T. Arnold, *Memorials of St Edmund's Abbey*, i, 43–6.

[2] If an abbot Ælfwig who attests once in 1018 (*Ordnance Survey Facsimiles*, iii, pl. 39) is the same person as an abbot of this name who occurs occasionally between 997 and 1012, and who is abbot of Westminster according to KCD 698, it cannot be the latter who became bishop of London in 1014.

[3] FW i, 173.

[4] ii, fos. 10–10b.

[5] *Chronicon Abbatiæ de Evesham*, ed. W. D. Macray, pp. 36–7, 81–5 and 314; *Chronicon Abbatiæ Rameseiensis*, ed. idem (RS, 1886), pp. 148–50, 157–8 and 198; a list of abbots on p. 340 refers to Ælfweard as *aureus episcopus*.

which benefited from Cnut's good will, for Cnut died soon after Ælfweard obtained London. Cnut gave to Evesham relics of St Wigstan, a black chasuble and other ornaments; also Bagby and Newnham, Northamptonshire, but as we are told later that these were given by Æfic the prior, Cnut may merely have confirmed the gift.[1] Ælfweard was able to recover the estates which Evesham had lost in its very chequered history, and the freedom lost when the abbey had been given to Ealdulf, bishop of Worcester, about 995; he also obtained that the prior Æfic should be *decanus Christianitatis* of the whole vale of Evesham. An Evesham lease of 1022–5,[2] which mentions 'the Lady Ælfgifu who rules the monastery' suggests that it was under the special patronage of Cnut's queen. Ælfweard also is said to have been on good terms with Earl Leofric and his wife.

Ælfweard was devoted to the cult of relics. He had a shrine of gold and silver made for the relics of St Ecgwine, the Evesham saint; he sent to Evesham the relics of a Frankish saint, Odulf, which he had bought from merchants in London, and he abstracted some relics of St Osyth from her shrine, presumably for St Paul's. The Ramsey chronicler regarded the illness (said to be leprosy) which caused him to retire from office, as a punishment for this act. He was refused asylum at Evesham, and went to Ramsey, taking with him chasubles, pallia, ornaments, pontifical books, and the jawbone of St Ecgwine and the blood-stained cowl of St Ælfheah, apparently purloined from Evesham and London respectively.

These monastic chroniclers are local in their interests. They are not concerned with Ælfweard as bishop of London. With no evidence from St Paul's, it would be unfair to assume from so one-sided an account that he neglected his see for his abbey, or that the many theological and grammatical books which he sent from London to Evesham were stolen from the St Paul's library. Only once do we hear of a public action, when he was a member of the mission sent to Flanders in 1040 to invite Hardecnut to England, and the Evesham chronicler tells us this only because Ælfweard was believed to have been saved from shipwreck on his way by a prayer to St

[1] The *Chronicon*, p. 75, says he gave to Evesham eight unnamed estates.

[2] AS Charters, no. LXXXI.

Ecgwine. For all we know, he may have played a part in other political affairs. He was probably present when Edward the Confessor was elected king at London in 1042. But at least we know that he was not one of those who carried out Hardecnut's shameful command to dig up the body of King Harold at Westminster and throw it into the Thames.[1] He is named in the address of some writs, attests a few charters, and was left Bentley, Essex, in a woman's will.[2]

When he retired in 1044 he was succeeded by Normans, first by Robert and then by William. If we ignore Sparrowhawk, elected in 1050 but never consecrated, Ælfweard was the last Anglo-Saxon bishop of London.

I have tried to suggest something of the gaps left in our knowledge of the see of London when we have thus mainly to depend on scattered and incidental references preserved elsewhere. Even so, London can claim four outstanding personalities, Eorcenwald and Theodred, Dunstan and Wulfstan, though the two last soon went on to higher things. From at least the early tenth century, the see of London was regarded as an important office, and one should not underestimate the political importance of its being given by Edward the Confessor to a Norman favourite. If we had better evidence, we might find that several of its other occupants were by no means nonentities.

[1] FW s.a. 1040.
[2] AS Wills, no. XXIX.

ABBREVIATIONS

The following abbreviations are used: ASC: *Anglo-Saxon Chronicle*; AS Charters: *Anglo-Saxon Charters*, ed. A. J. Robertson (2nd edn., Cambridge, 1956); AS Wills: *Anglo-Saxon Wills*, ed. D. Whitelock (Cambridge, 1930); BCS: *Cartularium Saxonicum*, ed. W. de G. Birch (London, 1885–93); CCCC: Corpus Christi College, Cambridge; *Councils: Councils and Ecclesiastical Documents relating to Great Britain and Ireland*, ed. A. W. Haddan and W. Stubbs (Oxford, 1869–71); *Crawford Charters*: *The Crawford Collection of Early Charters and Documents*, ed. A. S. Napier and W. H. Stevenson (Oxford, 1895); EETS: Early English Text Society; EHD: *English Historical Documents c. 500–1042*, ed. D. Whitelock (London, 1955); EHR: *English Historical Review*; FW: *Florentii Wigorniensis Monachi Chronicon ex Chronicis*, ed. B. Thorpe (London, 1848–9); Gibbs: *Early Charters of the Cathedral Church of St Paul, London*, ed. Marion Gibbs (Camden 3rd Ser., lviii, London, 1939); GP: *Willelmi Malmesbiriensis Monachi De Gestis Pontificum*, ed. N.E.S.A. Hamilton (RS, 1870); GR: *Willelmi Malmesbiriensis Monachi De Gestis Regum Anglorum*, ed. W. Stubbs (RS, 1887–9); Hart: *The Early Charters of Eastern England*, ed. C. R. Hart (Leicester University Press, 1966); HE: Bede's *Historia Ecclesiastica Gentis Anglorum*, quoted by book and chapter; KCD: *Codex Diplomaticus Aevi Saxonici*, ed. J. M. Kemble (London, 1839-48); RS: Rolls Series.

III

The Dealings of the Kings of England with Northumbria in the Tenth and Eleventh Centuries

ABBREVIATIONS

AS Wills *Anglo-Saxon Wills*, ed. D. Whitelock (Cambridge, 1930).
AS Charters *Anglo-Saxon Charters*, ed. A. J. Robertson (Cambridge, 1939).
AS Writs *Anglo-Saxon Writs*, ed. F. E. Harmer (Manchester, 1952).
BCS *Cartularium Saxonicum*, ed. W. de G. Birch (London, 1885-93).
EHD *English Historical Documents*, gen. ed. D. C. Douglas, vol. I, ed. D. Whitelock (London, 1955).
KCD *Codex Diplomaticus Aevi Saxonici*, ed. J. M. Kemble (London, 1839-48).
Sym. Dur. *Symeonis Monachi Opera Omnia*, ed. T. Arnold (Rolls Series, 1882-5).

THE purpose of this paper is to see if any conclusions may be drawn regarding the policy of the kings of England towards the northern Danelaw from hints scattered through the scanty records for this area in the period after the Scandinavian settlements.

It was not until the reign of Athelstan that a West Saxon king became the direct ruler of Northumbria. It is important for subsequent history to note that in the days of the Heptarchy, when one hears of kings who held what Bede calls an *imperium* over other kingdoms, a position which, judging by the Anglo-Saxon Chronicle, gave them the title of *Bretwalda*, this *imperium* did not extend to Northumbria, except, of course, when it was held (as it was in the seventh century) by a Northumbrian king. What was implied was dominion over the kingdoms south of the Humber. Even the strongest of overlords, Offa of Mercia, could not speak for Northumbria.

Only for very brief periods before Athelstan's reign did the Northumbrians admit the overlordship of a southern ruler. When the Chronicle tells us that Egbert of Wessex conquered the Mercians in 829, and calls him *Bretwalda*, it adds that he led an army to Dore against the Northumbrians, and that 'they offered him submission and peace there'. But this can hardly have led to great or prolonged interference by the West Saxon king in Northumbria, for the next year we read 'Wiglaf again obtained the kingdom of the Mercians', and charter evidence supports the view that this ended Egbert's overlordship in Mercia, without which control in Northumbria was impossible.[1] In 918, the Danish kingdom of Northumbria submitted to Æthelflæd, Lady of the Mercians, probably to obtain her support against the threat from the Irish-Norsemen.[2] But she died the same year, and the Norseman Ragnald established himself at York. He accepted King Edward as 'father and lord' in 920, but, when Edward died at the end of 924, Athelstan seems to have thought in terms of alliance rather than of overlordship, giving his sister in marriage to Ragnald's successor Sihtric. On the latter's death in 927, Athelstan drove out Guthfrith and took direct control of Northumbria. The previous history of the area does not justify an assumption that it would seem natural, even to the English-born section of the inhabitants, to be governed by a southern king. The chronicle attributed to John of Wallingford states that Sihtric's successor Guthred (i.e. Guthfrith) was persuaded to rebel against Athelstan by the Northumbrians, who declared that their country had always had its own king and had paid tribute under no king of the South Angles, and that it was well-known that from the coming of the English to Britain they were subjected to none of the kings of the English except Athelstan.[3] It is possible that this thirteenth-century writer is expanding the lost source which both he and Roger of Wendover used.[4]

It is not clear what part the Northumbrians played in 937, when Athelstan defeated a great combine of Scandinavian and Celtic leaders at *Brunanburh*, but, after his death in 939, when the Norseman Olaf Guthfrith's son recovered York, raided Tamworth, where he took prisoner a lady called Wulfrun, and escaped by night when besieged in Leicester by King Edmund, it was the belief of a later generation that he had the support and company of Archbishop Wulfstan I of York. Edmund recovered the lands as far as the Humber in 942, and Northumbria in 944, but, after his death in 946, though Archbishop Wulfstan and the Northumbrians pledged themselves to Eadred, 'within a short space

[1] See F. M. Stenton, *Anglo-Saxon England*, 2nd ed. (Oxford, 1947), p. 231 ff.

[2] See F. T. Wainwright, *EHR*, LXIII (1948), 145-69.

[3] ed. R. Vaughan, *Camden Miscellany*, XXI (1958), 45.

[4] See *EHD*, pp. 119 and 255-8.

they were false to it all'. They took as king a Norwegian prince, Eric Blood-Axe. They submitted when Eadred ravaged Northumbria, but in the following year they accepted Olaf Sihtric's son, and in 952 expelled him in favour of Eric. The archbishop is said to have been imprisoned by Eadred in this year. Eric was expelled, and killed, in 954, and the archbishop was reinstated, at any rate partially. Henceforth Northumbria was permanently under the English crown, but contemporaries naturally could not know that Eric was to be the last Scandinavian king to establish himself at York. The account which depicts the archbishop as disloyal is in a series of entries in the D version of the Anglo-Saxon Chronicle alone, probably added in the eleventh century, at York.[1] It need occasion no surprise that this should be unsympathetic towards Scandinavian rule and Northumbrian independence, for, as we shall see, York received after Wulfstan a line of archbishops from south of the Humber. Moreover, from about 993 to 1006, its earl was a Mercian, Ælfhelm, son of the Wulfrun captured at Tamworth in 940. We probably owe our knowledge of this incident to the interest taken at York in the earl's mother. The author of these annals regards the Northumbrian behaviour as treacherous, but there may well have been many Northumbrians, English or Danish, who looked with disfavour on subservience to a southern king.

Athelstan would naturally expect support from the Church, for, though the Danish settlers of the ninth century seem to have accepted Christianity, many of the Norse invaders from Ireland were heathen. He was generous to the churches of Ripon, Beverley, St Cuthbert's (then at Chester-le-Street), as well as to York. To this see, under Archbishop Wulfstan, who appears to have been his nominee, he gave in 934 the whole district of Amounderness, bought from the pagans with his own money, presumably that it might form a bulwark against the recent Scandinavian penetration into Westmorland and Cumberland.[2]

[1] See *The Peterborough Chronicle*, ed. D. Whitelock (Early English Manuscripts in Facsimile, vol. IV, 1954), pp. 28-30.

[2] *EHD*, pp. 505-8; *Early Yorkshire Charters*, ed. W. Farrer, I (Edinburgh, 1914), 1-5. A similar transaction seems to lie behind the name of the Cumberland barony of Copeland, 'purchased land', which Sir Frank Stenton suggests was brought under English rule by purchase from the Scandinavian armies in the tenth century. See *Royal Commission on Historical Monuments: Westmorland* (London, 1936), p. xlviii.

The story in the D text of the Chronicle that Wulfstan betrayed this trust receives some external support. The B manuscript of the Chronicle, s.a. 971, says that Oscytel was made archbishop of York 'by the consent of King Eadred and all his councillors', which would put him in control of York while Wulfstan, who survived Eadred, was still alive. Moreover, Amounderness did not remain a possession of the see of York. Domesday Book shows that Earl Tostig was the sole landowner there in the Confessor's reign. The area had been preserved united, but removed from the archbishops' to the earls' control. While it cannot be proved that this transfer was a sequence to Wulfstan's alleged disloyalty, this would afford a natural explanation of it.

An examination of the position of Wulfstan's successor Oscytel may provide support to the story. It is unfortunate that Wulfstan's reinstatement in 954 is expressed in ambiguous terms. It can be rendered: 'Archbishop Wulfstan again received a bishopric, of Dorchester.' As this was Oscytel's see, this, taken together with the statement in B that Oscytel was translated to York in Eadred's reign, would imply an exchange of sees. Wulfstan continued to sign with his archiepiscopal title until his death, but he was perhaps not trusted to return to Yorkshire. He died at Oundle, in the diocese of Dorchester, in 956. Alternatively, annal 954 can be read 'Archbishop Wulfstan received back his bishopric, at Dorchester', i.e. the reinstatement took place there. This entails the rejection of the evidence of B, a rejection made easier by the fact that B's companion manuscript, C, reads Edward for Eadred; for, though Edward is impossible, the discrepancy casts doubt on what was the reading of the common exemplar of these manuscripts.

If the story of Wulfstan's disloyalty can be accepted, it will supply a strong reason why later archbishops of York often held this see in plurality with one south of the Humber. This is normally accounted for by the impoverishment of the see of York after the Danish invasions, and this is certainly one factor in the situation. Yet the kings may also have reasoned that an archbishop drawing a large income from a southern see would be unlikely to work for an independent Northumbria. Such a view would be strengthened if it could be shown that this holding in plurality, which is certain in the cases of Oswald, Ealdulf and Wulfstan II, all of whom held Worcester, began already with

Wulfstan I's immediate successor. There is evidence that suggests that Oscytel did not relinquish Dorchester.

The investigation is hampered by the inadequacy of the episcopal lists. There is a gap in that of Leicester (the see moved to Dorchester because of the Danish invasions) between Alfred's reign and the middle of the tenth century, and Oscytel is not mentioned. From other sources four names can be recovered, the last being Oscytel. After this gap, the list begins with Leofwine, who, it says, united the sees of Leicester (i.e. Dorchester) and Lindsey in the reign of Edgar (958-75). Leofwine, however, is not simply Oscytel's successor at Dorchester, for his signatures begin while Oscytel is bishop there, before his translation to York. Hence Leofwine is usually taken to be at first a bishop of Lindsey alone, who, succeeding Oscytel when he became archbishop, thus united Lindsey and Dorchester. But, if this was immediately after Oscytel's translation, the list is wrong in assigning the union to Edgar's reign. One odd thing about the attestations should be noted: before Oscytel obtained York, he and Leofwine never attest the same document. Leofwine appears in two charters of 953, two of 955 and one of 956, all without Oscytel's name, while Oscytel attests a charter of 951, one of 952, five of 955 and forty-two of 956, which lack Leofwine's signature. They play cox and box so consistently in these years that one would suspect that we had to do with an individual with two names (remembering Æthelberht alias Coena of York, Ælfheah alias Godwine of Lichfield, Ælfstan alias Lyfing of Canterbury), were it not for the occurrence of Leofwine in four charters of 958, one of 965 and one spurious text of 966,[1] all attested by Archbishop Oscytel (as well as in two spurious texts, dated 958 and 961,[2] where Oscytel does not occur). If this is the same Leofwine, one must dismiss as coincidence a mention in the *Historia Eliensis* of an *Oschitellus alio nomine Leofwinus appellatus*.[3] This does not refer to the bishop under consideration, but to an abbot of Ely who succeeded c. 1019; yet, since he is otherwise known only as Leofwine, it is conceivable that the twelfth-century Ely historian misapplied the alias, which he could have found in an obit or in a list of benefactors, to an abbot of his house instead of

[1] BCS, no. 1179.
[2] BCS, nos. 1021 and 1073.
[3] ed. D. J. Stewart (Anglia Christiana Society, 1848), bk. II, ch. 80.

to an earlier bishop of the diocese. Leofwine's see is mentioned by name, *Dorcacistrensis*, only in a Crowland forgery, dated 966, which can be disregarded, but it was certainly north of the Thames, for the genuine charters he witnesses in 958 are issued by Edgar when he ruled this area only.[1]

But even if we take the Ely reference as a coincidence, and assume Leofwine to be a bishop of Lindsey who succeeded Oscytel to Dorchester, he need not have done so in Oscytel's lifetime. Oscytel may have held Dorchester along with York till his death in 971. This would explain why the episcopal list assigns to Edgar's reign the uniting of Dorchester and Lindsey, and also the rarity of Leofwine's signatures. One would not expect to find so important a see as Dorchester unrepresented in the vast majority of the charters.[2] This difficulty would vanish if Oscytel represents both sees until his death.[3] The fact that he died at Thame, an episcopal manor of the see of Dorchester, supports this surmise, as does the *Historia Eliensis*, for it shows him acting as bishop of Dorchester in an incident in Edgar's reign.[4]

It can be established that after Wulfstan I, of whose origin nothing is known, the men chosen for the northern archbishopric were all from south of the Humber, and mostly had connexions with the eastern Danelaw. Oscytel owned land in Beeby, Leicestershire, and included in his kindred Thurcytel, abbot of Bedford, the possessor of estates in Northamptonshire and Cambridgeshire.[5] Both Oscytel and Thurcytel are Scandinavian names. Oswald, who was Oscytel's successor to York,[6] was his kinsman, and nephew of Archbishop Oda, a man of Danish

[1] BCS, nos. 1040 and 1042-4.

[2] This should not be overstressed, for no bishop signs for Dorchester between Wynsige's last appearance in 934 and Oscytel's first in 951, unless one allots to this see an Æthelwold who attests from 945 to 949, and who occurs in no episcopal list.

[3] Oscytel, though holding York in 956, when Edwy gave Southwell (BCS, no. 1029), does not attest as archbishop before 958-9, except in a late copy. He appears in innumerable charters as bishop, signing some way down among the episcopal signatories. But it would be rash to connect his delay in receiving full archiepiscopal rights with his holding in plurality.

[4] bk. II, ch. 32.

[5] See D. Whitelock, *Saga-Book of the Viking Society*, XII (1937-45), 169-75.

[6] In northern sources, Oscytel was succeeded by an Æthelwold or Eadwold, who soon relinquished the see, desiring a quieter life. See J. Raine, *Historians of the Church of York* (Rolls Series, 1879-94), II, 340; Sym. Dur., I., 226. Nothing is known of him elsewhere.

extraction, probably from the eastern Danelaw. Oswald was succeeded by Ealdulf, a monk, and later abbot, of Peterborough. He was followed by Wulfstan II, bishop of London, whose generosity to the Fenland abbeys, especially Ely, where he was buried, suggests a previous connexion with this area. This preference for men from the eastern counties was probably not accidental. They would be familiar with the Anglo-Danish language and customs, and thus fitted to take charge of the Scandinavianized population of the diocese of York, while there would be little danger of their working for Northumbrian independence. The connexion with the eastern counties seems to have been broken with the appointment in 1023 of Ælfric Puttoc, prior of Winchester, but it was renewed with his successor Cynesige, who had patrimony in Rutland[1] and was a benefactor of Peterborough, where he was buried. The last Anglo-Saxon archbishop of York, Ealdred, a friend of the house of Godwine, had been a monk at Winchester, abbot of Tavistock, and bishop of Worcester, before his translation to York. Certainly no Northumbrian ecclesiastic was appointed to the northern archbishopric after the death of Wulfstan I. But, if political considerations played a part in the choice of archbishops, there may have been other factors in this avoidance of ecclesiastics trained in Northumbria. Such may have been regarded as inadequately educated for so high preferment. With the exception of Cynesige, a royal chaplain, all the archbishops were the product of the monastic revival;[2] but they did not succeed in establishing monastic houses in Northumbria, and it is only of Oswald that we hear of any attempt to do so.[3] Nevertheless, the appointment of these men, and the holding of York in plurality with a southern see over long periods, helped to break down the isolation of the north and brought it into contact with the new learning.

It is time to turn from ecclesiastical affairs to secular admin-

[1] *The Chronicle of Hugh Candidus*, ed. W. T. Mellows (London, 1949), p. 70.

[2] Oscytel, who was too early to be trained in a reformed monastery, gave a warm welcome to Oswald when he returned from Fleury.

[3] The *Vita Oswaldi* (ed. Raine, *op. cit.*, I, 462), after speaking of a shrine made by Oswald for St Wilfrid's relics, adds that he established monks in the place *in quo ejus pontificalis cathedra posita est*, which may refer to York rather than to Ripon. There is no further mention of monks at either place in pre-Conquest times.

istration. Athelstan's great courts, which he held in the early years of his reign, were attended by dignitaries from all parts of Britain, including two members of the English house which controlled from Bamburgh the districts north of the Tyne, and also by a number of *duces* with Scandinavian names, sometimes as many as eight in one year. But one cannot tell how many of these came from Northumbria, for some may belong to East Anglia or to the district of the Five Boroughs. Nor can one tell whether Athelstan handed over any rule in southern Northumbria to the house of Bamburgh. However, after Eric's expulsion in 954 this expedient was resorted to, and Osulf of Bamburgh was made earl of the whole of Northumbria.[1] In 963 an earl called Oslac was placed over southern Northumbria. According to the chronicle attributed to John of Wallingford, the decision to divide Northumbria into two earldoms was taken at a council held by Edgar at York, on the death of Earl Osulf, and the reason given is the king's unwillingness to let the whole area come to be regarded as any person's inheritance, *ne ad antiquam libertatem aspirantes Northimbri discordie fomitem inuenirent.*[2] The information that follows this, that the area from the Humber to the Tees was given to Oslac, and that from the Tees to *Mireforth* (the Firth of Forth) to Eadulf 'Evil-child', is contained also in the list of Northumbrian earls in the tract *De primo Saxonum adventu*,[3] which draws on the same lost source. Both these texts mention Oslac and Eadulf as the earls who, with Ælfsige, bishop of Chester-le-Street, escorted Kenneth, king of the Scots, to Edgar's court on the occasion of the cession of Lothian.[4] On the other hand, the list of Northumbrian earls incorporated into Simeon's *Historia Regum*[5] omits Eadulf and places the division into two earldoms in Osulf's lifetime.[6] It is in agreement, however, in

[1] Osulf witnesses as *dux* in 934 (BCS, nos. 701-3), as high-reeve in 946 (BCS, no. 815), and as high-reeve of Bamburgh in 949 (BCS, no. 883). See also BCS, nos. 880 and 882.

[2] *op. cit.*, p. 54.

[3] Sym. Dur., II, 382.

[4] Only Eadulf is mentioned by Roger of Wendover. See *Rogeri de Wendover Chronica*, ed. H. O. Coxe (London, 1841), I, 416; *EHD*, p. 258.

[5] Sym. Dur., II, 197.

[6] Eadulf and Oslac attest as *duces* a charter of 968 (W. Dugdale, *Monasticon Anglicanum* (London, 1846), II, 324), and another dated 978 for 968 (BCS, no. 1220), one dated 969 (BCS, no. 1230) and a dubious charter dated 970 (BCS, no. 1266). Oslac alone often witnesses from 966 to 975.

allotting to Oslac York and the territories dependent on it, leaving northern Northumbria as a separate earldom, but it names the Tyne, not the Tees, as the boundary.[1]

The northern recension of the Anglo-Saxon Chronicle records Oslac's appointment, putting it in 966, immediately after a statement that Thored Gunner's son ravaged Westmorland. Charters would appear to make Oslac earl before this date, for he witnesses a grant of North Newbald, Yorkshire, to a *dux* Gunner, which is dated 963,[2] and also three charters of 965;[3] but the Newbald charter is preserved only in a late cartulary, while the three charters of 965 are all in an Abingdon cartulary and couched in identical form, so may easily share an error in date. A contemporary charter of 966 may perhaps have a *dux* Thored,[4] and is certainly witnessed by an Oslac *minister*, thus supporting the Chronicle's date for his appointment as earl. The Chronicle calls him 'the famous earl' when telling of his banishment in 975, and Edgar's fourth code of laws entrusts him alone with the task of securing its observance in Northumbria. He must have been considered the superior of his colleague in the north. Charters show that there were other earls besides those mentioned in historical sources. Though one cannot safely allot to Northumbria all the *duces* with Scandinavian names,[5] Gunner, the recipient of Newbald, who signs from 949 to 963, and who may be identical with a *dux* Gunner appearing in Athelstan's charters, must belong there. Probably such men were subordinate earls, and they were perhaps local men; but such seem to have been avoided as the chief earls of southern Northumbria. Osulf was an Englishman from beyond the Tyne, and a reference in the *Historia Eliensis*[6] shows that Oslac was connected with the eastern Danelaw, for it mentions a son of Earl Oslac, Thorth, as concerned in an incident in Edgar's

[1] Probably because a Durham writer would not admit that anyone but St Cuthbert's had authority in County Durham.

[2] BCS, no. 1113.

[3] BCS, nos. 1169 and 1171-2.

[4] BCS, no. 1176. The name is only partly legible, but initial *þ* and what may be the remains of a *d* are visible.

[5] Scula, perhaps from East Anglia, signs a text of 942-6, in 947 and in 949; Urm, Morcar, Grim and Koll in 946 and 949, Urm also in 956 and 958, Morcar in 958; Leot in 956, 958 and 959; Halfdan in 958; Thurre in 963; Cytelbearn in the Newbald charter discussed above.

[6] bk. II, ch. 32.

reign, in a manner which implies his residence in Cambridgeshire. Thorth is a Danish name, and Oslac is often an Anglicized form of Old Norse Áslákr. As in their choice of archbishops, the kings may have considered Anglo-Danes from this region particularly suited for office in the northern Danelaw.[1]

By 979, at any rate, Oslac's successor was Thored (i.e. Thorth),[2] who gave to St Cuthbert's the Yorkshire estates of Crayke, Smeaton and Sutton.[3] He was one of the leaders of the abortive operations against the Danes in 992, after which he is not heard of again. It is possible that he was Oslac's son mentioned above, but this is not certain, for he may be the Thored Gunner's son who ravaged Westmorland in 966. If this act was, as Sir Frank Stenton suggests,[4] one of private violence, it is understandable that he should be out of favour for some time.[5] He may have become earl immediately on Oslac's expulsion after the death of Edgar in 975. He may even have had something to do with that expulsion, for which the Chronicle supplies no reason. That it was followed by troubled times in Yorkshire would appear from Archbishop Oswald's memoranda on the losses suffered by his see, if we interpret some partly illegible words near the end of the documents as 'and I held them all (i.e. the lost estates) until Thored came to power; then was St Peter robbed'.[6] The events

[1] Gaimar, *Lestorie des Engles*, ed. T. D. Hardy and C. Trice Martin (Rolls Series, 1888-9), ll. 3843-8, makes Edgar send Æthelwold, ealdorman of East Anglia, to York, and entrust to him the rule of all beyond the Humber. Though this part of the poem is based on a wild legend, it may preserve a memory of East Anglians as earls of Northumbria.

[2] KCD, no. 621. E. A. Freeman, *The Norman Conquest*, 2nd ed. (Oxford, 1875), vol. I, n. KK, suggests that the earl beyond the Tyne, Waltheof I, secured York for a brief space after Oslac's exile, since Symeon says *His* (i.e. Osulf and Oslac) *successit Walthef*; but Roger of Hoveden reads *Huic*, not *His*.

[3] *AS Charters*, no. 60.

[4] *Royal Commission on Historical Monuments: Westmorland*, p. li.

[5] See above, p. 78. Gaimar, *op. cit.*, l. 3587, says this raid cost Thored his life. This would rule out the identification with the later earl, but it may merely be Gaimar's invention.

[6] N. R. Ker, *Catalogue of Manuscripts containing Anglo-Saxon* (Oxford, 1957), p. 302, reads *ealle ic hy h[æfde o]ð þ[.]rað in com þa wæs sancte peter bereafod*, which would admit of the interpretation given above. In *EHD*, p. 522, I suggested expanding to *oð æþeræð* 'until Æthelred . . .'. One of the lost estates was Newbald, given by King Edgar to Gunner, so, if the suggestion that the alienator was Thored Gunner's son is correct, he may have reclaimed land which he thought wrongly alienated from his family.

immediately following Edgar's death are somewhat obscure, but it is clear that a reaction from his pro-monastic policy was led by Ælfhere of Mercia, and most strongly opposed by the magnates of the eastern counties. If we could assume that Oslac came from this region, and that his exile represents the victory of a member of a powerful Yorkshire family who was no friend to Archbishop Oswald, the supporter of monastic reform and an East Anglian by origin, the picture would become a little clearer. The choice of Thored as a leader in 992 shows his importance. He may have been King Æthelred's father-in-law, for Ailred of Rievaulx, who tells us so, was well placed for hearing traditions of the earls of Northumbria, and two of Æthelred's sons by his first marriage had close connexions with the thegns of the north.[1]

It seems likely that Thored lost his earldom because of the fiasco of 992. His successor Ælfhelm signs already in 993.[2] If Thored was a man of a local family, Ælfhelm's appointment indicates a change in policy. He was a Mercian, a son of the Wulfrun whose capture at Tamworth in 940 has been mentioned, the foundress of Wolverhampton. His brother, Wulfric Spot, deals in his will with extensive estates in English Mercia, as well as in the territory of the Five Boroughs, in south Lancashire, and in the West Riding of Yorkshire.[3] Ælfhelm's own lands may have been similarly widespread, but all we know is that he gave three estates in Northamptonshire to Peterborough.[4] As his daughter Ælfgifu, later Cnut's concubine and mother of his sons Swegn and Harold, is described as 'of Northampton',[5] it is probable that his main holding was in this county. His appointment seems to have much to recommend it; York would receive an earl familiar with an Anglo-Danish area, but with big stakes south of the Humber. His English origin seems stressed by his consistently receiving the title of *ealdorman*, whereas Thored is

[1] See *EHD*, p. 50.

[2] KCD, no. 684. Thored witnesses a number of charters from 979 to 988. Ælfhelm also attests frequently. He is called *Norðanhumbrensium provinciarum dux* in a spurious charter of 997 (KCD, no. 698) and *dux Transhumbranæ gentis* in Wulfrun's charter for Wolverhampton (Dugdale, *op. cit.*, vol. VI, pt. iii, pp. 1443-6).

[3] *AS Wills*, no. 17.

[4] Mellows, *op. cit.*, p. 69.

[5] *þære Hamtunisca*, ASC 1035 D; *Northamtunensis*, Florence of Worcester, *Chronicon ex Chronicis*, ed. B. Thorpe (London, 1848-9), I, 190.

called *eorl.* Ælfhelm's position in his earldom would be strengthened by Wulfric's bequest to him of Conisbrough, Yorkshire, shown by its name to have been a royal estate, since it probably already included the great area of sokeland surveyed with it in Domesday Book.[1] Wulfric also left to him and his son Wulfheah all his lands between Ribble and Mersey.

The will of Wulfric is interesting in that it reveals how there were by the end of the tenth century thegns in English areas who possessed also large estates in the districts settled by the Danes. Their lands may have been got together by purchase and inheritance, but one wonders whether Athelstan and his successors encouraged such infiltration into the Danish areas, as it is known Edward the Elder did.[2] It would clearly be to their interest to break down the isolation of the north by such means.

Ælfhelm's appointment was not a lasting success. In 1006 he was murdered and his two sons blinded, apparently by the king's orders.[3] The reason is unknown, but it is possible that Ælfhelm was suspected of pro-Danish sympathy, since his brother's will shows a connexion between this family and that of Morcar, a thegn of the Seven Boroughs (i.e. the Five Boroughs perhaps plus York and Torksey), who with his brother Sigeferth was murdered in 1015.

Meanwhile, north of the Tyne, Eadulf 'Evil-child' had been succeeded by Waltheof I, whose only attestation is in a charter of 994.[4] This is witnessed also by Ælfhelm and by an earl Northman, who in other references is connected with Durham. The *Liber Vitae* enters a gift by him to St Cuthbert's of Escomb with Ferryhill,[5] and the *Historia de S. Cuthberto* contains a list of estates, mainly in Durham, but including three in Cleveland, which Bishop Aldhun (990-1018) leased to three earls, Ethred, Northman and Uhtred.[6] Ethred is otherwise unknown, unless he is the Æthelred *dux* who attests two charters of 1019.[7] Northman

[1] See *Early Yorkshire Charters*, vol. VIII, *The Honour of Warenne*, ed. C. T. Clay (Wakefield, 1949), pp. 137-9.

[2] See Stenton, *Anglo-Saxon England*, p. 318 f.

[3] ASC gives no details. Florence (*op. cit.*, I, 158) places the murder at Shrewsbury and attributes it to Eadric Streona, but by Florence's time most acts of violence were put down to him. The sons' blinding he places at the king's residence at Cookham, by his orders.

[4] KCD, no. 687. [5] *AS Charters*, no. 68. [6] Sym. Dur., I, 213.

[7] KCD, nos. 729-30.

is probably to be identified with a man who attended a great meeting in London in 989 or 990, along with his brother Nafena and other northern dignitaries.[1] He may have been a subordinate earl, perhaps over part of Durham.

After Ælfhelm's murder the practice was revived of placing all Northumbria under an earl of the house of Bamburgh, now represented by Uhtred. The *De obsessione Dunelmi*,[2] a tract of about 1100 which includes legendary features, makes him succeed his father Waltheof after a successful battle against the Scots, an event dated 1006 by the Annals of Ulster.[3] But if Simeon of Durham correctly names him as earl when Bishop Aldhun transferred his see to Durham in 995,[4] Uhtred must have succeeded Waltheof in the north some years before he obtained the earldom of all Northumbria in 1006. The *De obsessione* says his first wife was Bishop Aldhun's daughter, whom he divorced in order to marry the daughter of a rich citizen, presumably of York,[5] called Styr Ulf's son, agreeing to kill Styr's enemy Thurbrand. This he did not do, and a second divorce followed, after which he married King Æthelred's daughter. The *De primo Saxonum adventu*[6] and the chronicle attributed to John of Wallingford[7] both have this last piece of information. Uhtred and all the Northumbrians submitted to Swegn Forkbeard in 1013, and in 1016, after campaigning for some time with the ætheling Edmund, he submitted to Cnut 'out of necessity', but was murdered by Thurbrand when entering Cnut's hall. Thus was started a feud which lasted until 1073.

Cnut then gave Northumbria to one of his generals, Earl Eric of Hlathir, though apparently northern Northumbria was left

[1] The bungled form read by E. Edwards, *Liber Monasterii de Hyda* (Rolls Series, 1866), p. 245, as *norwinan* and by A. J. Robertson, *AS Charters*, no. 63, as *norwinaai*, may represent *Norþman*, with the common errors of *wyn* for *þorn* and *m* misread as *in*, rather than *Norþwine*. Nafena is no doubt the father of Thurcytel who was killed along with Uhtred in 1016. A Northman called *princeps* who received Twywell, Northants., in 1013 (KCD, no. 1308) is more probably the brother of Earl Leofric, who was killed in 1017.

[2] Sym. Dur., I, 215-20.

[3] See A. O. Anderson, *Early Sources of Scottish History A.D. 500 to 1286* (Edinburgh and London, 1922), I, 525.

[4] Sym. Dur., I, 81. Uhtred first signs in 1009 (KCD, no. 1306).

[5] The family of his enemy, Thurbrand, is shown by Domesday and later evidence to have held property in York and lands in Yorkshire.

[6] Sym. Dur., II, 383.

[7] *op. cit.*, p. 59.

under the control of Uhtred's family, probably in subordination to Eric. The northern lists do not mention him, but let Uhtred be succeeded first by his brother Eadulf Cudel, then by his son Ealdred, and then, about 1038, by his younger son, another Eadulf. Eric last witnesses a genuine document in 1023,[1] and it is uncertain, owing to the scarcity of documents for Cnut's later years, who was earl of south Northumbria between this date and 1033, the year of Siward's first signature as *dux*.[2] Siward may be Eric's immediate successor, or Eadulf Cudel may for a time have had the whole of Northumbria.[3] All that is certain is that Siward became earl 'from the Humber to the Tweed' after Eadulf Cudel's nephew and namesake was murdered at Harthacnut's court in 1041, according to northern sources by Siward himself. Siward, a Dane of unknown origin, who had married Ælfflæd, the daughter of Earl Ealdred Uhtred's son, played a prominent part in the events of the Confessor's reign until his death in 1054.

His son Waltheof was too young to succeed him,but there were adult members of the house of Bamburgh. Yet King Edward passed them over and gave the earldom to Tostig Godwine's son. Sir Frank Stenton writes: 'It is not surprising that the king and his council took this unique opportunity of governing Northumbria through an earl in close association with the court.'[4] There was certainly precedent for bringing in an outsider as earl of southern Northumbria, but the lands north of the Tyne had always had an earl from the local family of Bamburgh. The Northumbrians rose against Tostig in 1065. The pro-Godwine writer of the *Vita Ædwardi* attributes his unpopularity to his efforts to suppress violence in an unruly province;[5] the Northumbrian point of view,

[1] KCD, no. 739.

[2] Cnut's grant of Patrington to York, KCD, no. 749.

[3] Freeman, *op. cit.*, vol. I, n. KK, considered this implicit in the statement in the *De obsessione Dunelmi* (*op. cit.*, p. 219) that Ealdred, Eadulf Cudel's successor, *solius Northumbriæ comitatum* (i.e. Northumberland) *suscepit*; but northern sources are unreliable for the history of the earldom of southern Northumbria. They know nothing of Ælfhelm, Thored, or Eric. A *dux* Sihtric witnesses in 1026 (KCD, no. 743) and in 1031 (*Ordnance Survey Facsimiles*, vol. II*: Exeter*, no. 11), but there is nothing to connect him with the north.

[4] *Anglo-Saxon England*, p. 562.

[5] *Lives of Edward the Confessor*, ed. H. R. Luard (Rolls Series, 1858), p. 421 f. An account of one of St Cuthbert's miracles depicts Tostig as refusing to release a malefactor in spite of the importunity of his kindred (Sym. Dur., I, 243 f.).

given by Florence of Worcester,[1] is that the north rose to avenge the deaths of its noble thegns, Uhtred's son Gospatric, whose death at court on 28 December 1064 was blamed on Queen Eadgyth, acting in the interests of her brother Tostig, Gamal Orm's son and Ulf Dolfin's son, both killed by Tostig's orders when visiting him at York under safe conduct. He is accused also of levying an unjust and immense tax. The rebels asked for Morcar, son of Ælfgar, earl of Mercia, for their earl, probably believing their best chance of success lay in enlisting the support of this powerful family.[2] Northumbria could no longer stand alone. Their choice was reluctantly ratified at Oxford on 28 October 1065. Morcar gave the lands north of the Tyne into the charge of Osulf, the son of the last Earl Eadulf. Morcar and Osulf were in office at the time of the Norman Conquest.

During the Confessor's reign the earldom of Northumbria began to be held along with one in the east Midlands.[3] Siward was earl of Huntingdonshire by 1050-2, but not before 1044, when it was held by Thuri, whom Florence of Worcester describes as *Mediterraneorum* in 1041, and perhaps not before 1051, when the same authority includes this county and Cambridgeshire in Harold's East Anglian earldom. Tostig's earldom included Northamptonshire[4] also, and Bedfordshire. On his expulsion this Midland earldom did not pass with Northumbria to Morcar, but to Siward's son Waltheof, who was an earl by 1066. Later evidence shows that it included Cambridgeshire. In view of the practice in Edward's reign of concentrating comital power in the hands of a few great families, it would be unwise to attach special

[1] *op. cit.*, I, 223.

[2] No connexion can be established between this family and that of Morcar, the thegn of the Seven Boroughs killed in 1015, though Earl Ælfgar's choice of this name for his son makes one suspect some link by marriage.

[3] See Freeman, *op. cit.*, vol. II, n. G; J. H. Round, *Geoffrey de Mandeville* (London, 1892), pp. 191-3; G. H. Fowler, 'The Shire of Bedford and the Earldom of Huntingdon', *Publications of the Bedfordshire Record Society*, IX, 24-34; *AS Writs*, pp. 574-6; F. S. Scott, 'Earl Waltheof of Northumbria', *Archaeologia Aeliana*, 4th ser., XXX (1952), 149-215.

[4] Siward had connexions in this part of the country, for by agreement with Peterborough he held Ryhall and Belmesthorpe, Rutland, which his wife Godgifu, who died soon after the marriage, left to the abbey (KCD, no. 927).

significance to the granting of an earldom south of the Humber to Northumbrian earls. Yet it must have helped to unite Northumbria with the south, and have added to the earls' resources when dealing with troubles in the north.

It was essential that the earls of Northumbria should be powerful, not only because of the turbulence of the inhabitants, but because of the danger of attack from Scotland and Strathclyde. Lands on both sides of the Solway which had belonged to Northumbria had been lost to Strathclyde during the period of Viking settlement, and north Lancashire and the Lake District received an influx of Irish-Norse settlers in the early tenth century.[1] We have already seen how Amounderness was made into a bulwark against them, and it is likely that the large holding held in Edward's reign by Earl Tostig in Lonsdale and in the parts of Westmorland and Cumberland which were surveyed with Yorkshire consisted of comital lands organized as a protection against inroads from the north-west. In the north-east, the Tweed became the boundary by the cession by Edgar of Lothian to Kenneth of the Scots. Several times the kings led their forces against the Cumbrians or the Scots. Athelstan received the submission of both at Eamont Bridge in 927, and took an army to Scotland in 934; Edmund conquered Cumbria in 945, making it over to Malcolm, king of the Scots, on condition that he should defend northern England from raiders, though this arrangement was short-lived; Edgar took his whole naval force to Chester in 973 and received pledges from Kenneth of the Scots and Malcolm of Strathclyde; Æthelred ravaged Strathclyde in 1000, though the fleet sent to co-operate with the army failed to establish contact; Cnut led an army to Scotland soon after he came back from Rome. Occasional references to the king's presence in the north may indicate unrecorded troubles. Athelstan was at York in 936,[2] and Æthelred at a date not before 1002.[3] Often, however, the earls had to deal with their enemies without the king's help. Uhtred won a battle

[1] On this and what follows see Stenton, *Royal Commission on Historical Monuments: Westmorland*, pp. xlviii-lv, also *Anglo-Saxon England*, pp. 328, 336-9, 354 f., 364 f., 373, 412 f. and 562; B. Dickins, *The Place-Names of Cumberland*, III (EPNS, vol. XXII, 1952), xxi-xxx.

[2] See *EHD*, p. 316, n. 5.

[3] Simeon names Wulfstan as the archbishop concerned; the *Historia de S. Cuthberto* has Ælfric, who was not archbishop in Æthelred's reign (Sym. Dur., I, 83 and 213).

against Malcolm in 1006,[1] but was defeated a few years later at Carham-on-Tweed;[2] about 1040 Duncan of the Scots unsuccessfully laid siege to Durham;[3] Siward in 1054 took a land force and a naval force into Scotland in support of Malcolm Duncan's son, and heavily defeated Macbeth.[4] He may be the earl who recovered the area of Cumberland which afterwards became the honour of Allerdale, but the writ of Gospatric (probably Uhtred's son who was murdered in 1064), which tells us that these lands had been Cumbrian, contains a hint that already Earl Ealdred had power there.[5] Tostig was on friendly terms with Malcolm, and escorted him to King Edward in 1059.[6] Yet he harried Northumbria while Tostig was on a visit to Rome in 1061.

In view of the distance of this vulnerable province from the centres of government, it is not surprising that Domesday Book reveals only what Farrer calls 'a trifling estate' of the Crown in 1066: 'under the earl, rather than the king, was a great crowd of thegns'.[7] Though it is only rarely that estates held by the earl by reason of his office can be distinguished from his private possessions, it must be significant that Morcar, the earl in 1066, had a much greater holding in Yorkshire than other big men. His fourteen great estates had an aggregate value of £618, whereas his brother Edwin's five estates were valued only at £176. Morcar's lands included Driffield, perhaps once belonging to the kings of Northumbria, since it was there that King Aldfrith died in 705, and Market Weighton, which included part of Goodmanham, the sanctuary of the kings of Deira. Mention has already been made of Tostig's lands in Amounderness, Lonsdale, etc. Some other lands entered as his in Domesday may have belonged to the

[1] According to the *De obsessione Dunelmi* this was at an unsuccessful siege of Durham, but this account suspiciously resembles that of the siege of 1040.

[2] On its date, see Stenton, *Anglo-Saxon England*, p. 412, n.

[3] Sym. Dur., I, 90 f.

[4] According to Gaimar, *op. cit.*, ll. 5043-5, Siward had been to Scotland in 1053 and made a treaty, which Macbeth broke. In this part of his poem Gaimar seems to have had access to some lost northern source.

[5] The Gospatric writ (Dickins, *op. cit.*, pp. xxvii-xxx; *AS Writs*, pp. 419-24) refers to rights held in the days of Eadred, and I agree with Professor Dickins that this is probably an error for Ealdred.

[6] Sym. Dur., II, 174.

[7] *Victoria County History of Yorkshire*, II, 134.

earldom. Hemingborough, for example, is shown by a charter of 1080-6 to have belonged to Siward before Tostig.[1]

It would not be strange if the kings of England were reluctant to put such power into the hands of an Anglo-Danish Northumbrian. In the middle of the tenth century the fear of the establishment of another Scandinavian king must have been real. Eadred does not include the Northumbrians when he makes bequests for the benefit of his people.[2] Edgar used a conciliatory policy, admitting the right of the Danes to their own laws: 'I have ever allowed them this and will allow it as long as my life lasts, because of your loyalty, which you have always shown me.'[3] He punished the men of Thanet for offences against York merchants.[4] Yet the presence of a Northumbrian hostage among Brihtnoth's household troops at Maldon in 991[5] is most easily accounted for on the assumption that the English government did not fully trust the Northumbrian Danes when Scandinavian invasions had recommenced. Attempts to secure their loyalty by diplomatic marriages may also have been made, seeing that Ailred of Rievaulx says that Æthelred's first wife was a daughter of Earl Thored, and northern sources assert that Uhtred married Æthelred's daughter.[6] An unpublished charter[7] shows Æthelred making a large grant to Morcar, the thegn of the Seven Boroughs, at a gathering which included an unusual number of thegns of the northern Danelaw in 1009, the year of Thurkil's great invasion. This looks like an attempt to buy the support of the northerners in this crisis.

If all this is indicative of uneasiness on the part of the English, there is evidence that their fears were not unfounded. In 993 the leaders of a force in the Humber region instigated flight from the Danes, and Florence of Worcester attributes this to Danish sympathies. The Northumbrians were among those who submitted immediately to Swegn at Gainsborough in 1013, and the fact that on his southward march he refrained from ravaging until he had crossed the Watling Street shows how strong the distinction between the English and Danish areas was still felt to be.

[1] *Early Yorkshire Charters*, ed. W. Farrer, II (Edinburgh, 1915), 303.
[2] *EHD*, p. 511 f.
[3] *ibid.*, p. 400.
[4] *ibid.*, p. 257.
[5] *The Battle of Maldon*, ll. 265-72.
[6] See above, pp. 80 and 82.
[7] William Salt Library, Stafford.

The men of Lindsey elected to throw in their lot with Cnut after Swegn's death and to join him in raiding English territory. The unexplained murders of Earl Ælfhelm in 1006 and of Sigeferth and Morcar in 1015 may have been actuated by a suspicion that they were disloyal to the English cause.[1] There is a true ring about the reason given in the *Vita Wulfstani* to explain the Northumbrian reluctance to accept Harold Godwine's son as king in 1066: *aquilonalem ceruicositatem australi ut dictitabant mollitiei subiugare non dignati.*[2] As late as 1066, after the Battle of Fulford, the men of York agreed to go south with Harold Hardrada to conquer the land.[3]

It is not within the limits of my subject to deal with the northern resistance to William. But one should note the argument put into Lanfranc's mouth in one account of the conflict between Canterbury and York over the primacy: 'That it was expedient for preserving the integrity and security of the kingdom that the whole of Britain should be subject to one primate; otherwise it could happen that a king might be created by the archbishop of York and the changeable and perfidious natives of his province, from the Danes, or Norwegians, or Scots, who were in the habit of coming to York with a fleet and infesting the kingdom.'[4] In spite of the scanty nature of our sources, I suspect that similar fears often beset the Saxon kings in the tenth and eleventh centuries.

[1] The murder of Sigeferth and Morcar caused a breach between Æthelred and his son Edmund, who in defiance of his father married Sigeferth's widow and seized all his lands and Morcar's. A very late source, *La Vie Seint Edmund le Rei*, ed. T. Arnold, *Memorials of St Edmund's Abbey* (Rolls Series, 1890-6), II, 246 f., says that these thegns had invited Swegn to England.

[2] *Vita Wulfstani*, ed. R. R. Darlington (Camden Society, 1928), p. 22.

[3] ASC 1066 C.

[4] Raine, *op. cit.*, II, 100.

IV

The Appointment of Dunstan as Archbishop of Canterbury[1]

In 1874 Bishop Stubbs rescued the reputation of St. Dunstan from the various misrepresentations which had grown up from grotesque legends told about him.[2] The favourable view put forward by Stubbs has prevailed ever since, and it is not the intention of this article to question its general accuracy. On certain matters, however, claims made by Stubbs can no longer be upheld. Dunstan cannot be given the credit for the so-called 'Canons of Edgar', since Jost has shown them to be the work of Archbishop Wulfstan II of York (1002–23).[3] There is no evidence in support of Stubbs when, wishing to clear Dunstan of any responsibility for the misgovernment of Ethelred's reign, he suggests that he had retired from public activities after Ethelred's accession;[4] charters show him present at meetings after Edgar's death as before it. His failure to prevent the decline is more probably because he never had had even in Edgar's reign the great influence in secular affairs which Stubbs assigns him, calling him the king's 'chief minister'—a view which tended to diminish the stature of the king himself and some effective lay magnates; the only evidence for Dunstan's political importance comes from the Lives of St. Dunstan, and it is the common practice of hagiographical writers to exaggerate the power of the saint about whom they are writing. Writers since Stubbs have laid more emphasis on the leading part Dunstan played in ecclesiastical concerns, especially in the monastic revival of the tenth century, and on the admiration accorded him both by contemporaries and by later writers.[5] It should not, however, be forgotten that no writings survive from those opposed to the monastic party, who might have given a different view.

There is one episode in his career, his appointment as archbishop of Canterbury, which received little attention until in 1962 Dom Thomas Symons at my suggestion included a brief discussion in an article on Dunstan.[6] A rather fuller treatment may raise a few points of interest.

The events leading up to Dunstan's appointment are as follows: He was driven into exile soon after Eadwig came to the throne in 955. The normally accepted view is that this was because he aroused the personal enmity of the young king by his behaviour at the coronation feast, when, according to the oldest Life of Dunstan, by a man whom we know only by his initial, 'B', he and Cynesige, bishop of Lichfield, forced Eadwig to return to the banquet which he had left for the society of the lady whom later he married, and of her mother.[7] But 'B', who was probably a foreigner, wrote the Life between 994 and 1004, perhaps early in that period, and a story can grow in some forty years. There appear to have been other rumours current about Eadwig and his wife.[8] Seeing that no action appears to have been taken by Eadwig against Bishop Cynesige, and that about the same time the queen-mother, Eadgifu, a keen supporter of monastic reform, was deprived of all her lands,[9] it is more likely that Dunstan's exile was brought about by the coming into power of a party which had resented the influence which he and Eadgifu had had over King Eadred. One must take seriously the evidence for a reaction against Eadred's ecclesiastical policy which is contained in an Old English tract known as 'King Edgar's Establishment of Monasteries',[10] for there is good reason to believe that it is the work of Dunstan's contemporary, Æthelwold, bishop of Winchester. According to this, Eadwig, 'through the ignorance of childhood, . . . distributed the lands of the holy churches to rapacious strangers.' Dunstan went to the monastery of Blandinium, Ghent.

In 957 the Mercians broke away from Wessex and elected Edgar as their king, and the Northumbrians soon followed suit. While still an atheling, Edgar had vowed that, if ever he became king, he would restore the ruined monasteries. He now recalled Dunstan from exile. Biographer 'B', while correctly ascribing this to the period when Edgar was king only of the Mercians and Northumbrians, wrongly places in the period after Eadwig's death, when Edgar had succeeded to the whole of England, a great council of the witan held at *Bradanford*, at which Dunstan was ordained bishop, by the election of all.[11] He implies that at first Dunstan was not elected to any particular see, and this is supported by a charter of 958 witnessed by Dunstan as bishop, along with Bishop Coenwald, his predecessor at Worcester, the first see which Dunstan held.[12] Edgar was still reigning only over the Mercians and Northumbrians when Dunstan became bishop of this Mercian see, and also when he was appointed to London, another Mercian see. This is shown clearly by a charter of 959, issued by Edgar as king of the Mercians, which is attested by Dunstan as bishop of London.[13] Dunstan retained Worcester; holding in plurality was contrary to canon law, but it was not uncommon in the tenth century, in part necessitated by the impoverishment of some sees during the Danish ravages of the previous century.

Oda, archbishop of Canterbury, died on 2 June, 958.[13a] He was succeeded by Ælfsige, bishop of Winchester, but he died of cold in the Alps on his way to Rome to fetch his pallium. A bishop called Brihthelm was then appointed. 'B' does not actually say that these events took place after Edgar's accession to the whole of England, though from the sequence of his narrative one might suppose so; charters show that Brihthelm's appointment was in Eadwig's reign.[14] 'B' then says that Brihthelm was made to withdraw by Edgar, and to return to his former see, and that Dunstan was then appointed to Canterbury.[15] As there are several bishops called Brihthelm at this time, it is necessary to try to sort them out.[16]

The Brihthelm appointed to Canterbury is called by 'B' *Dorsætiensium prævisorem*, i.e. bishop of Sherborne, but his name does not occur in the lists of bishops[17] of this see, and there is room only for a short episcopate between Wulfsige (called Alfsius by Florence of Worcester) who last attests a charter in 958,[18] and Ælfwold, whose first certain attestation is in 964[19], when he appears along with Ælfwold of Crediton, to whom the frequent attestations in 958–962 may belong. It is possible that 'B' has given a wrong name to Brihthelm's see. In annal 958 of Florence, it says that *Ælsius Dorsetiensium episcopus* was succeeded by Brihthelm, who is described in words which show that Florence is using the Life by 'B'. In the next annal, the manuscript of Florence at Corpus Christi College, Oxford,[20] reads: *Byrhthelmus Sumorsetensium episcopus ad archipresulatum Cantuuarie sedis deligitur*, but from *Sumorsetensium* to *archipresulatum* is on an erasure; Professor Darlington dates this hand as mid-twelfth-century;[21] the correction may possibly be by the author. The Lambeth[22] and the Dublin[23] manuscripts read *Dorsetensium*, not *Sumorsetensium*, which is the reading of the Bodleian manuscript.[24] Yet, though it seems clear that Florence originally agreed with 'B' in the name of Brihthelm's see, the alteration may be correct. There is a Brihthelm of Wells (i.e. Somerset) in the lists between Wulfhelm, who last attests in 956,[25] and Cyneward, who first attests in 974.[26] According to an obit given by William of Malmesbury,[26a] he had been a monk at Glastonbury. Even if 'B' was not in error in assigning Brihthelm to Sherborne, the same person could be meant, for Brihthelm may have held the see of Sherborne in plurality with that of Wells. An addition to the Oxford Corpus manuscript of Florence, which adds at the end of annal 958 the words *Wellensis episcopus* to the statement that a Brihthelm succeeded to Winchester when Ælfsige was appointed to Canterbury, is a late and mistaken identification.

It is, however, correct that Ælfsige was succeeded at Winchester by a Brihthelm, though not Brihthelm of Wells. Though his name is omitted in the lists of bishops in BM Cotton MS. Tiberius B.v, in the *Liber Vitæ* of Newminster and in Corpus Christi College, Cambridge, MS. 173, it occurs in that in MS. 140 of that college. He held the see until 963. He is certainly not the Brihthelm appointed to Canterbury, for two charters attested by the latter as bishop of the church of Canterbury[27] have also the attestation of Brihthelm, bishop of the church of Winchester. The latter is called the king's kinsman in charters of 960 and 961.[28]

There was also a Brihthelm who was Dunstan's predecessor at London. He is the Brihthelm who attests charters of 953 and 955,[29] and probably most, perhaps all, of the thirty-seven charters of 956 and the five of 957[30] prior to the division of the kingdom between Eadwig and Edgar, which are attested by only one bishop of this name. Some time during 956 a second Brihthelm appears; in one charter with two Brihthelms, one is called bishop of London.[31] There are five charters of 956[32] and two of 957[33] before the division, with two Brihthelms. The second is probably the bishop of Wells. After the division, when Eadwig's charters are witnessed only by bishops from south of the Thames, three texts of 957[34] and seven of 958[35] are attested by two bishops called Brihthelm. Armitage Robinson thought that one of these was still the bishop of London, but this would imply that, though London is a Mercian see, its bishop remained loyal to Eadwig when the kingdom was divided. The charters issued by Edgar as king of the Mercians and Northumbrians[36] do not include a certain attestation of a bishop of London until Dunstan is given this title in 959,[37] but in some of the texts of 958 where he appears simply as bishop, he may already have held London as well as Worcester. Armitage Robinson suggests that it was Brihthelm of London who received the see of Winchester late in 958, after Ælfsige went to Canterbury. If so, it would mean that Dunstan accepted London in his predecessor's lifetime, either because the latter had resigned, or because Edgar, understandably, expelled him in view of his attendance at Eadwig's councils.

Yet this is not the only possible interpretation of the evidence. The absence of Brihthelm of London from Edgar's charters in 958 need imply nothing more than that he was in failing health some time before he died; and there is another candidate for the position of the second bishop of this name in Eadwig's charters of 957 and 958. A spurious charter, dated 956,[38] purports to be a grant to a Bishop Brihthelm of Chichester (an obvious error, for the see was not moved from Selsey until after the Conquest); another text in the same cartulary claims to be a deed issued in 957 by Bishop Brihthelm, concerning the restoration of lands seized from Selsey.[39] Though neither text can be accepted as it stands, it seems improbable that the name Brihthelm would have been used unless some record survived at the see that there had been a bishop of this name. There is room for one between Alfred and Eadhelm in the Selsey list, for Alfred's last appearence is in 953[40] and Eadhelm's first in 963.[41]

In 956 Eadwig gave land at Stowe-Nine-Churches, Northamptonshire, to his kinsman Brihthelm, *ad episcopalem gradum electus*.[42] Since Brihthelm of Winchester did not receive that see until 958, it is usually assumed that this refers to Brihthelm of Wells, though he is not called the king's kinsman elsewhere. Yet it is possible that Brihthelm of Winchester, who certainly was the king's kinsman, was elected in 956, not to Winchester, but to Selsey, and then translated to Winchester after Ælfsige went to Canterbury. He may be the Bishop Brihthelm mentioned in the foundation charter for Eynsham[43] as the donor of Esher, Surrey, to Ealdorman Æthelweard, for he is described as the latter's kinsman, and Æthelweard was a member of the royal house. The estate given to the bishop-elect in 956, Stowe-Nine-Churches, was given by him to Abingdon. This makes it tempting to identify him with the king's priest Brihthelm, who in the same year received from King Eadwig land in Kennington, Berkshire,[44] which he exchanged with Æthelwold, abbot of Abingdon, for land at Curbridge, Oxfordshire; in the deed of exchange[45] he is called bishop.

However, as the king's priest is not described as the king's kinsman, this identification is uncertain. He could be the bishop of Wells, who became bishop in 956. In that case, we should have to reject the statement of William of Malmesbury that Brihthelm of Wells had been a monk of Glastonbury. If we accept it, it would at first sight appear to lessen the probability that it was Brihthelm of Wells who was appointed to Canterbury, for he would have been a monk when Dunstan was abbot of Glastonbury, and this would mean, if we accept the account of the dismissal as given by 'B', that Dunstan acquiesced in the summary treatment of a man who had been trained under him at Glastonbury. If, however, as suggested below,[45a] Brihthelm was willing to resign, this would be more understandable if he did so in favour of his former abbot. If we reject William of Malmesbury's statement as an error, and, identifying the king's priest with Brihthelm of Wells, take the latter to be the same person as the one called bishop of Dorset by 'B', we then reach the interesting result that Eadwig appointed to Canterbury a man who had been his chaplain a couple of years earlier. Even so, this would not be enough to prove correct Stubb's suggestion that the Brihthelm appointed to Canterbury 'was probably Edwy's prime minister, as Dunstan was Edgar's';[46] to claim for him political influence is to run counter to the description of his character given by 'B'. Stubbs believed him to be the king's kinsman, but this depends solely on the identification of him with the bishop-elect of *BCS* 986, which is uncertain; it would give Eadwig two kinsmen of this name who both became bishops.

Amidst much uncertainty, it is at least clear that Brihthelm of Canterbury had been bishop neither of London nor of Winchester. He may have been bishop of Wells, with the title bishop of Dorset given to him by 'B' either in error, or because he held Sherborne in plurality for a few years from 958. If we reject this identification, we must take Brihthelm of Canterbury to be a fourth bishop of this name, and assume that Eadwig appointed as archbishop a man who had only recently been given a bishopric, that of Sherborne, in 958. If so, the see to which he was sent back would be Sherborne, and he held it, at the latest, only until 964, when his successor certainly begins to attest charters.

The date of his appointment to Canterbury requires some discussion. Oda died on 2 June, 958; his attestation of a charter of 959 is doubtful.[47] In several charters of 958 he does not appear,[48] either because he was ill, or because they are later than his death. The episcopal signatories are usually headed by Ælfsige, his successor at Canterbury.[49] Then, still in 958, Ælfsige's name disappears, presumably because he had set out on his ill-fated journey to fetch his pallium. His place at the head of the list is now taken by Brihthelm,[50] who succeeded him at Canterbury, while another Bishop Brihthelm, lower down, must be Ælfsige's successor at Winchester, though perhaps as yet only bishop of Selsey. Next come two of Eadwig's charters attested by Brihthelm as *Dorobernensis ecclesiæ episcopus*. They have survived in cartularies from different houses, and there is no reason to suspect their authenticity. One, in the Athelney cartulary, is dated 958, but has an indiction for 959;[51] the other, in a Newminster cartulary, is dated 959.[52] This date is probably correct for both charters: they have the same episcopal signatories, in the same order and with the same titles, and may have been issued on the same occasion. Moreover, to accept a date 958 would imply that things moved very quickly; Ælfsige did not set out for Rome until so late that he met dangerous conditions in the Alps; the news of his death had then to be brought back; then his successor had to be appointed, and since Brihthelm does not attest as *electus*, he had apparently been enthroned. All this can hardly have happened before Christmas, 958, the date from which the new year was calculated. The use of *episcopus*, instead of *archiepiscopus*, implies that he had not got his pallium; for though there are a few examples of the use of the title bishop for an archbishop, especially in vernacular writing, there is evidence from about this time of the avoidance in Latin charters of the title archbishop until the pallium has been received. This seems to be why Archbishop Oscytel of York consistently attests as *episcopus* from 956 to 958, and almost consistently as *archiepiscopus* from then until his death in 971.[53] It is possible that Brihthelm had not held Canterbury long enough before Eadwig died on 1 October, 959, for arrangements to be made to obtain a pallium for him. If he had received one, it would surely have been difficult for Edgar to dismiss him.

It is unlikely to have been before late on in 959, at the earliest, that Edgar expelled Brihthelm. Dunstan attests one charter in 959 as archbishop; it survives only in the twelfth-century *Codex Wintoniensis*.[54] If it is genuine it would show Dunstan using the title archbishop before he got his pallium, unless, as is conceivable, a copyist altered the title. In a charter of 960 Dunstan attests merely as *episcopus*;[55] four others of this year,[56] in which he is *archiepiscopus*, may be after his return with his pallium late in 960.

According to 'B', Brihthelm was *mitis et modestus et humilis et benignus*, but was prevented by his gentleness of character from controlling the proud and rebellious; hence Edgar dismissed him and put Dunstan in his place.[57] Later Lives of Dunstan merely elaborate on this, without having any fresh evidence. Several sources ignore Brihthelm, and some ignore his predecessor Ælfsige as well. Thus the acrostic poem written for Dunstan by Abbo of Fleury in 985—8 mentions Oda as a predecessor without referring to intervening holders of the see.[58] The episcopal lists of archbishops of Canterbury[59] have Dunstan immediately after Oda. This may be because Ælfsige and Brihthelm did not receive the pallium; naturally they are not mentioned in the list telling which popes sent pallia to the archbishops of Canterbury, which represents the tradition current at Canterbury about 1100.[60] About this time, the F manuscript of the *Anglo-Saxon Chronicle*, written at Canterbury, says, under a wrong date, 961: 'In this year the good Archbishop Oda died, and Dunstan was elected archbishop.' If it were not for the Lives of Dunstan, Eadmer's Life of St. Oda, based on these, the two charters which Brihthelm attests as bishop of Canterbury, and the reference to Ælfsige (but not to Brihthelm) in the *Vita Oswaldi*[61] and in the *Gesta Pontificum* of William of Malmesbury,[62] we should have thought that Dunstan was Oda's immediate successor.

The charters are enough to show that 'B' was correct in letting Brihthelm precede Dunstan; but was he equally correct in representing Brihthelm's departure as the result of so arbitrary a dismissal? It is understandable that Edgar would wish to have an archbishop who was a strong personality and fully in favour of his own ecclesiastical policy, and he may not have shrunk from ruthless action to get his way, but would Dunstan have allowed himself to be thus intruded into the see in the lifetime of a duly appointed predecessor, unless the latter had resigned?

It may be of interest to compare the appointment of Oswald to the archbishopric of York. Archbishop Oscytel died on 31 October, probably in 970,[62a] and some sources[63] merely record the succession of the monastic reformer, Oswald, bishop of Worcester; but Symeon of Durham[64] and the 'Chronicle of the Archbishops of York'[65] place between Oscytel and Oswald an Archbishop Æthelwald (or Eadwald), who, they say, soon resigned his see because he preferred a quieter life. There seems no motive for the invention of this person by the northern writers. His resignation left it open for Edgar to put at York one of the monastic party which he favoured, and one wonders whether Æthelwald had not been encouraged to resign. It is possible that Brihthelm also was willing to resign, in Dunstan's favour,[65a] but that there was a suspicion in some quarters that he had been dismissed, and that it was this version which reached 'B'.

The later biographers of Dunstan had only the account in 'B' to go by. They do not appear to have been altogether happy about Dunstan's succession after the dismissal of a predecessor. Adelard, a monk of Blandinium, writing a series of lessons on St Dunstan before 1011, avoids the incident entirely, but he expands a story told by 'B' in a way which may bear on this matter. In 'B', Dunstan refused the see of Crediton offered to him by King Eadred, and then had a vision of the Apostles Peter, Paul and Andrew, in which the last chastised him for his refusal to accept episcopal office.[66] In Adelard, where the see concerned is called Winchester, the account is much lengthened and the chief rôle transferred to Peter, on whose sword words are inscribed which King Eadred is able to interpret as a prophecy that Dunstan will become archbishop.[67] Adelard also adds a story not in 'B'; this tells how Archbishop Oda, when consecrating Dunstan bishop of Worcester, made, by the inspiration of the Holy Spirit, a slip of the tongue, and consecrated him archbishop of Canterbury;[68] and when Adelard mentions Dunstan's appointment to Canterbury, he refers back to this incident in the words: 'with the election of the whole church he succeeded to the throne of the patriarchal office to which the Holy Spirit had at the time of his ordination named him in advance'. But, as we saw above, according to the Life by 'B', Dunstan was not first ordained as bishop of Worcester, but as a bishop without a see. These additions in Adelard, which are meant to show that it was, all along, the divine intention that Dunstan should become archbishop of Canterbury, may be directed against possible criticisms of the manner of his appointment. One cannot be sure whether they were already part of the Dunstan legend as it reached Adelard, or whether he himself added them, being disturbed by the implications of the account of Brihthelm's dismissal in 'B'; but the former is the more likely, since we can point to a similar development in England about the same time. Abbot Ælfric, in the Life of St Æthelwold which he sent to the bishop and monks of Winchester in 1005 or 1006, says that when Ælfheah, bishop of Winchester, consecrated on the same occasion Dunstan, Æthelwold and one other man as priests, he prophesied that two of them would become bishops, one in his own diocese, one in another.[69] But Wulfstan, the precentor of Winchester, whose Life of Æthelwold is probably later, was not content with this: he makes Ælfheah prophesy that Dunstan will become bishop of Worcester and archbishop.[70]

The post-Conquest biographers of Dunstan, namely Osbern, precentor of Christ Church, Canterbury, writing between 1070 and 1093, Eadmer, also at Christ Church, writing about 1100, and William of Malmesbury, writing about 1125, repeat these additions of Adelard, with only minor differences.[71] Osbern takes the presence of St Paul in the vision of the Apostles as a prophecy that Dunstan will become bishop of London; he is defending Dunstan's holding of the see in plurality. William of Malmesbury makes Dunstan refuse Crediton, as in 'B', and Winchester, as in Adelard, and be reluctant to accept London. Unlike Adelard, these authors do not ignore the appointment of Brihthelm; but they claim that the see of Canterbury was offered to Dunstan on Oda's death, and again on Ælfsige's, and was refused on both occasions.[72] It is extremely unlikely that Eadwig should have wished to appoint his brother's protegé, whom he had exiled, but these authors were unaware that Eadwig, not Edgar, was the king concerned. Osbern lets Brihthelm hold the see only for a few days, and leave not only by the king's command, but by that of all the people, and depart in shame, conscious of his unsuitability. Eadmer and William repeat the jist of this, and William makes Dunstan accept Canterbury only because of great pressure from the king, the bishops and the magnates. It is a hagiographical commonplace that a saint should be reluctant to take office, though of course there are cases where it is true; but the single refusal mentioned by 'B' has grown into four refusals in William's account, and a reluctance to accept London and Canterbury. Was William particularly concerned, in view of Dunstan's holding Worcester and London in plurality, to show that he was not an ambitious prelate? Since William thought that Brihthelm was appointed by Edgar, he explains that the king was persuaded to this act by others, but discovered within a few days that what he had taken for modesty was in fact inertia. If only 'B' had said that Brihthelm (like Æthelwald of York) had retired out of a desire for a quieter life, the visions, prophecies and blackening of Brihthelm's character would have been unnecessary.

These post-Conquest writers were writing after the eleventh-century papal reform, and were aware that the papacy had refused to ratify the appointment of Stigand to Canterbury after the flight of Archbishop Robert in 1052, and had granted the pallium to Ealdred of York in 1061 only on condition that he relinquished the see of Worcester.[72a] But there is no evidence that the circumstances of Dunstan's appointment raised any trouble at Rome. There was at any rate no great delay before he was granted the pallium. 'B' says he set out soon after he was appointed; we need not take this very literally, and in any case we do not know just how long it was after Eadwig's death on 1 October, 959, before Edgar could replace Brihthelm with his own nominee. From the authentic version of the privilege Dunstan received from Pope John XII,[73] we can date his reception of the pallium in Rome 21 September,[74] in the fourth indiction, i.e. in 960, for this indiction ran from 1 September 960 to 1 September 961. That the year is 960, and not, as some older scholars claimed, 961, is supported by the great number of charters witnessed by Oswald, bishop of Worcester, in 961, for he was not consecrated bishop of Worcester until after Dunstan's return from Rome, which can only have been late in the year in which he received his pallium. The rubric to the papal letter in the Paris manuscript tells us that Dunstan received the privilege from the pope's hands, but took the pallium from St Peter's altar.[74a]

If, as seems likely, Brihthelm had never received the pallium, and if his withdrawal could be represented as voluntary, and he made no appeal, there was no reason why Pope John XII should refuse the pallium to Dunstan on Brihthelm's account. Though objection was sometimes made to the translation of a bishop from a lesser to a greater see,[74b] this was normal in tenth-century appointments to Canterbury: all archbishops between Plegmund in 890 and Æthelnoth in 1020 were translated from other sees. As for Dunstan's plurality, he relinquished the see of Worcester soon after his return from Rome. The case of London is less clear, for one cannot distinguish Ælfstan of London from Ælfstan of Rochester until both appear, with their sees named, in a charter of 964;[75] it is probably Ælfstan of London who begins to attest in 961.[76] The pope may have made the grant of the pallium conditional on Dunstan's relinquishing his other sees, just as Nicholas II made Ealdred of York give up Worcester in 1061,[77] but this cannot be assumed. Dunstan may always have intended to consecrate successors to Worcester and London as soon as he had his pallium.

It must have been the same pope, John XII, who had granted the pallium to Oscytel, archbishop of York, a year or two earlier. In this case there was a considerable delay, and as the circumstances of Oscytel's appointment were unusual, it is possible that papal reluctance had to be overcome. Oscytel's predecessor, Archbishop Wulfstan I, had, according to the D version of the *Anglo-Saxon Chronicle*, which is much concerned with northern affairs, supported the Scandinavian usurpers in Northumbria against the English kings, and in 952 he was imprisoned. His re-instatement in 954 is ambiguously worded: *Wulstan arcebiscop onfeng eft biscoprices on Dorceceastre*. This could mean that he 'received back his bishopric, at Dorchester', i.e. that the ceremony of re-instatement took place there; but it seems more likely to mean 'received again a bishopric, that of Dorchester', i.e. that he was not trusted in Northumbria again.[78] It was at Oundle, in the diocese of Dorchester, that he was buried. The next archbishop was Oscytel, bishop of Dorchester, and it seems possible that he was given charge of the diocese of York, though perhaps not as archbishop, in Wulfstan's lifetime. Wulfstan used the title archbishop until he died.[78a] The date of his death is not quite certain: the northern version of the *Anglo-Saxon Chronicle* enters it 956 E, 957 D, but D is a year ahead in this portion; D adds the day as *xvii kł Ianuar'* (16 December): Florence of Worcester and the 'Chronicle of the Archbishops of York',[79] enter his death under 956, but on *vii kal. Ianuar* (26 December), which, seeing that the year changed at Christmas, means 26 December, 955. There are a great number of charters for 956 in which Wulfstan does not occur, but he could have been ill during the months before he died, and if we took the earlier date, we should have to dismiss the three charters of 956 with his attestation.[80] But even if we were to accept the earlier date, he outlived King Eadred, who died 23 November, 955, and the B manuscript of the *Anglo-Saxon Chronicle*, s.a. 971, says that Oscytel was consecrated archbishop of York by the consent of King Eadred and all his councillors. This would prove that Oscytel was appointed in Wulfstan's lifetime if manuscript C did not read *Eadweard* instead of Eadred; though this is impossible, it suggests that the name was not clear in their common exemplar, and it could have been Eadwig. Oscytel was certainly in control of York in 956, when Eadwig gave him the great estate at Southwell, Nottinghamshire, which always afterwards belonged to the see of York;[81] he is called bishop in the text, and the title archbishop given him in the witness-list is likely to be a copyist's alteration. For otherwise Oscytel attests merely as *episcopus*, not only forty times in 956,[82] when Wulfstan may still have been alive, but also in the charters of 957[83] and 958[84]. In that year, Edgar gave him an estate at Sutton, Nottinghamshire, speaking of him as his *pontifex*.[85] His first reliable attestation as archbishop is in a charter of 959,[86] issued by Edgar when still king only of the Mercians and Northumbrians; from then on he is almost consistently given the title of archbishop. This suggests that in 959, or late in 958, he had got his pallium. This agrees very well with a statement in the *Historia Ramesiensis*[87] that he went to Rome for his pallium, taking Oswald with him; for Oswald did not join him until soon after the death of Archbishop Oda of Canterbury on 2 June, 958; however, the failure of the *Vita Oswaldi* to mention this journey casts a doubt on whether it took place.

One is tempted to connect this delay in receiving the pallium with the circumstances of Oscytel's appointment, if this was in his predecessor's lifetime, especially as there is evidence that Oscytel continued to hold the see of Dorchester in plurality. But other explanations than papal disapproval are possible. It may be that the papacy was already trying to insist on a personal journey for the pallium, and that this was being resisted. There has survived part of a letter from the English bishops to an unnamed pope which claims that in earlier times the 'immense labour'[87a] of going to Rome had not been demanded, but the pallium had been sent;[88] it was probably drafted by Archbishop Wulfstan of York early in the eleventh century, but the demand against which it is a protest need not have been a new thing. Oscytel's successor Oswald did go to Rome for his pallium,[89] but not, apparently, the next two archbishops of York, Ealdulf and Wulfstan II. In any case, it was less urgent for archbishops of York to get the pallium; since they had only one suffragan, they did not often need it for episcopal consecrations.[89a] Ælfric, who succeeded in 1023, did not fetch his pallium until late in 1026, and Cynesige delayed from 1051 to 1055. They may, however, have been trying to insist on its being sent without their going to Rome.

Besides granting pallia to Archbishops Oscytel and Dunstan, Pope John XII had other dealings with King Edgar, if a letter addressed to him and all the English people by a Pope John is genuine.[90] It says that the king has asked, through Archbishop Dunstan, for permission to eject the secular canons from the Old Minster at Winchester, and it gives the required permission. It is usually assigned to Pope John XIII, though, as Dom Thomas Symons has shown,[91] this is most unlikely; for he did not become pope until 1 October, 965, and the canons were driven out on 20 February, 964. The wording of the letter is not that of a confirmation of something which had already taken place, more than eighteen months previously. If it is ascribed to John XII, it was probably written before his deposition on 4 December, 963, rather than in the period of his re-occupation of the papal throne from February to 14 May, 964.[92]

Somewhere about the same time as Edgar was seeking the pope's support for his policy of monastic reform, he was issuing regulations on the payment to Rome of Peter's Pence. Hitherto, it would appear that secular penalties were not attached to non-payment of this due: King Edmund speaks only of the excommunication of those who refused to pay *Rom-feoh*.[93] But Edgar, who calls it 'hearth-penny', lays down very heavy secular penalties in a code which cannot be later than 963. The man who has not paid his penny by St Peter's day is to take it to Rome himself, with 30 pence in addition, and to pay 120 shillings to the king on his return; on a second offence, he is to repeat the journey, and pay 200 shillings to the king when he gets back; on a third offence he is to lose all that he possesses.[94] These regulations show how great an importance Edgar attached to the link with Rome. It may never have been possible to enforce such exaggerated penalties: the laws of Ethelred and of Cnut drop the journeys to Rome[94a], and the references to increased penalties for a second or third offence.[95] In Danish areas in the early eleventh century, the penalty was *lahslit*,[96] a fine varying with the rank of the offender; by this the king's thegn would pay ten half-marks, i.e. 640 pence, which is more than the 120 shillings (i.e. 600 West Saxon pence) of Edgar's law, and the other ranks come off more lightly, six half-marks (= 384 pence) for the landowner, twelve ores (= 192 pence) for the *ceorl*. Another rate of fine is stated in a little text known as *Romscot*, namely 60 shillings and twelve times the original penny.[97] But even in these modified forms, Edgar's legislation must have encouraged prompt payment and have resulted in increased papal income from this source. It appears to have been valued at Rome; when Nicholas II raised difficulties over granting the pallium to Archbishop Ealdred of York, Earl Tostig is said to have threatened the withdrawal of Peter's Pence, and this is said to have caused consternation at Rome.[98]

Notes

1 The following abbreviations are used: *ASC* = *Anglo-Saxon Chronicle*; *BCS* = W. de G. Birch, *Cartularium Saxonicum* (London, 1885–93), cited by number of document; BM = British Museum; *EHD* = *English Historical Documents* c. *500–1042*, ed. D. Whitelock (vol. I of *English Historical Documents*, ed. D. C. Douglas, London, 1955); *Memorials* = Memorials of Saint Dunstan, ed. W. Stubbs (RS, 1874); RS = Rolls Series.

2 *Memorials*, Introduction.

3 K. Jost, 'Einige Wulfstantexte und ihre Quellen', *Anglia*, lvi (1932), 288–301.

4 *Memorials*, pp. cii–ciii.

5 See e.g. Dom David Knowles, *The Monastic Order in England* (Cambridge, 1949), *passim;* F. M. Stenton, *Anglo-Saxon England* (3rd, edit., Oxford, 1971), pp. 446–57; Dom Thomas Symons, 'Notes on the Life and Work of St. Dunstan', *Downside Review*, N.S. lxxx (1962), 250–61, 355–66.

6 *op.cit.* 360—2.

7 *Memorials*, pp. 32–4.

8 See *ASC* 958 D: 'Archbishop Oda separated King Eadwig and Ælfgifu, because they were too closely related'. A story in the *Vita Oswaldi*, that Oda drove from the country a mistress of King Eadwig, may be a late and garbled version of this (*Historians of the Church of York and its Archbishops*, ed. J. Raine, RS, I (1879), 402).

9 *Select English Historical Documents of the Ninth and Tenth Centuries*, ed. F. E. Harmer (Cambridge, 1914), no XXIII (= *BCS* 1064).

10 Ed. by O. Cockayne, *Leechdoms, Wortcunning and Starcraft of Early England* (RS, 1864–6), III, 432–44; translated in *EHD*, pp. 846–9. On its authorship, see D. Whitelock, in *Philological Essays in Honour of Herbert Dean Meritt*, ed. J. L. Rosier (The Hague, 1970), pp. 125–36.

11 *Memorials*, p. 36 f. One manuscript gives the name as *Brandanford*, which could be from a scribe's mistaking a length-mark over the first *a* as denoting a nasal. William of Malmesbury has *Bradford*. It is unlikely to have been Bradford-on-Avon, which was not in Edgar's part of the kingdom; Stubbs's other suggestion, Brentford, is ruled out by the early forms of this place-name.

12 *BCS* 1042.

13 *BCS* 1052.

13a On this date, see p. 236f. below.

14 See p. 236f. below.

15 *Memorials*, p. 38.

16 My conclusions differ in some respects from those of J. Armitage Robinson, *The Saxon Bishops of Wells* (British Academy Supplemental Papers, IV, London, 1918), pp. 62–7.

17 A convenient edition of the chief versions of Anglo-Saxon episcopal lists is that of R. I. Page, in *Nottingham Mediaeval Studies*, x (1966), 1–24; see also *Liber Vitae of*

New Minster and Hyde Abbey, ed. W. de G. Birch (London, 1892), pp. 14–21; and *Florentii Wigorniensis Monachi Chronicon ex Chronicis*, ed. B. Thorpe (London, 1848), I, 231–46.

18 *BCS* 1032.

19 *BCS* 1134; two bishops with this name attest *BCS* 1079, dated 961, but the second is probably an error for Abbot Ælfwold.

20 Corpus Christi College, Oxford, MS. 157.

21 Private communication.

22 Lambeth MS. 42.

23 Trinity College, Dublin, MS. 502. E5. 23.

24 Bodleian Library, Oxford, MS. 297.

25 *BCS* 923, 969·

26 *BCS* 1303.

26a *De Antiquitate Glastoniensis Ecclesiæ*, ed. T. Hearne, *Adami de Domerham Historia de rebus gestis Glastoniensibus* (Oxford, 1727), I, 94.

27 See p .236f. below.

28 *BCS* 1054, 1076.

29 *BCS* 899, 900, 903, 905, 908, 909, 911, 917.

30 *BCS* 987, 988, 1001, 1002, 1004: he is doubtless the Bishop Brihthelm to whom Eadwig granted an estate in Orsett, Essex, in an extract from a St Paul's charter made by Richard James, misdated 1457, probably a misreading of DCCCCLVII; see *Early Charters of the Cathedral Church of St. Paul, London*, ed. M. Gibbs (Camden Soc., 3rd series, lviii, 1939), p. 6.

31 *BCS* 966, dated 29 November.

32 *BCS* 927, 934, 966, 970, 974.

33 *BCS* 994, 999. This last is dated 9 May, showing that the division of the kingdom was after this date.

34 *BCS* 992, 998, 1005.

35 *BCS* 1022, 1027, 1028, 1030 (misdated 956), 1032, 1033, 1035.

36 *BCS* 1036, 1037, 1040, 1042–4, 1052.

37 *BCS* 1052. Charters do not usually name the sees of the signatories, but those of London and Winchester are sometimes named when others are not.

38 *BCS* 930.

39 *BCS* 997.

40 *BCS* 898–900.

41 *BCS* 1101, 1103, 1112, 1125.

42 *BCS* 986.

43 *Codex Diplomaticus Aevi Saxonici*, ed. J. M. Kemble (London, 1839–48), no. 714.

44 *BCS* 971.

45 *BCS* 972.

45a See p. 238 below.

46 *Memorials*, p. xcvi.

47 *BCS* 1046. Oda's name does not occur in the older version, in BM Cotton Claudius C.ix. The charter is suspicious: it is couched in language like that of Ethelred's charters, and is witnessed by the queen-mother, who attests no other charter of Eadwig. E. John, who defends this charter in *Orbis Britanniae* (Leicester, 1966), pp. 188–94, postulates a reconciliation between her and Eadwig late in his reign, but she herself complains at a later date that she could not get justice in a suit 'until Edgar came to power' (*BCS* 1064).

48 Oda appears in 958 only in *BCS* 1032 and in *BCS* 1021, which is suspect, having a wrong king's name. *BCS* 1029 should be dated 956.

49 *BCS* 1026–8, 1033, 1034 and 1022, with a wrong king's name.

50 *BCS* 1035; also *BCS* 1030, wrongly dated 956, but with the indiction for 958.

51 *Two Cartularies of the Benedictine Abbeys of Muchelney and Athelney*, ed. E. H. Bates (London, 1899), p. 145 f.
52 *BCS* 1045.
53 See p. 238 below. Lyfing, made archbishop of Canterbury in 1013, attests only as bishop until 1018. He was in Rome, perhaps to fetch his pallium, in or soon after 1017. In 1053, when neither of the archbishops had a pallium, the C version of the *ASC* says: 'There was no archbishop in the land, but Bishop Stigand held the bishopric in Canterbury at Christ Church and Cynesige at York.'
54 *BCS* 1051. *BCS* 1047, an alleged charter of Edgar, misdated 958, but with indiction for 959, is dubious.
55 *BCS* 1056; but here Oscytel of York also is called *episcopus*. Perhaps the drafter did not care to use a higher title for York than for Canterbury.
56 *BCS* 1053, 1054, 1055, 1058.
57 *Memorials*, p. 38.
58 *Ibid.*, p. 410.
59 The list in Corpus Christi College, Cambridge, MS. 173 appears to have been drawn up 984–8, that in BM Cotton MS. Tiberius B.v in 989–95.
60 It was added about 1100 to the Corpus MS. 173, and by the same hand in BM Cotton MSS. Faustina B. iii and Tiberius A. vi.
61 Raine, *op. cit.*, I, 408.
62 ed. N. E. S. A. Hamilton (RS., 1870), pp. 25 f., 165.
62a The year is given as 970 by Symeon of Durham; Oscytel's death is entered in the B and C versions of the *ASC*, without date in B, but in annal 971 in C. However, C seems to be a year wrong in this portion, for it dates 972 an event dated 971 or 970 in the other versions, and puts under 974 instead of 973 Edgar's coronation, although in the text of the annal it dates it, as do A and B, as 27 years before 1000. According to Symeon, Oswald succeeded in the following year, i.e. 971, and he attests a genuine charter (*BCS* 1270), dated 971, as archbishop of York. If this implies that he had already received his pallium, he could hardly have made the journey to Rome and back after 31 October 971, since one must allow some time for his appointment, even if we reject Symeon's evidence regarding the election and resignation of another candidate.
63 Florence of Worcester, *s.a.* 972; William of Malmesbury, *Gesta Pontificum*, ed. Hamilton, p. 247. But the *Vita Oswaldi* (ed. Raine, *op.cit.*, p. 435) mentions Oswald's appointment to York without saying who was his immediate predecessor.
64 *De archiepiscopis Eboraci*, in *Symeonis Monachi Opera Omnia*, ed. T. Arnold (R.S., 1882), I, 226.
65 Raine, *op.cit.*, II, 340.
65a On a possibility that Brihthelm had been a monk under Dunstan at Glastonbury, see p. 234 above.
66 *Memorials*, pp. 29–31.
67 *Ibid.*, p. 57.
68 *Ibid.*, p. 60.
69 *Chronicon Monasterii de Abingdon*, ed. J. Stevenson (R.S., 1858), II, 256; *EHD*, p. 833, where its relation to the Life by Wulfstan is discussed.
70 *Acta Sanctorum*, 1 August, I, 90.
71 *Memorials*, pp. 95–8, 103 f., 106, 185–7, 195–7, 199 f., 278–81, 292 f.
72 *Ibid.*, pp. 107 f., 197 f., 293–5. Eadmer omits the second offer.
72a See authorities cited in nn. 74[b], 77.
73 Preserved in a pontifical once at Sherborne, now Paris, Bibliothèque Nationale, Lat. 943, in a late-tenth-century hand; it is printed by J. Mabillon, *Acta sanctorum ordinis S. Benedicti* (Venice, 1733–40), V, 658, from which Stubbs prints variants to the text given in William of Malmesbury's Life of Dunstan (*Memorials*, pp. 296–8). William's

version, that in Eadmer's *Historia Novorum* (ed. M. Rule, RS, 1884, p. 274) and that in *BCS* 1069 all come from a form interpolated at Canterbury, and included in the collection of forged or interpolated documents made after the Norman Conquest during the quarrel with York about the primacy, which is preserved in BM Cotton MS. Cleopatra E.i.

74 *xi kalendarum Octobris*. The Canterbury versions read *i* instead of *xi*, but it is more likely that a copyist should have omitted than have inserted an *x* in error.

74a He was not accorded the special honour paid by Benedict VIII to Æthelnoth, archbishop of Canterbury, when, according to the D version of *ASC*, 1022, he gave him two pallia, one of which he himself took from the altar of St Peter, just as Pope Alexander II gave *ob signum præcipui amoris* two pallia to Lanfranc, one taken *Romano more* from the altar; see *Two of the Saxon Chronicles Parallel*, ed. J. Earle and C. Plummer (Oxford, 1892), I, 288.

74b It was raised against Ealdred of York in 1061 that he had moved *de sede ad sedem sine apostolica auctoritate* according to the alleged letter of Nicholas II (Raine, *op. cit.*, III, 7); this should be compared with the 'Chronicle of the Archbishops of York' (*ibid.*, II, 346) and with *Vita Ædwardi Regis* (ed. F. Barlow, London, 1962, p. 35), which says: *inuentus est a primo ordinationis sue episcopio ad aliud commigrasse contra canones.*

75 *BCS* 1134.

76 Six times in this year, beginning with *BCS* 1066. On *BCS* 1047, misdated 958, which is attested by a Bishop Ælfstan, see n. 54. Rochester was an unimportant see: Ælfstan's predecessor Burhric last attests in 946 (*BCS* 812, 813).

77 See *The Vita Wulfstani of William of Malmesbury*, ed. R. R. Darlington (Camden Society, xl, 1928), p. 16 f.; *Gesta Pontificum*, ed. Hamilton, p. 251 f.; and authorities cited in n. 74[b] above.

78 See D. Whitelock, 'The Dealings of the Kings of England with Northumbria in the Tenth and Eleventh Centuries', *The Anglo-Saxons. Studies . . . presented to Bruce Dickins*, ed. P. Clemoes (London, 1959), pp. 72–5.

78a Unlike Brihthelm, Wulfstan would have received his pallium, and this would make it difficult to depose him completely.

79 ed. Raine, *op. cit.*, II, 340.

80 Two, *BCS* 924 and 931, are dubious; the third, *BCS* 923, survives only in a late register.

81 *BCS* 1029 (= *EHD* no. 108), wrongly dated 958; the indiction is for 956, and the grant must have been made before the Mercians broke away from Eadwig in 957.

82 The only exception is *BCS* 937, which calls him *summus pontifex*. *BCS* 906, which calls him *primas* of the church of York in 955, is a forgery.

83 *BCS* 987, 988, 994, 997, 999, 1001, 1003.

84 *BCS* 1036, 1037, 1040, 1042, 1043, 1044.

85 *BCS* 1044.

86 *BCS* 1052. He has this title in *BCS* 1023, but it is undated and has a wrong king's name, Eadred. On *BCS* 1047 (958, for 959?), with Oscytel as *primas* and Dunstan as archbishop, see above, n. 54.

87 *Chronicon Abbatiæ Rameseiensis*, ed. W. D. Macray (RS, 1886), p. 24.

87a This is described by the Ramsey chronicler (see previous note) as *maris injurias, intemperiem aeris, prædonis insidias, et totius itineris suspecta pericula*. If Oscytel went to Rome, it must have been near the time when Ælfsige of Canterbury lost his life on the journey.

88 *Councils and Ecclesiastical Documents relating to Great Britain and Ireland*, ed. A. W. Haddan and W. Stubbs (Oxford, 1869–71), III, 559–61. On its date, see W. Levison, *England and the Continent in the Eighth Century* (Oxford, 1946), pp. 241–8; on its authorship, see D. Bethurum, 'A Letter of Protest from the English Bishops to the Pope', *Philologica: the Malone Anniversary Studies*, ed. T. A. Kirby and H. B. Woolf (Baltimore, 1949), pp. 97–104.

89 *Vita Oswaldi*, ed. Raine, *op.cit.* I, 435; 'Chronicle of the Archbishops of York', *ibid.*, II. 341; Symeon of Durham, *De archiepiscopis Eboraci*, ed. Arnold, *op.cit.*, I, 226.

89a The see of Chester-le-Street fell vacant only once in Oscytel's pontificate, in 968; see Symeon of Durham, *Historia Dunelmensis Ecclesiæ*, ed. Arnold, *op. cit.*, I, 78.

90 *Memorials*, p. 364; *BCS* 1275. This was first printed by Matthew Parker, *De Antiquitate Britannicae Ecclesiae* (London, 1572), p. 66 'ex archivis', from a text since lost, and later editors print from Parker. Copies survive in four late Winchester registers, on which see W. Holtzmann, *Papsturkunden in England* (Berlin, 1930—52), I, 127, II, 39, 40 and 42. The letter is accepted as genuine by, among others, W. Levison, *England and the Continent in the Eighth Century* (Oxford, 1946), pp. 196—8, who points out agreements with the papal formulare *Liber Diurnus*. Stubbs, *Memorials*, p. 364, was less certain, but regarded its failure to refer to the church as St Swithun's as in its favour; yet it would have been a very clumsy forger who would use this title for the church before the expulsion of the canons, seeing that it was held that Swithun's sanctity was revealed only after the canons had been expelled. The abusive terms in which the letter speaks of the secular canons look like Winchester writing, but could have been taken from the letter sent from England to request permission to expel them.

91 *op. cit.*, p. 357 f.

92 It would take some time for the papal letter to reach England, and it need not have been acted on at once. If it belongs to the period after Pope John's re-instatement, Edgar would appear to have acted before receiving it. The later date may be supported by John's calling Æthelwold his *coepiscopus*, for his consecration was on 29 November, 963; but the pope may not have waited to receive confirmation of this event before using the title.

93 I Edmund 2; F. Liebermann, *Die Gesetze der Angelsachsen* (Halle a, S., 1903—16), I, 184.

94 II Edgar 4—4.3; Liebermann, *op. cit.*, I, 198; translated in *EHD.*, p. 395 f.

94a Yet Archbishop Wulfstan retains this in a homily; see *Wulfstan: Sammlung der ihm zugeschriebenen Homilien,* ed. A. Napier (Berlin 1883), p. 311.

95 VIII Ethelred 10—10.1, I Cnut 9—9.1; Liebermann, *op. cit.*, I, 265, 292.

96 Edward and Guthrum 6.1; Liebermann, *op. cit.*, I, 130. On the date see D. Whitelock in *English Historical Review*, lvi (1941), 1—21.

97 Liebermann, *op. cit.*, I, 474.

98 See authorities cited n. 77 above.

V

WULFSTAN *CANTOR* AND ANGLO-SAXON LAW

Wulfstan, the precentor of the Old Minster, Winchester, composed a poem, *Narratio Metrica de Sancto Swithuno*,[1] which begins with a poetic epistle to Ælfheah, bishop of Winchester, 984-1005/6. As he says that the new church has been recently dedicated,[2] and that this ceremony was attended by Archbishop Siric, who died *c*. 28 October, 994,[3] and by Wulfsige, who became bishop of Sherborne in 992, the poem can be dated between 992 and 994, for had Siric died before the poem was composed the poet would surely have given some indication of this. The poem includes two passages of interest for the study of Anglo-Saxon law.

I

The more important of these is Book II, lines 440-465, which are prefixed to an account of the miraculous healing of a man unjustly mutilated for crime. It is as follows:

> Precipit interea rex iustus et inclitus Eadgar,
> quosque minis terrendo malos, lex staret ut ista
> gentis in Anglorum diffuso limite, quo si
> fur aliquis, seu predo ferox, inuentus eadem
> adforet in patria, crudelia dampna subiret
> lumine priuatus, miser et caecatus utroque,
> tortor eique simul nares precidat et aures,
> truncaretque manus plantasque securibus actis,
> subtraheretque simul capitis cum pelle capillos,
> seminicemque uirum poena cruciante peremptum
> proiceret canibus rabidis exactor edendum,

[1] See *Frithegodi Monachi Breuiloquium vitæ beati Wilfredi et Wulfstani Cantoris Narratio Metrica de Sancto Swithuno*, ed. A. Campbell (Zürich, 1950). Wulfstan's poem had been previously edited by P. Michael Huber, O.S.B., *S. Swithunus, Miracula Metrica auctore Wulfstano monacho*, I. Text (Beilage zum Jahresbericht des humanistischen Gymnasiums Metten, 1905/06).

[2] L. 219

[3] See K. Sisam, *Studies in the History of Old English Literature* (Oxford, 1953), p. 157 f.

nocturnisque auibus, coruis et edacibus, atque
membratim in uacuas caesum dispergeret auras.
Stat praedicta pii lex et sententia regis,
in commune bonum quam sanxerat ille benignus,
unus quisque suis securo ut pectore lucris
plena pace frui posset sine murmure damni.
Exploratores siluarum densa peragrant,
predonesque locis inuestigantur opacis,
et membris caesi prebent spectacula plebi,
perculerat terrorque animos formidine cunctos,
detestanda manus fuit et consumpta latronum,
sic ut ad extremum mater cum pignore posset
ire per anfractus securo pectore curuos
aequoris Eoi de finibus absque periclo,
litoris occidui donec contingeret oras.

Meanwhile the just and glorious King Edgar decrees, to terrify all evildoers with threats, that this law shall stand in the wide limits of the English people, that, if any thief or fierce robber should be discovered in that same country, he should undergo cruel punishments, deprived of light, wretched and blinded in both eyes, and also the executioner should cut off his nose and ears and lop off his hands and feet with axes, and also remove the hair of his head and the scalp as well; and the reeve[4] should throw the man, half-dead and wracked by the agonising punishment, to be devoured by savage dogs, and by birds of night[5] and greedy ravens, and should scatter the mutilated man limb by limb to the empty air. Thus stands the aforesaid law and pronouncement of the pious king, which he in his benignity had ordained for the common good, that everyone might with carefree heart enjoy in full peace his own goods without complaint of loss. Scouts traverse the thickets of the woods, and robbers are discovered in shady places, and, with their limbs mutilated, present a spectacle to the people; and terror struck all hearts with dread, and the detestible gang of brigands was destroyed, so that in the end a mother with her child could go through the winding ways with carefree heart, without danger, from the limits of the eastern sea until she might reach the margins of the western shore.

Some of the expressions in this lurid passage are, as Mr. Campbell points out, drawn from classical authors,[6] and the final four lines are obviously borrowed from Bede's description of the security which prevailed in the reign of Edwin of Northumbria: *ut, sicut usque hodie in prouerbio dicitur, etiam si mulier una cum recens nato paruulo uellet totam perambulare insulam a mari ad mare, nullo se ledente ualeret.*[7] One's first instinct is to dismiss most of the passage as wild poetic exaggeration, which in part it is. But a clause in the early eleventh-century code which goes under the name of the

[4] Or perhaps "executioner"; but *exactor regis* is how Æthelweard translates in his chronicle *se gerefa* of the *Anglo-Saxon Chronicle*, *s.a.* 787.

[5] Presumably owls. Cf. *Owl and Nightingale*, 11. 385-390, where the owl claims that she follows in the train of men going to war.

[6] Cf. 1. 450 *canibus rabidis* with Verg., *Aen.* vii, 11. 493-4 *rabidae ... canes*; 1. 455 *securo ... pectore* with Ovid, *Ars. Am.* ii, 1. 443 *securaque pectora*; 1. 452 in *uacuas ... auras* with Verg., *Aen.* xii, 1. 592 *vacuas ... ad auras*.

[7] *Historia Ecclesiastica*, Book II, ch. 16.

Laws of Edward and Guthrum[8] must give us pause. It reads: "If a mutilated maimed man, who might have been destroyed,[9] be abandoned, and after three days he is still alive, anyone who wishes to heal his wounds and his soul may with the bishop's permission help him afterwards." We may perhaps dismiss the poet's savage dogs and birds of prey, but this clause shows that, when mutilation had been substituted for the death penalty, it was only after three days that anyone was allowed to come to his help.

Parts of the passage in the poem reflect statements in Edgar's laws: in IV Edgar, which is mainly a measure against cattle thieves, we read: "This measure is to be common to all the nation, whether Englishmen, Danes or Britons, in every province of my dominion", and may compare: *lex staret ut ista/gentis in Anglorum diffuso limite*; the law continues: "to the end that poor man and rich may possess what they have rightly acquired", with which compare: *unus quisque suis securo ut pectore lucris/plena pace frui posset sine murmure damni*; the clause in the law ends: "that against their will they (the thieves) be so guarded against, that few of them shall escape";[10] the poem describes the result of the measure as *detestanda manus fuit et consumpta latronum*.

III Edgar, 7-7.3, enjoins that when men who are often accused and are unworthy of the people's trust fail to appear in court to answer a charge, men are to be chosen by the court to ride to them. The man who then cannot find anyone to act as surety for him is to be seized, alive or dead. This reminds one of the poet's words on the searching out of the criminals. But Edgar's injunctions end: "and no matter what refuge the proved thief, or the man who is discovered in treason against his lord, may reach, they are never to save their lives". He allows no alternative punishment for the death penalty.

There is little reference in Edgar's laws to mutilation as a punishment; the only instance is loss of tongue for false witness, a penalty taken over from Alfred's laws.[11] In the laws before Edgar, a thieving *ceorl* may lose a hand or foot in Ine 18 and 37; loss of a hand is the penalty for stealing in church in Alfred 6, and for coining false money in II Athelstan 14.1; III Edmund 4 prescribes the removal of the scalp and the mutilation of the little finger of slaves who have combined to commit theft, though the leader is to be hanged.

It is after Edgar's time that we get a close parallel to the passage in the poem. The motive that led to the tendency to substitute mutilation for the death penalty was the desire to allow the criminal a chance to repent and thus save his soul. Archbishop Wulfstan, in the laws which he drew up for King Ethelred, advocates to this end what he calls *friðlice* punishments, *i.e.*, punishments which do not put a man outside the

[8] See D. Whitelock, "Wulfstan and the so-called Laws of Edward and Guthrum", *English Historical Review*, LVI (1941), pp. 1-21.
[9] *þe forworht wære*. With F. Liebermann, *Die Gesetze der Angelsachsen* (Halle, 1903-16), vol. I, p. 133, I take *forworht* to mean "having incurred the death-penalty".
[10] IV Edgar, 2.2.
[11] III Edgar 4; cf. Alfred 32.

frið "peace" and make him liable to lose his life.[12] But it is not until he drafts the laws of Cnut[13] that he specifies the alternatives to the death penalty. The case considered is that of a much accused man who has to go through the threefold ordeal. It is stated:

(II Cnut 30.3b). And if he is then convicted, on the first occasion he is to pay two-fold compensation to the accuser and his wergild to the lord who is entitled to his fine, and to appoint trustworthy sureties that he will afterwards cease from all evil-doing.

(30.4) And on the second occasion there is to be no other compensation, if he is convicted, but that his hands, or feet, or both, in proportion to the deed, are to be cut off.

(30.5) And if, however, he has committed still further crimes, his eyes are to be put out and his nose and ears and upper lip cut off, or his scalp removed, whichever of these is then decreed by those with whom the decision rests; thus one can punish and at the same time preserve the soul.

This law gives exactly the same list of mutilations as does the poem, except that the law adds the cutting off of the upper lip. The poet could not have known this much later code, and he could not so accurately have forecast its pronouncements. Archbishop Wulfstan had a very high regard for Edgar's laws, and he makes great use of II and III Edgar when drafting the laws of Cnut. It seems likely, therefore, that the section quoted above was based on a lost edict of Edgar's which was known to the poet. This would mean that at some time after the promulgation of II and III Edgar, early in his reign, where no alternative for the death penalty is allowed,[14] Edgar came under the influence of that school of ecclesiastical thought which wished to substitute mutilation.

If this suggestion is rejected, it must at least be admitted that these mutilations were practiced long before the reign of Cnut. The poet certainly believed that Edgar had issued an edict to this effect, and he could not have held this opinion had these practices been recent innovations in his time. He is writing less than twenty years after Edgar's death. He did not, however, share the view of his later namesake Archbishop Wulfstan that they were intended as a mitigation of the laws against thieves, and surely such severities must have proved as strong a deterrent as death itself. The poet is not praising the king's leniency towards criminals, but his concern for the security of his people, and the efficacy of his measures against thieves and robbers.

It is interesting to compare his praise of the security in Edgar's reign with a passage in William of Malmesbury, who says: "He permitted no man, no matter what his rank, to evade the laws with impunity. In his day there was no secret thief, no public

[12] V Ethelred 3.1; VI Ethelred 10.1; II Cnut 2.1. The word *friðlic* is unique in Old English; it corresponds to Old Norse *friðligr*, the opposite of *friðlauss* "outlawed". Liebermann renders it *(Leben) schonende*; A. J. Robertson, *The Laws of the Kings of England* (Cambridge, 1925) "merciful".

[13] On Wulfstan's authorship see D. Whitelock, "Wulfstan and the Laws of Cnut", *English Historical Review*, LXIII (1948), pp. 433-452, and "Wulfstan's Authorship of Cnut's Laws", *English Historical Review*, LXIX (1955), pp. 72-85.

[14] Not in most manuscripts of the code. In Corpus Christi College, Cambridge, MS. 201, the words "unless the king allows them to preserve their lives" are added to III Edgar 7.3; but this is a Wulfstan MS., and this phrase is probably his addition.

robber, unless such as preferred to lose his life in attacking the property of others."[15] William knew of another work by Wulfstan the precentor, his prose *Life of St. Athelwold*, as well as a work which he calls *De Tonorum Harmonia*[16], but he does not mention the poem on the miracles of St. Swithun, and, if he had known it, it seems to me unlikely that he would have omitted to mention the mutilations in this passage of the poem. The tradition that Edgar dealt effectively with thieves and robbers must have reached William from some other source.

It seems to me that Wulfstan's poem affords evidence of a lost edict of Edgar. We certainly do not possess all the legislation of this reign. IV Edgar, a code directed only to the Danish areas of England,[17] must have been accompanied by a companion document addressed to the English areas, Wessex, Kent and South-West Mercia. In 2.1a it says: "Among the English, however, that is to be in force which I and my councilors have added to the decrees of my ancestors, for the benefit of all the nation", and in chapter 14, concerning one offence, it says: "Among the English, I and my councilors have decided what the punishment shall be", without, however, saying what they have decided. There must have been a lost code with specific instructions on this matter. Moreover, the extant code IV Edgar is not included in any of the great collections of Anglo-Saxon laws, and has come down to us solely in two manuscripts from Worcester,[18] one of the sees held by Archbishop Wulfstan. It is to the interest taken by this prelate in Edgar's legislation that we owe the preservation of this code.

Even if one were to reject the theory that this passage in Wulfstan's poem is based on a lost edict, it is even so not devoid of interest. It puts back the admiration for the efficiency of Edgar's rule to a period less than twenty years after his death, more than a dozen years before Archbishop Wulfstan begins to make his frequent complaints of the deterioration since Edgar died.[19] Moreover, it suggests that William of Malmesbury had good authority for the claims he makes concerning Edgar's strong government.

II

The second passage to be considered (Book II, lines 299-434) is a lengthy and very verbose account of how a man was saved at the ordeal by the intervention of St. Swithun. It is unnecessary to quote it in full. It tells how a certain noble, a well-known merchant of Winchester, Flodoaldus (whose name shows him to be a foreig-

[15] *De Gestis Regum Anglorum*, ed. W. Stubbs, vol. I, p. 177.

[16] *Ibid.*, I, p. 166f.

[17] Hence the only ealdormen concerned with its promulgation and enforcement are Oslac of Northumbria, Æthelwine of East Anglia, and Ælfhere of Mercia, all in charge of areas which include a Danish population.

[18] British Museum, Cotton MS. Nero E. i and Corpus Christi College, Cambridge, MS. 265.

[19] On these see D. Whitelock, "Wulfstan and the Laws of Cnut", p. 442 f.

ner),[20] had a slave to whom he was greatly devoted because of his loyalty. This slave was suddenly arrested for some crime and brought to the judgment-seat of the reeve[21] Eadric, who then held the royal vill of Calne. The reeve ordered the man to be guarded until his master could come, and pronounced that he must go to the ordeal of the red-hot iron. If there he were proved blameless, he should be released uninjured, but otherwise the executioner should behead him. The master hastened to the spot and begged the reeve to be merciful and remit the whole *iudicium*,[22] and to receive the slave as his own. The reeve refused, insisting on trial by ordeal. Flodoaldus went back to him with a gift, offering a pound of silver in addition to the slave to keep in his service for ever. But in spite of Flodoaldus's entreaties and of many presents offered him by the kinsmen of the slave, the haughty reeve, in his pride of office, insisted on carrying out his previous intentions. He commanded the man to be present, and as he stood there timidly, the judge ordered the officials to throw faggots on the fire and to put in an exceedingly heavy lump of metal. He then ordered the red-hot iron, glowing and emitting sparks, to be taken out of the fire and placed, according to custom, on a pair of posts. Soon he gave orders for the slave to carry the iron, which he did under compulsion, and immediately felt a great burning pain. His swollen hand was sealed up, according to custom, for three days. Flodoaldus lost hope, and, summoning his brother and all his companions, planned to go home rather than witness the execution. But then he turned to God, and exhorted all his following to pray that Christ would free the slave from death by the merits of St. Swithun, and he promised to give the slave to the saint. On the third day, when the slave was led in trepidation before the reeve, with both parties standing round he showed the hand which had been wrapped up and sealed. To the reeve and his followers the hand appeared clean, and they shouted: "This man is blameless. There is no guilt in him." But Flodoaldus and his party were astounded, for they saw the hand all burnt and swollen, and the man therefore deserving of death. The enemies who stood by with drawn swords ready to behead the man were silent, and the reeve stood blushing with shame, since he had scorned to remit the *iniquum iudicium* of his own accord, and now by the power of God was without the pound of silver and the slave, and must return home in confusion with his shame alone. The slave's friends bore him off rejoicing, and Flodoaldus gave him to St. Swithun, as he had promised.

When one compares this passage with the laws, one finds that it adds little to our knowledge of the conduct of the ordeal. We see the ordeal from the point of view of the accused, but the details given, *i.e.*, the placing of the iron on two posts after it is taken from the fire, the sealing of the hand for three days, and the presence of mem-

[20] Economic historians should note the presence of a continental foreigner living as a prosperous trader in Winchester.

[21] Eadric is called *preses*, *præfectus regis* and *iudex*. The second is a common title for a king's reeve, while *preses*, which occurs occasionally in charters, is glossed *gerefa*, *heahgerefa* in the mid tenth century (Wright-Wülcker, 465.41, 466.1) and *scirgerefa* by Ælfric (*ibid.* 110.13).

[22] This could mean "sentence" or more narrowly "ordeal".

bers of both parties, are all found in the small treatise called *Ordal*,[23] from which we learn that the iron was removed from the fire at the last collect of the mass and left on the posts until mass was ended and the accused had been given holy water to drink and had had his hand sprinkled with it. It says also that from the moment when the priest began the consecration in the mass, no more fuel was to be added to the fire. Each party was to be represented by an equal number of men. The account in the poem suggests that the reeve here plays a more active part than one would have gathered from the laws: he gives the orders for the stoking of the fire and for the removal of the iron from it, and he chooses the moment at which the accused must take up the iron. According to *Ordal*, once the fire was taken into the church, no one was to enter except the priest and the accused until the preparations were complete. Still, there is no real contradiction, since the fire could be stoked until the time of the consecration of the mass, and it is probable that it was the reeve's business to see that each incident in the ordeal took place at the correct moment.

What is interesting in this miracle tale is not the conduct of the ordeal but the negotiations before it. On the face of it, these look like a bare-faced attempt to bribe a royal official to alter the course of justice, and, if they were, the poem would form an interesting comment on the prevalence of bribery and on the attitude towards it. For it would show that a contemporary ecclesiastic regarded such a course as natural, and, instead of admiring the incorruptibility of the reeve, accused him of pride of office and rejoiced in his discomfiture.

It is not, however, necessary to interpret the incident in this way. The poet calls the *iudicium* unjust. Unfortunately, he is so vague with regard to the slave's crime that we cannot be certain on what he bases this charge of unfairness. Provided there was a sufficient reason to presume guilt, *e.g.*, an adequate accusers' oath or notorious ill repute on the accused's part, the reeve was right to prescribe the ordeal, for the man was a slave and hence not able to clear himself by oath. If what the reeve prescribed was the triple ordeal (and the mention of the exceeding weight of the iron may justify this assumption), the unfairness might lie here, if the crime were not serious enough for this. Yet the poet does not suggest that the offence was a trivial one. But even if the decision to refer the case to the triple ordeal was correct, the reeve may have erred in declaring that the crime, if proved by the ordeal, was to be punished by death, for he is thus allotting it to the category of *botleas* crimes, which allow of no alternative of redemption.

Chapter 2 of Ethelred's first code says that if a slave is found guilty at the ordeal, on a first occasion he is only to be branded, though on a second occasion "there is to be no other compensation than the head". This code is probably later than the poem, but II Athelstan 19 shows that death did not in that reign automatically follow the conviction of a slave for theft, for it states that if a slave is convicted at the ordeal, the stolen goods are to be compensated for and the slave scourged three times, or else the price

[23] F. Liebermann, *Die Gesetze der Angelsachsen* (Halle, 1903-16), vol. I, p. 386 f.

of the goods is to be paid a second time. We may also compare the *Leges Henrici Primi*, 59.23, where the penalty for theft of chattels worth less than eightpence by a slave is given as compensation to the plaintiff and scourging and branding of the slave; if, however, he is cought in serious theft he is to die just as a freeman must.

It is possible, therefore, that the unspecified crime in the present instance was one which did not fall into a category which justified the death penalty, and that this was where the reeve could be accused of unfairness. It may, for example, have been the man's first offence. Yet the reeve could perhaps have argued that he was of ill repute; at any rate, neither his master nor his kin seem to have any belief in his innocence, or else they had no faith in the reliability of the "judgment of God", expressed in the ordeal. The reeve might have pointed to the stern pronouncement of Edgar that the proved thief is never to save his life,[24] though probably this did not refer to theft by slaves.

If the slave's crime was not one to justify the death penalty, then it was open to his master to offer to compound for the ordeal on his behalf, by paying the compensation and fines which would redeem the slave from punishment if he were judged guilty. The possibility of paying the fines incurred instead of going to the ordeal is seen in Ine 62, which begins: "When a charge is brought against a man, and he is being driven to the ordeal, and he himself possesses nothing to give in order to avoid the ordeal; and another man comes forward and gives his goods instead, on what terms he can obtain. ..." This should be compared with II Athelstan 21: "And if anyone compounds for the ordeal, he is to compound what he can for the price of the goods, and not for the fine, unless he to whom it belongs will concede it." From this it appears that the reeve, representing the king to whom the fine belongs, could have accepted a composition from the slave's master, but we see also that he was within his rights in refusing to do so. And if he had, in this case, accepted the offer from the slave's master and kin, he would have been admitting that his former pronouncement that the offence was one punishable by death was wrong. He might then have found himself faced with the penalty laid down in III Edgar 3 for a judge who pronounces a wrong judgment, namely loss of office. If the poet's statement that it was a wrong judgment is correct, then presumably the slave's master could have brought an action against the reeve on this account, but perhaps the case was an arguable one, and in any case it may not have been easy to bring such an accusation against a powerful royal official.

It is not, in my opinion, a stumbling-block in the way of interpreting the offers to the reeve as a legal composition rather than a bribe that it is the reeve himself who would have profited by the gifts and who was to retain the slave in his own service. In theory, such compositions and fines belong to the king; but it is probable that already by this time a reeve might hold a royal manor in farm, paying to the king a fixed payment, and making what he could out of the profits of jurisdiction as well as

[24] See p. 85 above.

from other sources of income from the estate. There is no doubt that royal vills were farmed at a later period: the *Leges Henrici Primi*, 91.3, for example, refers to manors *de dominio et firma regis*. Liebermann[25] considers that this practice may be implied by Ine 73,[26] where offenders are to compensate "as they may compound with the king and his reeve". But this passage is not unambiguous; it could mean "with the king where he retains the profits of jurisdiction in his own hand and with the reeve where the latter holds them at farm"; it could also mean simply "with the king when he is present and with his representative, the reeve, otherwise". Reeves are no doubt included among the judges who, according to III Edgar 3, may, if the king permits it, buy back the position they have lost by giving false judgments,[26] and this implies that the office was a lucrative one; but it might well be this if the reeve were allowed to retain a proportion of the fines, similar to the earl's third penny, and so the clause is not safe evidence for the farming of the profits of jurisdiction by the reeve. Yet the tenor of this code, which has clauses against the imposition of excessive fines, suggests that it was not normally the king who stood to profit from such, but that Edgar was legislating to prevent those who would benefit from abusing their position. He may have in mind both private holders of immunities and reeves who are trying to make too much out of their farm.

Since the statements in the laws are not definite enough for one to pronounce with certainty that they refer to reeves who farm royal estates with the profits of jurisdiction attached to them, the poem is welcome in showing that here the reeve was expected to keep as his own property the compositions paid to him in the course of his exercise of justice — unless, of course, we are to take the offers of payment as bribes. There is evidence for the prevalence of bribery, but surely Wulfstan the precentor would not have openly poured scorn on a royal officer for refusing bribes. The acceptance of bribes was a heavy offence: in V Athelstan 1.3 a reeve who takes bribes is threatened with a fine of 120 shillings and loss of office,[27] and the same penalty is suffered in III Edgar 3 by a judge who gives a wrong judgment and cannot prove that he did so merely out of ignorance.[28] The poet would not wish to express open approval of those who offer bribes and lack of sympathy with an official who will not accept them.

The passage has a further interest, for it supplies clear evidence of the important part played by the king's officer in local pleas. It assumes that in this criminal suit the judgment was given by the reeve, who took sole responsibility and could have altered it had he been willing. There is no suggestion of the participation of the suitors of the court at this stage of the proceedings. Thus this passage can be added to other evidence which establishes that Asser, when he depicts King Alfred as calling his judges to answer for wrong judgments which they had given from ignorance or favor or

25 Vol. II: *Glossar*, *s.v. Vogt*, 2c, 12-12t, 19c.

26 See below, p. 90.

27 As shown by comparison with II Athelstan 25.

28 II Cnut 15.1, based on Edgar's clause, prescribes this penalty for giving a wrong judgment out of hatred or for bribes.

bribery, knew what he was talking about, although his accuracy has been called in question by scholars who believed that judgments were made by the assembled court and that the official presiding could not thus be held responsible.[29] Edward the Elder charges his reeves to judge right judgments,[30] as also does Cnut.[31] The most important text in this connexion is the clause from the laws of Edgar which states: "And the judge who pronounces a wrong judgment on another is to pay to the king 120 shillings as compensation, unless he dare declare on oath that he knew not how to do it more justly — and he is always to forfeit his 'thegnship', unless he may redeem it from the king, according as he will allow him. And the bishop of the diocese is to exact the compensation on the king's behalf."[32] The choice of the word "thegnship" rather than *folgað* "office", was probably dictated by the need to make the statute apply to holders of private courts as well as to royal officials, and the particular privilege of a thegn's position here envisaged is the right to hold a court. That the statute is meant to apply to royal officials also is shown by the assignment of the duty of exacting the compensation to the bishop; if it referred only to immunity holders, this duty could have been left to the secular officials. Wulfstan's poem shows the important part played by the reeve in a criminal suit, but Edgar's legislation is general, and there is no reason to doubt that in civil suits also the direction given by the president of the court is likely to have been decisive.[33]

[29] See *Asser's Life of King Alfred*, ed. W. H. Stevenson, Cap. 106, and cf. Stevenson's discussion, pp. 342-343. In the reprint of this work, 1959, I have discussed this question when defending the authenticity of the work against recent doubters. See especially pp. cxliii-cxlvii.
[30] I Edward, Prologue.
[31] Letter of 1019/1020, 11.
[32] III Edgar 3; this is repeated in II Cnut 15.1, with the addition that it applies in the area under English law, while in the Danelaw the penalty paid by the judge who cannot prove that he erred out of ignorance alone is to be *lahslit*, *i.e.*, 10 half-marks if the offender were a king's thegn, an amount equivalent to 128 West Saxon shillings.
[33] I am indebted to Sir Frank Stenton and Professor B. Dickins for reading and criticizing this article.

VI

The Anglo-Saxon Achievement

In contrast to the Duchy of Normandy, which came into being as the result of a grant to Rollo in 911, the Anglo-Saxon state had had a long and by no means inglorious history behind it in 1066. Its people, who usually called themselves 'the English', had begun to settle in Britain about the middle of the fifth century, and by about a century later the settlements had coalesced into a few kingdoms, those south of the Humber often acknowledging a single overlord, a *Bretwalda* 'ruler of Britain'. Before the end of the seventh century all had accepted Christianity, and the sharing of a common church reinforced the sense of common origin, giving the members of the various kingdoms a feeling of unity. Thus St Boniface appeals in 738 to 'all God-fearing catholics in common, sprung from the stock and the race of the English', and Bede's pupil Cuthbert, a Northumbrian, wrote in 764 to Lul, a West Saxon, as was Boniface, his predecessor in the see of Mainz, saying that 'the whole race of the English, in whatever provinces they are found' should give thanks to God for granting Bede to their nation. When in the ninth century the Vikings menaced all western Europe, the courage and tenacity of King Alfred saved Wessex, and, though much of the north and east of England passed for a time under Scandinavian control, and received numbers of Scandinavian settlers, these areas were brought back under English rule by Alfred's efficient successors, his son Edward, his daughter Æthelflæd, his grandsons, Athelstan, Edmund and Eadred. Athelstan was the first king who could claim to rule the whole of England; since he was recognized by some Celtic rulers, a charter refers to him as 'elevated by the right hand of the Almighty, which is Christ, to the throne of the whole kingdom of Britain'. He defeated at *Brunanburh* a great combine of Celts and Scandinavians, and he played some part in continental politics. Though there were short periods later when a Scandinavian king secured recognition in Northumbria, the last of these was killed in 954. Henceforward, we have the united kingdom of England. The renewed Danish attacks in the reign of a weak king, Ethelred, resulted in the conquest by Cnut in 1016, but, contrary to what might have been expected, he reigned as his predecessors had done, upheld the laws and supported generously the church; those of his followers who were not already Christian seem to have conformed. It is interesting to find, for example, a list of those who had entered into confraternity with the monks of Thorney Abbey, for the sake of their prayers, which begins with the names of Cnut's Danish earls, Turkil, Hacun, Eoric, Eglaf and his brother Ulf, followed by thirty-one Danish male names, presumably of their retinues. The English appear quickly to have civilized their Danish conquerors. The reigns of Cnut's sons were unpopular, but short, and in 1042 the English welcomed back a king of their old royal line. A vernacular writer at Bury St Edmunds writes: 'May the noble name of our Lord the Saviour Christ be honoured for ever into eternity. . . . He in these days has given and granted the fair island of the kingdom of Britain to King Edward, just as He did of yore to his kinsmen.' By this time England had recovered its prosperity after the ravages of the Danish wars and the heavy tributes, and had become a rich prize to tempt the Norman duke.

During these six hundred years there were periods when the

Anglo-Saxon contribution to learning, literature and art had been spectacular. In the early eighth century Bede's writings showed him the foremost scholar of his age, in theology, chronology and history, and his work had a profound influence on the subsequent scholarship of all western Europe. His older contemporary, the West Saxon Aldhelm, was a man of great erudition, whose works continued to be used for centuries both at home and abroad. This period produced also masterpieces of manuscript illumination, sculpture and metal-work, and many manuscripts and works of art produced in England were taken to the Continent in the eighth century by the missionaries, Boniface, Willibrord and numbers of other Anglo-Saxons, men and women, who took the Christian faith to the heathen Germanic tribes. They established monasteries in Frisia and in the Rhineland, in which Anglo-Saxon learning and art flourished, and from which it spread to other foundations. Anglo-Saxon influence was not confined to these spheres, however, for St Boniface was instrumental in persuading the Frankish rulers to reform their church and to enter into closer relations with the papacy.

In the mid-eighth century continental students came to study at York, under Alcuin, an Englishman trained at the school of York established by Bede's pupil, Archbishop Egbert, and in 782 Alcuin went, at the invitation of Charles the Great, to play an important part in the Carolingian revival of learning, and by means of his pupils, some of them Englishmen, to influence continental scholarship of the next generation. Thus King Alfred had reason to remember with patriotic pride 'how men from abroad came hither to this land in search of knowledge and instruction'.

This period in which the Anglo-Saxons were influential on the Continent seems to have been the time when, at home, the bulk of surviving vernacular poetry was composed. This includes *Beowulf*, a rich and subtle poem in which a vivid account of the raids of monsters is told on a background of historical or heroic legend, with an underlying theme of the relation of monsters to a divinely created universe and of the qualities of a Christian hero and deliverer. There is also a deeply moving poem describing a vision in which the Cross tells its own experience at the Crucifixion, and brings home to the dreamer the full significance of the Christian doctrine of redemption; also some shorter lyric poems poignantly depicting tragic situations, such as that of a deserted woman, or of a man who has lost his lord, or lamenting the decay of earlier and greater civilizations, in order to conclude that the only true security lies in faith in God. There survives also a number of more directly religious poems, of various kinds, biblical paraphrase, homiletic and doctrinal instruction, saints' lives, etc. This early poetry was still being entered in manuscripts of the late tenth and early eleventh centuries. It is probable that poetry of this kind formed the inspiration of the Christian poetry of the continental Saxons, the *Heliand* and the *Genesis*. One of the leading missionaries to the Saxons on the Continent, the Frisian Liudger, was educated at York, where he would be likely to hear some Anglo-Saxon Christian poetry and to realize its value in teaching the faith to laymen.

King Alfred's reforms were directed to improve the state of learning in his own land, partly by the provision of English translations of Latin books 'most necessary for all men to know'. These remained influential in England; rather surprisingly, the Old English version of Orosius was taken to the Continent in the eleventh century, and was used there at a date when a familiarity with this language is unexpected. Yet it was not until the latter part of the tenth century, after a great monastic revival under the leadership of Dunstan, archbishop of Canterbury, Oswald, bishop of Worcester and archbishop of York, and Æthelwold, bishop of Winchester, that we get another great period of activity in learning, literature and art. From this time on, Anglo-Saxon manuscripts and works of art were again taken in numbers abroad, and proved influential in some continental houses. This 'golden age', which, oddly enough, was at its heyday in the troubled reign of Ethelred, differed from the 'age of Bede' in that one of its great glories was its vernacular prose, as we shall see later. During this same period, the Anglo-Saxons were exerting an influence outside their own land in another way: they played an important part in the conversion to Christianity of the Scandinavian lands.

There was certainly much in their past history of which Englishmen in the eleventh century could be proud, if they were aware of it. It may be of some interest to consider how far they were aware of history further back than living memory could take them. Educated men, not only ecclesiastics who knew Latin, but also laymen of the upper classes who read English, would be aware of the contents of Bede's *Ecclesiastical History of the English Nation*: its influence can be seen in later authors; manuscripts of the Latin text continued to be produced, while the Old English translation, probably commissioned by King Alfred, which was used by Abbot Ælfric about 990, survives in two tenth-century manuscripts and three of the eleventh century. The writer of an Ely charter in the early eleventh century cites as his authority 'Bede, the teacher of the English people', while a marginal reference, by the late tenth-century glossator, in the Lindisfarne Gospels to *Beda ðe brœma bœcere* ('the famous scholar') sounds like a quotation from a poem. Among the results of a knowledge of Bede would be the consciousness that they were descended 'from three very powerful nations of the Germans, the Angles, Saxons and

Jutes' and the belief that it was by special divine favour that their ancestors were allowed to conquer Britain. Pride in this conquest is shown in the final words of the poem on the battle of *Brunanburh*: 'the proud assailants, warriors eager for glory, overcame the Britons and won a country.' Bede's book also kept them aware of their debt to Rome, whence Gregory, 'Apostle of the English' had sent them the true faith. They were not to know that in 1066 the papacy would bless the banner of a foreign usurper.

Bede's history would take them only to 731, but there was also available the Anglo-Saxon Chronicle, which was first compiled from earlier sources about 890 and circulated to some religious houses, and thereafter continued in some places. A version which reached the north was interpolated with material taken from Bede and from sets of northern annals. Two of the three surviving versions which were being kept up in the reign of the Confessor were continuations of this northern recension; one of these, however, was by this time at St Augustine's, Canterbury, while the other, which betrays a special interest in the affairs of Northumbria and of the diocese of Worcester which was sometimes held in plurality with that of York, was probably at York (though some scholars would place it at Worcester). A third version, not based on the northern recension, was being written at Abingdon. These three versions are at times independent, and at other times two of them share a common source. There were other copies of the Chronicle which were not actively kept up, but which would be available for consultation on past history, and we learn of some lost copies; others may have been lost without trace. Thus many men would have an opportunity of reading about the Danish raids of the ninth century, about Alfred's victories and about the tenth-century re-conquest of the Danelaw. They could read also of the calamities of the reign of Ethelred, but the older men would remember these, and the younger know of them from their fathers' reminiscences.

An interest in various English saints helped to keep alive some knowledge of earlier history and customs. Manuscripts of early Latin saints' lives, Bede's *Life of Cuthbert* and the anonymous *Life*, Eddius's *Life of Wilfrid* (*c.* 709), Felix's *Life of Guthlac* (730–40), continued to be produced, as were also tenth-century works like Frithegod's *Life of Wilfrid* and Abbo's *Life of Edmund*, and the *Lives* of the monastic reformers, Dunstan, Oswald and Æthelwold. Felix's *Life of Guthlac* was translated into English, and there were several short vernacular *Lives* of English saints, some of them intended to be preached on their festivals. Many an illiterate Englishman would have learnt about some of these saints, though his knowledge might include later legendary material which had grown up round the cult.

Men of Latin culture continued to use the non-historical works of Bede, and the writings of Aldhelm (*c.* 686), whose difficult and ornate diction was often supplied with glosses in Old English, an indication that it was much studied. Manuscripts containing letters and poems by Alcuin were written in England in the eleventh century, and his works 'On Virtues and Vices' and the 'To Sigwulf on Genesis' were translated into English, the latter by Ælfric (*c.* 1000). The fact that most of the pre-Viking age English poetry has come down to us in four manuscripts written in the late tenth and early eleventh centuries may point to a deliberate attempt to preserve from oblivion their early literature.

Yet, as far as one can judge, most Englishmen of the eleventh century would know little or nothing about what to modern scholars is one of the greatest of Anglo-Saxon achievements, the work of the missionaries on the Continent in the eighth century, especially that of Boniface. Since he is not mentioned by Bede or the Anglo-Saxon Chronicle, and since he was buried in Fulda in Germany and thus no English house could claim him as a wonder-working saint, little is heard of him in late English sources. No manuscript of any of the *Lives* of him appears to have been known in England, nor any of the collections of his correspondence and that of his successor Lul, which were made by their followers abroad. Only three of his letters can be shown to have been known in England at this time, and it was not interest in Boniface that preserved them. Two, in the original Latin, owe their preservation to the importance of their contents, for in one he and seven other missionary bishops attempted to persuade Æthelbald of Mercia to reform his ways, and in the other he sent decrees of a continental synod to Archbishop Cuthbert of Canterbury. A different type of interest led to the translation into English of a letter describing a vision of the next world seen by a monk of Wenlock, a type of literature which had a wide appeal. The scholar Archbishop Wulfstan II of York (1002–23) knew of some other eighth-century documents, but the average Englishman was probably quite unaware of this glorious period in his nation's past. Some who travelled abroad may have seen Anglo-Saxon manuscripts and treasures of the eighth century in continental houses; a far greater number of people would be aware that the productions in illumination, embroidery and metal-work of their own day were highly valued abroad.

Up till now, we have considered mainly what literate Englishmen in the Confessor's reign could read about past history. One must also reckon with oral tradition, which would reach far lower down the social scale. Some events may have been celebrated in poems, for it would be unwise to assume that the few historical poems which found their way into the Chronicle, and the single poem on a local hero, Byrhtnoth of Maldon, which a series of chances has preserved, are all which once existed: secular poetry had comparatively little chance of being written down. When King Ethelred's son Athelstan left to his brother Edmund in his will in 1015 'the sword which King Offa owned', we can well believe that he knew far more about this great eighth-century king than he could have learnt from the scanty entries in the Chronicle; the great dyke stood as a tangible memory of Offa's power and efficiency. Abbot Ælfric was probably not drawing on written sources alone when he selected as kings to compare with the Emperor Theodosius as being 'victorious through God', Alfred 'who often fought against the Danes, until he won the victory and protected his people', Athelstan 'who fought against Olaf and slew his army and put him himself to flight' and Edgar 'who exalted the praise of God everywhere among his people, the strongest of all kings over the English nation', for whom 'God subdued his adversaries, kings and earls, so that they came to him without any fighting, desiring peace'. Though not all the stories which reached the early twelfth-century historian William of Malmesbury are acceptable as history, there is no reason to disbelieve his claim that the places where Alfred suffered ill-fortune were still being pointed out by the local people. There must have survived a widespread admiration for Alfred as a man who snatched victory when in an apparently desperate position; otherwise we should not find two religious houses in the early eleventh century eager to secure the credit for their own saint: Durham attributed the victory to the help of St Cuthbert; St Neots claimed it for their saint, and in the vernacular *Life of St Neot* occurs the earliest recorded version of the story of the cakes, told to emphasize the depths of misfortune from which the saint rescued the king. Alfred lived on in popular memory also as the writer of books: when Ælfric speaks of the 'books which King Alfred wisely translated' he probably knew which these were, but the words of his contemporary, the chronicler Æthelweard, 'an unknown number of books', and those in the *Life of St Neot*, 'he composed many books through God's spirit', suggest a vaguer tradition. Middle English poetry shows that long after the Norman conquest the memory survived of Alfred as 'the wisest man that was in England'. Stories concerning Athelstan also reached William of Malmesbury; and as for Edgar, traditions concerning his care for justice, his organizing of the fleet and his reform of the coinage were eventually written down by post-Conquest writers.

We are therefore probably justified in believing that many people in Edward the Confessor's time were fully conscious that their nation had produced strong and victorious kings, and learned and saintly men; and they thought of their nation as a unity, in spite of local variations in customs and institutions. They would be unlikely to welcome the prospect of a ruler from an upstart state across the Channel; they would not consider their civilization and government inferior to that of Normandy, nor, as we shall see, had they any reason to do so.

It is hardly necessary nowadays to go to great trouble to refute earlier charges of decadence or incompetence levelled against the Anglo-Saxons of the eleventh century, for studies of surviving records and objects have already shed a favourable light on many aspects of their culture, and continue to do so. It is enough to let the facts speak for themselves. In the course of a long history, the monarchy had acquired greater powers than those possessed by most rulers in western Europe, and the kings in the tenth century, who were faced with the task of ruling the whole of England, had established a measure of uniformity in certain large matters, while permitting local differences in institutions and customs, especially between the Danelaw and the rest of England. The division into shires, which was ancient in Wessex, was extended over the whole country as far as the Tees, the shire-meeting being held twice a year. The division into hundreds, which may also have been ancient in some parts of the country, was spread everywhere, except in some Danelaw areas, where the functions of the hundred were performed by a district known as a weapontake; the hundred ordinance of the mid-tenth century secured uniformity in administration. Its court met every four weeks. Its duties included the maintenance of order by taking action against cattle-thieving, by ensuring that every man had sureties capable of bringing him to court, and by its jurisdiction over all but the gravest criminal suits. The hundred court also apportioned the incidence of taxation. There were also borough courts, which met three times a year, and we hear of courts where two or more hundreds were combined, while in the north there was a court of the riding. The shire court dealt with both criminal causes and civil causes concerning land, and it is in connexion with the latter that documents survive which supply us with vivid glimpses of the thegns of the shire settling local disputes. It is interesting to see how often they prefer to bring the parties to some measure of agreement rather than enforce the letter of the law. Typical is the statement in an account of a Worcestershire lawsuit between a certain Leofric of Blackwell and a man called Wulfstan: 'Then both Leofric's friends and Wulfstan's said that it would be better for them to come to an agreement than to keep up any quarrel between them.' Though many details of the working of the various courts are obscure, there is enough to show that there was an efficient system of local government in force, and this impression is supported by the insistence of the Norman kings that it should in essentials remain unchanged. Again and again we find them referring questions to the shire or the hundred, and a writ of Henry I in 1108 declares that the shire court and the hundred court are to be held in the same places and at the same fixed periods as they were held in the time of King Edward, and not otherwise. Though most suits were dealt with at these local assemblies, it was the king's justice they administered. The hundred was normally presided over by a king's reeve, the shire by the ealdorman or the sheriff, along with the bishop in suits which concerned the church. The increasing tendency in the later Saxon period for the ealdorman to be in charge of several shires led to greater responsibility of the sheriff for his own shire; but both ealdorman and sheriff were royal officials, and in addition, the king might sometimes send a special messenger to the meeting. There were some hundreds in private hands, which meant that the representative of the holder of the privilege presided, and that the profits of jurisdiction went to the latter; but these immunities were always derived from a royal grant. Moreover, there were certain serious criminal charges which were almost always reserved to the king, and not included in a grant of privilege, namely breach of the king's protection, forcible entry into a house, ambush, the harbouring of fugitives and the fine for neglect of military service. Only a very few highly privileged persons were allowed to handle these.

The law which the courts administered was a mass of customary law with various local differences, but supplemented and modified by the statutes of successive kings; for kings in England had been for centuries accustomed to legislate, and codes survive from seventh-century kings of Kent, from Ine of Wessex (688–94), from Alfred and from most of his successors up to Cnut. The laws of Offa of Mercia, which were known to King Alfred, have not survived. Archbishop Wulfstan II, who held the province of York 1002–23, speaks many times with admiration of the laws of Edgar, and made great use of the code which we cite as II and III Edgar when drafting several codes for King Ethelred and a comprehensive code for Cnut. This was the last Anglo-Saxon law-code, and when King Edward in 1065 had to yield to the Northumbrians in revolt against their earl, Tostig, we are told: 'and he renewed there the law of King Cnut.' When documents of the Norman kings insist on the observance of the laws of King Edward's time, they mean this code and established custom, and Cnut's laws are given the place of honour by the Latin writers who in the reign of Henry I translated and made compilations of the Anglo-Saxon codes and wrote treatises of the law. This was not done in a purely antiquarian spirit, for only a few changes had been introduced by William I, e.g. the murder-fine to protect his Norman followers, the use of the ordeal of battle as an alternative to the Anglo-Saxon methods, and a sharper differentiation between ecclesiastical and lay courts. The continued respect paid to Anglo-Saxon law is strikingly illustrated by the bringing of the aged bishop Æthelric of Selsey to the plea held on Pinnendon Heath in 1075 or 1076 in order to answer questions on Anglo-Saxon law. The two most comprehensive manuscripts of the Anglo-Saxon laws were compiled in Henry's reign, namely the *Textus Roffensis* and the St Pauls manuscript now in Corpus Christi College, Cambridge.

If William was content to make few alterations in the law, he also had little reason to be discontented with the royal rights held by his predecessors. Besides the profits of jurisdiction, the king had over the whole land the three public dues, fortress work, bridge work and military service. From these, immunity was hardly ever granted. Though the precise details of the amount of military service which could be demanded are uncertain, and seem to have varied in some places in accordance with individual agreements made with the king, there is no doubt that his rights were extensive. The Anglo-Saxon military organization was adequate to preserve the land reasonably secure from the Welsh and the Scots, and at Stamford Bridge a great army led by the foremost Scandinavian warrior of the time was utterly defeated. Even after the Norman kings had made arrangements for a feudal army, by granting estates to be held by knight-service, they still continued on occasions to call out the native levy.

The king possessed extensive royal lands in most parts of his kingdom, and they could be increased by the forfeiture of lands for grave offences, and by the royal right of inheritance after foreigners or others who died without heir. He had widespread rights to tolls, and from many estates he still received food-rents, relics from a time when this charge had been incumbent on all lands, though by the eleventh century the granting of land by charter, as 'bookland', which was freed from this payment, had greatly decreased the area which paid it. It was probably in relation to these food-rents and to military service that the country was first assessed in hides (in some Danelaw areas in carucates); but by the late Saxon period this assessment was mainly important for the collection of the geld.

This tax, one of the main sources of royal income, had originated from the need to buy off Viking invaders, but was later used to pay a standing army or navy, and eventually to meet any special need. To operate it, an efficient and flexible system had been evolved by which the geld was taken at a rate per hide which could be varied according to needs, and a sum was demanded from each shire according to the number of hides it was assumed to contain; this sum was then divided among the hundreds of the shire, and eventually among the estates in the hundred in relation to their assessment in hides. The collection of this tax, and the handling of the royal revenue from all its varied sources, imply an expert and centralized financial system in advance of its day; the Norman kings used it with little modification for a long period. They also inherited an excellent coinage: beside the Anglo-Saxon silver pennies the coins of the duchy of Normandy before 1066 make a poor show. From the eighth century onwards the high quality of Anglo-Saxon coins caused them to have influence on the Continent, and in the eleventh century a coinage on the English model was introduced into Scandinavia. A firm central control was kept; by the end of the period dies were cut at London, and circulated to the local mints, of which in Edward's reign there were about seventy; new issues were made at regular intervals, and the money paid by the moneyers for the new dies went into the royal coffers. A few ecclesiastics, e.g. the two archbishops and the bishops of Hereford and Rochester, were allowed their own moneyers. The fact that coins of Harold's brief reign survive from more than half of the known mints is evidence for the speed and efficiency with which the system worked. William took it over in full working order.

There was thus a high measure of centralized government, and its successful working was made possible by what Sir Frank Stenton has called 'the most efficient means of publishing the ruler's will which western Europe has so far known', that is the 'writ', a simple letter in the native language, authenticated by the king's seal, which gave instructions regarding the king's wishes or information regarding his acts. Numbers of these writs have survived, usually addressed to the bishop, earl, sheriff and thegns of the shire, or to the bishop, town-reeve and citizens of the borough. A casual reference in a late tenth-century homily, 'If the king sends his writ to any one of his thegns', suggests that it was common for the king to communicate by this means with individuals, but naturally the writs which had most chance of surviving were those which a religious house had an interest in preserving, those which made grants to them or re-established their claims to estates or privileges. For these purposes the writ began to supersede the older formal Latin 'diploma' as evidence of such rights, though diplomas of the old type could still be drawn up occasionally, even after the Conquest. The Norman kings took over the writ in order to communicate with their subjects for all manner of administrative purposes, though gradually it came to be written in Latin and supplied with a short list of witnesses. One writ of special interest just after the Conquest is not a royal one, but written in the name of the Confessor's widow, Edith, sister of King Harold: it is addressed to the hundred of Wedmore, informing it of a grant to the canons of Wells, which is the reason for its preservation; but in addition it asks 'that you will pronounce for me a just judgement concerning Wudumann to whom I entrusted by horse(s) and who has for six years withheld my rent'. No doubt numbers of writs dealing solely with ephemeral matters of this nature have perished without trace.

The powers of an Anglo-Saxon king were considerable, though during the later Saxon period the increasing tendency to combine several shires under a single ealdorman, or earl, as he was universally called by Edward's reign, gave this official more influence than had previously been the case. The politics of this reign were disturbed by the rivalry between the families of Earl Godwine and Earl Leofwine. Yet the notion of a hereditary earldom had not got very far. In principle, the earl was the king's nominee: Archbishop Wulfstan's statement, 'a thegn becomes entitled to an earldom by the king's gift', was copied in a manuscript about the time of the Conquest. In practice, something like a hereditary right of the house of Leofric to the earldom of the original Mercia seems to have been acknowledged, but this did not prevent small earldoms from being carved out of the great area which had formed the Mercian kingdom, and these were given to men of other families. For example, Swegn, Godwine's son, held the Mercian shires of

Gloucester, Hereford and Oxford along with the West Saxon shires of Berkshire and Somerset, and on his death Hereford and Oxford, at any rate, were given to the king's half-Norman nephew, Ralf. An earldom in the East Midlands was held along with Northumbria by Siward, and then it passed to Tostig, Godwine's son, in whose time it can be shown to include Huntingdonshire, Northamptonshire and Bedfordshire. It was only after Tostig's expulsion that it was given to Siward's son Waltheof. Godwine was earl of Wessex and Kent, and earldoms were created for his sons as they grew up: Swegn held the one already mentioned, Harold had East Anglia until he succeeded his father to Wessex, Tostig was appointed to Northumbria in 1055, Gyrth was given East Anglia when Ælfgar, Earl Leofric's son, who had succeeded Harold in this area, became earl of Mercia after his father, and Oxfordshire also was added to Gyrth's earldom, and finally, Leofwine, Godwine's son, held Essex, Hertfordshire, Middlesex and Buckinghamshire along with Kent and Surrey. Harold combined Herefordshire with his earldom of Wessex. The complicated re-arrangement of earldoms during this reign looks like deliberate policy: it would not weaken the house of Godwine as long as members of this held so many earldoms, but it would prevent the establishment of earldoms with settled boundaries in which sons might claim to succeed their fathers by right, instead of by royal gift. Without unduly minimizing the power of Godwine and his sons, especially after their triumphant return from exile in 1052, we should note that this return was made possible in part by the wish of both sides to avoid serious civil war. As the Anglo-Saxon Chronicle says: 'It was hateful to almost all of them to fight against men of their own race . . . and also they did not wish the country to be laid the more open to foreigners through their destroying each other.' Even after Godwine's victorious return, the king was no mere cipher, completely controlled by a powerful subject: loyalist attachment to the house of Alfred was strong, and, as we have seen, many institutions made the power of a central government felt throughout the country, mighty though the local earl might be.

Though powerful men, Osgod Clapa in 1049, Godwine and his sons in 1052, Earl Ælfgar in 1055 and 1058, Tostig in 1066, did not shrink from using armed force to recover their position after they had been exiled, the rivalries between comital families did not go as far as private warfare, and there was no need in England to establish a 'truce of God' as was done in Normandy to prevent private warfare during certain periods. Naturally, England was not free from deeds of violence. Northumbria in particular was a wild land, and we read of a long feud between two local families, in which the part played by a certain Thurbrand in the slaying of Earl Uhtred in 1016 was avenged by Uhtred's son Aldred, who then in his turn was killed by Thurbrand's son Carle; the last act in this drama was the slaughter by Aldred's grandson Earl Waltheof of most of Carle's sons in 1073. Yet this does not seem to have involved others than the families concerned, and in any case the north was exceptional. The Northumbrians who rose against Tostig in 1065 did great damage round Northampton while waiting for the king's reply: 'they killed people and burned houses and corn and took all the cattle that they could get at . . . and captured many hundreds of people and took them north with them, so that that shire and other neighbouring shires were the worse for it for many years.' Individual acts of treachery and cruelty are occasionally recorded, such as the blinding of the atheling Alfred in 1035, and Earl Swegn's murder of his cousin Beorn in 1049. Similar incidents can be found in all countries at this time, and perhaps what one should notice is how both these actions shocked contemporary English opinion: they were not taken as normal. Judged on eleventh-century standards, Anglo-

Saxon England must have appeared a comparatively peaceful place. The readiness of local thegns to settle disputes by compromise no doubt is one element in the comparative freedom from private conflicts. One gets the impression from the documents that the country was rich in good sense.

Without internal peace, England would not have recovered so rapidly from the devastations of the Danish wars. Its wealth is not disputed, and the bulk of surviving coinage implies a considerable amount of trade. Already in the reign of Ethelred we learn that English ships were to be expected in continental harbours, and English traders in Rome, while a document from about this time refers to the presence in London of traders from Normandy, Ponthieu, Flanders, Lorraine, France and the territories of the emperor. There was also considerable trade with Scandinavia, especially from York and the eastern ports, and Bristol and Chester handled trade with Ireland; one gets a casual reference to Irish traders with cloaks to sell in Cambridge. The imports seem mainly to have been luxury goods, wine, spices and incense, precious metals, gems, ivory and silk, rich robes, furs, glass vessels and some types of pottery; oil and blubberfish are mentioned also. We learn less about exports. Fine embroidery and metal-work of English manufacture were prized on the Continent, but the chief exports were probably wool and agricultural produce, especially cheese. The fact that these things could be produced in excess of home needs suggests that in some areas at least the land was being competently farmed according to eleventh-century standards. Both the law and the church forbade the sale across the sea of Christian men; yet some traffic of slaves to Ireland was carried on at Bristol as late as the reign of William I. The slave class was probably shrinking before the Conquest because of the frequency of manumission by the owners as a charitable act for the good of their souls. Manumission continued after the Conquest, and gradually the clear distinction between a slave and a free man of the lower classes on economically much the same level became blurred, since the Norman lords judged more by tenurial dependence than by the possession of a wergild (the price to be paid in compensation if a man were slain), which was in Anglo-Saxon times the mark of a freeman.

The increase in trade had been accompanied by an extension of urban life. This had received encouragement from the policy of Alfred and his son Edward the Elder of building fortified boroughs as a defence against the Danes, for these offered security as trading centres. It became increasingly common for landowners to possess at least one house in neighbouring boroughs, while important magnates, ecclesiastical or lay, usually had property in many large towns, and especially in London. Most citizens were regarded as tenants of the king, and in general he retained the main share of rents, services and profits of jurisdiction, though in many boroughs the earl had a third of the profits, and in some, as at York and Worcester, the archbishop or bishop owned part of the borough; it was common also for landowners with houses in a borough to have the right of jurisdiction over their own men occupying them. Boroughs were in charge of a town-reeve, and there was a borough court which King Edgar ordered to meet three times a year. It is not possible to access accurately the population of Anglo-Saxon towns, since Domesday Book gives only the number of messuages and we do not know how big an average of inhabitants one should allow to each. London and Winchester are not described in Domesday Book; York seems to have had some 1,800 messuages, Norwich 1,320, Lincoln 1,510, while several other towns, e.g. Chester, Oxford, Hereford, Gloucester, Worcester, Thetford, Ipswich, etc, though smaller, were by no means negligible. After the Conquest, and partly as a result of it, trade increased and with it the size of towns; but not uniformly nor immediately: Domesday Book reveals a decay in some towns between 1066 and 1086.

Criticism of the eleventh-century Anglo-Saxon church nowadays comes mainly from those who judge a church by its monastic fervour. The zeal of the reformers of the tenth century, which had led to the displacement of secular canons by monks in some places, and to the foundation or re-foundation of many Benedictine monasteries, had largely spent itself by the eleventh century, and the only sizable Benedictine houses to be founded then were Burton-on-Trent about 1004, and Bury St Edmunds, founded by Cnut in 1020, though there were also smaller foundations. An attempt was made in the laws of King Ethelred to insist on a communal dormitory and refectory in churches served by bodies of canons, and, though this did not become universal, some prelates of Edward's reign, such as Archbishop Ælfric at Beverley and Bishop Giso at Wells, imposed it. New foundations in this reign tended to be for bodies of canons, as were Stow, Lincolnshire, founded in the early eleventh century, and later endowed by Earl Leofric, and Waltham Holy Cross, enriched by Earl Harold, and the smaller foundations of Axminster and Cirencester. Throughout the period people also continued to be generous in gifts to the older establishments, in lands, money and ornaments. Lay donors include the earls, Siward, Ralf, Odda, Leofric, Tostig and Harold; and of particular interest are the many grants made by landowners to parish churches. Individual piety showed itself also in the prevalence of pilgrimages, to Rome and even to Jerusalem.

It became common in the eleventh century for bishoprics to be given to the king's priests, men who had served him in his writing office, whereas before the episcopate had had a preponderance of monks. This method of rewarding ecclesiastics who had carried on the essential civil service was not confined to England, nor does it follow that the king's priests who were thus advanced (and by no means all of them were) were unsuited for the episcopal office. Contemporary criticism seems levelled at only two of them, Ulf, a Norman whom Edward made bishop of Dorchester, and who would have been deprived at the Council of Vercelli (1050) if he had not had recourse to bribery (or so the Anglo-Saxon chronicler believed) and Stigand, a grasping prelate who held sees and abbacies in plurality, even after becoming archbishop of Canterbury. Most of the bishops appointed from among the king's priests appear to have given satisfaction, and not only as administrators. Leofric of Exeter collected books and enriched his church with them and with artistic treasures, as well as with land. On the other hand, when the choice fell upon a monk, as it not infrequently did, some of these proved active men of affairs. It is true that the reign of the Confessor produced no one of the stature of Archbishop Wulfstan II of York (1002–23), who combined deep scholarship with political and administrative ability, and carried out reforms in many aspects of religion, the effects of which reached far beyond his diocese, but the episcopate in 1066 included St Wulfstan of Worcester, a man of piety who was regarded as an ideal bishop, and Aldred of York, an outstanding administrator and political figure. Few appointments seem to have been made without good reason, though in England as elsewhere there was some danger of influence and simony. However, the English church did not appoint to sees mere youths related to the reigning house, as was sometimes done in the duchy of Normandy.

What is of particular interest in regard to the late Anglo-Saxon church is the amount of evidence showing a deep concern with the religious needs of the laity and with the condition of the parish priests in charge of them. A large number of homilies were produced, especially by Ælfric, abbot of Eynsham, to be preached by the clergy to bring home to ordinary men the central doctrines of the faith, to preserve them from heresy, and to inculcate proper Christian behaviour. Ælfric issued between 990 and 991 two volumes of homilies for the major festivals of the Christian year, and during the rest of his life he continued to revise these, and to add new homilies for Sundays not covered in his original work, as well as a series mainly of lives of saints, which might urge men to emulation of their virtues. From the manuscripts of these works which survive, it is clear that they were much used and copied. His contemporary, Archbishop Wulfstan II, also wrote many homilies, some of straightforward instruction on doctrine and morals, some of impassioned appeal for repentance. These too became widely known. Both these writers also produced works in Latin and in English which are directed towards the improvement of the secular clergy: Ælfric wrote for these pastoral letters, at the request of Bishop Wulfsige of Sherborne and of Archbishop Wulfstan, who himself is the author of sets of canons. One of Wulfstan's most interesting writings is a little tract on the need for more careful instruction and examination of candidates for orders. This is a practical document, and while it admits that there might be occasions when out of necessity one would have to ordain a 'half-trained' candidate, it insists that such a man must give an undertaking to continue his studies. Both Wulfstan and Ælfric, monks by training, make many appeals for a celibate priesthood, but with little obvious success; Wulfstan seems to have had to tolerate married priests in his northern diocese. His writings also consider the duties of bishops and of bodies of secular canons; there seems in fact no section of the church which he does not examine. Though after his death in 1023 the Anglo-Saxon church produced no one to equal him, a continued interest in these reforms is shown by the production of manuscripts of his work, as well as of Ælfric's, and of translations of canonical writings of continental authors. There is no reason to suppose that the average bishop neglected the spiritual needs of his diocese; care for these is not incompatible with vigilance over the temporal possessions of their church, though the nature of our surviving records makes this appear to loom more largely.

Latin scholarship had flourished after the tenth-century monastic revival, as is proved by saints' lives and canons written in this language, by the continued production throughout the period of manuscripts of Latin authors, and by the wide knowledge of these visible in the works of men like Ælfric and Wulfstan, who were familiar with many works of the Fathers and of Bede, Aldhelm and Alcuin, as well as with canonical writers, especially of the eighth and ninth centuries. For the teaching of Latin, Ælfric composed a Latin–English grammar, and an amusing colloquy to exercise his pupils in Latin vocabulary. Yet the glory of the late Anglo-Saxon period was its English writing. At a time when no vernacular prose of any distinction had appeared on the Continent, the Anglo-Saxons had developed a language of great copiousness and flexibility, capable of rendering Latin works on theology, philosophy and science. They had translated the gospels, most of the first seven books of the Old Testament, the Benedictine Rule and that of Chrodogang of Metz, some of Alcuin's treatises, and of the canonical writings of Amalarius of Metz and Theodulf of Orleans, and some of Bede's scientific work. These translations show a great advance in style on the renderings in Alfred's reign of Gregory's *Pastoral Care* and *Dialogues*, Augustine's *Soliloquies*, Boethius's *Consolation of Philosophy*, Bede's *Ecclesiastical History* and Orosius's *History against the Pagans*, which were still available. Many of Ælfric's homilies are based on Latin sources, but not slavishly; they show a control of language, a grace and a balance, which has never been surpassed. A different, but still a distinguished style was written by Wulfstan, capable of eloquence and force, and there are other excellent varieties of style in various anonymous authors. Strong and vivid narrative, not dependent on Latin originals, is found in the Anglo-Saxon Chronicle. Though the reign of Edward produced no writers of the calibre of Ælfric or Wulfstan, and though one can rarely date anonymous prose, the Chronicle and some charters show that the power to write good English prose not only continued until 1066, but survived in some places as late as the early twelfth century. But the copious vocabulary needed for abstruse subjects did not survive, since after the Conquest Latin was used for such themes. A distinguished foreign scholar has commented: 'It is almost pathetic to ponder on the expenditure of energy that was literally wasted, and the unrealised endeavour swept away by political change, through no inherent deficiency of its own.'[1]

No good Anglo-Saxon poetry later than the poem on the battle of Maldon, composed not long after the event of 991, has survived; the few later poems in the Chronicle and some didactic religious verse are of very inferior quality. As has been mentioned above, the chances of survival of secular poetry of the Maldon type are poor, and hence we cannot be sure that this poem was the swan-song in which the heroic ideals of loyalty and courage, of preferring death to flight, found their final expression. Yet one may feel that the ideals themselves were not dead, and that the stand made by some of Harold's followers after his death at Hastings would have lent itself to a similar treatment to that given to Byrhtnoth's bodyguard

[1] Otakar Vočadlo, 'Anglo-Saxon Terminology', *Studies in English*, iv, Prague, 1933.

at Maldon: 'Here lies our lord, all cut down, the hero in the dust. Long may he mourn who thinks now to turn from the battle-play.' What, however, we do know is that Anglo-Saxon poetry in the alliterative metre must have survived underground, to emerge again, with modifications, in Middle English in Lagamon's *Brut* and in the fourteenth-century alliterative poetry of the West Midlands.

The Benedictine revival of the late tenth century resulted in a great flowering of manuscript illumination, which owed much to continental models, but soon branched out in independence. It produced two main types: fully painted miniatures and pictures, often in a framework of acanthus-leaf design, in rich colours and gold; and outline drawing of great vivacity, characterized by delicacy of line and a remarkable power of imaginative suggestion. There survive a number of fine manuscripts from the last hundred years of Anglo-Saxon rule, mainly psalters, gospels, benedictionals and other books of ecclesiastical use, though there are others: the *Psychomachia* of Prudentius was often illustrated, and there is an illustrated copy of Gregory's Commentary on *Ezechiel*, one of Aratus's astronomical work, the *Phænomena*, one of Ælfric's *Heptateuch* and one of the Junius manuscript of Old English religious poetry in the Bodleian Library. Several illuminated manuscripts produced in England were taken abroad. Our records tell us of some donors, for example that Cnut and his wife Emma gave a sacramentary and a psalter to Cologne, that Emma gave a benedictional to Robert, abbot of Jumièges and that an abbot of Ramsey gave illuminated manuscripts to Fleury. But even without such references, surviving manuscripts would show the export of English illuminated manuscripts to the Continent, and their influence can be seen in the products of some continental houses, such as St Bertin's at St Omer and St Vaast at

Arras. In the latest pre-Conquest examples of English illumination, some of the earlier freedom and spontaneity has given way before an urge to stylization and pattern, but it remains an expressive and beautiful art. In some English houses, at least, its influence continued after 1066, all the more easily because the Normans had been familiar at home with the styles based on the Anglo-Saxon manuscripts which they had imported. Plate I reproduces one of many beautiful outline drawings contained in a psalter of about 1050.

Artistic products in other media had less chance of survival: objects in precious metal tended to be melted down in times of stringency, and textiles and wood are perishable materials. The richness of Anglo-Saxon England in works of art in these materials can be learnt mainly from references in our sources, in narratives, in wills and lists of benefactions, and in inventories, often of later date. We learn of crucifixes and images in, or covered with gold and silver, sometimes studded with precious stones, of valuable church plate and candelabra, of magnificent vestments, banners and tapestries: we read that 'English work' in precious metal and in textiles was valued abroad. The quality of English embroidery can be seen in the remarkable stole, made between 909 and 916, which was found in St Cuthbert's coffin, and the post-Conquest Bayeux tapestry is English work. Ivories also survive, and some smaller objects of metal, to show the artistry and skill of Anglo-Saxon craftsmen. Plates *2a* and *b* illustrate two ivory objects of the late tenth or early eleventh century. As for stone-carving, the date of some of the finest examples is disputed, but most experts now assign to the late Saxon period such dignified sculptures as the Langford and Romsey roods and the Barnack 'Christ in Majesty' (Plate 3).

No just appraisal of late Anglo-Saxon architecture can be made, seeing that none of the cathedrals or larger monastic churches have survived. It would appear, however, that even ambitious prelates had not been inspired to emulate the grandiose churches which were springing up on the Continent, and, as far as we know, that only Edward the Confessor's church at Westminster was built in the new fashion. The Anglo-Saxons seem to have been loath to sweep away earlier buildings long hallowed by religious use, and in some places the need for greater accommodation was met by the adding of a new church on the axis of one or more older churches. At St Augustine's, Canterbury, Abbot Wulfric planned to join two earlier churches by means of a great rotunda, but the Conquest intervened, and it was never completed. We have to judge, therefore, from the smaller churches. Far more Anglo-Saxon work survives in our parish churches than has hitherto been realized, and records show that several were being built right at the end of the period. We read, for example, of churches consecrated by Wulfstan, bishop of Worcester, 1062–95. Among the more impressive examples of late Anglo-Saxon architecture are the churches of Stow, Lincolnshire; Worth, Sussex; Hadstock, Essex; St Benet's in Cambridge; and the well-known towers of Earl's Barton and Barnack, Northamptonshire, and Barton-on-Humber, Lincolnshire, which afford good examples of the decoration by means of pilaster-strips, arcading and long-and-short work at the quoins, and of the double belfry windows, characteristic of this period.

It has not been the intention of this chapter to demonstrate how much of the civilization of the Anglo-Saxons survived the Norman conquest; this has been touched on here and there, when it was necessary to use post-Conquest evidence to prove that some aspect of this civilization was still vigorous in 1066. The Normans made many changes: a new aristocracy replaced the English higher classes, mainly holding its lands by knight service, and one result of this was to lessen the freedom with which women could hold land; the higher ecclesiastical offices were filled by Normans, and this brought the English church more rapidly into contact with continental developments in scholarship than would otherwise have happened; for a time Latin largely superseded English for official purposes, and Norman French as the spoken language of the upper classes. Yet, in the end, it was English, reinforced with much vocabulary from French, which conquered. William established a stronger monarchy than that of the Anglo-Saxon kings, but in doing so he was building on the foundations which these had laid. Yet, even if the Conquest had been as destructive of what went before as used once to be believed, the six centuries of Anglo-Saxon rule in England would remain a remarkable achievement.

VII

THE AUTHORSHIP OF THE ACCOUNT OF KING EDGAR'S ESTABLISHMENT OF MONASTERIES[1]

In the British Museum Cotton MS. Faustina A. x, immediately after a text of the Old English translation of the Rule of St.-Benedict, there occurs a unique Old English work describing the revival of monasticism in England in the tenth century. It is written in the same hand as the translation of the Rule, a hand dated by Dr. Ker as belonging to the first half of the twelfth century[2]; the language, however, is good West Saxon and could belong to the tenth century. This short text was published by Oswald Cockayne in 1866[3] and he attributed its composition to Athelwold, bishop of Winchester, in which view he was followed by Arnold Schröer in 1888[4]. I included a translation of this text as No. 238 in my *English Historical Documents* c. *500-1042* in 1955[5], and in my introduction to it I briefly defended its attribution to Athelwold against the criticism of this view by J. Armitage Robinson in 1923.[6] I have since come across information which has a bearing on this question and justifies a full re-examination of it.

The Old English rendering of the Rule of St.-Benedict is accepted as the work of Athelwold, on the evidence of the *Liber Eliensis*, Book II, c. 37, which says that King Edgar and his wife Ælfthryth gave to Athelwold the estate of Sudbourne, Suffolk, on condition that he would translate the Rule of St.-Benedict into English, and that Athelwold then gave the estate to Ely. The Ely historian had access to early

1 I am indebted to Dom Thomas Symons for calling my attention to the correspondence between this text and the New Minster charter, which caused me to reconsider the whole matter; also to Dr. Peter Clemoes for reading and criticising this article. The abbreviation BCS is used for W. de G. Birch, *Cartularium Saxonicum.*

2 *Catalogue of Manuscripts containing Anglo-Saxon*, No. 154.

3 *Leechdoms, Wortcunning and Starcraft of Early England*, III, pp. 432-444, henceforward cited as C, quoted by page and line.

4 *Die angelsächsischen Prosabearbeitungen der Benedictinerregel* (= *Bibliothek der angelsächsischen Prosa*, II), reprinted in 1964 with an appendix by H. Gneuss.

5 I omitted the section on the conversion of the English, as of little importance to the historian, and commenced after the lacuna mentioned below.

6 *The Times of St. Dunstan*, pp. 159-168.

reliable documents relating to the lands of the monastery, and he had seen a chirograph dealing with this transaction.[7]

We need first to consider what the text on the establishment of monasteries consists of. It begins on f. 148, not quite at the beginning of a line, after four blank lines. Armitage Robinson took this as a sign that the scribe had a mutilated exemplar[8], but Dr. Ker suggests tentatively that the space was left for a heading. The first sentence begins imperfectly: *...geard mid þæm leoman þæs halgan geleafan mildheortlice wearð gefylled* (C. 432. 8 f.). After the first leaf, either one leaf or three leaves are missing. As we shall see, it is possible to form some idea of what the missing section contained.

The beginning describes the conversion of the English through St.-Gregory, referring briefly to the story of the English youths in Rome, to Gregory's desire to convert the English himself, to his prevention by the Romans and to his sending of Augustine.[9] The author then says that Gregory by his messengers instructed Augustine to build monasteries and to teach the servants of God the same practice as that which the Apostles observed in the beginning of Christianity, and he quotes, as did Gregory in his answer to the first of Augustine's queries, Acts iv. 32.[10] He claims that this practice lasted long in the monasteries of England. The word 'but' follows, and then comes the lacuna mentioned above, obviously just as the author is about to describe a decline.

After the gap, the text resumes in the middle of a sentence with *(un)derstod ⁊ wiste getreowne dyhtnere his halegra cyricena ær he gewurþe mannum geswutelod. he him forþy mænigfealde ⁊ genihtsume æhta ⁊ mihta gesealde* (C. 434.21-23) '... understood and knew (him) a true steward of his holy churches before he was revealed to men. For that reason he gave to him manifold and plentiful possessions and power.' Cockayne assumed that the subject of *understod ⁊ wiste* is Edgar, and the *getreowne dyhtnere* Dunstan; but in my opinion a better sense is given if the subject is taken to be God, and the *dyhtnere* to be Edgar, for the rest of the section is concerned with God's granting of power to Edgar: 'Nor did he delay long, nor withhold power. It was not long before his brother (*i.e.* King Eadwig) ended the time of this transitory life.' We are then told of the accession and successful rule of Edgar.

We can guess that the missing portion first described the decay of monasticism. From later references in the text we can see also that it must have related an incident earlier in Edgar's life. That Edgar was mentioned in the lacuna is proved by his being called 'the aforesaid king' the first time he is mentioned in the extant text

[7] See *Liber Eliensis*, ed. E. O. Blake, p. 111, and pp. ix-xi of my foreword to this edition.

[8] *Op. cit.*, p. 158. Robinson was unaware that a later lacuna is to be attributed to the loss of one or more leaves in Faustina A.x, and not to a faulty exemplar.

[9] All this is from Bede, *Historia Ecclesiastica*, Book II, c. 1. Dr. Ker has recovered some additions made in faded ink, which expand the text with short extracts from Ælfric's homily on St. Gregory (*Catholic Homilies* II, pp. 116-132). Interesting in themselves, they are irrelevant to our present subject.

[10] *Historia Ecclesiastica*, Book I, c. 27.

(C. 436.2). Later, we are told that 'as soon as he was elected to his kingdom, he was very mindful of the promise which he had made as an atheling in his youth to God and St.-Mary, when the abbot invited him to the monastery.'[11] No abbot has been mentioned previously in the extant text, so this must refer to something in the gap, and there can be little doubt that the abbot meant is Athelwold, whose monastery, Abingdon, was dedicated to St.-Mary. The text continues: 'As we have said above, admonished by that promise he began in the beginning of his reign to be very intent on advancing that place just as he had promised in his childhood.' We learn of his endowing it richly, of his ordering a glorious minster[12] to be built within three years and to be consecrated to St.-Mary, and of his assembling there a great number of monks.

With this reference to the influence of an abbot on the young Edgar one should first compare a passage near the beginning of the prologue to the *Regularis Concordia*, the document drawn up in Edgar's reign, between 965 and 975, to establish uniformity of monastic practices in English monasteries, a document believed to have been drafted by Athelwold.[13] It runs: *Gloriosus etenim Eadgar... ab ineunte suae pueritiae aetate licet, uti ipsa solet aetas, diuersis uteretur moribus, attamen respectu diuino attactus, abbate quodam assiduo monente ac regiam catholicae fidei uiam demonstrante, coepit magnopere Deum timere, diligere ac uenerari.*[14] The text goes on to describe Edgar's restoration of monasteries. Dom Thomas Symons, in his note on this passage, discusses whether the abbot is Dunstan (as the late Edmund Bishop thought) or Athelwold, which, if the latter drew up the work, is suggested by the anonymous terms of the reference. This seems likely, and it could refer to the same incident implied in the Old English text we are studying. In itself, of course, it does not prove that Athelwold was the author of this, for the incident may have been well known.

Of greater interest, however, is a passage in William of Malmesbury's *Life of St.-Dunstan*,[15] for it tells of a promise by the young Edgar to restore a specific ruined monastery, and William gives as his authority the prologue to an English version of the Rule of St.-Benedict. Speaking of Edgar, he says:

Denique, ut in cujusdam prologo legi, qui regulam Benedicti Anglico enucleabat fuso, dum quadam die ludibundus sagittis exerceret animum, animadvertit procul ædificia magna, sed situ et ruinis deformia; consuluit ergo socios quid esset, indaginem veri sollicita mente rimatus: dictum est ab eis fuisse ibi monasterium olim magnificum, nunc, vel bellica hostium clade vel tyrannica regum destructum, raro incoli habitatore. Tum ille levatis in altum oculis huic se voto fecit obnoxium, ut si unquam regnaret, et istud et alia in statum

[11] C. 438.3-7: *to þæm munuclife*. Cockayne renders 'to the monastic life', which is possible, but less likely; the word often is used to mean 'monastery' at this time.

[12] C. 438.13-20 : or 'monastery'. The Old English *mynster* is used both of monasteries and of churches.

[13] As stated by Ælfric, who had been Athelwold's pupil. See *Regularis Concordia*, ed. Dom Thomas Symons, London, 1953, pp. li f.

[14] *Ibid.*, p. 1.

[15] This was noted and discussed by J. Armitage Robinson, *op. cit.*, pp. 164-168.

pristinum excitaret, per hæc Deo, Qui scrutatur interna, et hominibus qui præsentem indolem futuri boni viderent interpretem, carus, statim ut anni tulere ascitus est in regnum magna hominum felicitate.[16]

It is true that this passage does not fit exactly with the little we can learn about the incident described in the lost portion of our text. One has the impression in that that Edgar visited Abingdon by Athelwold's invitation when the restoration of the abbey had begun, whereas William makes the visit an accidental coming upon a complete ruin. But William of Malmesbury is quoting from memory,[17] and in any case is not always an accurate recorder. Moreover, if we had the full story, instead of having to make do with some back references in the Old English version and a summary by William of Malmesbury, we might find more agreement than appears. What is important is that William found in a prologue to an Old English version of the Rule of St.-Benedict a story with clear affinities with what must once have been in the missing portion of the text in Faustina A. x, where it follows a version of the Old English translation of the Rule. This need be no more than evidence that the text under discussion was associated in some places with the translation of the Rule. Alone, it is no proof of Athelwold's authorship of the account. Yet, if there is positive evidence pointing to his authorship, the fact that William found it as a prologue to the Rule adds support.

There can be no doubt that the abbot concerned is Athelwold, for a little later (C. 438.23-25) we learn that he was brought from Glastonbury, which is true of Athelwold. If the writer is not Athelwold himself, the absense of any term of praise in reference to the abbot is remarkable. J. Armitage Robinson, however, rejected the possibility of his being the author, because the account gives the impression that it was Edgar who first re-founded the monastery of Abingdon, and this is at variance with what we learn from Ælfric's *Life of St.Athelwold*[18] and from that by Wulfstan, the precentor of Winchester,[19] which attribute the re-founding to King Eadred, at the persuasion of his mother Eadgifu. Robinson finds it difficult to imagine Athelwold being 'faithless to the memory of his patron King Edred'.

Yet, if we possessed the missing portion of the Old English account, the discrepancy with what we are told by Ælfric and Wulfstan might not be so great. For the Old English writer's reference to the promise made by Edgar when still an atheling to 'the abbot' must surely show that he was aware that Athelwold had become abbot of Abingdon before Edgar came to the throne. The missing section might have described the small beginnings of Abingdon under Eadred's patronage. We should note that Ælfric refers to the poor buildings which Athelwold took over, and, though

16 *Memorials of St. Dunstan*, ed. W. Stubbs, p. 290.

17 See J. Armitage Robinson, p. 165.

18 *Chronicon Monasterii de Abingdon*, ed. J. Stevenson, II, pp. 253-266; translated by D. Whitelock, *English Historical Documents*, No. 235.

19 Mabillon, *Acta Sanct. ordinis S. Bened.*, Saec. V, pp. 608-624; *Acta Sanctorum* 1 August, pp. 88-98; Migne, *Patrologia Latina*, cxxxvii, col. 81-108.

he speaks of the great interest taken by Eadred in the planning of the house, he adds: 'Nevertheless, the abbot did not begin to construct the building assigned to him in the days of King Eadred, for he soon died, but in the reign of Edgar he built and completed in that place a noble temple in honour of St.-Mary, Mother of God'.[20] It was only after this that he sent a monk to Fleury to learn the customs of the Rule and then to teach them in Abingdon on his return. The statements in the English account that King Edgar became 'very intent on advancing that place just as he had promised in his childhood', that he endowed it so that it was not inferior to many houses advanced by his ancestors, and that he ordered a glorious minster to be built within three years, are not incompatible with the accounts in the Latin *Lives* of a commencement in Eadred's reign. The claim that Edgar assembled a great company of monks does not necessarily mean that there were none there before. Difficulty only arises when, immediately after this passage on Edgar's fulfilment of his youthful promise to Abringdon, the text continues:

ær þæm lyt (mu)neca wæs on feawum stowum on swa miclum rice þe be rihtum regule lifdon; Næs þæt na fealdre þonne on are stowe seo is glæstingabyrig gehaten; ðær his fæder eadmund cynincg munecas ærest gestaþolode; Of þære stowe wæs se foresprecena abbud genumen ⁊ gehadod to þæm foresædan mynstre þe eadgar cyning gestaþolode ⁊ mid munecum gesette; he þearle swiþe wearþ gegladod þurh þæt gastlice munyca angin (C. 438. 20 - 28).

(Before that there were (had been?) only a few monks in a few places in so large a kingdom who lived by the right rule. This was in no more places than one, which is called Glastonbury, where his father, King Edmund, first established monks. The aforesaid abbot had been[21] brought from that place and consecrated to the aforesaid monastery which King Edgar established and set with monks. He became very greatly gladdened by that spiritual beginning with monks).

If we take 'before that' to mean before Edgar, as king, built the minster at Abingdon, and hence that Athelwold was not brought from Glastonbury until Edgar's reign, this paragraph is certainly at variance with what Ælfric and Wulfstan tell us; but it is also at variance with the implications of the author's own reference to Athelwold as abbot when Edgar was only an atheling. It is surely preferable to interpret the words 'before that' more loosely, with reference to the whole sequence of events which began with Edgar's promise as a youth. If so, the 'spiritual beginning' which rejoiced Edgar could refer to what was happening at Glastonbury and Abingdon before Edgar came to the throne; yet, even if we take these words to refer to his encouragement of Abingdon when he became king, the author might have seen no more need to refer at this point to Eadred's work in Abingdon than to Edmund's in Glastonbury, which he has previously mentioned.

Armitage Robinson regarded with suspicion the statement that King Eadwig *halegra cyricena land incuþum reaferum todælde* (C. 434. 27 f.), holding that accusations

20 Stevenson, *op. cit.*, II. p. 258; Whitelock, *op. cit.*, p. 834.

21 The use of *wæs*, rather than *wearþ*, may suggest pluperfect.

of anti-monastic actions by Eadwig appear only in late writers such as Osbern of Canterbury and William of Malmesbury. This is arguing from negative evidence, and we should note that the study of the charters of Abingdon led Sir Frank Stenton in 1913 to the conclusion that, if we accept the evidence of Ælfric that Eadred gave to Abingdon a hundred *cassati*, 'the evidence of later charters will compel us to assume that the grant, if it ever took effect, was repudiated during the reign of Eadwig'.[22] He even thought it possible that Athelwold did not retain possession of Abingdon during that reign. In such circumstances, the tone of the writer's reference to Eadwig is understandable; and there may have been unrecorded instances of the alienation of church lands to explain the general nature of the accusation. It is possible that Ælfric and Wulfstan, writing some fifty years after Eadred's foundation of Abingdon, failed out of ignorance, or by design, to mention a break in its development between Eadred's death and Edgar's accession. The visit of the young Edgar was probably not, as William of Malmesbury implies, to a deserted site, but to one where Athelwold and his monks were occupying in Eadred's reign the 'few poor buildings' mentioned by Ælfric, in the midst of the ruins of the former abbey.

It would seem, therefore, that there is no reason to reject Athelwold's authorship on the ground that the writer betrays ignorance of the early history of Abingdon. It is now time to look at the positive evidence in favour of the attribution.

The text continues with an account of the foundation of monasteries by King Edgar, and of nunneries placed under the care of his wife Ælfthryth. This can be supported from the *Regularis Concordia.* We are then told of Edgar's request for a translation of the Rule of St.-Benedict, and the author justifies at some length the production of a translation. It is true, as Armitage Robinson says, that he does not expressly say that he is himself the translator; but if, as seems likely, this text was written as a prologue to a version of his translation, he may have thought this too obvious for statement. After warning his successors against the diminishing of God's patrimony, he addresses a passage to abbesses, warning them against giving away God's estates to kinsmen or secular great men. An interesting passage then follows:

Gif heora hwilc mid deofles costnunge beswicen. for gode oþþe for worulde gyltig biþ. ne gladige on þæt noþer ne cyning ne worulrica swilce him gerymed sy ⁊ antimber geseald þæt he god bereafige þe þa æhta ah. ⁊ nænne gylt næfre ne geworhte; Ne sy la nan eorþcund cyning mid gitsunge to þæm swiþe undergan þæt he þæm heofoncundum cyninge þe hine geworhte ne læte beon þæs ylecan rihtes weorþne þe he sylf is; Gif cinges gerefena hwylc gyltig biþ wiþ god oþþe wiþ men, hwa is manna to þam ungescead and ungewittig þæt he xæm cyninge his are ætrecce forþi þe his gerefa forwyrht biþ; Stande forþi on þæt ilice gerad on ecnesse swa hwæt swa þæm ecum criste geseald biþ on cyricena æhtum (c. 442.34 - 444.14).

(If any one of them, led astray by the temptation of the devil, be convicted of guilt against the Church or the State, let neither king nor secular lord be glad at it, as if the way were cleared and a reason given for him to rob God, who owns those possessions and who never

[22] *The Early History of the Abbey of Abingdon*, pp. 48 f.

committed any offence; nor, indeed, let any earthly king be so greatly undermined with avarice that he will not let the heavenly King who created him be intitled to the same rights as he is himself. If any of the king's reeves is convicted of any offence against God or against men, what man is so foolish or senseless as to deprive the king of his property because his reeve is convicted? Wherefore in the same way let whatever among the possessions of the churches is given to the eternal Christ stand for ever.)

This passage should be compared with one in the Golden Charter of King Edgar for New Minster, Winchester, British Museum Cotton MS. Vespasian A. viii.[23] This is not really a charter, but a book of forty-three leaves, the first thirty-three of which are in a tenth-century hand, in a script very close to that of the Benedictional of St.-Athelwold.[24] This lengthy document, written in gold letters, records the ousting by the king of the canons from New Minster, and their replacement under Bishop Athelwold by Benedictine monks. It was originally preceded by an illumination depicting Edgar, flanked by the Virgin and St.-Peter, offering his charter to Christ who is seated in glory above.[25] The sumptuous form of the book suggests that it was intended to be preserved on the altar, as Professor Wormald says.[26] He is undoubtedly correct also when he assigns the composition of the document to Athelwold, though it is issued in the king's name; his subscription is longer than the others and includes a 'modesty formula' only likely to be used by the author: 'I, Athelwold... by my modest self *(mea mediocritate)* have blessed with the sign of the cross the splendid munificence of the most illustrious king, the father abbot, and the monks whom I have taught, commending them to him'.[27] The document may have been drawn up after the event, not necessarily in 966, the date in the text.[28]

If this document was composed by Athelwold, part of chapter XXI, *quod nullius reatus hoc Domini privilegium minuere valeat*, is of interest for our purpose. A similarity with the Old English passage which I have quoted on p. 130 is seen in the paragraph:

Reatus quippiam si incitante demone seductus vel abbas vel fratrum aliquis fragiliter quod absit contraxerit. justitia purgante secundum regulæ preceptum abolitus damnetur. maneatque prefatæ munificentiæ libertas altithrono per nostram humilitatem oblata ad monachorum usus gratuite sibi famulantium inviolabilis æterna libertate jocunda. quia Deus qui hanc privilegii largifluam donationem locumque cum universa monachorum familia ruraque omnia sacro subjecta coenobio possidet. nunquam reatum commisit. nec ullo unquam tempore commitet.

23 BCS 1190.

24 See *The Benedictional of St. Ethelwold*, with an introduction and notes by Francis Wormald, London, 1959, p. 10.

25 Reproduced, *e.g.*, in T. D. Kendrick, *Late Saxon and Viking Art*, London, 1949, plate II; D. Talbot Rice, *English Art* 871-1100, Oxford, 1952, plate 46.

26 'Late Anglo-Saxon Art : Some Questions and Suggestions', in *Studies in Western Art* (Acts of the Twentieth International Congress of the History of Art), pp. 23-26.

27 Professor Wormald's rendering.

28 It is not certain whether it is later than the *Regularis Concordia*, with which it has agreements in wording.

(Let any offence, if the abbot or any of the brethren, led astray by the prompting of the devil, has weakly committed one — which God forbid — be abolished according to the precept of the Rule by purifying justice and condemned; and let the privilege of the aforesaid munificence offered through our humility to Him who sits on high remain inviolable, pleasant with eternal liberty, for the use of the monks freely serving Him; because God, who possesses this generous donation of privilege and the place with all the family of monks and all the estates subject to the holy monastery, never committed an offence and never will commit one at any time.)

Not only does this passage share with the Old English one a general theme, namely that the possessions of a monastery are not liable to confiscation on account of the behaviour of its superior or its members, but the expression has similarities. While that between *incitante demone seductus* and *mid deofles costnunge beswicen* could easily be accidental, for it is a commonplace, the same cannot be said of *Deus qui... rura... omnia... possidet, nunquam reatum commisit* which corresponds closely to *God... þe þa æhta ah ⁊ nænne gylt næfre ne geworhte*. In fact, though leases of church lands often have a brief clause stating that the estate cannot be forfeited for any crime committed by the leasee, I know only one other place where the possibility of offences by abbot or monks is envisaged, and it is surely significant that it is a charter issued to Athelwold and that it includes the very words *qui nunquam reatum commisit*.[29] But it is not in this alone that it can be connected with the Old English passage; it shares with this the parallel drawn with offences committed by king's reeves.

The charter is written in King Edgar's name and dated 971. It grants to Bishop Athelwold the estate at Barrow-upon-Humber, the site of Chad's monastery.[30] It declares that Athelwold gave this land to Peterborough, and the charter has come down in the cartulary of that house, Society of Antiquaries of London, MS. 60. Athelwold's other foundation, Thorney, must also have possessed a copy, for the forged foundation charter of that house is partly based on it.[31] It is possible, as Dr. Hart suggests, that Athelwold did not at first decide to give the estate to Peterborough. But even if we were to reject as a later addition the clause saying that he did, this would not affect the argument of this paper.

The passage with which we are concerned comes immediately after the statement that Barrow was given to Peterborough, and reads:

quatinus pro nullius altioris vel inferioris gradus hominis reatu rus præfatum a domini qui nunquam reatum commisit possessione privetur. Si vero crimen quod veniæ non sit dignum suadente diabolo quod absit loci procurator commiserit. agatur rationabiliter

29 The same idea is always differently worded in the Vulgate : Isaiah liii. 9 *iniquitatem non fecerit* ; I Peter ii.22. *Qui peccatum non fecit* ; II Corinthians v. 21 *qui non noverat peccatum* ; I John iii. 5 *peccatum in eo non est* ; Psalm xci.16 *non est iniquitas in eo* ; Zephaniah iii. 5 *non faciet iniquitatem*; &c.

30 BCS 1270. Athelwold's desire to restore the pre-Viking-age monasteries is well known; in addition to Ely, Peterborough and Thorney, we should note his obtaining the site of the eighth-century monastery at Breedon-on-the-Hill, Leicestershire, BCS 1283.

31 BCS 1297. A better text is in C. R. Hart, *The Early Charters of Eastern England*, pp. 165-172.

de eo quod de regis agitur præposito. ut videlicet reo rite decuriato[32] ac justo ordine depulso illi qui dignus sit Christi designetur uti regis solet præpositura a nullo decurium[33] violata.

(since the aforesaid estate may not, on account of the offence of any man of higher or lower rank be removed from the possession of the Lord who never committed an offence. If indeed the man in charge [34] of the place should by the persuasion of the devil have committed a crime which is not entitled to pardon — which God forbid — let there be done reasonably concerning it what is done concerning a king's reeve, namely, that when the offence has been duly tried (?)[35] and removed by the proper process, it (the estate) shall be assigned to him who is worthy of Christ; just as the office of a reeve[36] of the king is not wont to be violated by any one of the authorities (?).[37]

Though the meaning of some words is uncertain, and there may be some corruption, it seems to me that the general sense, that the estate of a monastery cannot be forfeited for the offences of anyone in charge of it, is clear, and that a comparison is being drawn with an estate managed by a royal reeve, which cannot be forfeited for the reeve's crimes. If so, its connexion with the Old English account is obvious. Moreover, I have found no parallels outside these two Latin texts connected with Athelwold. The agreement seems too close to be accidental; so, if the Old English is not by Athelwold, it must be by someone connected with him, or with one of his establishments, in which case the author would be unlikely to be as ignorant of the true circumstances of the foundation of Abingdon as Armitage Robinson held.

Agreements in vocabulary and phraseology between the Old English account and Athelwold's translation of the Benedictine Rule[38] may next be examined. Both use

32 In the version of the Thorney foundation charter printed by Birch, from a fourteenth-century *inspeximus*, this reads *securato*, but the other texts agree with the reading of the Barrow charter.

33 Professor Wormald, who kindly checked the passage with the manuscript, tells me that the scribe first wrote *securium*, and then altered *s* to *d* ; the *de* comes at the end of a line, and *curium* begins the next line. The reading in the Thorney foundation charter, which replaces the word by *secularium*, suggests that the original had initial *s*.

34 I have translated *procurator* vaguely, believing that the writer may have deliberately chosen a general term; *loci* could refer to the owning monastery rather than the estate in question; *locus* is often used in this sense, like Old English *stow*. For the meaning of *procurator* in this period, one should compare the glosses : *Uillicus, uel actor, uel curator, uel procurator, uel rector* : *tungerefa* (Wright-Wülker 111.13) ; and *Procurator* : *scirman* (ibid. 183.28). Perhaps *loci procurator* means the reeve in charge of the estate, not the head of the monastery, but it may be expressed vaguely to include both.

35 This meaning is given by the *Revised Medieval Latin Word-List* prepared by R. E. Latham, 1965, but it comes via Du Cange from Dugdale's version of the Thorney charter which is using this very passage. It is hence a contextual rendering, but it is difficult to see what else can be meant.

36 Since *præpositus* is one of the terms used for 'reeve', it seems likely that *regis præpositura* means the office of royal reeve, with all the lands and rights attached to it.

37 The reading *decurium* makes no sense, and my rendering accepts the alternative *securium*, since *securis*, in the plural, is sometimes used in the sense of 'authority'. There was a liking at this period for the revival of Latin terms for officials, such as *lictor, consul,* &c., and Athelwold shared it. Alternatively, *decurium* was perhaps a miscopying of *decurionum* ; *decurio* was another of those Latin terms revived in the late tenth century, e.g. BCS 1099, where Edgar grants land *cuidam decurioni mihi oppido fideli Ælfsige* ; the West Saxon Gospels render it *gerefa*.

38 Cited as RB, with references to page and line in Schröer's edition.

the word *canonicas*, the account using it of the canons driven out by King Edgar, the Rule mentioning *arwyrðum canonicum* (RB. 111.6) in a chapter on the reception of foreign guests. Armitage Robinson, who held that the presence of this word in the account was an argument against Athelwold's authorship, claiming that neither it nor the Latin *canonici* occur before the early eleventh century, except in some foreign context,[39] makes no reference to the occurrence in the translation of the Rule, presumably because here it refers to foreigners. He rightly notes that the Parker manuscript of the Anglo-Saxon Chronicle, *s.a.* 964, uses *preostas*, which is replaced by *canonicas* in the Domitian version, about 1100. Yet in Athelwold's known vernacular writings he had no occasion to refer to secular canons in England; we cannot be certain that he would have preferred *preostas* to the learned term *canonicas* when writing for monks. If he is the author of the account, he anticipates by some twenty-five to thirty years the first datable occurrence, 1008;[40] this does not seem difficult to believe.

The account shares with the translation of the Rule several usages which are unrecorded or very rare elsewhere. Thus *awlacian* 'become lukewarm' occurs only in *welm awlacige* (C. 442.20) and *frumwylm... awlaciaþ* (RB. 135.6); *ungescead* as an adjective, 'foolish', 'unreasonable' (C. 444.7) is unique, but the Rule has several instances of the adverb *ungesceadlice* 'unreasonably'; *gesinlice* 'continually', 'diligently' (C. 440.4) is otherwise recorded only in RB. 97.14 and 127.9; *cildgeong* 'young' (C. 436.8; 438.5) is a favourite word in the Rule, but rare otherwise except in verse; *æsce* 'enquiry' (C. 432.27) occurs in RB. 3.16, but is only once recorded in this sense elsewhere; *geryman* 'to open a way' (C. 442.36) is used in the same rare figurative sense in RB. 103.19; the rare verb *tostencan* 'to disperse' (C. 434.26) may be compared with the noun *tostencenness* (RB. 128.6). One should set the phrase *on gleawscype swiþe bescawede ⁊ forewittige* (C. 436.11 f.) beside *foregleaw ⁊ welbesceawod* (RB. 121.14 f.), noting that *welbesceawod* 'very prudent' occurs also in RB. 121.2 and once in a gloss, while *besceawod* is otherwise unrecorded; and also that *gleawscipe* in the sense 'wisdom' is not uncommon in the Rule but rare outside it.

Not quite so rare, but still not very common, are the following: *misfon* 'to make a mistake' (C. 442.3, 11), *gefadung* 'disposition' (C. 440.25), *gespelia* 'representative' (C. 434.7, 11), *þæslic* 'pleasing', 'suitable' (C. 434.8), all of which occur fairly frequently in the Rule; also *formænig* 'very many' (C. 438.11: RB. 138.26; 139.19), *talu* 'excuse' (C. 442.3, 10: RB. 92.5), *hafenleast* 'poverty' (C. 442.19: RB. 65.6) and *antimber* in the abstract sense of 'occasion', 'cause' (C. 444.1: RB. 124.13). Very many of the favourite words of the Rule occur in the account, and, though they are not uncommon, many of them are words for which synonyms could easily have been used, and hence they are evidence of a similar selection among possibilities. They include words fairly common in our short account, such as *myn(d)gung* 'admonition' (5 times), *an(d)weald* 'dominion' (7 times), *(ge)fyrþrian* 'to advance' (5 times),

39 *Op. cit.*, pp. 170 f.
40 In the laws of Ethelred, V.7, VI.2.4.

angin 'beginning' (4 times); also common in the Rule are *mærsian* 'to glorify' (C. 432.18; 436.28), *geferræden* 'community' (C. 434.14; 438.18), *fremful* 'beneficial' (C. 436.21) and *fremfullice* (C. 436.22) *munuclif* 'monastery' (C. 438.7), *tæcing* 'instruction' (C. 438.20) *gegladian* 'to gladden' (C. 438.28), *(ge)weman* 'to attract' (C. 440.24; 442.6), *endebyrdness* 'arrangement' (C. 440.26), *woroldmonn* 'layman' (C. 440.33; 442.1), *geþafung* 'consent' (C. 442.24), &c.

More important are some identical expressions. The phrase *no þæt an* which occurs twice in our short text (C. 440.6, 9) is a mannerism in the Rule (*e.g.* 2.1; 14.7 f.; 31.3). Note also *ærest þinga* (C. 438.29: RB. 1.9), *to fulfremedum ende* (C. 442.14 f. RB. 1.10), *for hellewites ogan* (C. 440.33: RB. 19.17; 31.20), *mid deofles costnunge beswicen* (C. 442.33: RB. 103.2) *mid ungesceade* (C. 442.32: RB. 130.7) and *halgan þeowdom*, describing obedience to the Benedictine Rule (C. 440.35: RB. 19.16 f.). One may compare with *ænigne incan sece* (C. 442.17), with *inca* as 'cause of complaint', *nænne incan ne secen* (RB. 103.18), and note also that *þæt la ne geweorþe þæt* (C. 444.13) occurs in the identical form in RB. 36.4, and is similar to *þæt na næfre ne geweorþe* (RB. 103.4; *cf.* 105.4)[41] with which we may compare *þæt la næfre ne gelumpe* (C. 442.21).[42] Without making a claim that these expressions cannot be found elsewhere, one may yet suggest that, considering the shortness of the account, the number that occur in it and in the only known vernacular work of Athelwold is remarkable.

It is never easy to pronounce with absolute certainty whether even a considerable amount of agreement between two works in phraseology and in choice of vocabulary is to be ascribed to identity of authorship, or to the influence of one work on another, or to the similarity of expression by writers trained in the same school. The writer of a prologue to the translation of the Rule might well have been steeped in its language. Yet the amount of agreement will support an attribution to Athelwold if there are other grounds for such an attribution, and it is difficult to explain otherwise the writer's failure to bestow any words of praise on the abbot. When we add the close connexion both in content and wording with parts of two Latin documents which there is reason to believe that Athelwold drafted, it seems to me that the cumulative evidence for his authorship is strong.

If this account is by Athelwold, its date lies between the marriage of Edgar and Ælfthryth (964 or 965) and Athelwold's death on 1 August 984. It shares some information with the preface to the *Regularis Concordia*, another work probably

[41] *Cf.* also *swa hit na ne weorþe* (RB. 74.19), which is used like Latin *quod absit*.

[42] c. 434. 15-18 quotes in full Acts iv. 32; RB. 57. 5-9 translated part of this text quoted in the Latin Rule. As it seems unlikely that any writer would need to consult a previous rendering, either by himself or anyone else, of so simple a passage, the agreement, in that *aliquid suum* is rendered *syndrige æhta* in the one text, *ænig þing syndries* in the other, and that the account has *furþum ne gecwæþ* for *nec...dicebat*, the Rule *furþon þæt word gecweþe* for *dicat*, is, if not accidental, to be ascribed to quoting from memory.

drafted by Athelwold,[43] but he would not have needed to take it from that work. There is nothing odd, in my opinion, in his failure to mention his promotion to the see of Winchester in 963, for there is no place in the account where such a reference is called for, and he seems not to have been addicted to self-praise. He was certainly writing late enough for the success of Edgar's reign to have been widely realised: men would not be commenting on the unwonted peace of a reign until it had lasted some years. There is nothing in the text to prove that Edgar was alive when it was written. In fact, the high praise of his rule, and the claim that his success was God's reward to him for his advancement of the cause of the monks, could fit well into the period of anti-monastic reaction and inefficient rule which followed Edgar's death in 975. The fact that this text is found in only one manuscript of the translation of the Benedictine Rule would suggest, if William of Malmesbury is right in regarding the text he saw as a prologue to such a translation, that it it did not form part of the original version, but was added after the translation had begun to be circulated.[44]

If the conclusions of this paper are acceptable, we can add a few pages to the known work of one of the greatest of Anglo-Saxon ecclesiastics, and see what he could write when not restricted by a Latin original, as he was when translating the Rule. The text becomes a primary source for the establishment of monasteries, written by one of the main movers in monastic reform. Along with the two Latin documents, it illustrates the difficulty men found in grasping the distinction between lands belonging to monasteries, which could not be forfeited by individuals in charge of them, and lands in private ownership. Finally, the agreement in wording between an Old English text by Athelwold and two Latin charters issued in the king's name in favour of his monasteries supplies evidence to support the view that at this period royal charters were sometimes drafted by the beneficiary.

43 I have not used this agreement in support of Athelwold's authorship, for anyone could have used the widely-known *Regularis Concordia*. The two Latin charters, on the other hand, would not be likely to be available outside Athelwold's foundations.

44 Since all manuscripts of the translation contain some feminine pronouns and titles, it is held that the first translation was for women, and that it was only later adapted for use in male communities.

VIII

A NOTE ON THE CAREER OF WULFSTAN THE HOMILIST

THE Lupus who is the author of several Old English homilies which survive in eleventh-century manuscripts, including the famous *Sermo Lupi ad Anglos*,[1] was identified by Wanley [2] with the Wulfstan who held the sees of Worcester and York in the early years of the eleventh century, and this identification is undoubtedly correct and has always been accepted by subsequent scholars. On some points relating to his career there seems, however, to be a difference of opinion: the date of his accession to Worcester and York is variously given as 1002 or 1003, and, while some writers follow Freeman [3] in stating him to have been bishop of London previous to this date, this is emphatically denied by many scholars,[4] because Florence of Worcester [5] refers to him as abbot in 1002; and Becher [6] finds the signature of a *Wulfstan abbas* in the same charter as one of Bishop Wulfstan and takes this as conclusive proof that the homilist was not bishop of London, but this name is an error of the printed version.[7] I myself, when editing *Anglo-Saxon Wills*, assumed that the Bishop Wulfstan mentioned in the will of Archbishop Aelfric of Canterbury [8] as the executor of a bequest

[1] I am about to publish an edition of this text, with an introduction collecting references to the author.

[2] In Hickes' *Thesaurus*, ii. 140 f. Wanley attributed to Wulfstan many sermons that are not his, and A. S. Napier's *Wulfstan* is an edition of all homilies attributed to him. The question of a canon of his writings will be briefly considered in my edition of the *Sermo ad Anglos*.

[3] *Norman Conquest*, 3rd ed., i. 314, note; so also W. G. Searle, *Anglo-Saxon Bishops, Kings and Nobles*, p. 32, J. P. Kinard, *A Study of Wulfstan's Homilies*, p. 13, and G. T. Flom, *Introductory Old English Grammar and Reader*, p. 334.

[4] So first J. Earle and C. Plummer, *Two of the Saxon Chronicles Parallel*, ii. 182, followed by W. Keller, *Die litterarische Bestrebungen von Worcester*, p. 41, note, and recently by R. R. Darlington, *Ecclesiastical Reform in the Late Old English Period*, *ante*, li. 400, note. Moreover, W. G. Searle, *Onomasticon Anglo-Saxonicum*, p. 519, and W. Stubbs, *Registrum Sacrum Anglicanum*, 2nd ed., pp. 31 f., 232, 242, do not identify Wulfstan, bishop of London, with the archbishop of York and bishop of Worcester of the same name.

[5] ed. Thorpe, i. 156. [6] C. F. R. Becher, *Wulfstan's Homilien*, p. 10.

[7] I.e. no. 707 in J. M. Kemble, *Codex Diplomaticus Ævi Saxonici* (henceforward cited as K. with the number of the document). The Charter Roll from which it is taken has *Wlfstar*, and Brit. Mus. Egerton MS. 2104 has *Wulfgar*, i.e. the abbot of Abingdon who signs most charters of the period. There is no doubt that it is he who is meant, for the Charter Roll also writes *Ælfstar* for Ælfgar, bishop of Elmham.

[8] *Op. cit.* pp. 52 f.

was a different person from the Archbishop Wulfstan to whom a small bequest is made, and the date I assigned to the will rests on this assumption, accepting Stubbs' date, 1003, for Wulfstan's consecration to York and Worcester.[1] I have since come across evidence that makes me doubt the correctness of this assumption, and it is perhaps worth while to reconsider the whole question. As far as this will is concerned, it is natural that a testator should make a bequest to an executor, and the difference in title need not imply that different persons are meant, for it is not uncommon to find an archbishop referred to as bishop in Anglo-Saxon times,[2] and a similar inconsistency to the one in this will occurs in a late tenth-century charter [3] which speaks of Dunstan now as archbishop, now as bishop.

Freeman based his identification on the evidence of signatures, but without discussing this in detail. It is, however, as follows: a Wulfstan signs as bishop from 996 on, and in 1002, besides witnessing a charter [4] which Ealdulf signs as archbishop of York, he witnesses two charters [5] in which no archbishop of York appears. When, however, we get the first signature of Wulfstan as archbishop, in K. 1296, dated 1002, no bishop of London signs. This would certainly fit well with a translation of Wulfstan from London to York towards the end of 1002, but we must first consider two charters which appear to have a Bishop Wulfstan of London at a later date. One, K. 715, is dated 1006, but the witnesses show that this date is wrong and that it cannot be later than 1002.[6] The other is no. 36 in the third volume of the Ordnance Survey Facsimiles, and is dated 1003; yet it is noteworthy that no archbishop of York appears and that the indiction (15th) and the epact (4th) are at variance with the date, while correct for 1002. In view of this, I do not think this one charter sufficient evidence for denying the identity of the bishop of London with the archbishop of York, even if we accept 1002 as the date of Wulfstan's accession to York. If, however, we date this event in 1003,[7] this charter presents no difficulty; but

[1] In any case the will cannot be before 1002, when Aelfric received Dumbleton, one of the estates mentioned in the will, from the king.

[2] e.g. on p. 94 of my *Anglo-Saxon Wills* (= K. 953) or on p. 148 of A. J. Robertson, *Anglo-Saxon Charters* (= K. 1315).

[3] *Ibid.* p. 84 (= K. 1288).

[4] K. 707. See note 7 on p. 460 *supra*.

[5] K. 1295 and 1297.

[6] Its authenticity has been questioned, but even if genuine or copying a genuine list of witnesses, these do not belong to 1006. The ealdorman Leofsige, who is included in the list, was exiled in 1002. Moreover, there are too many signatures of Aelfhun, Wulfstan's successor at London, in charters of 1004 and 1005, for us to accept Wulfstan's signature as bishop of London in 1006. The Old English version of this charter is undated.

[7] *Sic* Stubbs, *op. cit., loc. cit.*, although he gives 1002 as the date of Ealdulf's death. He says Wulfstan signs from 1004 to 1022, but apart from the charter of 1002, Wulfstan signs as archbishop in K. 1299, dated 1003. K. 1294, which is also witnessed by him, has an impossible list of witnesses for its date, 1000 (see *infra*, p. 462, n. 2).

as Florence of Worcester merely says that Wulfstan succeeded Ealdulf, whose death he has dated 6 May, in the twenty-fifth year of Ethelred, 15th indiction (i.e. 1002), and as I can see nothing to indicate that K. 1296, which contains Wulfstan's signature as archbishop in 1002, has been dated too early,[1] I think it probable that this earlier date is correct.[2] The later date is suggested by the thirteenth-century *Chronicle of the Archbishops of York*,[3] which states that Wulfstan died on the 5th of the Kalends of June 1023, in the twentieth year of his episcopate, but although this would certainly put the beginning of his episcopate in 1003, I do not consider it independent of a passage just before it, referring to the death of Ealdulf, where the chronicler, though giving the date, regnal year, and indiction exactly as in Florence, adds that this was the twelfth year of his episcopate. As there is clear evidence that Ealdulf succeeded in 992,[4] the chronicler appears to be placing his death in 1003. Naturally, then, he takes this date as the basis for his calculation of the length of Wulfstan's episcopate. Yet 1002 is the year of Ealdulf's death in the Anglo-Saxon Chronicle [5] as well as in Florence, and the absence of his signature from some of the charters of this year supports their evidence.[6]

Whichever of these two dates we accept, however, the evidence of signatures does not prove the identification of Wulfstan, bishop of London, with Wulfstan, archbishop of York and bishop of Worcester, to be impossible ; and in my opinion, the identification does not depend on this evidence. What seems to me significant is that Wulfstan of London refers to himself as *Lupus*, i.e. the name assigned to the homilist by the rubrics to his sermons, and that penitential letters issued by him under this name while bishop of London are preserved in a manuscript

[1] Its indiction does not agree with its date, but it would be still further out if we assume a later date for the charter.

[2] It is supported also by K. 1294, which has the signatures of Wulfstan as archbishop and Aelfhun, Wulfstan's successor, as bishop, along with that of the ealdorman Leofsige, which cannot be later than 1002. This would be conclusive evidence if the charter had not an impossible date, 1000, and may perhaps have been tampered with.

[3] J. Raine, *Historians of the Church of York and its Archbishops*, ii. 342. Professor F. M. Stenton, who has kindly read this article, called my attention to this reference.

[4] e.g. *Anglo-Saxon Chronicle*, 992E, and Florence of Worcester, i. 149.

[5] *sub anno* 1002E.

[6] Ealdulf's death occurred soon after he had translated the bones of St. Oswald, his predecessor. It is noteworthy that William of Malmesbury, *Gesta Pontificum*, Rolls Series, p. 250, places this translation *post xii annos*, and Eadmer, *Miracula S. Oswaldi*, in Raine, *op. cit.* ii. 46, in the twelfth year after Oswald's death. Can this have arisen from a misinterpretation of Florence's regnal year ? There is great uncertainty as to whether Ethelred succeeded to the throne in 978 or 979 (see Earle and Plummer, *op. cit.* ii. 166). Florence calculates from 978, but any chronicler beginning the reign in 979 would take the twenty-fifth year as 1003, and might therefore reckon an extra year to Ealdulf's episcopate.

from Worcester, now at Corpus Christi College, Cambridge.[1] This might mean little if these formed part of a collection of letters of Anglo-Saxon bishops, but on the contrary the only other letters are from various popes and are addressed either to Archbishop Wulfstan, or to an unnamed archbishop, or, once only, to Archbishop Aelfric of Canterbury, whom we know to have been on friendly terms with Wulfstan. This interest shown at Worcester in the penitential formulae of one solitary bishop of London is difficult to account for, unless he is to be identified with their own bishop of this name.

Moreover, this is not the only manuscript to betray an interest both in a Bishop Wulfstan of London and an Archbishop Wulfstan. The Cotton MS. Vespasian A. 14, fo. 179, has as the last entry a letter addressed to Wulfstan, bishop of London, and on fo.148v it contains a Latin poem in honour of Archbishop Wulfstan, who has caused to be drawn up the book for which the poem was composed.[2] Birch suggested that the letter and the poem referred to the same person, but took the archbishop concerned to be Wulfstan I, archbishop of York from 931 to 956, and therefore suggested that the bishop of London in question was the bishop of this name who occurs in Florence's list of bishops of London [3] between Theodred and Brihthelm. But it is extremely unlikely that the poem is addressed to Wulfstan I, the primate who sided with the Scandinavian kings of York against the West-Saxon royal house, and who was imprisoned in 952 and not restored until 954. We have no evidence whatever that he had literary interests, and it would be most unexpected to find activity in book production at York so early in the tenth century. To identify him with the contemporary bishop of London is almost impossible.[4] Birch was led into these difficulties by assigning too early a date to the handwriting, which he declares ' contemporary ', i.e. mid tenth-century, whereas it is actually early eleventh century.[5] It is therefore almost certain that Stubbs is right in taking the archbishop in the poem to be Wulfstan II, i.e. the homilist,

[1] It is no. 265 and the letters are on p. 110. See M. Bateson, *A Worcester Cathedral Book of Ecclesiastical Collections, ante*, x. 728. Wanley knew of these letters, but subsequent writers on Wulfstan have ignored them.

[2] The letter is printed in Stubbs, *Memorials of St. Dunstan*, pp. 404 f., but with a wrong reference to Vespasian B. 14. The poem is given in *ibid.* p. liv, note. W. de G. Birch, *Cartularium Saxonicum*, has the poem as no. 896 and the letter as no. 897.

[3] ed. Thorpe, i. 232.

[4] Wulfstan I of London can only have had a very short episcopate, for Theodred signs as late as 951 and Brihthelm already in 953 (Birch, *op. cit.* no. 887, which has the latter's signature in 950, is wrongly dated : it includes Alfwold, who did not become bishop of Crediton until 953). It is more than improbable that the see should have been handed over to the northern primate, a man of doubtful loyalty, to be held in plurality for this brief period, and that, if so, a correspondent should have addressed him simply as bishop of London.

[5] Mr. C. E. Wright of the British Museum has kindly dated this manuscript for me.

and though we cannot be sure that the book mentioned there is Vespasian A. 14, for the poem could have been copied from another manuscript, yet the contents of the manuscript, namely letters of Alcuin, records of ecclesiastical synods, &c., are such as may well have appealed to Wulfstan, and the handwriting does not contradict such a conclusion. Even if Wulfstan is not responsible for this compilation, it is extraordinary that any scriptorium should show this interest in one archbishop of York and one bishop of London, if they really are different persons, at the same time ignoring all other prelates of the period; particularly when we see that the letter to Bishop Wulfstan is of a private nature, and not at all likely to have been circulated. It is from an unnamed writer and is an apology for refusing to translate into Latin some secret matters (*archana*) at the bishop's request, because of his unfitness in comparison with the bishop's own qualities (as an author ?): 'sed revera postmodum diligenter dulcissimam eloquii vestri considerans sagacitatem, decenterque dispositae narrationis prolixitatem, simulque profunditatem, me ad hec transferenda nullam reputo habere facultatem'. Surely this fits well with an identification of the recipient with the homilist, and against this identification there remains only Florence's statement, that Abbot Wulfstan succeeded Ealdulf, to be considered.

Even in itself, Florence's statement cannot be accepted without hesitation, for in the years preceding 1002, though there are a number of charters extant and they are usually witnessed by several abbots, there is no trace of an Abbot Wulfstan [1]. If Florence is right, then Wulfstan must have been promoted from some minor and obscure foundation direct to the joint sees of York and Worcester. I find it easier to believe that Florence's sources failed to mention Wulfstan's comparatively short episcopate in London, than to account for the preservation of documents relating to Wulfstan of London in manuscripts connected with Archbishop Wulfstan, and in no others, in any other way than I have suggested.

I believe, therefore, that the homilist Wulfstan succeeded Aelfstan in the see of London in 996, and Ealdulf in the united sees of York and Worcester in the latter half of 1002.[2] Whether he immediately relinquished London is uncertain, as his successor's first certain signature does not occur until 1004.

[1] See note 7 on p. 460 *supra*.

[2] Florence places Ealdulf's death on the *secundo nonas Maii*, and this is repeated by later chroniclers. The calendar in the Worcester MS. Hatton 113 has entered it on the second of the nones of June, and this is supported by the Peterborough calendar in Lambeth MS. 198, which enters his *obit* in June, though, as Miss I. J. Churchill has verified for me, on the nones.

If we can accept this identification as proved, the results are not quite so trivial as might at first appear. Wulfstan had much influence on the legislation of Ethelred's reign [1] and, mainly indirectly, on that of Cnut's ; his homilies are often used as evidence of contemporary conditions. It is surely then of interest to know what type of experience he had had,[2] and a six years' episcopate in the trading metropolis must have given him a varied knowledge of his countrymen. Moreover, we can no longer take 1002 as the earliest date of a *sermo Lupi episcopi*, and it may well be that Wulfstan began to write eschatological homilies before the year 1000, though he certainly continued in this strain when this year was over. Finally, if we can take the letter in Vespasian A. 14 to be written to the homilist, we have a contemporary opinion of his style.

[1] I discuss this matter in my edition of the *Sermo Lupi ad Anglos*.

[2] Beyond the mere reference to his having been an abbot nothing is known for certain of his career before he became a bishop. In my edition of the *Sermo* I consider whether there is any evidence that throws light on this point.

IX

WULFSTAN AND THE SO-CALLED LAWS OF EDWARD AND GUTHRUM[1]

A CODE of Anglo-Saxon laws concerned mainly with the penalties for certain ecclesiastical offences is often called 'the Laws of Edward and Guthrum', or some similar title,[2] to distinguish it from the treaty between Alfred and Guthrum which immediately precedes it in one manuscript.[3] It is not a happy title, for the code cannot be precisely dated, and in its preamble it does not claim to be issued in the reign of Edward the Elder but to be a further series of regulations drawn up by Alfred and Guthrum, and afterwards reissued by Edward and Guthrum, whom the author of the preamble erroneously imagines to have been contemporary rulers. Liebermann, who devotes several columns of closely reasoned argument to considering its date,[4] concludes that it was probably promulgated between

[1] I wish to state my debt to Professor F. M. Stenton, Professor B. Dickins, and Mr. K. Sisam for reading this article and giving me the benefit of their criticism and encouragement. In this article codes are cited by the abbreviations used by Liebermann, *Die Gesetze der Angelsachsen,* i.e. Af = Alfred, AGu = the Laws of Alfred and Guthrum, As = Athelstan, Atr = Ethelred, Eg = Edgar, EGu = the Laws of Edward and Guthrum, Em = Edmund, Ew = Edward, Had = *Hadbot,* Northu = *Norðhymbra Preosta Lagu.* In addition the following abbreviations are used :—

ASC = Anglo-Saxon Chronicle.
BCS = W. de Gray Birch, *Cartularium Saxonicum,* 1885–93.
KCD = J. M. Kemble, *Codex Diplomaticus Aevi Saxonici,* 1839–48.
Napier = A. S. Napier, *Wulfstan : Sammlung der ihm zugeschriebenen Homilien nebst Untersuchungen über ihre Echtheit,* 1883.
Robertson = A. J. Robertson, *Anglo-Saxon Charters,* 1939.
Sermo Lupi ad Anglos = my edition in Methuen's Old English Library, 1939.

[2] E.g. Lambarde, *Archaionomia* (1568), fos. 51*b*–56*a*, heads it *Foedus Edouardi & Guthruni :* B. Thorpe, *Ancient Laws and Institutes of England* (1840), i. 166 ff., 'The Laws of Edward and Guthrum'; Liebermann, *op. cit.* i. 128 ff., 'Eadwards Gesetz nach Erwerbung von Guthrums Gebiet'; F. L. Attenborough, *The Laws of the Earliest English Kings* (1922), pp. 97, 102 ff. '(The Laws of) Edward and Guthrum'.

[3] I.e. Corpus Christi College, Cambridge, MS. 383 (Liebermann's B). The other Old English version is in the *Textus Roffensis* (H). Both manuscripts are of the first half of the twelfth century. A Latin version is contained in *Quadripartitus* (Quadr). On the question of Lambarde's supposed access to a lost manuscript, see Appendix. In this article the text of B is given except when otherwise stated, significant variations being given in the footnotes.

[4] *Op. cit.* iii. 86–9.

921 and 939 and that the preamble was added subsequently, but certainly not later than 975, and probably not later than 950, though he would allow that the phrase *7 Gyþrum cyng*, which makes Edward and Guthrum contemporary rulers, may be an even later interpolation. His arguments fail to convince me and I shall examine them in detail later. One thing, however, emerged in the course of his discussion to which he appears to have attached little significance, but which seems to me very important. It is the extraordinarily strong influence exercised by this code on legislation from the time of Ethelred's fifth and sixth codes,[1] that is to say, from 1008. The following parallels will make this clear :—

EGu Prol. 1. Ðæt is [2] ærest þæt hi gecwædon þæt hí ænne God lufian woldan 7 ælcne hæðendom georne aworpen.	V Atr 1. Ðæt is [3] þonne ærest þæt we ealle ænne God lufian 7 wurðian 7 ænne Cristendom georne healdan 7 ælcne hæðendom mid ealle awurpan (cf. V Atr 34 = Northu 47, 67 ; VI Atr 1, 6 ; VIII Atr 44 ; IX Atr Expl. ; X Atr 1 ; I Cn 1. The last clause is also in Napier, p. 40, l. 1 f.).
EGu 1. . . . þæt cyricgrið binnan wagum 7 cyninges handgrið stande efne unwemne.[4]	VI Atr 14. 7 sy ælc cyricgrið binnan wagum 7 cyninges handgrið efen unwemme (cf. Grið 2 ; I Cn 2. 2 ; Napier, p. 266, ll. 10 f.).
EGu 2. . . . gylde swa wer swa wite swa lahslite, be ðam ðe seo dæd sy.	V Atr 31. . . . gilde swa wer swa wite swa lahslite, a be þam þe seo dæd sy (cf. VI Atr 38).
EGu 5. 1. 7 ealle Godes gerihte fyrðrie [5] man georne . . .	V Atr 12. 2. 7 ealle Godes gerihta fyrðrige man georne . . . (= VI Atr 21. 1 = VIII Atr 14 = I Cn 14).
EGu 6. 7. 7 gyf he gewyrce þæt hine man afylle, þurh þæt he ongean [6] Godes riht oððe ðæs cynges geonbyrde, gyf man þæt gesoðige, licge ægylde.	V Atr 31. 1. 7 gif he ongean riht þurh æhlyp geonbyrde 7 swa gewyrce þæt hine man afylle, licge ægylde eallan his freondan (cf. VI Atr 38).

[1] These are variant versions of a code issued in 1008.
[2] *Ðæt is* : *Ðis* H.
[3] *Ðæt is* : *þis* D.
[4] *unwemme* H.
[5] *gerihto forðige* H.
[6] *he ongean* : *hine man gean* H.

EGu 9.

Ordel 7 aðas syndon tocwedene freolsdagum 7 rihtfæstendagum.

V Atr 18.

7 ordol 7 aðas sindon tocweðen freolsdagum 7 ymbrendagum . . . (cf. VI Atr 25, where MS. K adds 7 *wifunga* after *aðas*, and I Cn 17, to which MSS. G and A add 7 *rihtfæstendagum*; also Napier, p. 117, ll. 14 f., from I Cn 17).[1]

EGu 11.

Gyf wycan [2] oððe wigleras, monsworan oððe morðwyrhtan, oððe fule, afylede, æbære horcwenan ahwar on lande wurðan agytene, ðonne fyse hi man of earde 7 clænsie þa ðeode, oððon [3] on earde forfare hy mid ealle, buton hig geswican 7 ðe deoppor gebetan.

VI Atr 7.

7 gif wiccan oððe wigeleras, scincræftcan oððe horcwenan, morðwyrhtan oððe mánsworan ahwar on earde wurðan agytene, fyse hy man georne ut of þysan earde 7 clænsige þas þeode, oþþe on earde forfare hy mid ealle, butan hy geswican 7 þe deoppor gebetan (cf. II Cn 4a).

Many minor correspondences could be added, in vocabulary and in phraseology, but the foregoing is more than sufficient to show a close connexion between the 'Laws of Edward and Guthrum' and Ethelred's fifth and sixth codes. Parallels with other codes are as follows :—

EGu 12.

Gyf man gehadodne oððe ælþeodigne ðurh ænig ðing forrǽde æt féo oððe æt feore, ðonne sceol him cing beon—oððon eorl þær on lande —7 bisceop ðære ðeode for mæg 7 for mundboran, buton he helles [4] oðerne hæbbe ; 7 bete man georne be ðam ðeo [5] seo dæd sy Criste 7 cyninge, swa hit gebyrige ; oððe ða dæde wrece swiðe deope ðe cyning sy on ðeode.

VIII Atr 33.

And gif man gehadodne oððe ælþeodigne man þurh ænig þinc forræde æt feo oððe æt feore, oððe hine bænde oððe hine beate oððe gebismrige on ǽnige wisan, þonne sceal him cyngc beon for mæg 7 for mundboran, buton he elles oðerne hæbbe (cf. II Cn 40, 42 ; Geþyncðo 8).

VIII Atr 34.

And bete man ægðer ge him ge þam cynge, swa swa hit gebirige, be þam þe séo dæd sy, oððe he ða dæde wrece swiðe deope (cf. II Cn 40. 1).

EGu 3. 1.

7 gyf mæssepreost folc miswissige æt freolse oððe æt fæstene, gylde xxx scill' mid Englum 7 mid Denum ðreo healfmarc.

Northu 11.

Gif preost folce miswissige æt freolse oððe fæstene, bete wið God 7 gilde xii or.

[1] The passage is connected with the 'Canons of Edgar' (1001–8) : cap. xxiii : And we læræð, þæt freolsdagum 7 rihtfæstendagum ænig geflit ne beo betweox mannum (ealles to swiðe, Junius MS.) ; cap. xxiv : And we læræð, þæt man freolsdagum 7 fæstendagum forga aðas 7 ordela ; cap. xxv : And we læræð, þæt ælc wer forga his wif freolstidum 7 rihtfæstentidum.

[2] *wiccan* H. [3] *oððe* H. [4] *elles* H. [5] *ðe* H.

EGu 3. 2.

Gyf preost to rihtandagan crisman ne fæcce, oððe fulluhtes forwyrne ðam ðe ðæs ðearf sy, gylde wite mid Englum ⁊ mid Denum lahslit, þæt is twelf oran.

Northu 8.

Gif preost fulluhtes oððe scriftes forwyrne, gebete þæt mid xii ór ⁊ huru wið God þingige georne.

Northu 9.

Gif preost to rihtes timan crisman ne fecce, gilde xii ór.

EGu 4. 2.

⁊ [1] gyf gehadod man hine forwyrce mid deaðscylde, gewylde hine man ⁊ healde to bisceopes dome.

II Cn 43.

Gyf gehadod man hine forwyrce mid deaðscylde, gewylde hine man ⁊ healde to bisceopes dome, be þam þe seo dæd si.

EGu 5.

⁊ gyf deaðscyldig man scriftspræce gyrne, ne him man næfre [ne wyrne].[2]

II Cn 44.

Gif deaðscyldig man scriftspæce gyrne, ne wyrne him man næfre.

EGu 6. 4.[3]

Gyf hwá ænigra godcundra gerihta forwyrne,[4] gylde lahslitt mid Denum, wite mid Englum.

II Cn 48.

Gif hwa mid wige godcundra gerihta forwyrne, gilde lahslit mid Denum, fullwite mid Englum, oððe geladige hine—nime xi ⁊ beo sylf twelfta.

EGu 6. 6.

Gyf he man to deaðe gefylle, beo he ðonne uthlah, ⁊ his hente mid hearme ælc ðara ðe riht wylle.

II Cn 48. 2.

Gif he mann afylle, beo he utlah, ⁊ his hente mid hearme ælc þæra þe riht wylle.

EGu 6. 7.

⁊ gyf he gewyrce, þæt hine man afylle, þurh þæt he ongean Godes riht oððe ðæs cynges geonbyrde, gyf man þæt gesoðige, licge ægylde.

II Cn 48. 3.

Gyf he gewyrce þæt man hine afylle, þurh þæt þe he ongean riht geondbyrde, gif man þæt gesoðige, licge ægilde.

EGu 7. 1.

Gyf friman freolsdæge wyrce, ðolie his freotes oððe gylde wíte, lahslite. Ðeowman ðolige his hyde, oþþe hydgyldes.

II Cn 45. 1.

Gyf freoman freolsdæge wyrce, þonne gebete þæt mid his halsfange, ⁊ huru wið God bete hit georne, swa swa man him tæce.

II Cn 45. 2.

Þeowman, gif he wyrce, þolige his hyde oððon hydgyldes, be þam seo dæd sy.

EGu 7. 2.

Gyf hlaford his ðeowan freolsdæge nyde to weorce, gylde lahslitte

II Cn 45. 3.

Gyf hlaford his þeowan freolsdæge nyde to weorce, þolige þæs

[1] Omitted in H. [2] From H; accidentally omitted in B.

[3] V Atr 31 has the same substance, but different wording, while *ibid.* 31. 1 shows the influence of EGu 6. 7. It is, however, further removed from it than is II Cn 48. 3.

[4] *Sic* H. B *forwyrna.*

se hlaford [1] inne on Dæge lage [2] 7 wite mid Englum.

þeowan; 7 beo he syððan folcfrig; 7 gylde lahslit se hlaford mid Denum, wite mid Englum, be ðam þe seo dæd sig; oððe hine geladige.

EGu 8.

Gyf friman rihtfæsten abrece, gylde wite uel [3] lahslite. Gyf hit ðeowman gedó, ðolie his [hyde] [4] oððe hydgyldes.

II Cn 46.

Gif frigman rihtfæsten abrece, gilde lahslit mid Denum, wite mid Englum, be þam þe seo dæd sy.

II Cn 46. 2.

Gif hit þeowman gedó, þolige his hyde oððe hydgyldes, be þam þe seo dæd sy.

EGu 9. 1.

Gyf man wealdan mæge, ne dyde man næfre on Sunnandæges freolse ænigne forwyrhtne, ac wylde 7 healde, þæt se freolsdæg agan sy.

II Cn 45.

Gyf man wealdan mæge, ne dýde man æfre [5] on Sunnandæges freolse ænigne forwyrhtne man, butan he fleo oððe feohte; ac wylde 7 healde, þæt se freolsdæg agan sy.

In fact, there are only two chapters of EGu for which one cannot cite close parallels in one of the above-mentioned codes. These are chapter 4, on the punishment for incest,[6] and chapter 10, on the assistance that may be given to a mutilated criminal.

In codes previous to 1008 one looks in vain for such parallels. It is true that II As 6, like EGu 11, deals with witchcraft, but in completely different terms; and though II As 24. 1 undoubtedly, as Liebermann says, goes back to the same Old English source as EGu 7, I see no reason to assume that EGu represents an older version. The passages are as follows:

EGu 7.

Sunnandæges cypinge gyf hwá agynne, ðolie ðæs ceapes 7 xii ore mid Denum 7 xxx scill' mid Englum.

II As 24. 1.

7 ðæt nan cyping ne sy Sunnondagum; gif hit ðonne hwa dó, þolige ðæs ceapes 7 gesylle xxx scll' [to wite].[7]

Nor can I agree that Athelstan's codes are the first to use the style of EGu. There are no close correspondences, either in vocabulary or phraseology, such as we find between EGu and the later codes.[8] Athelstan's laws are nearer to EGu than are previous codes, merely because they are written in a fuller, less elliptical style. Even when dealing with similar subject-matter, the laws of Athelstan, Edmund and Edgar betray no sign of influence from EGu.

[1] H omits *se hlaford*. [2] *Sic* MS. for *Dæne*, H *Deone*.

[3] H *oððe*. [4] From H; omitted in B. [5] B *næfre*.

[6] Ethelred's codes and Cnut's refer to incest, but do not specify the penalties (see VI Atr 12 = I Cn 7, and Cn 1020. 15, II Cn 51). Codes before V, VI Atr do not mention it.

[7] Added in the margin. [8] See *infra*.

The sudden influence exerted by this code from the year 1008 surely requires some explanation. Now it is precisely in Ethelred's codes of this year that we first get the influence of Archbishop Wulfstan of York, an influence so strong that all this king's subsequent codes are couched in phraseology similar to that in Wulfstan's homilies;[1] the vocabulary that now comes into use appears also in the laws of Cnut and in the eleventh-century private codes. We might therefore conjecture that it was Wulfstan, obliged as he must have been by his office to be familiar with regulations regarding religious observance in the Danelaw, who brought this treaty into such prominence. Even if we were to accept Liebermann's localization of the code in East Anglia, the probability of a connexion with Wulfstan is hardly lessened, for this prelate, who was a benefactor of two Fenland abbeys and who elected to be buried at Ely,[2] had clearly some close connexion with the eastern counties.

The correspondence between the 'treaty of Edward and Guthrum' and codes from 1008 on is closer, however, than can be explained by this hypothesis. It is not merely a question of the borrowing of whole chapters of the treaty by the later codes. There is an amazingly close agreement in terminology and phraseology, even in quite different contexts. It can hardly be accidental that over and over again words and phrases completely alien to the legislation before 1008 are found in this supposedly tenth-century treaty and in the eleventh-century laws. Sometimes they are otherwise unrecorded in Old English, often they only occur, outside these codes, in the writings certainly or probably due to Wulfstan.

For example, a striking characteristic of Wulfstan's style, also found in the laws from V, VI Atr onwards, namely the excessive use of certain intensives, is also prominent in the treaty, where we get *fullice*, *mid rihte*, *mid ealle*, *georne* (this last four times in a fairly short code), nowhere necessary to the sense and all common expressions in the Wulfstan style.[3] *Elles*, another favourite expression of his,[4] usually redundant, occurs three

[1] For a discussion of Wulfstan's connexion with V, VI Atr, see my edition of his *Sermo Lupi ad Anglos*, pp. 15 f. In my opinion the last six codes of the reign are his work.

[2] See my *Sermo Lupi ad Anglos*, pp. 6 f.

[3] Cf. *fullice*, Napier, p. 14, l. 7, p. 132, l. 14, p. 162, ll. 8, 10; VIII Atr 27: *mid rihte*, Napier, p. 36, ll. 19, 22, p. 39, l. 16, p. 65, l. 20, &c.; V Atr 7, 9, &c.; VIII Atr 25, 30, &c.; I Cn 2. 1 &c.; II Cn 65. 1: *mid ealle*, Napier, p. 27, l. 10, p. 33, l. 8, p. 40, l. 1, &c.; V Atr 1, 34; VIII Atr 40, 44: *georne*, *passim* in Wulfstan's work; I have counted over a hundred instances in his homilies and V Atr has eighteen examples. In tenth-century codes there are in all only two instances of *georne* (VI As 8. 9, IV Eg 16), two of *mid rihte* (II Edw 2, I As 5), in both cases with unweakened meaning, and none of *mid ealle* or *fullice*.

[4] E.g. Napier, p. 10, l. 12, p. 12, ll. 4, 10, p. 33, ll. 12, 13, p. 35, l. 1, &c.; V Atr 15, 28. 1; VIII Atr 4 (MS. G).

times. Moreover, the treaty has several of the formulae common in late laws and in Wulfstan's homilies, but absent from tenth-century laws, for example, *be ðam ðe seo dæd sy*,[1] *wordes oððe weorces*,[2] *for Gode 7 for worulde*,[3] *swa he sceolde*,[4] *gemæne Criste 7 cynge*,[5] *gecuran 7 gecwædon*,[6] *to friðe 7 to freondscipe*.[7] The expression *buton hig geswican 7 ðe deoppor gebetan* of EGu 11 occurs in Wulfstan's so-called Pastoral Letter[8] and, in the singular, in another genuine homily;[9] while *ahwar on lande* in the same chapter of the treaty is closely akin to the Wulfstan phrases *æghwær on þeode*,[10] *ahwar on worulde*,[11] *æghwar on earde*,[12] *æghwær mid mannum*.[13] Finally, both Ethelred's and Cnut's codes use the *swa (be) wer(e) swa (be) wite swa (be) lahslite* of the treaty[14] in passages not repeated from it.[15]

Similarly, the codes under discussion have agreements in vocabulary over against all earlier Anglo-Saxon laws. Thus the term *cyninges handgrið* (EGu 1) is used only by VI Atr,

[1] This occurs three times in this treaty. It is common later, e.g. V Atr 31 = VI 38; VIII Atr 4, 4. 1, 27. 1, 29; II Cn 30. 4, 40. 2, &c.; Had 1. 2, 9. II Cn 43, 45. 2, 3, 46, 46. 2, add it to passages borrowed from EGu.

[2] Though not confined to him, the contrast between *word* and *weorc* is a favourite one with Wulfstan, and in particular, instances of the formula with these words in the genitive case come mainly from works at least influenced by him, e.g. Napier p. 67, l. 16, p. 278, l. 31, p. 279, l. 2; VI Atr 30; II Cn 84. 4b (MS. B). It is inserted into Ælfric's *De Septiformi Spiritu* by the reviser in the Wulfstan manner (Napier, p. 54, ll. 3 f.). It does not occur in the earlier laws. Cf. also *wordes 7 dæde* in Wulfstan's *Sermo Lupi ad Anglos*, ll. 69 f., 135 (= Napier, p. 160, ll. 3 f., p. 163, l. 18) and in V Atr 26, II Cn 84, 4b (MSS. GA).

[3] This is a formula common from the latter part of the tenth century on. See e.g. my *Anglo-Saxon Wills*, p. 30, l. 17, p. 38, l. 2, p. 60, l. 30, and Liebermann, ii. *Wörterbuch*, s.v. *God* 11. It is very frequent in the laws that are in Wulfstan's style, e.g. V Atr 1. 2, 4, 33. 1; VI Atr 8, 8. 2, 36, 39, 40. 1, 53; VIII Atr 38; X Atr Prol.; and in Wulfstan's homilies, e.g. Napier, p. 13, l. 9, p. 55, l. 7, p. 68, ll. 9 f. &c. It occurs also in the Anglo-Saxon Chronicle, 959 DE, in a poem which Jost (*Anglia*, xlvii. 105–23) believes to be Wulfstan's work. In the laws before 1008 it occurs only once (III Eg 1. 2) and then with the two parts of the phrase separated. Harmer, *English Historical Documents of the Ninth and Tenth Centuries*, p. 24, l. 12, has the formula in a ninth-century document, which is, however, preserved in twelfth-century cartularies only. Apart from this instance, the earliest example is in A. J. Robertson, *Anglo-Saxon Charters*, p. 58, l. 6, dated 955, but this again survives only in a late cartulary, and I suspect it to be a later translation of a Latin original of 955.

[4] This is a very common Wulfstan mannerism, e.g. *swa (swa) hy* (or *ge, we*) *scoldan*, Napier, p. 13, l. 16, p. 47, l. 16, p. 92, ll. 7 f. &c., *swa hit* (or *he, man*) *scolde*, *ibid.* p. 46, l. 21, p. 48, l. 8, p. 82, l. 10, &c. In the laws, apart from this treaty, it appears only in the eleventh-century codes *Geþyncþo* 7 (*swa swa he scolde*) and *Grið* 21 (*swa swa hy sceoldan*).

[5] Exactly as in VIII Atr 15, 38. Cf. also *Criste 7 cyninge*, *ibid.* 36; *þam cyninge 7 Criste*, *ibid.* 2; *healf Criste, healf þam cynge*, Northu 48, 58; *Crist 7 cyningc*, *ibid.* 54. 1, 59; *lahriht Cristes oððe cyninges*, V Atr 31.

[6] Exactly as in VI Atr Prol. Cf. *gecoren 7 gecweden*, VIII Atr 6.

[7] Cf. V Atr 1. 1 = X 2. 1.

[8] Napier, p. 115, l. 4.

[9] *Ibid.* p. 12, ll. 7 f.

[10] *Sermo Lupi ad Anglos*, l. 150 = Napier, p. 164, l. 13.

[11] Napier, p. 91, l. 8, p. 105, l. 1.

[12] V Atr 26. 1.

[13] *Sermo Lupi ad Anglos*, l. 62 = Napier, p. 159, l. 15.

[14] EGu 2, 3, 4. 1.

[15] V Atr 31, II Cn 49.

I Cn, and *Griđ*, but not by the tenth-century codes. Even Ethelred's third code expressed the conception differently, i.e. *his* (the king's) *griđ . . . þæt he mid his agenre hánd sylđ. Lahslit*,[1] used frequently in EGu, appears otherwise only in V, VI Atr, II Cn and the eleventh-century *Norđhymbra Preosta Lagu* (Northu). *Deone lage* [2] is another term in agreement with eleventh-century usage, for the first datable occurrence is VI Atr 37 and it does not appear again until Cnut's laws.[3] The tenth-century codes used instead the phrase *mid Denum*, which occurs often in EGu and is held by Liebermann to indicate an early date for the composition of this document. But, though it is true that by Cnut's time *in Denalage* is the more normal expression, even Cnut's laws use *mid Denum* once in a passage not derived from any extant earlier code [4] and several times when quoting EGu, while there is insufficient material for any opinion to be formed of the usage in Ethelred's reign.[5] Professor Stenton has mentioned to me his misgivings at the use of the term 'Danelaw' at as early a date as that to which Liebermann assigns this treaty.

Two other terms first recorded in EGu differ from those we have been discussing in that they describe something not mentioned at all in dated codes before 1008. The first is *sibleger* 'incest',[6] which also occurs in Wulfstan's writings [7] and in Cnut's laws,[8] but not elsewhere. The offence itself is not dealt with in other laws, so one cannot judge if the term is an innovation. Yet it is perhaps worth noting that the penitential literature does not use it, but some much more wordy expression.[9] The

[1] In Northu 51-53 *lahslit* is a penalty that increases in amount with the rank of the offender, 10 half-marks for the king's thegn, 6 half-marks for other landowners, 12 ores for the *ceorl*. In EGu it is defined in one place only (3. 2) as 12 ores, where an offence by the priest is being considered which costs 12 ores in Northu also. I do not believe that this necessitates the assumption that elsewhere in EGu a fixed rate of 12 ores is meant when *lahslit* is mentioned. More probably, as with the accompanying *wer* and *wite*, a payment variable with the rank of the offender is implied, hence the need for definition in the one case where a fixed sum, the *ceorl's* rate of *lahslit*, is meant.

[2] *Sic* MS. H ; B has *Dæge lage* (for *Dæne lage*).

[3] An undated code, *Mirce*, has an imitation of the expression, *Myrcna laga*. In my opinion Liebermann antedates this code, underestimating the antiquarian spirit of Anglo-Saxon private compilations. Even he, however, admits that it has come down to us in the standard language of late West Saxon. No importance is to be attached to *Dena laga* in Lambarde's version of *Norđleod* 6.

[4] II Cn 71. 3.

[5] *On Dena lage* occurs once (VI Atr 37) and VIII Atr 5. 1 has *on Engla lage*. *Inne mid Englum* is used by the eleventh-century *Griđ* and we may also compare *mid Englum, mid Bryttan*, of Wulfstan's *Sermo Lupi ad Anglos*, ll. 196 f. (= Napier, p. 166, n.), though the situation is not quite parallel.

[6] EGu 4.

[7] E.g. *Sermo Lupi ad Anglos*, l. 143 and p. 40 n. = Napier, p. 164, l. 5, p. 165 n.

[8] Cn 1020. 15, II Cn 51.

[9] E.g. *Se đe mid his meder ođđe swustor ođđe dohtor hæme* (Conf. Ps.-Egberti, 6a) ; or *Be þam men þe on his magan gewifađ* (Poen. Ps.-Egberti, 18).

second innovation, the *leohtgesceot* of EGu 6. 2, seems more significant, for the absence from tenth-century legislation of any reference to a payment for lights is strange if this due was already in existence, seeing that three codes, I As, I Em and II Eg all give comprehensive lists of church dues. II Eg in particular gives a very detailed survey, which is borrowed by codes from V, VI Atr onwards,[1] but these always [2] add to Edgar's list the *leohtgesceot* first mentioned in EGu. Moreover, the so-called 'Canons of Edgar', dated by Jost [3] 1001–8, do not mention this payment, though it is added to a version of them in an eleventh-century manuscript. Wulfstan, in his 'Pastoral Letter' refers to the necessity of paying this due.[4]

These instances by no means exhaust the correspondence in vocabulary between the treaty and Wulfstan texts. *Ægylde* (EGu 6. 7) and *morðwyrhta* (EGu 11) are otherwise recorded only in Wulfstan's homilies and in codes directly or indirectly influenced by him; [5] the verb *fysan* (EGu 11) perhaps from Old Norse **feysa*,[6] occurs once as a gloss to a Prudentius manuscript, but all other instances, including the compound *tofesian*, come from Wulfstan's writings; [7] in EGu 10 *limlæweo* (H), *limlǽþeo* (B), *límeþeo* (Quadr) has obviously given trouble to the scribes, and small wonder, for the word *lǣw* of which it is a derivative is extremely rare, occurring as *lewe* (dat.) in the *Sermo Lupi ad Anglos*,[8] and in the compounds *synleawa* in the same text and *limlæwa* in a penitential document.[9] Wulfstan uses also the rare derivative verb *lǣwan*.[10] Another word in the treaty has worried the scribe of the *Textus Roffensis* version, namely *genydmagas*, 'close kinsfolk', of chapter 4. 1, which he gives as *genyhe magas*.[11] It is an interesting word for our purpose, for it is unique and can be compared only with the *nydmaga*, 'near kinswoman', of the *Sermo Lupi ad Anglos* [12] and VI Atr 12 (= I Cn 7) and with the *nydmæg*, 'near kinsman', which replaces

[1] V Atr 11. 1, VI Atr 16–19, VIII Atr 9–12, I Cn 8. 1–12.

[2] Except Cnut's proclamation of 1027, 16.

[3] *Anglia*, lvi. 288 ff.

[4] Napier, p. 113, ll. 10 f.

[5] *Ægylde* in V Atr 31. 1, II Cn 62. 1, and *Sermo Lupi ad Anglos*, l. 107 = Napier, p. 162, l. 8. Other codes use instead *or-* or *ungilde*. *Morðwyrhta* in VI Atr 7 (= II Cn 4a), VI Atr 36 and in Napier, p. 26, l. 16. Cf. also *morðorwyrhtan*, *Sermo Lupi ad Anglos*, l. 169 = Napier, p. 165 n.

[6] See K. Luick, *Historische Grammatik der englischen Sprache*, § 384. 4.

[7] *Sermo Lupi ad Anglos*, l. 115 = Napier p. 162, l. 18; *ibid.* p. 132, l. 21, p. 133 l. 5; ASC, 975 D; VI Atr 7 = II Cn 4a.

[8] l. 164 = Napier, p. 165, l. 9. It is worth noting that here, too, it has worried three out of the five scribes.

[9] B. Thorpe, *op. cit.* ii. 278 n.

[10] *Sermo Lupi ad Anglos*, l. 167 (and note) = Napier, p. 165 n. Perhaps our code should read *limlæwed*, 'mutilated'.

[11] It is unlikely that this represents the original reading, for no adjective *geneah* is recorded. *Nih*, for *neah*, occurs in the Kentish Glosses.

[12] l. 118 (see note) = Napier, p. 162, l. 21.

the simple *mæg* of Ælfric's Pastoral Letter [1] in MS. D, a version of the letter revised in Wulfstan's style, very probably by Wulfstan himself.[2] *Nyd-* is not otherwise used in this sense in Old English, but in Old Norse the cognate *nauð-* has this meaning in *nauðleyti*, 'close relationship'. Apart therefore from the treaty we are discussing all English instances of the usage come from works in the Wulfstan style.

Not only the words, but also some usages are most uncommon outside the set of writings under discussion. For example, *fela* (*manna*) [3] with a singular verb is Wulfstan's normal usage,[4] but this does not occur in tenth-century laws; *gebugan*,[5] when governing a direct object and meaning 'submit to' is otherwise only in V Atr 29 and II Cn 35; *steor* is rare in the plural except here and in Wulfstan texts.[6] The impression of close connexion is deepened by the number of words which, while not confined to the Wulfstan style, are yet words which seem to have come naturally to his mind, for example *afyllan*, 'to slay',[7] *forrædan*, 'to betray',[8] *forfaran*, used transitively, 'to destroy',[9] *wyrdan*, 'to injure',[10] all fairly common in Wulfstan and texts influenced by him, but not frequent elsewhere and absent from the legal language of the tenth century. It is naturally possible that one or other of these correspondences of word and phrase is accidental, but there are surely too many for all to be explained away. Finally, there are some general stylistic similarities with Wulfstan's prose. The list of criminals in EGu 11 is very like those so common in Wulfstan's homilies,[11] of which one feature is their arrangement in alliterating pairs, as here, *wycan oððe wigleras*,

[1] Ed. B. Fehr, *Die Hirtenbriefe Ælfrics*, p. 76, cap. 15.

[2] See K. Jost in *Englische Studien*, lii. 105 ff.; Fehr, *op. cit.* pp. lxiv-lxxxii.

[3] EGu Prol. 2.

[4] See, e.g., Napier, p. 54, ll. 11 f., 23, p. 78, ll. 17 f., p. 110, l. 5; *Sermo Lupi ad Anglos*, ll. 11 f. = Napier, p. 156, ll. 10 f. In the instance in EGu it appears to have worried the scribes, one of whom partly, the other completely, turned the following clause *swa hi sceolden* into the singular also, B as *swa he sceolde*, H as *swa hy sceolde*.

[5] EGu Prol. 2, EGu 3.

[6] Cf. with the *woruldlice stéora* of EGu Prol. 2 the *friðlice steora* of V Atr 3. 1 (= VI Atr 10. 1), *þurh grimlice steora*, Napier, p. 133, l. 19. Wulfstan uses the word, singular or plural, very often. With the reading in EGu cf. *mid worldlicre steore*, VIII Atr 15 and Napier, p. 169, l. 8.

[7] EGu 6. 7; cf., e.g., Napier, p. 132, l. 20, p. 162, ll. 8, 10; V Atr 31. 1 = VI Atr 38, II Cn 20, 39, 62. 1. In earlier laws it occurs only in Af 12 (MS. B, Rb), where death is caused by a falling tree.

[8] EGu 12; cf. Napier, p. 17, l. 19, p. 22, l. 20; *Sermo Lupi ad Anglos*, ll. 76, 78 = Napier, p. 160, ll. 11, 13; VI Atr 10 = II Cn 2. 1.

[9] EGu 11; cf. *Sermo Lupi ad Anglos*, p. 33 n. = Napier, p. 160 n.; V Atr 2 = VI Atr 9 = II Cn 3. In Napier, p. 106, l. 11, this word replaces the *acwellan* of the Ælfric original.

[10] EGu 2; cf. Napier, p. 67, l. 21, p. 168, l. 8; II Cn 15. 3, 83; *awyrdan* also occurs several times in these texts.

[11] Cf., e.g., *Sermo Lupi ad Anglos*, ll. 166 ff. and note, and instances there cited. See also Jost in *Anglia*, lvi. 267 f.

monsworan oððe morðwyrhtan. There is nothing similar in tenth-century laws. Alliteration appears in other parts of the code, and not merely in set legal formulae; note, for instance, *to friðe 7 to freondscipe fullice fengon* (Prol.).[1] Rhyme occurs in *gebugan mid rihte to bisceopa dihte* (Prol. 2) and may be compared with the following examples from Wulfstan's homilies, where the rhythm also is similar: *7 healdan unwemme 7 a butan glemme,*[2] *weorðaþ to wlance 7 ealles to rance,*[3] *wealdan eow blisse 7 micelre lisse.*[4] There is also much more tautology in this code than in those of any king before Ethelred. The very fact that whole passages from it can be inserted almost word for word in the laws of Ethelred and Cnut without our being conscious of a change of style would suggest that there is no gap of some sixty years (at least) between the writing of these codes.

The most likely explanation of the similarities we have noted, taken together with the absence of any evidence for the use of EGu before 1008, would surely be that this code, in its present form, dates from the early eleventh century, and in my opinion the resemblance to the certain works of Wulfstan is so close as to make it highly probable that he had a hand in its compilation. A theoretically possible alternative, that Wulfstan was so impressed by the style of an earlier code that he modelled his own very characteristic rhetorical style on it, is unlikely, and fails to explain the neglect of the code by earlier legislators. But before we can accept the more natural explanation it will be necessary to examine Liebermann's reasons for dating the code so early. As one cannot differ lightly from so great a scholar, a detailed consideration of his views is called for. One or two of his points have already been met above.[5]

First, however, the localization of the code must be considered, for features that would help to fix the date of a purely East Anglian code may be inapplicable if the code applies to a wider or different area. Liebermann ascribes it to East Anglia, because in chapter 12 there is mentioned, as an alternative to the king as protector of a wronged ecclesiastic or stranger, *oððon eorl þær on lande*; secondly, because Guthrum, mentioned in the preamble, was king in East Anglia. Liebermann argues from the first point that the code applies to a district under a single earl, and cannot therefore be intended for the whole of the Danelaw. This is surely reading too much into the passage,

[1] The use of alliteration in Wulfstan's homilies is too common to need illustration, but it is worth noting that in the revisions of Ælfric's work in the Wulfstan manner additions are often made for the sole purpose of obtaining alliteration, e.g. (*mod-staðolnysse 7*) *modes strencðe*, Napier, p. 53, l. 10 (*wærne 7*) *wisne, ibid.* p. 52, ll. 29 f.

[2] *Ibid.* p. 67, ll. 17 f.

[3] *Ibid.* p. 81, ll. 14 f.

[4] *Ibid.* p. 132, l. 23. Cf. also I Cn 26. 3, *to swyðe ne slite ne to fela ne abite.*

[5] See pp. 5, 8.

which can equally well refer to the particular earl in whose area the crime has been committed and need tell us nothing about the number of earls in the district affected by the code.[1] His second argument, the mention of Guthrum in a prologue which is admittedly later, and contains erroneous information in other respects,[2] would not be a very strong argument even if it were certain that the author of this prologue meant it to be thus interpreted. He may well, however, have been thinking of Guthrum, not so much as an early king of East Anglia, but as the representative of the Danes when first a *modus vivendi* between Danes and English was reached. Any traditional regulations regarding the position of the Danes in England may well have been attributed to him. Certainly, as Liebermann himself notes, the reference to bishops in the plural later on in the preamble shows that the author is not speaking then of East Anglia alone.[3] It is therefore unjustifiable to date this code from the conditions that prevailed merely in that province.

The preamble begins as follows :

> And ðis is seo gerædnyss eac, ðe Ælfred cyng ⁊ Guðrum cyng ⁊ eft Eadward cyng ⁊ Gyþrum cyng gecuran ⁊ gecwædon, ða ða Engle ⁊ Dene to friðe ⁊ to freondscipe fullice fengon ; ⁊ ða witan eac, ðe syððan wæron, oft ⁊ unseldan þæt seolfe geniwodon ⁊ mid gode gehuhtan,[4]

i.e. in Mr. Attenborough's translation, 'This also is the legislation which King Alfred and King Guthrum, and afterwards King Edward and King Guthrum, enacted and agreed upon, when the English and the Danes unreservedly entered into relations of peace and friendship. The councillors also who have been [in office] since then, frequently and often have re-enacted the same, and added improvements thereto.' Liebermann considers that, after the accession of Edward the Martyr in 975, an author referring to Edward the Elder would have given him some distinguishing epithet, but I doubt whether in such a context confusion with a young king who reigned less than three years and issued no law codes would have been anticipated.

[1] Any more than II Cn, for example, refers to a single diocese because in 53. 1, 54. 1, &c., it speaks of 'the bishop'. In any case, if we assume that *eorl* would not be used in tenth-century East Anglia of an English *ealdorman* (see p. 14 below), we have no evidence that this province was administered by a single *eorl*; and, if the passage is to be interpreted as Liebermann takes it, Southern Northumbria might be meant, unless other grounds force us to assign it to East Anglia.

[2] E.g. the claim that it was drawn up by Alfred and Guthrum is patently impossible ; see Liebermann, iii. 87, § 5.

[3] East Anglia consisted of two sees before the Danish invasions, but there is no evidence that it ever had more than one afterwards. At the time to which Liebermann would assign this code it appears to have been held by Theodred, bishop of London ; see my *Anglo-Saxon Wills*, p. 99.

[4] *Sic* B ; *gehihtan* H. Both represent *geīhtan*, past tense of *geīcan*.

There would, of course, be no possibility of confusion if the words *7 Gyþrum cyng* are original, and they occur in both Old English versions.[1] Liebermann would, moreover, prefer a date not later than 950 on the grounds that Guthrum's name was unlikely to be remembered, except by Danish colonists, after the time of his younger contemporaries. Even if this were true, which I think unlikely, it hardly applies to the author of a preamble so antiquarian in spirit, who may well have been familiar with the Anglo-Saxon Chronicle and who possibly had before him the earlier treaty, beginning *Ðis is ðæt frið ðæt Ælfred cyninc 7 Gyðrum cyning.*[2] Nor do I find, with Liebermann, the absence of reference to Athelstan strange if the preamble is later than his death. The author seems concerned to establish the antiquity of the regulations he is about to state. It is enough for him to show that they go back to the earliest negotiations and have continually been re-enacted since. The chronological error, by which Edward is made to rule at the same time as Guthrum,[3] who had died nine years before Edward's accession, would be improbable during the reigns of Edward's sons and grandsons, but understandable if the preamble dates from the early eleventh century. There is no manuscript evidence for the assumption that it is due to later interpolation.

The preamble closes with the statement, in language very like Wulfstan's: *7 ða woruldbote hig settan gemæne Criste 7 cynge, swa hwár swa man nolde godcunde bote gebugan mid rihte to bisceopa dihte*, i.e. 'And they fixed secular amends which should be divided between Christ and the king wheresoever people would not legally submit to the amends required by the church and determined by the bishops'. As VIII Atr 36-37 regard the division between 'Christ and king' a wise arrangement of the past, neglected since Edgar's time, Liebermann holds that our code, which enjoins it, must be previous to the latter's death. It may, however, equally well be part of legislation of Ethelred's reign re-enforcing this arrangement, apparently with success, for we get division between ecclesiastic and secular authorities, not only in his codes, but also in Cnut's and in the eleventh-century *Norðhymbra Preosta Lagu.*[4] In short, there is nothing in the preamble incompatible with an eleventh-century date.

To turn from the preamble to the regulations themselves, we must bear in mind the possibility of their being repeated from an

[1] While Quadr omits, not this phrase alone, but the reference to Edward also.

[2] At any rate the common original of H and B had our text just after AGu, for both begin: *And þis is seo gerædnis eac.*

[3] That it is the same Guthrum, and not an otherwise unknown successor, who is meant, is made clear from the context, as Liebermann points out.

[4] See passages cited above, p. 7 n., and add II Cn 36, *þæt sy gemæne hlaforde 7 bisceope*, and Northu 49, *healf Criste 7 healf landrican.*

earlier code, even if re-written in the terminology of a later period. Yet I do not think that Liebermann's arguments for an early date will hold. We have seen above that the use of the phrase *mid Denum* has no significance for dating. Another of Liebermann's arguments is the use of *eorl*, for this term is not recorded in use as the title of the East Anglian *ealdorman* Æthelstan 'Half-king' (932–) or his successors.[1] But it is only if the code is an East Anglian one that this argument has any weight. In Northumbria the term *eorl* [2] continued in use beside *ealdorman*. The men who sign charters with this designation between 946 and 949 [3] are probably Northumbrians. Oslac, of South Northumbria, is *se mæra eorl* in the Anglo-Saxon Chronicle, 975 DE, and *eorl* in IV Eg 15 ; Thorod, who must be connected with the north, is *eorl* in 992 [4] and in a charter of about 979–992 ;[5] Uhtred is called *eorl* in 1013 [6] and his province was southern Northumbria. After Cnut's accession the term is used of the Danes to whom he gave these offices,[7] and by about 1040 it has ousted the English designation.[8] All that its occurrence in our code need mean is that a Danish area, presumably Northumbria, is included. It is quite analogous to the use of *eorles* in III Atr 12, a code that applies to a Danish area, especially to the Five Boroughs, and it is no more indicative of an early date in EGu than in this code.

When Liebermann claims that a tenth-century code is required because 'die Taufe ist noch für Erwachsene nicht selten erfordert', he is reading too much into the text,[9] which runs: *Gyf preost . . . fulluhtes forwyrne ðam ðe ðæs ðearf sy*, i.e. 'if a priest refuse baptism to him who is in need of it'. In his note to this chapter Liebermann says, 'an adult heathen may be

[1] Even local vernacular documents, such as wills, refer only to *ealdormenn*; see *Anglo-Saxon Wills*, XIII–XVI, and the Peterborough documents, Robertson, *op. cit.* XXXIX f. Apart from the poem on the Battle of Maldon, which cannot be precisely dated, and which may be influenced by the poetical use of the word, we get no reference to an *eorl* in the eastern counties before the Dane, Thurkil, from 1017 on. *Eorles* in *Vlf eorles suna*, Robertson, XL, is probably a personal name. It cannot apply to the East Anglian ealdormen, none of whom had a son Ulf.

[2] In its use to designate an official, it is influenced by the cognate ON *jarl*. The OE word, which means a man of the upper classes, was out of date by this time except in set legal phrases. See H. M. Chadwick, *Studies on Anglo-Saxon Institutions*, pp. 161 ff.

[3] BCS 815, 883. [4] ASC DE. [5] Robertson, LX = BCS 1255.

[6] ASC. On the other hand, Ælfhelm, who was ealdorman of Southern Northumbria to 1006, is never called *eorl*, not even in ASC 1036 E, when referred to retrospectively at a period when *eorl* was the only term then current.

[7] Thurkil of East Anglia, Eric of Northumbria, Eglaf, &c.

[8] The earliest datable use of *eorl* for an English holder of a province outside the Danelaw is 1036 (ASC CE). From then on instances are common. The latest instances of *ealdorman* that I have found are from about 1023, e.g. Robertson, LXXXI (= Earle, p. 235) and LXXXIII (= KCD 898), both referring to Leofwine *ealdorman*. Ranig is given this title in Robertson, LXXVIII (= KCD 755), between 1016 and 1035.

[9] EGu 3. 2.

meant ', and he thinks that the briefer statement in Northu 8 is a deliberate exclusion of this possibility. Yet it is more probable that the author of EGu has in mind merely the baptism of a sickly infant. There is a parallel in the addition, probably by Wulfstan, of the phrase *gif þearf bið*, ' if it is necessary ', to the statement in Ælfric's Pastoral Letter [1] that a deacon may baptize a child.

It is also dangerous to assume from the omission of any express injunction regarding clerical marriage that the code is previous to the monastic revival, for, though Ethelred's and Cnut's codes repeatedly state that the priest has no right to marry, clerical marriage was not uncommon throughout the Anglo-Saxon period.[2] It is not forbidden, and, moreover, its existence is implied, in the *Norðhymbra Preosta Lagu*, an eleventh-century compilation applying to the diocese of York.

There remain to be examined some matters where the injunctions of EGu have been thought to differ from those in codes of the second half of the tenth, and the eleventh centuries, and the conclusion has been drawn that EGu represents an older phase of legislation. Non-observance of festivals by a freeman is punished in EGu 7. 1 [3] with either loss of freedom or monetary payment. The codes which use this passage, II Cn 45. 1, Northu 57, omit the reference to loss of freedom, punishing by monetary payment only, the former by *healsfang*, the latter by 12 ores.[4] Liebermann points out that loss of freedom for legal offences is not mentioned in the laws after Athelstan's sixth code, except in the private compilation *Grið*.[5] Yet, as the actual existence of the penal slave at any rate as late as 1015 can be proved from the will of the Ætheling Æthelstan,[6] which states that his executors are to set free *ælcne witefæstne mann þe ic on sprǽce ahte*,[7] we can only assume that failure to meet legal liabilities automatically meant servitude even when the laws fail to mention this alternative. The omission of the clause from the codes which copy EGu need not imply any change of law.

Another discrepancy is claimed with regard to the punishment of clerical offences. Here again, I consider it more apparent

[1] Version D. See Fehr, *op. cit.* p. 108, cap. 107. Phrases meaning ' if necessary ' are frequent in the Wulfstan style. An exact parallel to that in EGu 3. 2 occurs in a different context in VI Atr 53.

[2] See Liebermann, ii. *Glossar*, s.v. *Cōlibat.*

[3] As in Ine 3. 2, where, however, only breach of Sunday is mentioned.

[4] These are probably the amounts meant by *wite* and *lahslit* in EGu 7. 1. On *lahslit* see above, p. 8 n., and on *healsfang* see A. J. Robertson, *The Laws of the Kings of England from Edmund to Henry I*, pp. 297 f.

[5] Cap. 16. Liebermann's statement is badly worded and suggests that these texts deal with non-observance of festivals, which is not the case.

[6] *Anglo-Saxon Wills*, p. 56, ll. 14 f.

[7] I.e. ' every penally enslaved man whom I acquired in the course of jurisdiction '.

than real. Theft, fighting, perjury, or adultery committed by a priest incur monetary payments and ecclesiastical penance in EGu 3, and the offender must find surety or go to prison. VIII Atr 27 enjoins deprivation of office for such offences, but only if the offender does not 'make amends the more deeply towards God and men', and surety is to be produced. These injunctions are repeated in I Cn 5. 3. I see no contradiction here: Ethelred adds what happens if the offender will not pay the fine and do penance, EGu states more definitely what the 'amends towards God and men' consist of. Then in EGu 4. 2 the case of a priest who has committed a capital crime is referred to the bishop's decision, and this is repeated in II Cn 43. VIII Atr 26, repeated in II Cn 41, gives as the penalty for homicide or other great crime committed by a priest deprivation of office, exile, and pilgrimage as far as the pope appoints for him. This probably refers only to serious, but not capital, crimes; for, if it were meant to supersede EGu 4. 2, it is strange that Cnut's law includes both statutes. Even if a change of law is implied, it is unnecessary to assume a great lapse of time between the two statements.

Purely ecclesiastical offences, i.e. misdirection about festivals and fasts, neglect of duty, incur in EGu 3.1, 3.2 a fine of thirty shillings *mid Englum* and three half-marks *mid Denum*. Such offences, according to Liebermann, normally incur only spiritual consequences and degradation. They are not mentioned in any king's legislation after Wihtred of Kent.[1] They do, however, occur in the *Norðhymbra Preosta Lagu* [2] and with the same penalty, twelve ores,[3] as in EGu. In so far, therefore, as EGu derives support from other laws, it comes from an eleventh-century code.

Finally, there is some difference in severity in the penalties for failure to pay Peter's pence and other church dues. In EGu 6–6.4 it is given as *lahslit* among the Danes, *wite* among the English, and this is supported in part by the *Norðhymbra Preosta Lagu* [4] which, in case of failure to pay Peter's pence, has a fine of 10 marks for the king's thegn and for the *landrica*, of 12 ores for the *tunesman*, both of these amounts being payments in the *lahslit* scale.[5] The fine for withholding tithe in this code is the same, except that the *landrica* pays only 6 marks, i.e. the usual *lahslit* for a man of this class. Contrary to these injunctions, II Eg 4.1 enjoins a fine of 120 shillings to the king for failure to pay Peter's pence, in addition to a journey to Rome and a thirty-fold payment there, with increased penalties for a second

[1] Wi 6, where the punishment is suspension from office.

[2] Caps. 8, 9, 11.

[3] Twelve ores are equivalent to three half-marks.

[4] Caps. 58, 59. They are not borrowed from EGu and there is no reason to believe them to be merely antiquarian.

[5] See above, p. 8 n.

offence and loss of all property on a third occasion, while II Eg 3. 1 punishes refusal to render tithe with loss of nine-tenths of one's harvest. VIII Atr 10. 1 and I Cn 9. 1 repeat the injunctions about Peter's pence, but omit the journey to Rome; VIII Atr 8 and I Cn 8. 2 have the regulations on tithe unchanged. From the *Norðhymbra Preosta Lagu* it is clear that these severe regulations were not effective in Northumbria in the eleventh century and that we need not assume EGu to be anterior to Edgar's legislation because it refers to *lahslit* in this connexion. There is, however, a very great discrepancy between the penalties in Edgar's law and that paid 'among the English' according to EGu, if, with Liebermann, we take *wite* to mean a fine of thirty shillings throughout the code. But does it mean anything more than 'the recognized fine for such an offence'? This is clearly its meaning in VIII Atr 9 and 12, where tithe of young stock and plough-alms are to be paid by set times *be wite*, i.e. on pain of incurring the fine. Elsewhere in Anglo-Saxon law *wite* refers to a fine of 30 shillings, 60 shillings and 120 shillings.[1] The fact that in two places in the code the *wite* among the English is stated to be 30 shillings when the Danes pay 12 ores does not compel us to believe that *wite* necessarily means this sum throughout the code, any more than *lahslit* need denote a fixed rate of 12 ores except when this is expressly stated.[2] The code is mainly concerned with a Danish province and I should interpret *lahslit mid Denum, wite mid Englum* to mean that the Danes incurred a penalty varying, according to the rank of the offender, on a fixed scale, when the English paid the fine laid down elsewhere for such an offence. But, even if we accept the theory that *wite* in EGu is always 30 shillings, is it safe to assume from the resulting discrepancy with Edgar's legislation that EGu antedates this, when we remember how Ethelred's laws complain of undesirable alterations made since Edgar's time?[3]

To sum up, we have found that the code under consideration has only one very questionable case of disagreement with the extant legislation of the eleventh century, and that even this need not imply an early date; that it introduces a church due, *leohtgesceot*, lacking from all documents before 1008; that from that date it is frequently used by all codes, whereas no previous code shows familiarity with it; that in its terminology, phraseology, and style it is in close agreement with the writings that

[1] See Liebermann, iii. *Wörterbuch* s.v. *wite*.

[2] The first offence incurring a 30 shilling fine in the code is one not mentioned elsewhere; the second, trading on Sunday (EGu 7), has this penalty in II As 24. 1.

[3] VIII Atr 37: . . . *æfter Eadgares lifdagum, Cristes lage wanodan 7 cyninges laga litledon*. Cf. *Sermo Lupi ad Anglos*, p. 26 n., and the poem, attributed by Jost to Wulfstan, in the ASC *s.a.* 975 D.

show the influence of Archbishop Wulfstan, including the law-codes of Ethelred and Cnut ; and that again and again it uses formulae not on record before the eleventh century. There is nothing in the code to rule out an early eleventh-century date except the claims made in the preamble, which have been shown to be erroneous. Moreover, there is nothing in the code to force us to assume that the author is revising an earlier document.

It would naturally be difficult to prove the negative—that he is not using an earlier code. It is more than probable that in general the code represents regulations of considerable antiquity, or otherwise the author's claim that they went back to Alfred and Guthrum would have been too demonstrably false. That more than one treaty between the English and the Danish settlers once existed is shown by II Ew 5. 2, which runs, in Mr. Attenborough's translation : 'If the offence is committed in the eastern or northern kingdoms, compensation shall be paid in accordance with the provisions of the treaties '. The reference is, however, to an offence not treated of in either AGu or EGu, namely the harbouring of a fugitive. The author of our code may have had earlier written sources, but I doubt very much whether any English king in the first half of the tenth century could enforce such stringent ecclesiastical rules on the recently converted people of the Danish provinces, and I hold that we cannot take this code as a proof that he could.

If I might be allowed to reconstruct the probable course of events, I should suggest that when Wulfstan was translated to York in 1002 he found his diocese backward in ecclesiastical matters and failing to observe regulations which he regarded as of long standing. We know that about this period he was sufficiently interested in the reform of ecclesiastical practice to write to Ælfric asking him many questions about it, and that, when Ælfric wrote two pastoral letters for him,[1] he revised one in his own style, whether for circulation or oral delivery is not known. His homilies show him to be greatly concerned at the amount of 'heathenism' he considered prevalent.[2] It seems likely, therefore, that about the same period he should compile some regulations concerning the observance of ecclesiastical laws and the penalties for their violation, providing a preface to explain that they were not innovations, but had been in force since the first days of the Danish settlement. He may well have written this preface in good faith. That he should use this compilation, with only slight alterations, when drawing up law-codes for Ethelred at a later date, is entirely in accordance with what we know of Wulfstan's methods. In that case we could date the code between Wulfstan's translation to York in 1002

[1] Fehr, *op. cit.*

[2] See *Sermo Lupi ad Anglos*, p. 36 n.

and the promulgation of V, VI Atr in 1008. This seems to me a very likely course of events, but I am aware that it stops short of proof. What is clear at least is that the affinities of the code are with eleventh-century legislation, that it is written in the Wulfstan style, and that it contains nothing to make us date it much before 1008, the date of the first code to make use of it.

This means that we have no longer any evidence that the Scandinavian settlers in East Anglia were brought so quickly under the control of the church as has been supposed, and we may need to modify our opinion as to the extent of the West Saxon kings' authority in that province in the first half of the tenth century. Moreover, the results of this re-dating are not without importance for the study of legal formulae. Hitherto, our code has supplied in many cases a disturbingly early example of what otherwise seemed a late development. Similarly, we need no longer assume such an early fusion of English and Danish inhabitants as was necessary to account for the early adoption of so many ON words. Of loan-words that have been thought to appear first in this code, and so to have been borrowed before 950, the earliest datable examples are now as follows: *lahslit, Dena lagu* in Ethelred's code of 1008; *eorl*, as an official under the English king, in the documents mentioned on page 14, i.e. 946–949; *utlah* in a charter of 963–975[1] and in I Eg 3. 1; *grið* in II Em 7. 1; *ora* perhaps first in a Peterborough document of 963–992,[2] and then in III Atr. The only really early loan-word in this code is *lagu*, which occurs in the phrase *on Godes lage* already in I As 2[3] and again, but with reference to the Danes only, in IV Eg 2. 1, 12.

APPENDIX

On the supposed lost manuscript used by Lambarde

While admitting that Lambarde mainly depends on B, Liebermann thought that he also had access to a version now lost, going back on an Old English version from which *Quadripartitus* is derived and which he calls *lq*. Mr. Sisam showed convincingly in *Modern Language Review*, xviii. 100 ff., and again in *ibid.* xx. 253 ff., when replying to Liebermann's objections in *Anglia-Beiblatt*, xxxv. 214 f., that it was unlikely that Lambarde had access to any such manuscript and he accounted otherwise for those features said to be derived from this lost manuscript. Since then,

[1] Robertson, XXXVII = BCS 1131. [2] *Ibid.* XL = BCS 1130.

[3] If this very early and isolated example is not due to later alteration. The code survives only in late manuscripts.

Mr. Sisam's views received remarkable confirmation when the British Museum acquired a transcript of Nowell (see R. Flower, ' Laurence Nowell and the Discovery of England ', *Proceedings of the British Academy*, xxi, especially note 16). It will therefore be sufficient to show here that in this code also the variants from extant manuscripts are nothing more than what an Elizabethan scholar could produce without access to another version. Leaving aside mere meaningless alterations, such as the addition or omission of a final *e*, the variants are as follows:

1. The omission of *And* and *eac* from the introductory words of the preamble. As Lambarde separates this treaty from that of Alfred and Guthrum, which immediately precedes it in B, he may easily have felt that ' and also ' was no longer to the point, and have followed Quadr in omitting it.

2. In cap. 3 where B has *carcer gebuge*, H *carcern gebuge*, Lambarde reads *on carcerne gebuge*. The construction of *gebugan* with a direct object is rare, and Lambarde has ' normalized ', having the *in carcere* of Quadr and the *on carcerne* of Af 1. 2 (which he prints earlier in the book) to go by.

3. Lambarde begins cap. 3. 2 *Gyf mæssepreost* where the manuscripts have *Gyf preost*, but this is merely bringing it into uniformity with the preceding clause of the code.

4. Similarly, he has inserted *swa be were* into the phrase *swa be wite swa be lahslite* in cap. 4. 1, to bring it into line with the formula used elsewhere in the code.

5. Where H in cap. 5 reads *ne him man næfre ne wyrne*, Lambarde has *ne forwyrne him man næfre*. The B text, which he used, accidentally omits *ne wyrne*. Lambarde could gather the meaning required from Quadr *negetur*, and no doubt selected *forwyrne* from its use in cap. 6. 4, but naturally he could not guess the original position of the verb.

6. In cap. 6. 5, Lambarde replaces *weres* by *feorhes*. He may have thought the Quadr reading, *uita*, gave a better sense, and translated it.

7. In 6. 6, *sylle* for the manuscripts *gefylle* is, of course, due to the easy misreading of *f* as *s*.

8. In cap. 6. 7, *licge he orgylde* for the manuscripts *licge ægilde* may be accounted for as a substitution of the *licgge he orgilde* of Alfred 1. 5 for an unfamiliar expression. Nowell's manuscript dictionary (on which see Sisam, *op. cit.* p. 103) has under *ægild* ' vnpayd for ', w *orgild*. One version of Quadr (i.e. Br) has, however, *orgilde* in EGu here.

9. He naturally rectified B's omission of *hyde* in cap. 8, from the identical phrase in 7. 1.

10. In cap. 11 the manuscripts have *fyse hi*, where Lambarde has *fyrsie*. *Fysan* is a rare word and it is not in Nowell's dictionary, which has, under *f*, *afyrsian*, ' to drive away, to putte away '. As this gives the required sense, Lambarde probably thought his text corrupt and emended it.

11. Finally, there remain two minor variants considered significant by Liebermann, of which one is *þære* for B's *ðæne* in cap. 4. Liebermann says that Lambarde's form is the proper gender. If it is not a mere misreading of B's *n* as *r*, it could result from reasoning similar to Liebermann's own. The other variant is the ' weakening ' of the name

Guðrum to *Guðrun*, a point hardly strong enough in itself to prove access to a lost manuscript.

If Lambarde had no other OE text than B, we must allow no authority to the chapter rubrics, which occur in his text alone. For the purpose of this article I am robbed of the support of a second manuscript to the reading *genydmagas*, but on the other hand the alternatives to *fyse* and *œgilde* are shown to have no early authority.

X

TWO NOTES ON ÆLFRIC AND WULFSTAN

(i) *The Date of Ælfric's Death*

In 1856 Dietrich expressed the opinion that the death of the homilist Ælfric occurred between 1020 and 1025,[1] and this has been so frequently repeated, usually without any reference to Dietrich's evidence, that it is well on the way towards being accepted as ascertained fact. It seems therefore desirable to point out how slender is the evidence on which this opinion is based. Dietrich believed that Ælfric survived so long into the eleventh century solely because of the occurrence of an Abbot Ælfric among the witnesses to an Old English will (K.C.D. 972) which he dated 1020, deliberately differing from Kemble, who dated its Latin confirmation (K.C.D. 1300) 1004. Dietrich's date is given because the list of witnesses includes Archbishop Æthelnoth (1020–38), Archbishop Wulfstan (1002–23) and Bishop Ælfhun of London, whom he erroneously believed to have been alive in 1020, when in fact his successor Ælfwig was consecrated early in 1014[2] and signs from 1015 on. This document is no. XXII in my *Anglo-Saxon Wills* and I have discussed its date there. It has an impossible list of witnesses, including, along with the above-mentioned ecclesiastics, Ealdorman Ælfhere who died in 983 and Ealdorman Brihtnoth who was killed in 991. It is a late version from a St Paul's register which is now lost, and it is obvious that the list cannot be genuine as it stands. In the body of the document the king's name is Æthelred, and it is difficult to see why this should have been substituted for Cnut as it must have been if Dietrich's dating is correct. Possibly the St Paul's scribe eked out an original list of the first decade of the eleventh century with a sprinkling of famous persons; possibly the original will had no witnesses and this deficiency was remedied by compiling a list from at least three documents of different dates. In any case, there is no good reason for supposing that Abbot Ælfric belonged to the same list as Archbishop Æthelnoth. His immediate predecessor is Ælfhun, Bishop of London from 1004 to 1014. As evidence for the survival of the homilist as late as 1020 the document is clearly worthless.

Even if it could be proved that Archbishop Æthelnoth and Abbot Ælfric witnessed the same document, the question whether this abbot is necessarily the homilist would remain open. The name is extremely common and our knowledge of the succession of abbots to even the more important abbeys is

[1] 'Abt Aelfrik. Zur Literatur-Geschichte der angelsächsischen Kirche.' Part II. In Niedner's *Zeitschrift für die historische Theologie*, Neue Folge xx, 247 f.

[2] *Anglo-Saxon Chronicle*, 1014 D.

by no means complete. This should be borne in mind when considering other signatures claimed for him. One of these can be easily dismissed, namely, the alleged occurrence of his attestation to the Eynsham foundation charter of 1005.[1] The better text given by Salter[2] shows that Kemble's *Ælfric* is *Ælfrie* in the manuscript, and this is an error for *Ælfsige* both here and later on in the list, Anglo-Saxon *s* and *r* being easily confused. Two abbots called Ælfsige normally witness charters of this period. It is not remarkable that the newly appointed abbot does not witness the foundation charter of his abbey. The same is true at the almost contemporary foundation of Burton-on-Trent, where the abbot, Wulfgeat, is not one of the witnesses to the foundation charter of 1004 (K.C.D. 710).

Another signature has been attributed to the homilist by Dietrich, that of an abbot who witnesses a royal charter (K.C.D. 1307) of July 1012, dealing with lands in Oxfordshire. It is clear that it was witnessed by a gathering of the witan, but we are not told where. It does not follow that the Abbot Ælfric belongs to the same locality as the estates granted, any more than the other abbots, who probably represent the houses of Thorney, the New Minster at Winchester, either Ely or Peterborough, and Evesham. Wulfgar of Abingdon is there, but as he witnesses almost every charter of the period, we need not assume he is here in the capacity of a local abbot. It is possible that the Abbot Ælfric of this charter is identical with the one who witnesses a charter in favour of Evesham in 1016 (K.C.D. 723), not mentioned by Dietrich, no doubt because Kemble marked it as doubtful. It is true that its list of witnesses starts unpromisingly, after the king's name, with Archbishop Dunstan (died 988); but apart from this name and the title of bishop, instead of archbishop, given to Lifing (Archbishop of Canterbury, 1013–20), the list fits the year 1016 so well that it can hardly be the work of a late forger. Probably the scribe of the cartulary has substituted Dunstan for Wulfstan (Archbishop of York, 1002–23) and therefore deprived Lifing of his correct title, realizing that there could not be two archbishops of Canterbury. If we make this adjustment, the list can be dated as after 1012, the date of the accession of Ælfsige to Winchester,[3] of Æthelstan to Hereford and of Brihtmer to the Abbey of Newminster, Winchester, and before the death of the Ealdorman Ælfric in 1016. All the other identifiable witnesses are in agreement with this date and the indiction is correct for the date given in the charter.

In both these charters the signature of Abbot Ælfric follows immediately on that of Abbot Wulfgar, and as both texts are from later cartularies, we may suspect confusion, as in the Eynsham charter, with the Abbot Ælfsige who occupies this position in a number of charters about this time. There is,

[1] K.C.D. 714.
[2] *Eynsham Cartulary*, ed. by H. E. Salter in *Oxford Historical Society Publications*, xlix, 19 ff.
[3] See A. J. Robertson, *Anglo-Saxon Charters*, p. 393.

however, one document attested by an Abbot Ælfric which was unknown to Dietrich, and this survives in a contemporary version and so is not open to the above explanation. It is a royal charter to Archbishop Ælfstan of Canterbury, dated 1018 and witnessed by three abbots, Ælfric being one.[1]

Thus it is established that an Abbot Ælfric was alive in 1018, and it is possible that he is the witness of the 1012 and 1016 charters; but it is very doubtful whether he can safely be identified with the homilist. Eynsham was not an important house, whose abbot would naturally attend the meetings of the witan. There are gaps in the lists of abbots of several abbeys, including Chertsey, Pershore, Muchelney and Milton Abbas, at this time. Athelney had an Abbot Ælfric about 1007,[2] and there is no reference to another abbot until mention is made of an Æthelwine about 1023.[3] Matthew Paris has an Ælfric in his history of the abbots of St Albans who is generally assumed to be merely a duplication of the earlier abbot of this name, who became Bishop of Ramsbury in 990 and later Archbishop of Canterbury;[4] if this second Ælfric ever existed, his abbacy must be placed about this time. In any case it seems clear that our knowledge of the succession of abbots in the early eleventh century is too fragmentary for any certain identification with the homilist to be made.

We are therefore thrown back on the internal evidence of the works. None of these can be dated with certainty later than the homily *In natale unius confessoris* which he dedicated to Æthelwold II, Bishop of Winchester from 1006 to 1012, for Dietrich's opinion that the second pastoral letter for Wulfstan was issued in 1014 or later is based on an error.[5] Most of Ælfric's work can be dated before 1007, the major works belonging mainly to the period before he came to Eynsham in 1005. His *De Vetere et Novo Testamento* was long enough after this event for him to have become closely acquainted with the Oxfordshire thane Sigwerd, and his letter to the Warwickshire thane Wulfgeat of Ilmington need not be as early as 1006, a date which depends on the identification of this Wulfgeat with Æthelred's favourite whose estates were forfeited in this year, an identification for which there is no evidence. But even if we give a late date to these two works, there is very little to fill the long period between the *Vita S. Athelwoldi* in 1006 and the normally accepted date of his death. We should have to suppose that he almost ceased from literary activity during the latter part of his life. It would, of course, be difficult to disprove this, but it seems at least as likely a hypothesis that Ælfric's death occurred many years earlier than has been assumed.

[1] *Ordnance Survey Facsimiles*, III, no. 39.
[2] *Somerset Record Society Publications*, XIV, 147.
[3] Ibid., XIV, 141. Cf. A. J. Robertson, op. cit., pp. 412 f.
[4] See *Victoria County History of Hertfordshire*, IV, 370 f.
[5] B. Fehr, *Die Hirtenbriefe Ælfrics* (*Bibliothek der angelsächsischen Prosa*, IX), pp. xlvi ff., lxviii.

(ii) *Gildas, Alcuin and Wulfstan*

In my edition of the *Sermo Lupi ad Anglos*,[1] I suggested that when Wulfstan refers to Gildas as his authority for the sinful state of the Britons at the time of the English invasion and draws a moral for his contemporaries, he owes a debt to Alcuin's letters such as the one published in Haddan and Stubbs, *Councils and Ecclesiastical Documents*, III, 510. There is, however, another of Alcuin's letters on the same theme which is certainly Wulfstan's immediate source. It is addressed to Archbishop Æthelheard and contains the following passage:

> Legitur vero in libro Gildi Brettonum sapientissimi, quod idem ipsi Brettones *propter rapinas et avaritiam principum, propter iniquitatem et iniustitiam iudicum, propter desidiam et pigritiam praedicationis episcoporum, propter luxoriam et malos mores populi patriam perdiderunt.* Caveamus haec eadem nostris temporibus vitia inolescere; quatenus benedictio divina nobis patriam conservet in prosperitate bona, quam nobis in sua misericordia perdonare dignata est.[2]

Wulfstan translates very freely, expands and alters to suit his purpose, but the debt remains clear, as will be seen on comparing the italicized passages:

> An þeodwita wæs on Brytta tidum, Gildas hatte, se awrat be heora misdædum, hu hy mid heora synnum swa oferlice swyþe God gegræmedan þæt he let æt nyhstan Engla here heora eard gewinnan ⁊ Brytta dugeþe fordon mid ealle. ⁊ þæt wæs geworden, þæs þe he sæde, *þurh ricra reaflac ⁊ þurh gitsunge wohgestreona, þurh leode unlaga ⁊ þurh wohdomas, þurh biscopa asolcennesse ⁊ þurh lyðre yrhðe Godes bydela, þe soþes geswugedan ealles to gelome ⁊ clumedan mid ceaflum þær hy scoldan clypian. þurh fulne eac folces gælsan ⁊ þurh oferfylla ⁊ mænigfealde synna heora eard hy forworhtan* ⁊ selfe hy forwurdan. Ac wutan don swa us þearf is, warnian us be swilcan.[3]

Alcuin's letter is contained in three manuscripts connected with Wulfstan,[4] Cotton Vespasian A. XIV and Corpus Christi College, Cambridge, 265 and 190, and in the last this particular sentence[5] is copied separately on another folio, to be soon followed by the Latin passage *De tribulationibus*,[6] probably used by Wulfstan for his *Sermo*. This suggests that he collected and recorded material for this homily as we know that he did for others.[7]

A point of interest arises out of the comparison of this Old English passage with its Latin source. I have quoted it from the version in Nero A. 1. The Hatton text, which most editors have taken as the basis of their text, has several phrases scattered through the homily which do not occur in other manuscripts. Thus in the passage under discussion it adds *þurh gelæredra regolbryce ⁊ ðurh læwedra lahbryce* after *þæs þe he sæde* and ⁊ *unsnotornesse*

[1] Methuen's Old English Library, 1939, p. 41 note.
[2] M.H.G., Abt. IV, *Epistolae Karolini Ævi*, II, 47.
[3] Ll. 184 ff. of my edition.
[4] See my 'Archbishop Wulfstan, Homilist and Statesman' in *Transactions of the Royal Historical Society*, 4th series, XXIV, 30 ff.
[5] See M. Bateson, *E.H.R.* x, 718. While the manuscript remains inaccessible one cannot be sure just how much was extracted.
[6] Ibid., p. 731.
[7] See K. Jost in *Anglia*, LVI, 265 ff.

after *þurh biscopa asolcennesse.* There is nothing equivalent in the Latin original, an indication that the additional matter does not go back to the author's first draft.[1]

OXFORD

[1] Miss D. Bethurum's article, 'Archbishop Wulfstan's Common-place Book' (*P.M.L.A.*, LVII, 916 ff.), reached me only when this article was at press.

XI

Archbishop Wulfstan, Homilist and Statesman[1]

When Wulfstan II, archbishop of York from 1002 and bishop of Worcester from 1002 to 1016, alias *Lupus episcopus*, died at York on 28 May 1023, his body was taken for burial to the monastery of Ely, in accordance with his wishes. From the twelfth-century historian of this abbey we get the only medieval account of the prelate,[2] a brief, and in some respects unreliable, account. Among other things, it states that miracles were worked at his tomb, but there is no hint elsewhere that Wulfstan had any special claims to sanctity. There was certainly never any question of canonisation; hence there was little motive for the writing of his life by his contemporaries or successors. When we consider how little we should know of the activities of Dunstan or Oswold if we had been denied the contemporary lives of these saints, it is perhaps not remarkable that political historians of the period refer to Wulfstan, if at all, merely as the author of a sermon, the famous *Sermo Lupi ad Anglos*,[3] revealing contemporary conditions in England, or as the consecrator of Cnut's church at Ashingdon. Even in ecclesiastical histories Wulfstan is given no prominent place. Some mention his appointment to York, some his refoundation of St. Peter's at Gloucester and his consecration of Ashingdon, none, except recently Professor Darlington, who calls him an ardent reformer,[4] suggest that he had any influence on the Anglo-Saxon Church of his time or later.

Yet, leaving aside as biased by private considerations the claims of the Ely historian, we find scattered references to the archbishop in the records of the period that suggest that he was not without influence on

[1] I wish to thank Professor B. Dickins for reading and criticising this article.

[2] *Liber Eliensis*, ed. E. O. Blake (Camden Third Series XCII), ii, cap. 87, pp. 155–7.

[3] See my edition of this text in Methuen's Old English Library, 3rd edn., 1963, to which subsequent references refer, unless otherwise stated.

[4] *E.H.R.*, li. 392.

affairs. Legal historians have, of course, noted that he is mentioned in connection with Ethelred's code issued at Enham, though they are guarded as to the precise nature of this connection. In general, however, the fact that we can to some extent reconstruct his life is due to his being an author as well as a churchman. The identification of him with the author of the *sermones Lupi*, first made by Wanley in 1705,[1] and since proved beyond any reasonable doubt,[2] is the starting-point for any real knowledge of his work and its significance. It is for this reason that I place the homilist before the statesman in the title of this paper, in which I propose to summarise what can be learnt about this prelate and to consider his place in the history of his time. Enough progress has been made in the last twenty years for it to be worth while to take stock of the results. A final estimate can be given only when we have critical editions of all the genuine homilies and of the work known as the *Institutes of Polity*, both of which are in the hands of excellent scholars, Miss Dorothy Bethurum and Professor Karl Jost.[3] It might have been possible to take the subject a little farther today if conditions did not deny one access to several manuscripts of primary importance in this investigation.[4]

Wulfstan might long ago have been given his proper position if Napier had brought out the volume of notes and introductions to his edition of 1883,[5] which contained all the homilies claimed for Wulfstan by Wanley, and a few others. It is quite clear that several homilies in Wanley's list are not by Wulfstan, and Napier showed in 1882[6] that only the two homilies that immediately follow the rubric *Incipiunt sermones Lupi episcopi* in all the three manuscripts in which it occurs, together with two others with separate rubrics ascribing them to

[1] In G. Hickes, *Liguarum Veterum Septentrionalium Thesaurus*, ii. 140 f.

[2] Despite the *Dictionary of National Biography*, which considers the identification made without 'any convincing reason'.

[3] These works have now appeared: *The Homilies of Wulfstan*, ed. Dorothy Bethurum, Oxford, 1957; *Die 'Institutes of Polity, Civil and Ecclesiastical'*, ed. Karl Jost (Swiss Studies in English 47), Berne, 1959.

[4] See my *Sermo Lupi ad Anglos*, pp. 17–37; Bethurum, *op. cit.*, pp. 24–49, 69–101; and work cited p. 47, n. 5 below.

[5] *Wulfstan: Sammlung der ihm zugeschriebenen Homilien nebst Untersuchungen über ihre Echtheit*, quoted in this article by the number of the homily.

[6] *Über die Werke des altenglischen Erzbischofs Wulfstan.*

Lupus, can be proved genuine by the evidence of rubrics. There are, however, several texts[1] in a style so similar to that of the 'four genuine homilies' that no one would doubt Wulfstan's authorship but for a theory that there were 'Wulfstan imitators'.

The 'Wulfstan style' is very distinctive and has been frequently described.[2] It is a forcible, trenchant style, pre-eminently suited for preaching. It uses a few simple rhythmical patterns and it obtains a strong emphasis, chiefly by the frequent use of intensifying phrases such as *mid ealle* 'entirely', *georne* 'eagerly', *ealles to swiðe* 'all too greatly'. It possesses a characteristic vocabulary and syntactical peculiarities. Lists of words, often arranged in pairs, are a frequent feature, as, for example, in this passage from a homily based on a chapter of Leviticus: 'Then to your harm shall poverty and misery increase, strife and persecution, devastation and famine; and your hearts shall be greatly afraid and the might of your enemies shall grow grievously strong, and, driven asunder, terrified, you will often flee as cowards from a little band. And bad harvests shall oft come upon you through storms, and theft and pestilence shall bring you low, and you shall be given into the power of enemies, who will impoverish and greatly oppress you';[3] or in the descriptions of hell that are not rare in his work: 'There is everlasting fire cruelly stirred up, there is everlasting terror, there is everlasting pain, there is sorrowing and lamentation, and ever unceasing complaint, there is moaning and groaning, there is every misery and the throng of all devils.'[4] Some of these traits would be easy to imitate, and, if Wulfstan was the forceful person I believe him to have been, it would be strange if he exercised no influence on his followers. Every text with a sprinkling of the phrases mentioned above need not be his.[5] But when

[1] Including the so-called pastoral letter (Napier, xix–xxii), which begins in one version 'Wulfstan archebisceop'.

[2] See my edition of the *Sermo Lupi ad Anglos*, pp. 17 f., and the works cited, *ibid.*, p. 17, n. 3.

[3] Napier, xxviii (p. 133).

[4] *Ibid.*, xxii (p. 114). It is not possible in translating to give the effect obtained by rhyme and alliteration, e.g., *sorgung 7 sargung 7 á singal heof; wanung 7 granung*, etc.

[5] Even the Lord's Prayer is not proof against their insertion: one Old English version (Napier, xxvi) is equivalent to 'Lead us not into temptation all too greatly'.

we find works possessing not only the obvious characteristics of his style but also the minor syntactical mannerisms and the preferences in vocabulary, it is more probable that Wulfstan himself is the author. This can hardly be doubted when the work in question reveals an independence of mind incompatible with slavish imitation in style, or when its influence on later laws and canons is so strong as to suggest that it emanated from a person of high standing.[1] Wulfstan had a reputation as a stylist already by 1002, for an anonymous ecclesiastic, writing to him in Latin no later than this year,[2] speaks of 'the most sweet sagacity of your eloquence and the prolixity as well as the profundity of your elegantly arranged narrative'. As he uses Wulfstan's attainments as his excuse for declining to undertake some translation himself, he apparently did not think them easy to imitate.

An article by Professor Jost, published in 1932,[3] has greatly advanced Wulfstan studies. It not only establishes the authenticity of two important homilies, *De baptismate* and *De cristianitate*,[4] but it throws light on Wulfstan's scholarship and methods. For each of these homilies is based on a series of extracts[5] from Latin canonists, and, whereas it had hitherto been assumed that the collection was made by someone else for the homilist's use, Jost points out that the translator reveals familiarity with the original works, sometimes translating parts of the contexts of the selected passages. This suggests that he had made the compilation himself, and for these two homilies alone he read works of Theodulf of Orleans, Jesse of Amiens, Amalarius of Metz, Atto of Vercelli, St. Augustine, as well as Alcuin's *Liber de virtutibus et vitiis*, the Benedictine Rule and the *Poenitentiale Pseudo-Ecgberti*. In one place in the homily *De cristianitate*, instead of translating a simple passage of his original,[6] the author replaces it by a quotation from another work in the Wulfstan style, the unpublished *De regula canonicorum*, a translation of a chapter of

[1] See Jost, *Anglia*, lvi. 305.

[2] See my note in *E.H.R.*, lii. 460 ff.

[3] 'Einige Wulfstantexte und ihre Quellen', *Anglia*, lvi. 265 ff.

[4] Napier, v and x. Jost has found an earlier version of v in C.C.C.C. MS. 302, which is closer to the Latin original.

[5] Napier, iv and ix.

[6] I.e., *seniores honorate, iuniores diligite*. See Jost, *op. cit.*, p. 287.

Amalarius.[1] As the meaning is exactly the same, it is difficult to see why a different author should have troubled to do this; and this fact, taken together with strong stylistic evidence, makes it extremely probable that the *De regula canonicorum* is Wulfstan's work. Jost goes on to show that this text can hardly be divorced in authorship from the so-called 'Canons enacted under King Edgar'[2] which use the same source with the same omissions and the same explanatory addition. Though neither text is derived from the other, both have Wulfstan phrases. The canons survive in two manuscripts perhaps from Worcester, and only one describes them as *Eadgares geradnes*. As Ælfric's pastoral letter for Wulfsige (993–1001) has been used, this rubric is an error.[3] We may notice that it is these canons that are the main reason for Stubbs's statement, 'The ecclesiastical laws of the period [i.e. Dunstan's time] are of the same constructive and progressive stamp.'[4] It seems that we must give the credit to Wulfstan, not, with Stubbs, to Dunstan.

This picture of Wulfstan as a man well versed in canonistic literature, excerpting carefully from Latin authors before writing his vernacular sermons, can be strengthened by noting the relationship between a series of Latin extracts from Isaiah and Jeremiah and his homily VI, between a similar series from Leviticus and homily XXVIII, between a collection of references to Antichrist[5] and homily XII.[6] Work on Wulfstan's sources is still in its infancy. To those mentioned by Jost can be added a sermon of Abbo of St. Germain[7] and the letters of Alcuin.[8]

[1] Now edited by Bethurum, *op. cit.*, pp. 192 f.

[2] Viz., the first of the five texts printed by Thorpe under this title and the only one with the slightest claim to it, i.e. the rubric in one manuscript.

[3] Wulfstan himself seems to have looked back on Edgar's reign as a golden age of law and order. See VIII Atr 37 and ASC 975D. Perhaps there was a tendency in later times to attribute undated codes to his reign.

[4] *Memorials of St. Dunstan* (R.S., 1874), p. cvi.

[5] Napier, xi.

[6] On pp. 13 f. of my first edition of the *Sermo Lupi ad Anglos*, I suggested that these homilies were authentic, judging by style alone. Since then, I have found their Latin sources in manuscripts otherwise connected with Wulfstan.

[7] Cf. *infra*, pp. 47 f., 50.

[8] Cf. *infra*, p. 59.

An examination of early manuscripts also adds to our knowledge of Wulfstan's learning and interests. As early as 1874 Stubbs[1] noted that Vespasian A. xiv contained a Latin poem of panegyric addressed to Wulfstan, under whose patronage the book had been written. No one troubled to follow up this information. It gives us definite proof of Wulfstan's interest in manuscript compilation, and the manuscript in question contains texts that tally with his interests as we know them from other sources, for example the canons of the Synod of *Celchyth* of 816,[2] of the Council of Hertford,[3] various papal letters, the Constitutions of Odo[4] and several letters of Alcuin, including one which Wulfstan uses in his *Sermo Lupi ad Anglos*.[5] A manuscript hitherto unknown to Wulfstan scholars[6] is the Copenhagen MS., Gl. kgl. S. 1595 (4to), of the early eleventh century. In addition to a group of penitential letters written by or addressed to Wulfstan, it contains the complete version of a homily of Abbo of St. Germain, of which Wulfstan used an extract for his homily XXXII;[7] the series of Latin excerpts above mentioned that are the sources of homilies V, VI and XII; the two pastoral letters written for Wulfstan by Ælfric; two copies of the chapter of Amalarius which is the source of Wulfstan's *De regula canonicorum*;[8] and several Latin texts that occur also in a Worcester manuscript (C.C.C.C. 265).[9] The only Old English in the manuscript is a short passage in the Wulfstan style,[10] and I have Mr. Ker's permission to mention his discovery

[1] *Op. cit.*, p. liv.

[2] A. W. Haddan and W. Stubbs, *Councils and Ecclesiastical Documents relating to Great Britain and Ireland*, iii. 579–84.

[3] *Ibid.*, iii. 118–21.

[4] D. Wilkins, *Concilia Magnae Britanniae et Hiberniae*, i. 212–14.

[5] See *infra*, p. 59. On this and other manuscripts connected with Wulfstan, see my article 'Wulfstan at York', *Franciplegius: Medieval and Linguistic Studies in Honor of F. P. Magoun, Jr.*, eds. J. B. Bessinger, Jr., and R. P. Creed (New York, 1965), pp. 214–31; also works cited, p. 43, n. 4 *supra*.

[6] I owe my knowledge of it to Mr. Neil Ker, who pointed out that it contained the penitential letters mentioned below.

[7] Cf. *infra*, p. 50.

[8] The extract is contained in C.C.C.C. 265.

[9] See next paragraph.

[10] Published, not quite accurately, by F. Holthausen in *Zeitschrift für deutsches Altertum*, xxxiv (Neue Folge, xxii), 228, repeated by Karl Jost, *Wulfstanstudien* (Swiss Studies in English 23, Berne, 1950), pp. 268 f.

that this is in the same hand as the poem in Vespasian A. xiv addressed to Wulfstan. There can be little doubt that the manuscript was compiled for Wulfstan's use or by his instructions. In addition to works already mentioned, it has several more homilies by Abbo of St. Germain, Amalarius's *Ecloge de officio misse*, another treatise on the mass and some homilies as yet unidentified, apparently mainly concerned with practical instruction rather than abstruse theology.

It has long been recognised that C.C.C.C. 265, called by Miss Bateson 'a kind of theological commonplace book specially intended for a bishop's use',[1] is a Worcester book. It shares a number of texts with the Copenhagen manuscript, sometimes in the same order.[2] Among them is the source of Wulfstan's *De regula canonicorum*, and the group of penitential letters. Mr. Ker assigns this manuscript to the mid-eleventh century, later therefore than Wulfstan's episcopate, but as, in addition to the texts mentioned above, it has the source of homily V and a continental canon which is probably the source of a chapter in the laws of Ethelred issued under Wulfstan's influence,[3] it appears to be at least partially made up of material collected at Worcester during his time.[4] Its other contents include letters of Alcuin, a large collection of canons and penitentials from various sources, and in particular the work known as the *Excerptiones Pseudo-Ecgberti*. One secular code written in Old English and Latin appears among these items of purely ecclesiastical interest. This is Edgar's fourth code, but its inclusion ceases to appear strange when we remember that it was issued on account of the plague of 962, this misfortune being attributed to the people's sins. It enforces a stricter payment of Church dues. As its tone closely resembles much of Wulfstan's writing, this code may well have had a special interest for him.[5]

[1] *E.H.R.*, x. 712. See D. Bethurum, 'Archbishop Wulfstan's Commonplace Book', *P.M.L.A.*, lvii (1942), 916–29.

[2] Like the Copenhagen manuscript, it has Ælfric's two Latin pastoral letters immediately followed by the source of Wulfstan's homily *De baptismate* and a treatise on the Mass. The two manuscripts share also Amalarius, *Ecloge de officio misse*.

[3] *Infra*, pp. 52 f.

[4] Or at York; see the article cited, p. 47, n. 5.

[5] It is perhaps the interest taken in this code by Wulfstan which has preserved it for us, for the only other manuscript is Nero E. i, probably from Worcester.

Several of the texts in this manuscript, including the *Excerptiones Pseudo-Ecgberti*, though in a different version, appear also in Nero A. i, a manuscript containing many Anglo-Saxon laws and some of Wulfstan's homilies. One of these is a version of the *Sermo Lupi ad Anglos*, annotated, according to Mr. Ker, by the hand he has detected in the Copenhagen manuscript and in Vespasian A. xiv, as we have already seen, and he would date this hand as early eleventh-century.[1] This supports Keller's opinion that the manuscript is from Worcester, the most likely scriptorium to have produced three manuscripts all with some connection with Wulfstan.[2]

Another manuscript that shares many texts with those under discussion is C.C.C.C. 190, given by Bishop Leofric to Exeter. Fehr considers it so closely connected with Ælfric that he would bring it from Eynsham.[3] His strongest reason is that it contains a Latin text in the abbreviated form in which Ælfric used it when writing his second pastoral letter for Wulfstan. But on the other hand, it has the shortened form of the Benedictine Office which is the immediate source of the Old English version in the Wulfstan style[4] and Fehr explains the presence of this in an Ælfric manuscript by suggesting that Ælfric had supplied Wulfstan with this curtailed version. Fehr seems not to have

[1] It used to be dated late eleventh-century.

[2] I now consider York equally possible; see p. 47, n. 5.

[3] *Englische Studien*, xlvi. 337 ff. His other arguments are not very cogent. The manuscript contains Ælfric's pastoral letter for Wulfsige as well as those for Wulfstan, but so does the undoubtedly Worcester manuscript Junius 121. It has a text made up of passages from Athelwold's *Regularis concordia* and Amalarius, the authorities combined by Ælfric when writing for monks at Eynsham. This is an argument for the authorship of the work, but not for the provenance of the manuscript, for the compilation for the Eynsham monks has been preserved only in a Worcester manuscript, C.C.C.C. 265, and if Ælfric sent a copy of the one work, he may easily have done the same with this one. Since writing this article Fehr has realised that the version of the *Excerptiones Pseudo-Ecgberti* in C.C.C.C. 190 is not the one used by Ælfric. See his *Die Hirtenbriefe Ælfrics in altenglischer und lateinischer Fassung*, p. cv. This greatly weakens his case for an Eynsham origin for this manuscript.

[4] See E. Feiler, *Das Benediktiner-Offizium. . . . Ein Beitrag zur Wulfstanfrage* (Anglistische Forschungen 4), Fehr, *Englische Studien*, xlvi. 337 ff., and *The Benedictine Office*, ed. J. M. Ure, Edinburgh, 1957.

noticed that the manuscript has also the single sentence from one of Alcuin's letters that Wulfstan translated in his *Sermo Lupi ad Anglos*,[1] followed by a passage *De tribulationibus*, a probable source of this homily, and also the extract from Abbo's sermon *De coena domini* translated by Wulfstan in homily XXXII,[2] the complete sermon being in the Copenhagen manuscript. If Fehr's theory is right, we can only assume that Ælfric made a practice of supplying Wulfstan with catenae ready for his use. But, taking into consideration what we now know of Wulfstan's activity in excerpting passages from Latin authors, and remembering that he had access to the complete works in question in Vespasian A. xiv and the Copenhagen manuscript, it is surely more probable that the manuscript under discussion is based on a collection made at Worcester, and that the shortened version of the source for Ælfric's pastoral letter was sent to him by Wulfstan when he commissioned the letter. Something similar may have happened with regard to the *Excerptiones Pseudo-Ecgberti*, as Fehr once believed,[3] but this cannot be determined until a detailed study has been made of this text. We have, however, evidence that Wulfstan did once send to another ecclesiastic some Latin passages for translation, for the letter quoted above[4] is a refusal to undertake such a task. Wulfstan may have repeated this action in his dealings with Ælfric. Intercourse between Ælfric and Wulfstan is shown also by their both using the decalogue in the form in which it occurs in the Boulogne-sur-Mer MS. 63, Wulfstan in his *De cristianitate*,[5] Ælfric in his second pastoral for Wulfstan.[6] This manuscript has the only surviving copy of Ælfric's letter[7] in reply to a lost letter of Wulfstan's, but of course either sender or recipient might have put this on record.[8] Other contents show some connection

[1] Cf. *infra*, p. 59.

[2] Wulfstan does not use the first paragraph (as printed in Migne, *Patrologia Latina*, cxxxii. 764 ff.), but begins with the section *Vere, fratres charissimi, hoc debetis scire unde fuit incoeptum hoc exemplum*, i.e. the passage in C.C.C.C. 190.

[3] *Englische Studien*, xlvi. 344. Cf. *infra*, p. 51.

[4] Cf. *supra*, p. 45.

[5] Jost, *Anglia*, lvi. 278 f.

[6] Fehr, *Die Hirtenbriefe Ælfrics . . .*, p. xi.

[7] *Ibid.*, pp. 222–7.

[8] On the relations of Wulfstan with Ælfric, see my *Sermo Lupi ad Anglos*, pp. 22 f.; P. Clemoes, 'The Old English Benedictine Office, Corpus Christi

with the Worcester group of manuscripts, but at this stage of the investigation it is impossible to decide which way round the influence was exerted. This examination of the manuscripts makes no claim to be exhaustive, but I think that enough has emerged to show great activity in the compiling of manuscripts at Worcester under Wulfstan's influence. To some extent an answer is provided to Miss Bateson's questions:[1] 'Who collected these manuscripts? Where were they collected?'

In view of all this, I cannot agree with Fehr's estimate of Wulfstan in the introduction to his edition of Ælfric's pastoral letters.[2] He feels that the answers given in the private letter, which Ælfric wrote in reply to one from Wulfstan, imply considerable ignorance on the part of the questioner, and he withdraws a previous suggestion that Ælfric owed his knowledge of the *Excerptiones Pseudo-Ecgberti* to Wulfstan with the statement: 'the monk or abbot could not learn much from the archbishop'. It must be remembered that Wulfstan's letter does not survive and we do not know for what purpose he wrote, whether asking for information on matters of which he was ignorant or for support against the views of opponents. Most of the answers relate to ecclesiastical practices current in England though forbidden by the canons and we need not assume abysmal ignorance on Wulfstan's part if he consulted Ælfric on the precise attitude of the canons. Not all the subjects are of an elementary nature;[3] to some queries Ælfric replies that he has never read anything relating to them; to one query, on the number of times a day a priest may celebrate mass, he can refer only to the usage of his teacher, Bishop Athelwold.

Although Wulfstan was evidently active in religious reform by his

---

College, Cambridge, MS. 190, and the relations between Ælfric and Wulfstan: A Reconsideration', *Anglia*, lxxviii (1966), 265–83. On Boulogne-sur-Mer MS. 63, see Enid Raynes in *Med. Aev.*, xxvi (1957), 65–73.

[1] *Op. cit.*, p. 713. [2] P. cix.

[3] The letter deals with a range of subjects, the bars to entry into the priesthood, the limitation of the consecrating of the chrism to Holy Thursday, the abuse by which wine is mixed with water at baptism, the participation of the clergy in battle, etc. The passage in which Ælfric discusses the lawfulness of Caesarian section must have some connection with the Ely tradition that Wulfstan was born in this way.

own studies, by encouragement of manuscript compilation, by the issue of a rule of life for canons and a code for the priesthood in general, by the circulation of pastoral letters for the clergy of his diocese and by the preaching of homilies to the laity, he had energy left for other activities. His influence on secular legislation must now be considered. Ethelred's code promulgated at Enham in 1008, which has come down to us in two variant Old English versions[1] and in a Latin paraphrase, is said in the last to have been issued at the instigation of the archbishops Ælfheah and Wulfstan. Freeman, who had a high opinion of this code, arbitrarily ignores Wulfstan's influence when he says: 'The whole tone is at once pious and patriotic; the piety is of a kind which, while it strictly enforces every ecclesiastical observance by no means forgets the weightier matters of the law, judgment, mercy and truth. In all this we can hardly fail to trace the hand of good Archbishop Ælfheah.'[2] The Latin paraphrase concludes with the statement: 'I, Wulfstan, archbishop by the grace of the disposing God, set down in writing these same things,[3] for the memory of those who come after and also for the benefit of those of the present day and those to come, spurred on namely by the love of God and my neighbour.' It has been suggested that this statement refers to the Latin version alone, but this seems unnecessary caution when the vernacular codes are, like all subsequent codes of Ethelred, undoubtedly in the Wulfstan style: a style already fully developed in the original version of homily V and in homily X, both of which are earlier than the code. Moreover, the sources used include the so-called Canons of Edgar, probably, as we have seen above,[4] a work of Wulfstan's, and the so-called Laws of Edward and Guthrum, which I have suggested elsewhere to be another of his works;[5] also the Capitula of Theodulf of Orleans, a text used by Wulfstan on another occasion,[6] and probably a continental canon against the too ready application of the death penalty which occurs

[1] Ethelred's Vth and VIth codes. On these and the Latin version, see K. Sisam, *Studies in the History of Old English Literature*, pp. 278–87.

[2] *Norman Conquest*, i. 368.

[3] I.e. the edicts which all the *optimates* have sworn to keep.

[4] Cf. *supra*, p. 46.

[5] *E.H.R.*, lvi. 1 ff.

[6] See Jost, *Anglia, lvi.* 293 f.

only in the Worcester manuscript discussed above, C.C.C.C. 265.[1] The great use made by Wulfstan of this code in his later work must also be considered. His most famous homily, the *Sermo Lupi ad Anglos*, is largely based on it.[2] Unless we allow that Wulfstan was the author of the Old English code we are forced to assume that he set his name to a Latin version of a vernacular code written by someone else in his style, and later used his imitator's work for his own impressive homily. This is not very probable and it seems therefore, that if, with Freeman, we wish to attribute the 'weightier matters of the law' to Archbishop Ælfheah, we must nevertheless allow Wulfstan credit for the language in which it is couched and familiarity with the sources from which it is drawn. A rather similar employment of Wulfstan to draw up a legal document is on record in a charter[3] where, after a transaction has taken place 'with King Ethelred's leave and the cognisance of Archbishop Ælfheah and Archbishop Wulfstan and all the councillors who were alive at that time in England', it is stated that 'the king commanded Archbishop Wulfstan to draw up a charter to this effect'.

Though 1008 is the first year in which Wulfstan is mentioned by name in connection with legislation, I believe, for reasons that I have

[1] The sentiment has not been expressed in general terms in previous legislation. The English code does not translate the Latin, but gives a summary in its own words, and borrowing is therefore more difficult to prove. In my opinion there is enough similarity to make it highly probable. The most relevant passage reads: '*Castigandi sunt enim rei diris flagris vel vinculis et in carcerem mittendi sunt et trabibus includendi et plumis piceque perfusi ad spectaculum publicum in cippum mitti debent et diversis penis cruciandi sunt* ne anime pro quibus ipse dominus passus est, in eterna pena dispereant.' The Old English statute (V Atr 3, 3. 1) reads: '7 *ures hlafordes gerædnes* 7 *his witena is, þæt man Cristene men for ealles to lytlum to deaðe ne fordeme; ac elles geræde man friðlice steora folce to þearfe*, 7 ne forspille for litlum Godes handgeweorc 7 his agenne ceap þe he deore gebohte', in which *friðlice steora* seems to summarise the various alternatives of the Latin canon. Wulfstan has already given a closer rendering of the last phrase of the Latin in the previous statute: *þæt man þa sawla ne forfare þe Crist mid his agenum life gebohte*. For the complete canon, see M. Bateson, *op. cit.*, pp. 726 f.

[2] See pp. 36 f. of my edition of this homily.

[3] KCD 898; A. J. Robertson, *Anglo-Saxon Charters*, lxxxiii.

stated in full elsewhere,[1] that he had already composed a code of regulations concerning ecclesiastical observance in the Danelaw, or in part of it. To this code he wrote a preamble explaining that the regulations had been in force since the earliest days of the Danish settlement, being agreed on first by Alfred and Guthrum, and afterwards by Edward and Guthrum. This is the document known as the 'Laws of Edward and Guthrum' and frequent use is made of it by the codes of Ethelred written in the Wulfstan style, and also by those of Cnut. Previous to 1008 no code betrays any knowledge of it. His work continued to influence legal writings in the reign of Cnut, whose codes share many passages with the Wulfstan homilies.[2]

Wulfstan's authorship has been claimed by Jost[3] for the 'poems' in the Anglo-Saxon Chronicle 959 D E and 975 D (where E has substituted a prose summary). There are the familiar Wulfstan phrases, e.g. in 959, *hit godode georne*, 'things improved greatly', *swa him þearf wæs* 'as was needful for him', *Godes lage lufode* 'he loved God's law'; while in 975 there is a Wulfstan ring about *Godes wiþærsacan Godes lage bræcon* 'God's adversaries broke God's laws'. This is, however, clearest in the passage: *7 wydewan bestryptan oft and gelome, 7 fela unrihta 7 yfelra unlaga arysan up siððan, 7 áá æfter þam hit yfelode swiðe,* 'and they plundered widows oft and again, and many wrongs and evil injustices rose up afterwards, and it grew greatly worse ever after'.[4] The similarity recognised by Earle[5] between the 959 passage and Ælfric's Book of Judges is almost certainly borrowing on the part of the Chronicle, not vice versa. Whether these passages, summaries of the reigns of Edgar and Edward the Martyr respectively, are due to an imitator or to our

[1] *E.H.R.*, lvi. 1 ff.

[2] In two articles, *E.H.R.*, lxiii (1948), 433–52, and lxix (1955), 72–85, I have demonstrated that Wulfstan drafted Cnut's laws.

[3] *Anglia*, xlvii. 105 f.

[4] I print as prose, since phrases of an approximately equal length, with almost a verse rhythm, are a feature of Wulfstan's style. See A. McIntosh, 'Wulfstan's Prose', *Proc. Brit. Acad.*, xxxv (1949), 109–42. Jost prints *Institutes of Polity* in verse lines. Einenkel, in *Anglia*, vii. Anzeiger (1884), pp. 200 ff., suggested that the *Sermo Lupi ad Anglos* is a poem.

[5] C. Plummer and J. Earle, *Two of the Saxon Chronicles Parallel*, ii. 152 (hereafter cited as Plummer).

author himself, they cannot be earlier than the extreme end of the tenth century. If Plummer's suggestion that the original of D and E was by this time in the Worcester diocese be accepted, this addition was more likely to be made at Worcester itself than at Evesham;[1] but in view of the close connection between Worcester and York, it is not necessary, in order to account for matters of Worcester interest, to assume that this version had left the north. If still in the north, this Wulfstan insertion speaks for York in preference to Ripon.[2]

Having considered the evidence for Wulfstan's varied activities, we are in a better position to reconstruct his career. Of his early training nothing is known. William of Malmesbury's opinion that he was not a monk[3] is offset by the Ely historian's statement that he was,[4] and Florence of Worcester[5] gives him the title of abbot in 1002, and this, though incorrect at this date, may have been true at an earlier period. In later life Wulfstan showed great interest in the Fenland abbeys and perhaps this implies some early connection with the region. Our first clear evidence about him is his consecration to the see of London in 996.[6] As bishop of London he issued penitential letters, which he later included in a small collection of such letters intended to be used as formulae.[7] It is at this time that he received the letter from an anonymous ecclesiastic refusing to translate some *archana* from Old English at the bishop's request, being debarred by the thought of Wulfstan's eloquence.[8] I have suggested elsewhere[9] that some of the eschatological homilies, regarding the end of the world as imminent, may be what

[1] See also the strong case for a Worcester rather than an Evesham origin of the later part of D made by Sir Ivor Atkins, *E.H.R.*, lv. 8 ff. His case against a York origin is less cogent.

[2] See *The Peterborough Chronicle*, ed. D. Whitelock (Early English Manuscripts in Facsimile, iv, Copenhagen 1954), 29 f.; *The Anglo-Saxon Chronicle: A Revised Translation*, ed. D. Whitelock, with D. C. Douglas and S. I. Tucker (London, 1961), pp. xiv–xvi.

[3] *Gesta pontificum* (R.S. 1870), p. 250.

[4] *Historia Eliensis, loc. cit.*

[5] Ed. B. Thorpe, i. 156.

[6] ASC 996 F. On the identity of this bishop of London with the homilist and later archbishop, see my article in *E.H.R.*, lii. 460 ff.

[7] See *supra*, pp. 47 f. The group occurs also in the Bodleian MS Barlow 37, fo. 12.

[8] See *supra*, pp. 45, 50.

[9] *Sermo Lupi ad Anglos*, 1st edn., pp. 12 f.

obtained him this reputation; as, for example, homily XII: 'for the greatest evil shall come upon mankind, when Antichrist himself shall come, that ever has been in the world; and it seems to us that it is very close to that time, for this world from day to day grows ever worse and worse. Now is there a great need for all God's messengers that they often warn God's people against that terror which is about to come on mankind, lest they be taken unawares and then too quickly ensnared by the devil.'[1]

In the penitential letters, Wulfstan calls himself *Lupus*, translating the first element of his name, and this name is used in the rubrics to some of his homilies. As he is never given it elsewhere, and as he always signs charters as *Wulfstan(us)*, I am inclined to think that it is a nom de plume rather than a nickname, and I suspect him, in using a literary *alias* at all, to be copying the Carolingian group of scholars, for he certainly was familiar with Alcuin's letters. I have sometimes wondered whether he could have had any thought of Lupus of Ferrières in his mind, but he is unlikely to have known enough about this author to have noticed the similarity of their interests.[2]

It is after his translation in 1002 to the combined sees of Worcester and York that we have evidence of great reforming zeal on Wulfstan's part, zeal no doubt occasioned by his realisation of the laxity of his northern province. He corresponded with Ælfric on canonistic matters and commissioned him to write two pastoral letters for him and to translate them into Old English. One of them he rewrote in his more emphatic style. He translated Amalarius *De regula canonicorum* and for the secular clergy he issued the so-called 'Canons of Edgar'. He addressed a general exhortation to the 'thanes, ecclesiastical and lay, entrusted to his direction in spiritual concerns', a document often called his pastoral letter.[3] His 'Laws of Edward and Guthrum' are concerned with breaches of church regulations primarily in a Danish area; and probably some homilies of clear exposition of the essentials of the

[1] Napier, p. 79.

[2] Even if he knew of the manuscript of German customary law which Lupus wrote for Count Eberhard of Friuli, or of his composition of synodal acts, we have no evidence for Wulfstan's own legal activities as early as his use of the name Lupus.

[3] Napier, xix–xxii.

Christian faith,[1] with tirades against heathenism, belong to this period. It would be in line with his other activities if the Law of the Northumbrian Priests had been drawn up at his instigation.[2] In 1008 he drew up the statutes issued by the king and witan and his influence lies behind all the later codes of this reign. Among them is an ordinance[3] enjoining a three-day fast on the nation, which is closely connected with a homily surviving in two versions.[4] This, which amplifies the code and illustrates divine retribution from the Old Testament, reads like a sermon preached about the time of the promulgation of the ordinance. A similar attitude is shown in homilies based on the denunciatory passages in the prophets and Leviticus, and the culmination is the *Sermo Lupi ad Anglos*, preached after Ethelred's exile, and probably in 1014, as is shown by the passage: 'and a very great treachery it is also in the world that a man should betray his lord to death or drive him, living, from the land; and both have happened in this land: Edward was betrayed and then slain and afterwards burned, and Ethelred was driven out of his land'.[5] Wulfstan's disapproval of the acceptance of Swegn is clear, and it would be interesting to know what action he took during the few months while Swegn was king in Northumbria. All that can be ascertained is that he was in York within a fortnight of Swegn's death, for he consecrated Ælfwig bishop of London there on 16 February.[6]

From time to time, we get glimpses of Wulfstan's participation in public affairs.[7] Like other bishops of Worcester, he issues leases of the estates of the see, one even after Leofsige had been appointed to succeed him in 1016. He appears as legatee in two wills and as executor in one of them. In 1012 the monks at Sherborne asked him to be their advocate before the king when the ætheling Edmund wished to obtain one of

[1] E.g. Napier, ii and iii.

[2] See D. Whitelock, *English Historical Documents* c. *500–1042*, pp. 434 f. and the article cited on p. 47, n. 5.

[3] Ethelred's VIIth code.

[4] Napier, xxxv and xxxvi.

[5] Ll. 75–80. See also note to ll, 79 ff.

[6] ASC 1014 D. Homily xxxvii, a sermon preached at the consecration of a bishop, may belong to this occasion or to his consecration of Æthelnoth as archbishop of Canterbury in 1020 or of Edmund as bishop of Durham about the same year.

[7] See *Sermo Lupi ad Anglos*, pp. 8–14.

their estates, a fact which supports other evidence for his influence with the king. He consecrated Cnut's church at Ashingdon in 1020 and consecrated Æthelnoth as archbishop of Canterbury, writing to Cnut to inform him that he had done so. He placed monks in the monastery of St. Peter at Gloucester, according to the cartulary of the abbey, in 1022.

Enough remains on record of this prelate for us to see him as a man of fiery zeal who, convinced that the misfortunes of his country were a retribution for sin, strove by all means to bring about reform, not confining himself to impassioned denunciation, though of this he was a master. He toiled to improve the standard of learning and morality of the clergy and to bring all classes to an understanding of the Christian faith and a due observance of the laws of the Church, and to put an end to the abuses of contemporary life.

It was a misfortune that Ethelred's reign produced no secular leader of Wulfstan's calibre who could have followed up this religious and moral reform with strong measures for repelling the invader and keeping internal order. The principles stated in the codes composed by Wulfstan are excellent, and agree too closely to the sentiments of his homilies for us to accept Freeman's assumption that Ælfheah is alone responsible.[1] If at times they read more like a treatise on legal principles than a code of statutes, as, for example, 'but every deed shall be carefully distinguished and judgment meted out in proportion to the offence, as shall be justifiable in the sight of God and acceptable in the eyes of men',[2] or if there is sometimes a note of rather vague appeal, as when, after listing crimes including 'shameful frauds and foul adulteries, and horrible perjuries and devilish deeds such as murders and homicides, thefts and robberies, covetousness and greed, etc.'[3] it continues lamely, 'and lo, let it be clearly understood that all such things are to be censured and not approved',[4] it is only fair to note also that the code can be explicit enough about the penalties where new law is

[1] For example, I take it that in referring to the mercy shown in this code Freeman is thinking chiefly of the attempt to stop the slave trade (V Atr 2, VI. 9) and to limit the application of the death penalty (*supra*, pp. 52 f). The first subject cccurs in the *Sermo Lupi ad Anglos*, the second comes from a continental canon preserved at Worcester in a manuscript with other Wulfstan sources.

[2] VI Atr. 10. 2. [3] *Ibid.*, 28. 2 f. [4] *Ibid.*, 29.

being created, as in the statute on desertion from the army,[1] or on plotting against the king's life.[2]

In holding that the Viking raids were a divine retribution, Wulfstan is taking the same stand as Alcuin had done. In one passage on this theme he is actually translating from a letter of Alcuin's: 'There was a historian in the time of the Britons, called Gildas, who wrote about their misdeeds, how by their sins they so excessively angered God that finally he allowed the army of the English to conquer their land and entirely destroy the flower of the Britons. And that came about, as he said, through robbery by the powerful and through greed for wrongful gains, through the lawlessness of the people and through false judgments, through the slackness and base cowardice of God's messengers, who kept silent about the truth all too often, and mumbled with their jaws where they should have cried aloud. Also through the foul wantonness of the people and through gluttony and manifold sins they destroyed their country and themselves they perished.'[3] In other places also there are signs of Alcuin's influence.[4] If Wulfstan took up a purely ecclesiastical attitude to the problems of his time, this would have been in accord with a body of contemporary opinion; but the terms in which Ælfric's letter to him deprecates any interference by a bishop in secular affairs imply that Wulfstan held a different point of view. Ælfric says: 'take heed, lest perchance it is said to you by Christ: who constituted you judge of thieves or robbers?'[5] And a little later: 'and Paul said: no soldier of God is to involve himself in secular concerns'. We cannot now know whether Wulfstan paid heed to this and kept himself aloof from secular administration, or whether he strove for reform in this also, but, faced with the inertia and corruption of the lay magnates, worked without any noticeable result during Ethelred's reign.

[1] V Atr. 28. [2] *Ibid.*, 30.

[3] *Sermo Lupi ad Anglos*, ll. 184 ff. Cf. Alcuin to Archbishop Æthelheard, M.G.H., Abt. iv, *Epistolae Karolini Ævi*, ii. 47. The letter is contained in full in C.C.C.C. MSS. 190, 265, and in Vespasian A. xiv, and the sentence in question is entered separately on fo. 139 of C.C.C.C. MS. 190; see *supra*, p. 50.

[4] For example, he frequently stresses the cowardice of bishops who do not preach to the people of their sins, using the texts quoted by Alcuin again and again when writing to contemporary bishops: *clama et ne cesses; exalta quasi tuba vocem tuam; canes muti non valentes latrare.* [5] Fehr, *op. cit.*, p. 226.

In conclusion, we may turn to the estimate of later generations. In the west midlands, he left no good reputation. Worcester cartularies call him *impius*, *reprobus*, and one accuses him of having robbed the monks.[1] William of Malmesbury speaks rather slightingly of him. The monks of Worcester may have thought that he subordinated their interests to those of his northern see. There is at any rate no record of any personal aggrandisement at their expense. One of his charters, it is true, leases a Worcester estate to his brother, but Oswold had settled a whole series of relations on the lands of the see without any aspersions being cast on his sanctity. We ought, however, to notice that Ælfric's letter to Wulfstan mentioned above[2] concludes rather curiously after the valediction, begging him remember the words of the prophet Micah on justice,[3] and regretting the absence from England of justice free from bribery: 'we are all blinded by gifts and pervert judgments as gifts instruct us, *non habentes retributionem uere iusticiae a deo*'.[4] The position of this warning, away from its natural context where the corruption of bishops has been mentioned in general terms, seems a little pointed, as if Ælfric, if not actually aware of a streak of cupidity in Wulfstan's nature, at least thought him exposed to particular temptation.

There is no suggestion of any flaw in his character in the Ely account.[5] He is 'an excellent man', 'strong in good qualities', 'all his qualities and deeds served religion'. As he had been a benefactor of the abbey and it possessed (and still possesses) his body, exaggeration of his importance and his virtues is to be expected. Yet I think we may claim that the following passage, in spite of its extravagant expression, is not entirely without foundation: 'by them (the kings, Ethelred, Edmund and Cnut), he was loved as a brother and honoured as a father, and frequently summoned to the highest affairs of the realm, as being the most learned of counsellors, in whom spoke the very wisdom of God, as if in some spiritual temple'.

[1] *Sermo Lupi ad Anglos*, pp. 8 f. Atkins, *op. cit.*, p. 19, calls attention to the scarcity of information about him in Worcester documents.

[2] *Supra*, pp. 50 f.

[3] Micah vi. 8.

[4] Fehr, *op. cit.*, p. 227.

[5] *Historia Eliensis, loc. cit.*

XII

WULFSTAN AND THE LAWS OF CNUT[1]

A. The Version of Cnut's Laws in C.C.C.C. MS. 201

WHEN Liebermann assembles the evidence for dating the laws which he cites as I and II Cnut,[2] he dismisses rather hastily the evidence of the version contained in manuscript D (Corpus Christi College, Cambridge, 201), stating that it consists only of fragments and that it arbitrarily changes both the text and the order of the chapters. A detailed examination of this version shows that it is more interesting than Liebermann supposed.

The content of the D version

Apart from an introductory paragraph, which, along with an addition to I Cnut 1, we will leave for later consideration, the version in D begins with I Cnut 1–2.2, which is concerned with the peace of the Church and is in part derived from VI Ethelred 1, 1.1, 13 and 14.[3] It then passes on to II Cnut 1–4.2, 6–7.1,

[1] I wish to express my thanks to Professor Sir Frank Stenton, Mr. K. Sisam, and Professor B. Dickins for their encouragement and helpful criticism.

F. Liebermann's great work, *Die Gesetze der Angelsachsen*, 1903–1916, is cited as *Gesetze* : A.[S]. Napier's *Wulfstan : Sammlung der ihm zugeschriebenen Homilien*, 1883, as Napier (roman figures referring to the homilies).

[2] 'Wulfstan und Cnut', *Archiv für das Studium der neueren Sprachen und Litteraturen*, ciii. 47 ff. ; *Gesetze*, iii. 194.

[3] It would probably be more accurate to say 'from a text that lies between V Ethelred and the only version of VI Ethelred that has survived, in one manuscript'; for, while the text used by Cnut's laws generally agreed both in content and wording with the surviving version of VI Ethelred, it seems occasionally to have had closer affinity to V Ethelred. Thus Cnut's laws include V Ethelred 16, missing from VI Ethelred, and omit VI Ethelred 5.2, which is neither in the Latin paraphrase of this code, nor in V Ethelred. (On some further omissions by the D version see *infra*, p. 436, n. 4.) I Cnut 6.3 is closer to V Ethelred 10 than to VI Ethelred 11. Moreover Cnut's laws have the chapters almost exactly in the order of V Ethelred. Liebermann suggested that Cnut's laws used both these codes, but it seems unlikely that the compiler should have given in the main the wording of one code while using the order of another. The relationship between V and VI Ethelred is puzzling. Liebermann's final opinion (*Gesetze*, iii. 167) was that both are variants of a code issued at Enham in 1008, V being closest to the original. This is generally accepted, but, while I would agree that V is the older version, it seems less certain that the promulgation of V Ethelred in 1008 occurred at the Council at Enham mentioned in the Latin paraphrase of VI Ethelred, without reference to any year. It is possible that the assembly at Enham was later than 1008, though before the autumn of 1011, when Archbishop Ælfheah, who attended it, was taken prisoner by the Danes, and that a revision of

which express in general terms a determination to rid the land of malefactors, though with the exercise of discrimination and mercy. This part is drawn from VI Ethelred 8, 8.1, 10.2, 10.3, 10, 10.1, 9 and 7, but it adds general exhortations and lists of types of criminals very similar to those that occur frequently in the homilies of Archbishop Wulfstan. II Cnut 5, 5.1, which interrupts the context by giving details of heathen practices in the middle of a catalogue of criminal types, is omitted. Our text then leaves II Cnut, where, with chapter 8, the general injunctions give place to details about the coiners of false money ; it returns to I Cnut 6–7.3, concerned with clerical celibacy and the ecclesiastical laws on marriage, all taken from VI Ethelred 2, 2.2, 5, 5.1, 5.3, 11, 12, 12.1, 12.2, with only small variations.

From then on, for a considerable space and without any new paragraph—in fact, without so much as a capital letter—the version in D copies VI Ethelred 16–40.1, but omits several chapters. Liebermann, who prints this as a version of VI Ethelred and so detaches it from what precedes and follows in the manuscript, does not mention that the chapters omitted are those that are not used by Cnut's laws.[1] All the chapters of Ethelred's code that occur in D at this point occur also in Cnut's code ; moreover, with one exception,[2] they are in the same order, though they are there often separated from one another by material from other sources, and individual chapters are expanded. After VI Ethelred 40.1, which there is reason to regard as the original conclusion of this code,[3] and which is used by II Cnut 11.1, the version in D puts II Cnut 15.1–15.3, partly derived from III Edgar 3. Then follow chapters 42–9 of the matter which has been added to VI Ethelred in our only complete version of this code, but which is not an integral part of it.[4] These are not used by Cnut's laws.

The contents of the D version may be summarized as follows :

Introduction.

I Cnut 1–2.2 [VI Ethelred 1, 1.1, 13, 14].

II Cnut 1–4.2, 6–7.1 [VI Ethelred 8, 8.1, 10.2, 10.3, 10, 10.1, 9, 7].

V Ethelred was undertaken for it. If the extant version of VI Ethelred represents this revision, the author of Cnut's laws may have used an earlier draft ; but it is also possible that the transcriber of the only extant text of VI Ethelred is responsible for changes in wording and order. It should be noted that one of the homilies in Napier's edition of homilies attributed to Wulfstan, No. L, seems to use VI Ethelred, but to arrange its topics in the order of the D version of Cnut's laws. This homily requires a separate investigation.

[1] There are also two minor omissions rectified in the full code of Cnut. See *infra*, p. 436, n. 4.

[2] VI Ethelred 26.1 which enjoins that a widow must be allowed to marry whom she pleases after a year's space, is moved to II Cnut 73, to follow a series of clauses concerned with a dead man's estate.

[3] Liebermann, *Gesetze*, i. 256.

[4] See *infra*, p. 445, n. 3.

I Cnut 6–7.3 [VI Ethelred 2, 2.2, 5, 5.1, 5.3, 11–12.2].
VI Ethelred 16–40.1 (omitting 28.2, 28.3, 29, 33–39).
II Cnut 15.1–15.3 [III Edgar 3].
VI Ethelred 42–49.

The relation of the D version to the complete code

It is difficult to see why a later compiler should select from Ethelred's sixth code just the sections used by Cnut's laws and sandwich them between portions of those laws, instead of using Cnut's expanded version throughout. He could have produced the text preserved in D only by a laborious comparison of the two codes, and this seems a motiveless proceeding. It is much easier to suppose that we have in D a selection from VI Ethelred with a few additions, which was afterwards expanded with further matter from other sources and partially rearranged to form Cnut's laws. Fortunately, we are not left to judge the matter on a balance of probability; a study of the text of the individual chapters seems to me to put it beyond doubt that the version in D lies between VI Ethelred and I and II Cnut. This will be seen most clearly in a columnar arrangement, in which the agreement with VI Ethelred is emphasized by italics, that with Cnut's code by clarendon type.

VI Ethelred	D	I and II Cnut [2]
14[1] 7 sy ælc cyricgrið binnan wagum 7 cyninges handgrið efen unwemme.	**þonne is swiðe rihtlic þæt Godes** ciricgrið binnon wágum 7 **Cristenes** cynges handgrið stande efen unwæmme.	I Cnut 2.2. **þonne is swiðe rihtlic þæt Godes** ciricgrið binnon wagum 7 **Cristenes** ciningces handgrið stande efen[3] unwemme; 7 se ðe aðor fulbrece, þolige landes 7 lifes butan se cininge gearian wylle.
8. 7 *witena gerædnes is,* þæt man rihte laga up arære [for Gode 7 for worolde][4] 7 æghwilce unlaga georne afylle.	*And witena gerædnes is,* þæt man rihte laga upp arǽre, and æghwilce unlaga georne afille, **and þæt man awéodige 7 awyrtwalige æghwilc unriht, swa man geornost mæge, of þisan earde** 7 **arære up Godes riht.**	II Cnut 1. Ðæt is þonne ærest, þæt ic wylle þæt man rihte laga upp arære 7 æghwylce unlaga georne afylle, 7 **þæt man áweodige** 7 **awyrtwalige æghwylc unriht, swa man geornost mæge, of þysum earde** 7 **arære up Godes riht.**

[1] This chapter comes from Edward and Guthrum 1, and D and Cnut's code are nearer to this than to VI Ethelred in reading *stande*, not *sy*; but as they draw their neighbouring clauses from the latter code, *stande* may have stood in the version used. Knowledge of the *Laws of Edward and Guthrum* is, however, shown in the preliminary paragraph of D, and in the complete code. See *infra*, pp. 440, 447.

[2] The text is from Nero A.1 (G), except when otherwise stated. Only significant variants from the other manuscripts are given.

[3] *Sic* Harley 55 (A). G reads *æfre*.

[4] The phrase in brackets is missing from V Ethelred 1.1, which, in its second version in G, otherwise agrees very closely with VI Ethelred 8.

VI Ethelred	D	I and II Cnut
8.1 7 þæt man heonan forð læte manna gehwylcne, ge earmne ge eadigne, folcrihtes wyrðe.	7 heonan forð læte manna gehwilcne, ge earmne ge eadigne, folcrihtes wurðe beon.[1]	II Cnut 1.1. 7 heonon forð læte manna gehwylcne, ge earmne ge eadigne, f o l c r i h t e s weorðne 7 him man rihte domas deme.
10.2 Ac æghwilce dæde toscade man wærlice 7 dom æfter dæde *medemige* be mæþe swa for Gode sy gebeorhlic 7 for worolde aberendlic.	And witena gerædnes is, **þæt, þeah hwa agilte 7 hine silfne deope forwyrce, þonne** *medemige* **man þa stéore,** swa hit for Gode sy gebeorhlic 7 for worlde aberendlic.	II Cnut 2. And we lærað, **þæt, þeah hwa agylte 7 hine sylfne deope forwyrce, þonne** g e f a d i g e **man [ða]**[2] **stéore,** swa hit for Gode sy gebeorhlic 7 for worulde aberendlic.

It is clear that these passages in D, all chosen from the sections which Liebermann regards as extracts from Cnut's laws, are from a version closer to the source. Similarly, when we turn to that part of the text in D which he prints as a version of VI Ethelred, we find that it takes up a middle position ; in several places it has readings that differ from this code and are shared by Cnut's laws, and yet it is equally obvious that it could not have been assembled from the latter. For example, it agrees with I Cnut 19.3 in replacing the *þonne wyrð þysse þeode sona God milde* of VI Ethelred 30 with *þonne wurð us Godes miltse þe gearuwre*, and with II Cnut 10 in shortening the second part of VI Ethelred 32.3 ; but on the other hand it lacks the addition made by II Cnut 8 to VI Ethelred 32.1, 7 *þæt nan man ne forsace*, and it is much closer to VI Ethelred 25 [3] than to I Cnut 17 which is based on it.[4] The natural explanation of the relationship of the text in D to both VI Ethelred and Cnut's code is that D is a copy of a compilation used by the author of Cnut's laws, whether compiled with this end in view or for some other purpose.

[1] The last word is presumably added by the scribe of D. [2] Omitted in G.

[3] It is still closer to the corresponding chapter V Ethelred 18, this being one of the places mentioned above (p. 433, n. 3) where the surviving text of VI Ethelred differs from that available to the author of Cnut's laws.

[4] At a first glance, it looks as if II Cnut 15.1 ff. afforded evidence pointing in the opposite direction, for several lines are missing from the version in D and yet are in the source, III Edgar 3. Yet this can easily be explained as an accidental omission by the rather careless scribe of D, owing to homoeoteleuton ; he has continued after the second instead of the first occurrence of *scyldig* and has thus upset the whole balance of the passage. He is no doubt responsible for the alteration of *hwæs he sylf gyrne* in II Cnut 2a into *hwæt he æt us sylf gyrne*, to the detriment of the sense, and for the blunder *unræd* for *hundred* in II Cnut 15.2 ; but he is not to blame for the omission of VI Ethelred 18.1, 7 *cyricsceat to Martinus mæssan* and of 7 *scipfyrdunga* from VI Ethelred 32.3, for these are missing in V Ethelred also. The author of Cnut's code could have supplied the first from VIII Ethelred, which he uses elsewhere. In V and VI Ethelred, *scipfyrdung* was dealt with in the following chapter, which was not used by D ; it was therefore necessary to add a reference to it and the author of Cnut's laws, who shows himself very familiar with Ethelred's codes, was capable of making the correction. The fact that he introduces the reference differently from the surviving text of VI Ethelred suggests that this was not his source.

The authorship of the D version

Before we examine this compilation further, it is desirable to notice a few things about the manuscript in which it is preserved. It is the Wulfstan manuscript which Napier calls C, and it probably was written in the middle of the eleventh century. While it does not always give the best text of the works it contains, it has Wulfstan material that survives in no other manuscript. Thus, besides containing many of his homilies, the codes which he compiled for King Ethelred, the so-called *Canons of Edgar* shown by Jost to be his work,[1] and the version of the Benedictine Office written in the Wulfstan style [2]—all works that occur elsewhere—it alone has the version of Ælfric's *Pastoral Letter* which Wulfstan re-wrote in his own style,[3] and it is the only manuscript to preserve the work known as Wulfstan's *Pastoral Letter* with its epistolary beginning, 'Wulfstan arcebisceop greteð freondlice þegnas on ðeode', &c., when other manuscripts have it simply in homiletic form.[4] This manuscript tends to note the occasion for which its texts were composed: it alone preserves the Old English version of VII Ethelred, an enactment enjoining prayers and fasting on a definite occasion 'when the great army came to the country', and it is the sole manuscript to give a date, 1014, for VIII Ethelred. It must be admitted, however, that its dates cannot always be relied on. By a mere scribal error, it reads 1009 instead of 1014 in the rubric to the *Sermo Lupi ad Anglos*, but inserts a passage into the text stating that this homily was composed four years before Ethelred died, a date which cannot be correct for the text in the form in which it has come down to us.[5]

The law-codes in this manuscript which are not of Wulfstan's own composition are codes of special interest for him, i.e. Athelstan's ordinance to his reeves on the payment of tithe, which survives otherwise only in another Wulfstan manuscript,[6] Edmund's first code, concerned exclusively with ecclesiastical matters, and Edgar's code, divided into an ecclesiastical and a secular section (II and III Edgar), which Wulfstan drew on very frequently for his own compilations. There is also a series of five short legal statements,[7] all concerned with the rights of

[1] 'Einige Wulfstantexte und ihre Quellen', *Anglia*, lvi. 265 ff.

[2] See E. Feiler, *Das Benediktiner-Offizium . . . Ein Beitrag zur Wulfstanfrage* (Anglistische Forschungen 4), 1901.

[3] B. Fehr, *Die Hirtenbriefe Ælfrics*, 1914, pp. lxiv-lxxxii; K. Jost in *Englische Studien*, lii, 105 ff.

[4] Napier, XIX–XXII.

[5] See D. Whitelock, *Sermo Lupi ad Anglos*, 1939, p. 5.

[6] Nero A, 1.

[7] I.e. as divided by Liebermann, namely what he cites as *Geþyncðo*, *Norðleod*, *Mirce*, *Að*, and *Had*, but the two last are treated as a single document both in D and in C.C.C.C. 190.

different classes of society, especially of the clergy ; the first and the last are written in the Wulfstan style, and the three last occur also in C.C.C.C. 190, a manuscript with Wulfstan connexions.[1] Finally, D has the unique copy of the eleventh-century *Norðhymbra Preosta Lagu*, a code for the diocese of York that is dependent on the codes composed by Wulfstan. That this manuscript draws on material collected by Wulfstan is further suggested by its containing various sets of excerpts from Latin authors used as material for his homilies.[2] It is important for this study of the compilation that lies behind Cnut's laws to bear in mind that it survives in a manuscript full of Wulfstan's writings and their sources.

It is inherently probable that Archbishop Wulfstan should have been consulted by Cnut on the compilation of his laws. He was the acknowledged expert who had composed codes for Ethelred and many ecclesiastical canons ; he appears to have been on cordial terms with Cnut, who employed him on other occasions, for example to consecrate his foundation of Ashingdon in 1020. Liebermann admitted the probability of his influence,[3] but believed that direct influence on Cnut's code was excluded by the date of this, a matter to which we shall have to return. The compilation in D is written in the style for which Wulfstan had achieved a reputation already in his own day. As far as the extracts from VI Ethelred are concerned, it could not be otherwise, for this is almost certainly a piece of his own writing ; but his phraseology is equally visible in the parts not from this source. Of the smaller additions, some are the familiar Wulfstan tags, such as *æfre, georne, mid rihte, ealles to swiðe, ofer ealle oðre þingc, us selfum to þearfe ;* or else a sentence from some other Wulfstan work is inserted, as in I Cnut 6*a*, where the phrase *⁊ dæges ⁊ nihtes oft ⁊ gelome clipian to Criste*, added to the source, VI Ethelred 2.2, is found in a chapter on the same topic in the 'appendix' to this code (VI Ethelred 41) which is omitted from the compilation in D, as well as in *Institutes of Polity*,[4] and with slight variations in several Wulfstan texts. Again, the wording

[1] D. Whitelock, 'Archbishop Wulfstan, Homilist and Statesman', *Transactions of the Royal Historical Society*, 4th series, xxiv. 32 ff.

[2] Nos. IV, VI, IX, XI in Napier's edition.

[3] 'Wulfstan und Cnut', p. 50.

[4] That is the work, henceforward cited as *Polity*, given this title by B. Thorpe, *The Ancient Laws and Institutes of England*, 1840, ii. 304–41. It consists of chapters on the duties and rights of the various orders of society, occurring, though in various arrangements and with different degrees of completeness, in the three Wulfstan manuscripts, C.C.C.C. 201 (D), Nero A. 1, and Junius 121. Thorpe's text does not follow exactly the order of any manuscript, nor is it complete. The work is in the Wulfstan style, but Liebermann held that it had used Cnut's laws and was therefore later than Wulfstan's death. This question needs re-examination, but it is best to wait for Jost's edition to appear.

wurð us Godes miltse þe gearuwre of I Cnut 19.3, which is repeated almost exactly in the complete code at II Cnut 84.4*b*, and which is not in the source of either passage, may be compared with *swa byð . . . Godes mildheortnes him micle þe gearwe* of a Wulfstan homily.[1] Of the major insertions made by the compilation in D, the one in II Cnut 4.1–7.1 is merely a variant of the catalogues of kinds of sinners and malefactors that are met with again and again in the acknowledged works of Wulfstan.[2] The list here adds *wiðersacan 7 utlagan Godes* and *liceteras 7 leogeras ;* the first pair of terms occurs in a different context in a Wulfstan code, VIII Ethelred 41–2, while *licetere* is a very favourite word of his [3] and *leogere* also belongs to his vocabulary.[4] The other large addition is in II Cnut 15.1–3, an expansion of III Edgar 3. Here locutions are added that make their first appearance in the Wulfstan code known as the ' Laws of Edward and Guthrum ',[5] such as *gilde he lahslite, on Dena lage*, &c., while the phrase *þe oðrum woh deme* of Edgar's law is replaced by *se þe unlaga arære oððe undom deme*, which contains an expression common in the Wulfstan texts.[6] I find it easier to imagine Wulfstan himself altering the perfectly adequate terminology of Edgar's law into agreement with his own method of expression than to think of an imitator going to such trouble ; moreover, the compilation includes words that Wulfstan used readily, such as *griðian*, ' to protect ', *mæð* ' respect ', *wirdan* ' to injure ', *aweodian* ' to root out ', this last word being unrecorded outside his writings.[7] At any rate, there can be no doubt that the compilation was made by someone well versed in the Wulfstan style.

The authenticity of the preliminary matter

If it can be regarded as established that D has preserved a compilation earlier than Cnut's laws, the introductory part takes on a new interest, for we must reckon with the possibility that it is an integral part of the text and thus a contemporary authority

[1] Napier, p. 155, ll. 14 f.

[2] E.g. *ibid.* p. 26, ll. 14 ff., p. 40, ll. 6 ff., p. 114, ll. 12 ff., p. 164, ll. 10 ff. ; Edward and Guthrum 11. Cf. Cnut 1020, 15.

[3] Napier, p. 52, l. 30, p. 54, ll. 5, 14, 18, p. 89, l. 18, p. 93, l. 8, &c.

[4] *Ibid.* p. 79, l. 4. *Liceteras 7 leogeras* occurs also in Homily L (Napier, p. 266, ll. 28 f.) and in one of the entries in the York Gospels (*ibid.* p. 310, ll. 3 f.), which also includes *godcundnessæ wiðersacan 7 godes lage oferhogan*, approximately synonymous with the first pair of terms quoted above. It seems uncertain which way round the borrowing took place. See *infra*, p. 452, n. 1.

[5] See *ante*, lvi, 1 ff.

[6] Cf. Napier, p. 47, l. 26 : *þe ræreð unriht to rihte 7 undom demeð*. See also p. 128, l. 10, p. 268, ll. 1, 18, &c. The phrase in the Anglo-Saxon Chronicle, 1052 C, D ; *þe ær unlage rærdon 7 undom demdon* may be taken from Cnut's laws. No occurrence of *undom* outside these writings is recorded.

[7] Napier, p. 73, l. 2, p. 243, l. 19.

for the reign of Cnut, not merely the theorizing of the scribe of D or some intermediate copyist. It runs as follows :

> In nomine Domini. Đis is seo gerædnes þe witan gerædon 7 be manegum godum bisnum asmeadon ; and þæt wæs geworden sona swa Cnút cyngc mid his witena geþeahte frið 7 freondscipe betweox Denum 7 Englum fullice gefæstnode 7 heora ærran saca ealle getwæmde. *þonne is þæt ærest,* þæt witan gerædan *þæt hi ofer ealle oðre þingc ænne God æfre wurðodon*[1] 7 *ænne Cristendom anrædlice healdan* 7 *Cnut cingc lufian mid rihtan* 7 *mid trywðan*[2] 7 Eadgares lagan geornlice folgian. And híg gecwǽdan þæt hi furðor on æmtan smeagan woldan þeode þearfe mid Godes filste, swa hi betst mihton. Nu wille we swutelian hwæt us mæg to ræde for Gode 7 for worlde, gime se þe wille. *Uton swiþe georne fram sinnan acirran* 7 *ure misdæda geornlice betan* 7 ænne God rihtlice lufian 7 wurðian 7 ænne Cristendom anrædlice healdan 7 ælcne hæðendom georne forbugan.

(The passages in italics are also in the complete code, at I Cnut 1 and 18.1 respectively ; the rest is peculiar to the D version.) In translation, it reads :

> 'This is the ordinance which the councillors determined and devised according to many good precedents ; and that took place as soon as King Cnut with the advice of his councillors completely established peace and friendship between the Danes and the English and put an end to all their former strife. *In the first place, the councillors determined that above all other things they would ever honour one God and steadfastly hold one Christian faith, and would love King Cnut with due loyalty* and zealously observe Edgar's laws. And they agreed that they would, with God's help, investigate further at leisure what was necessary for the nation, as best they could. Now we wish to make clear what can benefit us in religious and secular concerns, let him pay heed who will. *Let us very resolutely turn from sins and eagerly atone for our misdeeds* and duly love and honour one God and steadfastly hold one Christian faith and diligently avoid every heathen practice.'

The first sentence is partly based on the preamble to II Edgar, but the writer seems also to have had in his mind the preamble to the Wulfstan code, ' Edward and Guthrum ', which, like this passage in D, is an explanation of the occasion for the statutes that follow. There is a reminiscence of its words *þa þa Engle* 7 *Dene to friþe* 7 *to freondscipe fullice fengon,* and in both documents the same injunction follows, though the text in D has it in the slightly expanded form in which it occurs in VI Ethelred. It may also be the influence of ' Edward and Guthrum ' that caused our compiler to commence his code proper with the statute on

[1] *Sic,* for *woldan lufian* as in I Cnut 1.

[2] Probably an error for the usual phrase *mid rihtan getrywþan,* as, for example, in I Cnut 1, and so I have translated it.

the peace of the Church, which occupies this first place in 'Edward and Guthrum' but does not appear until chapters 13 and 14 in VI Ethelred; the wording of the statute suggests knowledge of its form in both these Wulfstan codes.[1] But it is not only when drawing from them that the author of this passage writes in the Wulfstan style; he uses it consistently throughout: *swa hi betst mihton, for Gode 7 for worlde, gime se þe wille,* are its familiar formulæ, *hwæt us mæg to ræde* contains a turn of phrase common in Wulfstan's writings,[2] and expressions such as *saca . . . getwæmde,*[3] *lagan geornlice folgian,*[4] *smeagan . . . þearfe,*[5] can be paralleled in these and hardly occur outside them. And per contra there is nothing in the vocabulary or phraseology alien to his style.

The resemblance to Wulfstan's style is not confined to obvious features that would be easy to imitate. It has never been convincingly proved that he had imitators who could so consistently and exclusively imitate his diction and phrasing. It is particularly difficult to envisage a writer many years after Wulfstan's death going to considerable trouble to find a Wulfstan expression for everything he wished to say; yet, if the paragraph is not authentic, but merely the conjecture of a later writer, we must surely allow some passage of years for the real origin of the compilation to have been forgotten. There seems no motive for deliberate falsification, and if, as Liebermann suggests, the writer had drawn his reference to Edgar's laws either from Cnut's proclamation of 1020 or from the Anglo-Saxon Chronicle, one would have expected him to refer also to the place, Oxford, where, according to both these authorities, they were accepted. Moreover, there is an indication that the last sentence, 'Let us very resolutely turn from sins and eagerly atone for our misdeeds and duly love and honour one God and steadfastly hold one Christian faith and diligently avoid every heathen practice', was already present when the text was used by the author of Cnut's complete code. I Cnut 18.1 is closer to this sentence than it is to VI Ethelred 1, from which both are ultimately derived, and the borrowing is not likely to be the other way round, considering that the sentence in D occurs in its proper context, as in Ethelred's code, from which Cnut's code isolates it. We may set it out as follows:

[1] Use has also been made of the text *Be griðe 7 be munde* (*Grið*), a document in the Wulfstan style surviving only in Nero A.1, unless the borrowing is in the reverse direction.

[2] Cf. *mæg . . . to steore,* Napier, p. 168, ll. 5 f.; *mæg to bysne,* p. 44, ll. 20, 24, p. 48, l. 12, p. 170, l. 14.

[3] Cf. *ibid.* p. 118, l. 3; V Ethelred 19 = VI 25.1 = I Cnut 17.2; X Ethelred Pre. 1; Cnut 1020 4. The author of the passage under consideration could have taken the locution from I Cnut 17.2 in the compilation before him.

[4] E.g. VI Ethelred 42.2.

[5] Cf. *smeagan ure þearfe,* Napier, p. 132, l. 6.

VI Ethelred 1	D	I Cnut 18.1
Þæt we ealle fram synnum georne gecyrran, þæs þe we don magan, 7 ure misdæda andettan georne 7 geornlice betan, 7 ænne God rihtlice lufian 7 weorðian 7 ænne Christendom anrædlice healdan 7 ælcne hæðendom georne forbugan.	Uton swiþe georne fram sinnan acirran 7 ure misdæda geornlice betan 7 ænne God rihtlice lufian 7 wurðian 7 ænne Cristendom anrædlice healdan 7 ælcne hæðendom georne forbugan.	Ac uton swiðe georne fram synnum gecyrran 7 ure ælc his misdæda urum scriftum geornlice andettan 7 æfre geswican 7 geornlice betan.

It is possible that the scribe of D has omitted *andettan georne* 7 after *ure misdæda*, but in any case it is not a strange coincidence that Cnut's code should expand the text of D just at the point where the source is fuller, for, as we shall see later, the author of Cnut's laws was very familiar with Ethelred's codes. Unless the similarity here between D and I Cnut is accidental, part of the introductory passage in D must belong to Cnut's reign, and I see no cogent reason for separating this sentence from what precedes it.

There is no need to assume that the author of this preliminary matter took his reference to Edgar's laws from some other document. It is a commonplace of the Wulfstan texts to bewail the deterioration since Edgar's death. For example, one version of the *Sermo ad Anglos* adds the phrase ' since Edgar died ' to the statement that the ' laws of the people ' have deteriorated, and similar complaints are made in the codes which Wulfstan drew up for Ethelred [1] and in the passage in his style which occurs in manuscript D of the Anglo-Saxon Chronicle ; [2] this version of the Chronicle, whatever its precise place of origin, certainly comes from one of Wulfstan's two dioceses. He seems to have regarded the codes he composed for Ethelred as part of a movement to re-establish ' Edgar's law '—that is, perhaps, the practice of Edgar's time [3]—against later abuses ; one of these is specifically mentioned in *Institutes of Polity*, chapter 12, namely unjust exactions by reeves, which have arisen ' all too much since Edgar died '. He emphasizes the need to ' take as our example what former secular rulers decreed for our benefit—Athelstan and Edmund and last of all Edgar ',[4] and he makes constant use of Edgar's codes for his own compilations.[5] It would only be

[1] VIII Ethelred 37. Note also the mutilated marginal emendation to X Ethelred Prol. 3, which probably referred to some adoption of Edgar's laws.

[2] I.e. Tiberius B.4. Jost first drew attention to Wulfstan's style in this version, in *Anglia*, xlvii. 105 ff.

[3] Liebermann (' Wulfstan und Cnut ', p. 52) takes *lagu* as ' Verfassung ', ' Rechtszustand ', not ' Gesetz ' in this clause.

[4] VIII Ethelred 43.

[5] The codes issued in Edgar's name have come down to us mainly in Worcester or York manuscripts ; II and III Edgar in Harley 55, which includes memoranda concerning the lands of the see of York, in C.C.C.C. 201 (= D), and in the Wulfstan

natural, if Wulfstan or one of his close circle drew up the compilation in D, that a reference to Edgar's laws should be made in an explanatory introduction, even though the text itself is drawn almost entirely from Ethelred's legislation ; this was Edgar's law in the Wulfstan sense. In fact, although Wulfstan was not alone in regarding Edgar's reign as a golden age,[1] all references to a return to Edgar's law occur in texts that have some connexion with him, for Cnut's proclamation of 1020 with its mention of *Eadgares lage . . . þe ealle męn habbað gecoren 7 to gesworen on Oxenaforda* shows signs of Wulfstan's influence in its style, and is preserved only in an addition to the York Gospels, in a hand that may be as early as Wulfstan's lifetime ; [2] the addition of the words 'to Edgar's law' to the account in the Anglo-Saxon Chronicle of the agreement reached at Oxford in 1018 is made only in the D manuscript of the Chronicle, which has the passages in the Wulfstan style mentioned above.

There seems no reason why one should regard the preliminary matter to the text in D as a spurious later addition. There is nothing at all improbable in its statements to prevent us from taking them at their face value, and as the text itself is certainly earlier than Cnut's laws, it seems permissible to accept the very reasonable account of its origin given in the introductory statements, namely, that it resulted from the decisions of the council made, presumably at Oxford in 1018,[3] after agreement between the Danes and English had been reached. The document could then be used as the basis of Cnut's code, which may represent the fulfilment of the promise 'to investigate further what was necessary for the nation '.[4] A detailed examination of the relationship between the two texts strengthens the case for Wulfstan's authorship, as it will be the purpose of the second part of this article to demonstrate.

part of Nero A.1, though the loss of some folios leaves this version incomplete. The same manuscript has also a complete version, but on folios that may once have belonged to a separate work. IV Edgar is in the Worcester manuscript C.C.C.C. 265, and also in Nero E.1, where it follows some leaves of a Worcester cartulary, though not an original part of the same volume.

[1] Note in particular the beginning and the conclusion of Ælfric's homily on St. Swithun (W. W. Skeat, *Ælfric's Lives of Saints*, 1881, i. 440, 468 f.) and the conclusion of his translation of *Judges* (S. J. Crawford, *The Old English Version of the Heptateuch*, 1922, pp. 416 f.)

[2] I am indebted to Mr. N. D. Ker for this dating. See also W. H. Stevenson, *ante*, xxvii. 14, who dates this hand about 1030.

[3] This seems indicated by the reference to Edgar's law, as in the account of this assembly in the Anglo-Saxon Chronicle, 1018 D. Otherwise it would be tempting to connect it with the entry for 1017 in Florence of Worcester, which runs, in wording very similar to that in the preamble under discussion : ' Foedus etiam cum principibus et omni populo ipse, et illi cum ipso percusserunt, et amicitiam firmam inter se juramentis stabilierunt, omnesque veteres inimicitias postponentes sedaverunt '.

[4] If this text in D was intended only as an interim measure until a fuller code could be produced, its survival only in one manuscript is easy to understand.

As it can hardly be doubted that the archbishop would himself be present at this important gathering at Oxford, the establishment of his authorship of the preliminary matter of the D version would permit us to regard it as first-hand evidence of what took place there. What is even more significant, it would also give us for once an authentic glimpse of the procedure by which Anglo-Saxon law-books were made. They are known to have been 'ordained' by the counsel of assemblies of the *witan*, and it would be reasonable to assume that their form and wording would have to be drafted by clerks, that is, by ecclesiastics. In the present case, it would seem that the drafting was done by no less dignified an ecclesiastic than Archbishop Wulfstan.[1] If we could take this as typical of the usual practice, we could conclude that Anglo-Saxon law-books were drawn up by some prominent ecclesiastic, bishop, or abbot, who was present at the particular assembly in which they were enacted. In this connexion, the passage at the end of the eleventh-century Latin paraphrase of VI Ethelred may well be illustrative of contemporary practice :

> Haec itaque legalia statuta uel decreta, in nostro conuentu sinodali a rege N [Æþelredo] [2] magnopere edicta, cuncti tunc temporis optimates se obseruaturos fideliter spondebant ; idcircoque ego N [Wulfstanus],[2] gratia Domini disponente Eboracensium archiepiscopus, *eadem ad sequentium memoriam, necnon et ad praesentium uel futurorum salutem, litteris infixi* Domini uidelicet proximique dilectione conpunctus.[3]

B. The Complete Code

The influence of Edgar's code

The compiler of Cnut's laws added to the version in D a large amount of new matter. There is also a change in plan, the reason for which is not far to seek. He decided to imitate the code usually cited as II and III Edgar, and so he divides his work into two parts, ecclesiastical and secular. He copies Edgar's preambles :

II Edgar	I Cnut
Þis is seo gerædnes þe Eadgar cyngc mid his witena geþeahte gerædde, Gode to lofe 7 him silfum to cynescype 7 [4] to þearfe.	Ðis is seo gerædnys þe Cnut ciningc [5] mid his witena geþeahte gerædde, Gode to lofe 7 him sylfum to cynescipe 7 to þearfe ; 7 þæt wæs on ðære halgan midewintres tide on Winceastre.

[1] K. C. D. 898 shows the king asking Wulfstan to draw up another type of document. See D. Whitelock in *Transactions of the Royal Historical Society*, 4th series, xxiv. 37.

[2] Inserted in another hand, also of the eleventh century.

[3] *Gesetze*, i. 257. Cf. D. Whitelock, *op. cit.* pp. 35 ff.

[4] Harley 55 (A) and Nero A.1 (G) add *eallum his leodscipe*, missing from D.

[5] G adds *ealles Englalandes ciningc 7 Dena cining.*

III Edgar	II Cnut
Þis is ðonne seo worldcunde gerædnes þe ic wille þæt man healde.	Þis is (þonne)[1] seo woruldcunde gerædnes ðe ic wylle, mid minan witenan ræde, þæt man healde ofer eall Englaland.

After its preamble, III Edgar has some chapters which were used by VI Ethelred 8.1, 10.2, and from there copied into the compilation in D to follow the section which became I Cnut 1–2.2; they, and the section containing them, were now removed by the compiler of Cnut's laws to follow the preamble to II Cnut, that is to say, to the position corresponding to the one they had held in Edgar's code. Otherwise Cnut's laws follow the order of the text in D with only minor modifications,[2] using it as far as II Cnut 15.3. The few remaining clauses in D, from VI Ethelred 42–49, are not used for the long code, probably because they are in the main a repeat of what has gone before.[3] Instead, the author of Cnut's code continues to draw on III Edgar beyond that part of it on which II Cnut 15.3, the last clause to be taken from D, is based. Moreover, in two places where he repeats clauses from VI Ethelred as given in D, he shows that he is aware of their eventual source in III Edgar by adding phrases from this code which VI Ethelred had omitted, namely ⁊ *him man rihte domas deme* in II Cnut 1.1 and ⁊ *þæt nan man ne forsace* in II Cnut 8.

The Sources of I Cnut[4]

The compiler filled out the text in D from other sources. As I Cnut 2.3–3.2 he inserted VIII Ethelred 1.1–5.1, that is, the whole section of this code (except for a short final sentence) which also survives separately with the title *Be cyricgriðe* in the Wulfstan manuscript Nero A.1 with some variant readings which agree with Cnut's laws. I Cnut 5–5.4 is from VIII Ethelred 19–27.1, with some small additions, and it may be the influence of the same code that accounts for the addition to I Cnut 9 and 10, both from VI Ethelred as in D, of the penalties for non-payment of *Romfeoh* and *cyricsceat*. I Cnut 8.2 uses both II Edgar 3.1 and the modified form of this in VIII Ethelred 8, and it adds an explanatory clause very like one in VIII Ethelred 7. I Cnut 16 seems to represent II Edgar 5.1 with an addition perhaps from VI Ethelred 23. The compiler certainly knew his way about the codes of these two kings.

[1] *Sic* A and C.C.C.C. 383 (B), missing in G. [2] See *supra*, p. 434, n. 2.

[3] This section was not an original part of VI Ethelred (see *supra*, p. 434, n. 3). It occurs also in the homily headed *Sermo Lupi* in the York Gospels (see *infra*, p. 452, n. 1) where it ends at the same point as in D, without the further matter added to VI Ethelred. All three versions seem to be derived independently from a common source. Some of the clauses, with other matter, are also in Napier No. XXXVII.

[4] The following sections owe much to Liebermann's work on sources. I use only those parallels where verbal similarities make borrowing certain.

No other codes are used for the ecclesiastical part of Cnut's code, but much homiletic matter is inserted, some of it from extant homilies by Wulfstan. Thus I Cnut 18*a*–18*b* comes from his 'Pastoral Letter';[1] I Cnut 18.2 is found in his tenth homily, *De cristianitate*,[2] and this is also the source of I Cnut 25;[3] I Cnut 20 seems developed from a passage in this homily on loyalty between lord and follower.[4] I Cnut 22–22.4 consists of clauses from Wulfstan's *De fide catholica*,[5] not from the abbreviated version of the same passage in his *Canons of Edgar*, though the two paragraphs that follow immediately in Cnut's laws are taken from this work;[6] thus we are afforded another example of the combination of two sources by the compiler of Cnut's laws. There are also passages shared by *Institutes of Polity*,[7] but Liebermann claimed that this work was the borrower and it is best to reserve judgement until Jost's edition has appeared. Other legal treatises and homilies are considered to have used Cnut's code, but the whole question requires a fresh investigation; in some cases a reverse influence is possible.[8] Finally, there are a few passages for which no parallel is forthcoming, but which are closely akin to Wulfstan's known work in sentiment and are uniformly written in his style. It will not have escaped notice that of the sources used by the ecclesiastical section of Cnut's code the only one which does not come from the Wulfstan school is Edgar's code which Wulfstan drew on frequently when composing laws for Ethelred.

The sources of II Cnut

The secular part of Cnut's code uses a wider range of royal laws, but the method followed is the same. As far as II Cnut 15.3 it uses the compilation in D, inserting a section on heathen

[1] Napier, p. 113, ll. 14 ff.

[2] *Ibid.* p. 67, ll. 2 ff.

[3] *Ibid.* p. 75, ll. 6 ff. There is a closer, in fact almost identical, parallel in Napier XXXVII, p. 179, ll. 13 ff., but it is not certain that the second part of this homily, missing from all manuscripts but one, is independent of Cnut's laws.

[4] *Ibid.* p. 74, ll. 9 ff. A passage identical with that in Cnut's laws occurs in Napier XXIV, and one with slight variations is in a fragmentary homily, Napier LVIII, apparently borrowed from XXIV, for it follows it with an expanded version of the next paragraph in that homily. The possibility of the opposite line of development should be left open until more work has been done on *Polity*, which LVIII seems to use.

[5] Napier, p. 20, ll. 10 ff.

[6] Chapter 22; but see *infra*, p, 452, n. 1. Yet if, as I there suggest, the laws are not derived directly from these two sources, but from an intermediate work which already combined them and which was used also by the homily in the York Gospels, the author of Cnut's laws nevertheless went back to the *De fide catholica* for further expansions.

[7] I Cnut 2, 2.1 = *Polity* XXV; I Cnut 4.1–3 = *Polity* XIX: I Cnut 26–26.4, i.e. the concluding paragraphs of I Cnut = *Polity* VI.

[8] E.g. there is a connexion between I Cnut 4 and *Hadbot* 1.3, and between I Cnut 2.1, 26 and *Grið* 1, 19.1. See also *supra*, p. 433, n. 3, and n. 4 above, and *infra*, p. 452.

practices (5, 5.1), which employs some of the words also in Wulfstan's tirades on the same subject,[1] and adding some chapters (12—15) which enumerate the king's rights in the various provinces of the kingdom. When it ceases to use the text in D, it continues with the same source, III Edgar, drawing from there II Cnut 16–18.1 and 25–26. Other royal codes are drawn on : II Athelstan supplies II Cnut 13.2, 28, 28.1 ; I Ethelred is responsible for II Cnut 30–33.2, IV Ethelred perhaps for II Cnut 62, 62.1 ; Alfred's laws have been used in II Cnut 57–59, though with considerable modifications ; II Cnut 55 is from Wihtred 4 and there are other less certain indications that the compiler knew the laws of Kent. A combination of different sources is seen in II Cnut 40–48.3, chapters based on the *Laws of Edward and Guthrum* but with readings and additions from VIII Ethelred, which also borrowed from this code, so that again we find the compiler drawing simultaneously from two Wulfstan works.[2] It is to be noted that, while Edgar's and Ethelred's laws are usually left almost unchanged, earlier laws are frequently re-worded, so that there are cases where it is uncertain whether the author was influenced by previous statutes on the same subjects. Between the sections that can be assigned to extant codes are others that are probably derived from lost laws ; except for odd phrases here and there, they are not in the Wulfstan style. As the code advances, identifiable legal sources become rare and subjects are dealt with that are not treated in extant earlier laws. Some of these statutes may be original.

Throughout, as in the ecclesiastical section, there are insertions in the Wulfstan homiletic style. A text *De confessione* which occurs in manuscript D and elsewhere,[3] has supplied most of II Cnut 38, 38.1, 68.1*a*–68.3. The conclusion of the code (84–84.4*b*) is identical, except for one short additional phrase, with the conclusion of a hitherto unnoticed short work in the Wulfstan style. This is a text headed *Be sacerdan* which in D follows immediately on the compilation of laws. It is only in its first few lines that it coincides with the chapter in *Institutes of Polity* to which it is usually assigned.[4] It has other connexions with Cnut's code, for two phrases that are added in D to the text of VI Ethelred, namely *þegenlage wyrðe* which in I Cnut 6.2*a* replaces *þegenweres ⁊ þegenrihtes wyrþe* of the source, VI Ethelred

[1] See Napier, p. 11, l. 5, p. 12, ll. 3 f., p. 40, ll. 13 ff. ; *Canons of Edgar*, 16. Cf. also *Norðhymbra Preosta Lagu*, 48, 54.

[2] If this instance stood alone, one might suspect that the author of Cnut's law had access either to a common source of these two codes or to an intermediate version, but all the passages in Cnut's laws which combine different sources cannot be explained in this way.

[3] Thorpe, *op. cit.* ii. 260.

[4] *Polity* XIX (= I Cnut 4.2, 4.3). The few lines which run parallel to this in *Be sacerdan* have some variant readings.

5.3, and *7 wið ðone weallendan bryne þe wealleð on helle*, a Wulfstan phrase added to I Cnut 6.1, are contained in it. While it would be unsafe to be dogmatic on the question which text is the borrower, we may note that the concluding section is at least as suitable to a treatise on the respect due to the clergy as to a code of secular laws, and that the position of this text immediately after a document which was a source of Cnut's laws may perhaps suggest that it too was part of the material used in their composition. II Cnut, like the ecclesiastical section, has passages in the Wulfstan style for which no exact source is known. I have found no trace of the use of the writings of other homilists.

The authorship of Cnut's code

It would be possible to account for the Wulfstan features [1] in these homiletic passages by assuming that all are borrowed from his works, lost or extant ; but the familiar intensitives and formulae, e.g. *georne, ealles to swyðe, þe deoppor gebete, be þam þe seo dæd sy*, are scattered also through the parts that come from legal sources. If this were all, it might indicate nothing more than that the fashion in framing statutes set by Wulfstan continued after his death. These passages contain some of the less obvious characteristics of his style, such as his use of *gebugan* 'to submit to' with a direct object, and many of his favourite words, including *woroldlagu, weofodþegn, ægylde*, otherwise unrecorded in works outside his sphere of influence.

It has emerged from this investigation that both the earlier compilation and the complete code are the work of some one so well versed in the codes which Wulfstan composed for Ethelred that he knew from what sources the individual chapters had been taken and could add matter from the source while keeping in the main to the derived version ; some one who moved easily about all the Wulfstan writings, sometimes choosing to substitute or add the wording of a different work from the one he is at the moment using. Jost has shown that Wulfstan behaved in a similar way when he inserted a quotation from his *De regula canonicorum* into his homily *De cristianitate*, instead of translating his source, though no change of meaning resulted, and those familiar with Jost's important article [2] will have noticed that the relation of the compilation in D to Cnut's code is akin to that between the collection of materials for Wulfstan's *De baptismate* and *De cristianitate* and the complete works. For these homilies

[1] In addition to more obvious examples, note *deofles scyfe*, I Cnut 23 (cf. Napier, p. 103, l. 21) ; *godcunde ðearfe*, I Cnut 26 (cf. Napier, p. 75, l. 4, p. 104, l. 6) ; *deoflum ætweneð*, II Cnut 84.2a (cf. Napier, p. 38, l. 24) ; *beorgan*, used absolutely, II Cnut 38 (cf. Napier p. 165, l. 10).

[2] *Anglia*, lvi. 265 ff.

he used collections of excerpts from Latin authors, but he also drew on parts of the sources not included in the selection. From this, Jost concluded that he had compiled the sets of excerpts for himself, and it seems to me probable on the same reasoning that the author of Cnut's code was using a compilation of his own making when he based his work on the text that survives in D. If this author is not Wulfstan himself, it must be a follower who has learnt to copy his method of work as well as to reproduce his style, and has studied both his legal and his homiletic writings until he knows them as well as their author himself.

This is perhaps possible, but not probable. There is, however, another consideration that seems to weigh the balance in favour of Wulfstan's authorship. It is an insertion into a statute borrowed from I Ethelred 1.6. Where this code has the death penalty for the often accused man who has failed at the threefold ordeal, II Cnut 30.4–5 substitutes mutilation, and justifies it with the remark: *swa man mæg styran* ⁊ *eac ðære sawle beorgan* 'thus one can punish and also preserve the soul'. The codes of Wulfstan's composition tend to limit the application of the death penalty,[1] lest 'the handiwork of God and what he purchased for himself at a great price be destroyed for trivial offences',[2] and that this represents his own attitude is suggested by the occurrence of the Latin canon from which this passage is derived in a Worcester manuscript containing many of his sources.[3] This canon does not expressly mention mutilation among the alternatives it suggests to the death penalty, but it could be covered by the phrase *diversis penis crucianda sunt*, and this is actually rendered ⁊ *hwilum eac limlæwa* 'and sometimes also mutilation' in a paraphrase of a part of this canon inserted into the text of *Be dædbetan* in the Worcester manuscript Junius 121,[4] the term used being one that occurs only in Wulfstan's writings.[5] The increased tendency of Cnut's laws to punish by mutilation thus arises from a Christian archbishop's desire that malefactors should be given an opportunity to expiate their crimes in this world.

If we summarize the evidence for Wulfstan's authorship of Cnut's laws,[6] we find that the complete code and an earlier compilation on which it is based are written in the Wulfstan style and use methods of work known from other evidence to agree

[1] E.g. twice, in VI Ethelred 35 and 36, the death penalty is omitted where V Ethelred 28, 29 demand it.

[2] VI Ethelred 10.1 (= II Cnut 2.1), in A. J. Robertson's translation.

[3] See D. Whitelock, *Transactions of the Royal Historical Society*, 4th series, xxiv. 36.

[4] Thorpe, *op. cit.* ii. 278.

[5] See *ante*, lvi. 9.

[6] J. P. Kinard claimed this in 1897, in *A Study of Wulfstan's Homilies: Their Style and Sources*. His opinions were opposed by Liebermann, whose view was accepted by legal historians and writers on Wulfstan, including myself. Professor D. Bethurum has told me that her own studies have led her to the conclusion that Wulfstan wrote these laws.

with his ; they draw very largely on his writings and use no other known author's work, except for the codes of previous kings ; the respect paid to Edgar's laws is in agreement with frequently expressed views of Wulfstan's ; in at least one particular, the complete code changes existing law in a direction towards which he had long been working ; the earlier compilation is preserved only in a manuscript which contains many of his texts and sources;[1] that he should be commissioned to compose codes for Cnut is in itself extremely probable. This seems enough accumulative evidence to suggest that Cnut's laws had at least received their general shape before Wulfstan died on 28 May 1023.

Apart from the question of date, Liebermann used another argument against Wulfstan's authorship.[2] He considered that the archbishop, given the opportunity of producing an ecclesiastical code for an energetic young king, would not have been content to supply what is on the whole only a patchwork of earlier writings. This is to judge the matter from too modern a point of view. The age attached little value to originality, and Wulfstan in particular had no objection to repeating a passage again and again. He would doubtless welcome the chance to re-issue in the name of a more effective monarch many of the injunctions that he had put into code after code of Ethelred's legislation, and many of the moral exhortations that fill his homilies. If the chief aim was a return to the conditions of Edgar's reign, we should hardly expect much innovation, and he would see no reason to disguise old matter under new methods of expression, once he was satisfied with a previous wording, especially when he was writing for a king who was anxious to appear to be following the tradition of English kings.

The date of Cnut's laws

If we wish to retain Liebermann's date for Cnut's laws, 1027, or 1029–34, we may assume that the project moved very slowly, or was laid aside altogether, for some years, perhaps because of Cnut's other preoccupations, perhaps because Wulfstan had been the prime mover and it was not easy to find a successor to complete the code. But is it necessary to date the code so late ? There is nothing in it to force us to do so, for the title *Norþrigena cyningc* in the heading in one manuscript is, as Liebermann takes it, certainly a later addition. The statement that the code was issued at Christmas at Winchester leaves 1018, 1020–26 as possible

[1] It is perhaps only coincidence that two of the three texts of the complete code should be bound up with manuscripts with Wulfstan associations, Nero A.1 and Harley 55. There is unfortunately nothing to show that these texts had early connexions with Worcester or York.

[2] ' Wulfstan und Cnut ', pp. 50 f.

years. Cnut is called 'King of the Danes', but his brother had died in 1018 and Cnut made himself effective king in 1020. Liebermann bases his dating on two main considerations: that William of Malmesbury lets the code follow, undated, on the proclamation of 1027,[1] and that this proclamation makes no use of Cnut's code.

To take the second point first; while Cnut's proclamation of 1020 contains places where one might have expected a reference to his own code if it had already existed, the proclamation of 1027 does not give me this impression. I see no reason why Cnut should not be including his own code in the expression *secundum leges* of the last paragraph, and when, in the paragraph before, he speaks of the payment of church dues *secundum legem antiquam*, it is to make it clear that these demands are in accordance with long-established rules, and are not innovations.[2] It would be unsafe to conclude from the absence of any reference to II Cnut 69.1 in paragraph 12 of the proclamation that the code was not yet in existence: the proclamation deals comprehensively with abuse of power by royal officials, the code mentions only extortion by royal reeves; in any case, Anglo-Saxon legal documents rarely trouble to state that they are repeating injunctions made elsewhere. It is a pity that the vernacular version of this proclamation has not survived, for it might have supplied an answer to the question whether, after Wulfstan's death, he had imitators who could compose documents in his style.

As for William of Malmesbury, his unsupported evidence does not count for much. It would be natural for him to assume that Cnut's promises of good government made in the proclamation of 1027 were fulfilled by the issue of his code. If, however, William is right, having evidence denied to us, and Cnut first issued his code in 1027 or later, I would claim that he used a version that in its essential features was composed some half dozen years earlier. It is possible that it received minor insertions.

The possible re-dating of a code of laws by a few years might be a small result from a lengthy investigation, but it is obvious that our estimate of Cnut's character is greatly affected if it can be established that he was so much influenced by the veteran archbishop who had loyally supported Ethelred and striven against the disorder of the reign. The re-dating also has rather far-reaching implications for Wulfstan scholarship, for it makes it unnecessary to deny Wulfstan's authorship of texts that appear

[1] *De Gestis Regum Anglorum,* R.S. i. 224. The date 1028 given in a continental chronicler may be an assumption from William's words and of no independent authority. *Sic* Liebermann, *Gesetze,* iii. 194.

[2] That a letter should give a less exhaustive list than a code does not seem to me evidence of prior date.

to be using Cnut's laws. Even if we were to keep the late date for the actual promulgation, Wulfstan may have drawn on the materials collected for this code. One of the texts considered dependent on Cnut's laws can actually be shown to have used either an earlier draft or a common source, for where any passage in it can be traced to its source, this text is closer to it than is Cnut's code.[1] This text is the first of the homilies entered in the York Gospels by the scribe who entered also Cnut's proclamation of 1020. It thus affords another instance of the survival of material underlying Cnut's codes in a manuscript which it is natural to connect with Wulfstan, for I no longer see any reason to reject the evidence of a rubric written at his own see by a man who could have been his contemporary, and this homily is headed *Sermo Lupi*.

[1] The homily, No. LXIX in Napier, is almost entirely made up of passages that occur elsewhere, *Polity* XVIII, I Cnut 21, 22, 22.5, 22.6, 23, 24, 7, 7.1, 7.3, 25, and the clauses that are also in the compilation in D, VI Ethelred 42–49 (see *supra*, p. 445, n. 3). Its text of I Cnut 22–22.6 occupies a middle position between the code and its sources, being closer in its wording to the *Canons of Edgar* than is Cnut's law, and omitting some of the intervening clauses from *De fide catholica* which Cnut's law inserted at this point. Moreover, the homily omits I Cnut 7.2, which already the compilation in D added to VI Ethelred 12 (see Liebermann, *Gesetze*, iii. 199). There is even less evidence that the two other homilies in the York Gospels used Cnut's code. Napier LX, *Be hæðendome*, could have taken *leogeras* ⁊ *liceteras* from it, but the laws may on the contrary have used a homiletic source ; LXI, *Be cristendome*, seems to be a combination of parts of X (and its Latin source IX) with VIII Ethelred, differing from this in stating the times at which *leohtscot* must be paid. It disagrees with other statements, e.g. I Cnut 12, Napier XXIII and XLIII, and an addition to the *Canons of Edgar* in the Junius manuscript 121, in having Christmas instead of All Saints, and may therefore be independent of them.

XIII

WULFSTAN'S AUTHORSHIP OF CNUT'S LAWS[1]

IN two previous articles in this REVIEW I have attributed to Wulfstan, archbishop of York and bishop of Worcester, the authorship of law-codes. In 1941 I suggested, arguing both from style and content, that a document usually cited as the 'Laws of Edward and Guthrum' was in reality a work of the early eleventh century, probably by Wulfstan himself.[2] In 1948 I examined in detail a text on pages 126 to 130 of MS. 201 of Corpus Christi College, Cambridge (henceforward cited as D) which Liebermann regarded as a later combination of parts of VI Ethelred and Cnut's code, and therefore printed in separate parts scattered through his work.[3] In my article [4] I brought forward reasons for believing that this text is not a compilation later than Cnut's laws, but a text lying between these and VI Ethelred,[5] and that it was used by the compiler of the laws of Cnut as one of his sources. It may be convenient here to repeat the table previously given in order to show the relationship of the text in D to other codes. Its contents are as follows:

Introduction (to be discussed below).
I Cnut 1–2.2 (based on VI Ethelred 1, 1.1, 13, 14).
II Cnut 1–4.2, 6–7.1 (based on VI Ethelred 8, 8.1, 10.2, 10.3, 10, 10.1, 9, 7).
I Cnut 6–7.3 (based on VI Ethelred 2, 2.2, 5, 5.1, 5.3, 11–12.2).
VI Ethelred 16–40.1 (omitting 28.2, 28.3, 29, 33–39, none of which clauses, except 37, on which see p. 83, were used by the compiler of Cnut's laws).
II Cnut 15.1–15.3 (based on III Edgar 3).
VI Ethelred 42–49 (a text that was probably not an integral part of VI Ethelred, and which survives separately in the Wulfstan homily Napier LIX.[6] It is not used in Cnut's laws).

Thus the text in D includes all the clauses of VI Ethelred which were used by the compiler of Cnut's laws, except clause 37, which

[1] I am greatly indebted to Sir Frank Stenton, Dr. K. Sisam, and Professor Dorothy Bethurum for reading and criticizing this article.

[2] 'Wulfstan and the so-called Laws of Edward and Guthrum', *ante*, lvi. 1–21.

[3] *Die Gesetze der Angelsachsen*, I, 278, 280; 308, 310, 312; 288–91; 252, 254, 256; 318; 256, 258. I quote the order in which the passages occur in the manuscript.

[4] 'Wulfstan and the Laws of Cnut', *ante*, lxiii. 433–52.

[5] I use this term for convenience, though the compiler of the D text may have had before him this code with some minor differences from its form in the only surviving manuscript of it. On this see *ante*, lxiii. 433, n. 3.

[6] See p. 82 *infra*.

owes its presence in Cnut's laws to a specific reason.[1] Moreover, it carefully avoids the sections of Cnut's laws drawn from other sources, even when they intervene between the chapters based on VI Ethelred, except only for the clauses based on III Edgar 3. If the D text is a later compilation, then we must assume that the compiler had both VI Ethelred and Cnut's laws before him, and was deliberately extracting the clauses common to both. He did not even fail to notice that VI Ethelred 26. 1, omitted by Cnut's laws at its original context, was nevertheless used in II Cnut 73, long after the indebtedness to VI Ethelred had ceased at II Cnut 11.1.[2] He might well have overlooked this, for it is only the second part of a clause in Cnut's law; yet he allows it, and the preceding introductory clause VI Ethelred 26, not used by Cnut, to remain in its proper place in his selection from VI Ethelred. Since it is difficult to conceive of a motive that would drive a compiler to so complicated a proceeding, it is surely better to regard the text in D as a set of extracts from VI Ethelred, to which some material from other sources has been appended, and to account for its agreements with Cnut's laws by the hypothesis that it was used by the author of these. This view is strengthened by the fact that several of the clauses in the D text are in their wording midway between Cnut's laws and VI Ethelred.[3] If we do decide that the D text is an earlier document than Cnut's laws, we are only saying that it is what its own introduction claims it to be, when it states that it is an ordinance made ' as soon as King Cnut with the advice of his councillors completely established peace and friendship between the Danes and the English '.

In the same article I went on to demonstrate that the additions made in the D version to its sources are in the style of Wulfstan; moreover, the D manuscript is one that contains much Wulfstan material.[4] If the document is what it claims to be, an ordinance issued early in Cnut's reign, it is only natural that it should have been drafted by the archbishop who, as most scholars agree, drew up codes for King Ethelred. A detailed examination of the style, sources and content of Cnut's laws led me to conclude that these, too, are Wulfstan's work; and the manner in which they treat the D version is in complete agreement with Wulfstan's method of work in other places, where we find him using his own earlier work in later writings. Liebermann's arguments for dating Cnut's law late in his reign, and so after Wulfstan's death, do not seem to me valid.[5]

[1] See p. 83 *infra*. It is II Cnut 57.

[2] Except for II Cnut 57, on which see p. 83 *infra*.

[3] See *ante*, lxiii. 435 f.

[4] See *ante*, lxiii. 437. It has information preserved nowhere else, such as the original beginning of his pastoral letter, and the rubrics on the occasions of the issue of VII and VIII Ethelred.

[5] Liebermann, *op. cit.* III. 194. For discussion of these, see *ante*, lxiii. 450 f.

In 1950, however, in an important book of Wulfstan studies,[1] Professor Jost refused to admit the possibility of Wulfstan's authorship of Cnut's laws, or of the priority of the D version. As he is a scholar who has made valuable contributions towards the establishment of the canon of Wulfstan's writings,[2] his views must be given serious consideration, especially as this matter is one of great importance both for the understanding of the career of one of the foremost of Anglo-Saxon statesmen and for a correct interpretation of Cnut's character and of the course of events at a critical moment of Anglo-Saxon history. It would be regrettable if historians were, in view of the complicated nature of the evidence, to dismiss the whole subject as too controversial for their consideration.

It will first be necessary to consider Jost's views on VI Ethelred, for his arguments concerning Cnut's laws depend in part on his attitude to this text. Moreover, by his detailed and illuminating work on the sources that lie behind V and VI Ethelred and the Latin text which Liebermann calls a paraphrase of VI Ethelred, he has added much to our knowledge of the way laws were drawn up in Ethelred's reign, and has placed on a sounder basis the discussion of the relationship between these three texts. Among his firmer conclusions must be mentioned his proof first that V Ethelred was used by the author of the Latin document, who had, however, also access to the excerpts from Latin sources which this code had used; secondly, that VI Ethelred, while it repeats unchanged much of V Ethelred, also uses the Latin document, agreeing with it in the order of its topics as well as in some matters of detail; [3] thirdly, that the method of compilation in all three texts agrees with that employed by Wulfstan elsewhere, and thus confirms the already widely held attribution of all three texts to the archbishop. His authorship of the Latin document, which is indicated by the remark: *Ego N (Wulfstanus) . . . Eboracensium archiepiscopus, eadem* (i.e. *haec legalia statuta uel decreta*) . . . *litteris infixi*,[4] is confirmed by the similarities which Jost has noted between this text and the penitential letters composed by Wulfstan. One may agree also that this Latin document gives an historically acceptable account (*relatio*) of the proceedings at the council of Enham, and that it has

[1] *Wulfstanstudien* (Swiss Studies in English 23), Berne, 1950. He deals with this matter on pages 94–103. It is difficult to decide from this book whether the author does or does not accept my attribution of the ' Laws of Edward and Guthrum ' to Wulfstan. A footnote on page 73 may imply, but does not state, acceptance of it. He does not include this text in his list of genuine texts, yet nowhere in his very detailed examination of the features of Wulfstan's style does he suggest that this code departs from his usage.

[2] See, besides this new work, articles in *Anglia*, xlvii. 105 ff., lvi. 265 ff., and a review in *Englische Studien*, lii. 105 ff.

[3] Liebermann, *op. cit.* III. 168, regarded the Latin as a paraphrase of VI Ethelred, but Jost shows that the Latin is nearer to the sources than is the Old English code.

[4] Liebermann, *op. cit.* I. 257.

a particular interest for the light it sheds on how councils were conducted.

Jost draws some further conclusions from the evidence he has collected which cannot so easily be accepted without discussion. He holds that the council of Enham was held at Whitsuntide, 1008, and that V Ethelred is far and away the best text of the statutes issued at it; that the Latin document is a record of the proceedings which was voluntarily drawn up by Wulfstan, and that VI Ethelred is merely a private work of his, based on V Ethelred and the Latin account, and gives a code 'not as it had actually been decided at Enham, but as he subsequently would have wished it'.[1]

The Latin text gives us the name Enham as the place of assembly, and Whitsuntide as the season. Neither it nor VI Ethelred gives the year. The rubric to one of the versions of V Ethelred contained in MS. Nero A. 1 gives the date as 1008. Liebermann's final view was that V and VI Ethelred were variant versions of a set of statutes issued at Enham at Whitsuntide, 1008, and the Latin version a paraphrase of VI Ethelred.[2] There are considerable differences between V Ethelred on the one hand, and VI Ethelred and the Latin version on the other. V Ethelred lacks several injunctions which are in the other versions: for example, that those who persist in the practice of magic and idolatry are to be driven from the land (VI. 7);[3] that church-scot is to be paid at Martinmas (VI. 18.1); that those who damage warships are to make good the damage and pay the king's *mund* (VI. 34); that anyone who violates a nun or ravishes a widow is to pay heavy amends to Church and State (VI. 39).[4] On the other hand, V Ethelred has some things which are missing in the other versions: the feast of St. Edward is to be celebrated over all England on 18 March (V. 16); a deserter from the army when the king is not with it is to pay 120 shillings (V. 28.1).[5] Even if one were to explain these differences as due to accidental omissions by copyists, one would be left with other discrepancies which cannot be accounted for in this way, for there are clauses in V Ethelred which contradict those in VI Ethelred. Thus V. 28 prescribes the death penalty or payment of wergild for deserting the army when the king is with it, whereas in VI. 35 only loss of property is involved; and similarly, when in V. 29 it is stated that an excommunicated man who comes into the king's presence

[1] Jost, *op. cit.* p. 36: 'nicht wie es zu Eanham tatsächlich beschlossen worden war, sondern wie er es nachträglich gewünscht hätte.'

[2] Liebermann, *op. cit.* III. 166–71.

[3] Unless otherwise stated, the Latin version is in substantial agreement with VI Ethelred.

[4] The Latin version gives the penalty as loss of goods, and does not mention the ecclesiastical penalty.

[5] This is in the two texts of V Ethelred contained in Nero A. 1, but is omitted in that in the D manuscript.

endangers his life or property, only property is mentioned in VI. 36, which deals with this offence.[1] Another difference is the express injunction in VI. 23 that the Ember fasts are to be observed as St. Gregory prescribed for the English nation, to which the Latin version adds that other nations have a different practice, whereas V. 15 merely makes the general injunction that festivals and fasts are to be observed as they were best observed in the past. If we accept both V and VI Ethelred as emanating from a single council, these differences require some explanation.

Yet I do not think that Professor Jost's interpretation of the relationship between the versions removes the difficulty; for if we were to agree that V Ethelred represents the statutes as issued at Enham, that the Latin text is Wulfstan's own account of what took place there, and VI Ethelred a set of statutes as he would have liked them to have been issued, are we then to accuse him of deliberate falsification in his account in the Latin text? We know that he was in favour of avoiding the death penalty, but would he have gone so far as tacitly to ignore its imposition for two major crimes at a council whose proceedings he is recording?

It is not necessary to discuss this matter at length, for the whole problem has since been ably and fully considered by Dr. Kenneth Sisam,[2] who suggests a much more acceptable solution, namely, that while V Ethelred gives the statutes promulgated at Enham,[3] Wulfstan was there empowered to issue a version for his Danelaw province with some modifications. His Latin version would then be a learned record meant to guide his higher clergy, and VI Ethelred be intended for wider circulation among the clergy of his province, for them to make its injunctions known. Dr. Sisam shows convincingly how the variations between the versions can be accounted for on this hypothesis, having regard to the historical situation. It seems to me probable that he has supplied the correct solution,[4] and it is certainly to be preferred to Jost's. It is very difficult to envisage a busy archbishop going to considerable pains to compose in the name of the council a set of statutes for his own private satisfaction. At the very least, he would hope to get it adopted on some future occasion. So even if Jost were right in regarding VI Ethelred as a mere private compilation, there would be nothing odd in Wulfstan's using it as the chief basis of an

[1] It replaces the words ' excommunicated man ' by ' murderers, perjurers or proved homicides '.

[2] *Studies in the History of Old English Literature* (Oxford, 1953), pp. 278–87.

[3] Dr. Sisam shows that all three texts of V Ethelred come from a copy in some respects faulty, and he would attribute to scribal carelessness the absence of the clauses on payment of church-scot and on the damaging of ships. He regards the clause on St. Edward's festival as a later interpolation.

[4] It seems a better explanation of the facts than my suggestion *ante*, lxiii. 433, n., that, while V Ethelred was issued in 1008, the council of Enham was later than this year, and that a revision of V Ethelred was produced at it.

agreement drawn up between the English and Danes in Cnut's reign, as he did, if my interpretation of the D version of Cnut's laws is correct. Jost asks: 'Was VI Ethelred in Wulfstan's eyes the only usable law?'[1] Not at all, but on Jost's theory it was a set of statutes as he would have liked them to have been issued. Why then should he not use it when he had to draw up terms to be laid before the assembly at Oxford in 1018? His choice is equally easy to understand if we accept Dr. Sisam's hypothesis. A code modified to suit the Danelaw might well afford a basis for an agreement with the Danes.

We may now reconsider the authorship of Cnut's laws, and the nature of the version above mentioned contained in manuscript D. Jost admits that the compilation of this text out of VI Ethelred and the laws of Cnut 'must have been very laborious and seems to have no sensible meaning'.[2] We have seen above[3] just how laborious a task it would have been. He would consider the absence of motive for so laborious an undertaking a very weighty argument against its having arisen in this way if similar 'to our way of thinking purposeless work'[4] did not occur in pseudo-Wulfstan homilies. He therefore attributes the D version of Cnut's laws to 'the pedantic sport of a compiler'.[5]

A comparison with homiletic writings, however, is not valid in this connexion. It is true that some of these are simply a patchwork from other sources, though not necessarily on this account 'purposeless work'. We need not believe that in Anglo-Saxon times men went to great trouble to produce texts of no practical use out of a passion for compilation. Such compilations provide material for sermons, pastoral letters, &c. With laws the position is different. A set of statutes is valueless until it has authority behind it. It is fair to assume that a person who at great labour compiles a set of statutes in the name of the council has at least a hope of obtaining authority for its promulgation. If, therefore, the D version arose in the way Jost postulates, this would in my opinion imply that at some date after the promulgation of Cnut's long code a set of statutes was required (or someone thought one might be required) which would repeat such parts of VI Ethelred as had received Cnut's sanction, with only a little additional matter,[6]

[1] *Op. cit.* p. 99: 'War in den Augen Wulfstans VI Atr. das einzige brauchbare Gesetz?'

[2] Jost, *op. cit.* p. 100: 'müsste sehr mühsam gewesen sein und scheine keinen vernünftigen Sinn zu haben.' [3] P. 73.

[4] Jost, *loc. cit.*: 'für unser Denken zwecklose Arbeit.'

[5] *Ibid.*: 'der pedantischen Spielerei eines Kompilators.'

[6] Namely, III Edgar 3, and the text which follows as an appendix to VI Ethelred. This text is also in a homily in the York gospels. It is possible that it was a later addition both in VI Ethelred and in the text in D under consideration. See p. 80 *infra*.

ignoring the rest of Cnut's code. It is extremely difficult to imagine any historical context which would fit such a supposition. Cnut's laws seem to have been regarded subsequently as the final statement of Anglo-Saxon law; they form the chief basis of the work of the Anglo-Norman legists, namely, the authors of *Quadripartitus*, the *Consiliatio Cnuti* and the *Instituta Cnuti*. It is not until one comes to the spurious *Leges Edwardi Confessoris* that Cnut's laws are ousted from this position of eminence, by a writer who makes the demonstrably false claim that law had slumbered between the reign of Edgar and that of Edward the Confessor. It should also be noted that in 1065, when the northern rebels drove out Earl Tostig and marched south, and King Edward sent Earl Harold to make terms with them, he ' renewed there Cnut's law '.[1] Unless, therefore, one is content to leave the D version as an entirely motiveless piece of work, as Jost does, it is difficult to account for its compilation *after* the issue of the full code of Cnut's laws.

We have not yet exhausted the difficulties involved in the acceptance of Jost's view of this text. It remains to examine the introductory matter with which the D version is provided, and it will be as well, for clarity's sake, to give a full translation: [2]

> This is the ordinance which the councillors determined and devised according to many good precedents; and that took place as soon as King Cnut with the advice of his councillors completely established peace and friendship between the Danes and the English and put an end to all their former strife. *In the first place the councillors determined that above all other things they would ever honour one God and steadfastly hold one Christian faith, and would love King Cnut with due loyalty* and zealously observe Edgar's laws. And they agreed that they would, with God's help, investigate further at leisure what was necessary for the nation, as best they could. Now we wish to make clear what can benefit us in religious and secular concerns, let him pay heed who will. *Let us very resolutely turn from sins and eagerly atone for our misdeeds* and duly love and honour one God and steadfastly hold one Christian faith and diligently avoid every heathen practice.

Only the parts in italics could have been taken from Cnut's full code; [3] the rest is peculiar to the D version. If we accept Jost's view that the D version is later than the full code, we must explain this introduction in one of two ways: either it represents the work of the compiler himself, in which case it can only be deliberate deception, for he must have known that his own compilation was not what the preface claims it to be; or secondly, it is the addition of a later writer, who, realizing that this compilation in content lay between Ethelred's laws and Cnut's, jumped to the conclusion

[1] Anglo-Saxon Chronicle, 1065 D.

[2] Reprinted from *ante*, lxiii. 440.

[3] Cnut 1 and 18.1.

that it represented the agreement reached between the English and Danes early in Cnut's reign. The first explanation is improbable, for it is hard to see who could benefit by such a false claim. The second alternative would allow us to believe that the introductory matter was written in good faith. But why then should this unknown writer have gone to the trouble of searching out Wulfstan phrases in which to express his belief? *Swa hi betst mihton, for Gode and for worlde, gime se þe wille. hwæt us mæg to ræde, saca . . . getwæmde, lagan geornlice folgian, smeagan . . . þearfe* are all Wulfstan expressions.[1] Jost does not believe that there were persons who deliberately tried to write in Wulfstan's style, and I fully agree with him. What are we then to think of a passage so completely couched in his phraseology? If it really were composed after Cnut's full code, and if we were to accept Liebermann's date of 1026 or later for this, Wulfstan had been dead for several years before it was written. Surely then we would have to assume that the author collected his Wulfstan phrases in order to give colour to a false claim. And again one would ask: 'Who could benefit by such falsification?'

Far less difficulty is involved in the view that the D version is earlier than Cnut's code, and was one of the sources of it; and that the introductory passage is genuine, and is expressed in Wulfstan's phraseology because he wrote it himself. It remains then to consider whether Jost has brought any positive objections that might be held to invalidate this interpretation. Naturally, one can never actually *prove* that what looks like an intermediate text *could not* have arisen by a later compilation of two versions, but textual critics normally work on the assumption that this is the less likely happening unless there is some motive for it.

It will be convenient to take Jost's objections one by one, except in as far as they have already been considered. He finds the absence of Cnut's name from the statutes in the D version, most of which begin: 'and the ordinance of the councillors is . . .', a difficulty in the way of accepting the D version as what its introduction declares it to be. He considers that a strong king like Cnut would not have been content to let enactments be made in the name of the councillors alone, when even the weak king Ethelred had never done so. But this last claim is true only if we accept Jost's opinion that VI Ethelred, whose chapters use the same commencing formula, is merely a private work. In any case, the situation at the beginning of Cnut's reign was unprecedented, and to argue from the procedure of his predecessor may not be legitimate. Cnut was a foreign king recently established, to whom the support of the English councillors must have been highly important. The number of executions and outlawries of Saxon

[1] See *ante*, lxiii. 441.

notables, including King Ethelred's son Eadwig, in 1017, suggests that Cnut did not feel himself very secure. He had brought into England a large number of foreign followers, many of whom were heathen; it cannot have been an easy matter to ensure peaceful relations between them and the Christian English, and it seems likely that much preliminary work was necessary before, in the words of the Anglo-Saxon Chronicle, 1018, 'Danes and English reached agreement at Oxford'.[1] I find no difficulty in supposing that the witan were instructed to draw up a set of statutes likely to win general acceptance and to bring them before the king at the assembly; and that in such an event, the task of drafting would fall mainly to Archbishop Wulfstan, as it had in the previous reign.

Jost's next objection arises from the content of the D version. Its conclusion, a mere repetition of VI Ethelred, Appendix 42–49, occurs also in a homily at the end of the York Gospels, which both Jost and I accept as a genuine Wulfstan work.[2] He believes that the passage in question is in its original form in this homily, and that it is improbable that Wulfstan himself added it either to VI Ethelred or to the D version of Cnut's laws, since it repeats some matter already in these two texts.[3] The question of the nature of the D version is not affected either way by the problem of who added this passage to VI Ethelred; we are concerned only with deciding whether its presence in the D version of Cnut's laws prevents our taking this version to be prior to Cnut's laws and to emanate from Wulfstan. I do not think we are forced to reject it because its content overlaps that of the rest of the document in some particulars, but even if we do reject it, it does not follow that the rest of the D version must be a compilation later than Wulfstan's time, for this concluding section could have been tacked on later in the mid-eleventh-century manuscript which is our only source for the D version.

Jost objects also to the section immediately preceding the concluding section, a passage drawn, unlike most of the text, from Edgar's laws instead of Ethelred's. He considers that it gives the impression of an intrusion, because it states the precise amount to be paid for certain offences, whereas money-compensations are not mentioned in the rest of the text. It seems to me that a practical reason for the presence of this section becomes clear when we notice what offences are singled out for this divergent treatment,

[1] *Dene and Engle wurdon sammæle æt Oxnaforda.* Only the version of the Chronicle in Tiberius B. IV adds here: *to Eadgares lage.* On this, see *ante*, lxiii. 443.

[2] See *ante*, lxiii. 452; Jost, *op. cit.* pp. 86–94.

[3] The question of the nature of the D version of Cnut's laws is not affected by the fact that this does not derive its version of this passage from the addition to VI Ethelred, for we do not know when this addition was made, nor did the D version use the actual manuscript of VI Ethelred which survives.

namely, the promoting of injustice or giving of wrong judgements out of personal enmity or for bribes, and the refusal to obey the judgement of a court. When the anarchy and corruption of Ethelred's reign are remembered, it does not seem strange that men should desire a precise re-statement and enforcement of the penalties laid down for these great offences in Edgar's law, even though on other matters they were content with a more general statement, for the time being, at any rate.[1] It is possible that this section represents the contribution of other members of the council who, thinking that Wulfstan's proposals lacked precision, were determined that immediate practical injunctions should be made to suppress these serious and wide-spread abuses. This cannot be more than conjecture; it would, however, explain why the D version does not end where VI Ethelred does, as Jost thinks it would if Wulfstan had been the author of both texts. It was perhaps because the passage borrowed from Edgar's law does not make a good conclusion that the concluding section from the York homily was added, consisting of a general exhortation to each individual to cease from sin and restrain the wrongdoing of others, to remember his Christian faith, to respect and frequently visit the church, to pay church dues, to observe festivals and fasts, to refrain from markets on Sundays, to obey and honour the clergy, to be kind and generous to the poor, to widows and orphans, foreigners and strangers, and, finally, to do to others as he would be done by. There would be many Danes at that gathering to whom these exhortations would not be oft-repeated commonplaces.

I am ready to admit that the D version of Cnut's laws is by no means a well-planned and polished piece of work; the passage from Edgar's laws breaks the unity of tone, the concluding injunctions repeat some things already dealt with. But should one expect a finished piece of writing in the circumstances in which I believe the code to have been composed? Jost perhaps thinks too readily of Wulfstan, the scholar in his study, and too rarely of Wulfstan, the veteran archbishop, engaged in multifarious activities at a time when a foreign conquest and an influx of heathern and semi-heathen settlers was endangering the Christianity of his country. His activities in preparation for the assembly of 1018 must have included far more than the drawing up of statutes. I could easily believe that directions to a secretary to copy certain marked passages may in general have been all he had time for. That would account for the exact copying of some of his earlier work. Jost claims that Wulfstan cannot be shown to have ever slavishly excerpted from his own work, but I doubt whether we are justified in assuming that at all periods of his life and in all circumstances he

[1] The introduction to the D version promises further legislation at leisure.

used precisely the same method of work. By 1018 he was an old man, and doubtless filled with anxiety as to the effect on the Church of the new régime. I would suggest that stylistic niceties did not weigh very heavily with him on this particular occasion.

Jost has pointed out that in one section both the D version and Cnut's complete code go back, not directly on VI Ethelred, 12, 12.1, but on the somewhat different wording of this by Wulfstan in his homily LIX. If my theory of the origin of the D version is the correct one, this would mean that Wulfstan, while mainly using VI Ethelred, preferred in this part his later statement on the same topic. This is quite in line with his method of procedure in his other works. If Jost is right in taking the D version as later than Cnut's laws, we must then take it that it was the compiler of these who preferred at this point to depart from VI Ethelred (his main source in this section) in favour of a Wulfstan homily. I do not see why this should be easier to accept.

Next, Jost accuses the compiler of the D version, if he is writing prior to Cnut's laws, of inconsistency in his attitude to different parts of his source, VI Ethelred. Whereas he makes many additions to the chapters dependent on VI Ethelred 13, 14, 8, 2.2, 5, he leaves those from 16 on practically unchanged. This is true; but the parts where considerable modification has been made come all at the beginning of the D version. Its compiler would not be the first nor the last author to find that he had begun to work on too time-consuming a method, and to content himself with a simpler procedure as his work advanced. The author of Cnut's full code leaves the earlier sections of the D version much as they stood, but modifies those chapters borrowed from VI Ethelred which the D version had left unaltered. This does not suggest to me a different author. Why not the same author, working under different conditions, with leisure,[1] that is, to complete what he had only had time to begin before the assembly of 1018? And when Jost asks, why, when the introduction to the D version asserts that a return to Edgar's law is the goal of this code, was no single decree taken over from Edgar's laws,[2] has he not forgotten that he has himself rejected as an intrusion the part of the D version which does come direct from those very laws? I have already indicated that I consider it an integral part. Moreover, I am still of my previously expressed opinion [3] that Wulfstan's aim in the codes which he drew up for Ethelred was a return to the conditions of Edgar's reign, and so he would not regard quotations from

[1] Cf. *on æmtan* in the introduction of the D version.

[2] Jost, *op. cit.* p. 99: ' Und wenn, wie die Einleitung zu Cn D vorgibt, die Rückkehr zu Eadgars Rechtsordnung der Zweck dieses Gesetzes war, warum wird dann aus Eadgars Gesetzen keine einzige Verordnung übernommen? '

[3] See *ante*, lxiii. 442 f.

those codes as contradicting the statement that the councillors determined to observe Edgar's laws. That the complete code of Cnut should in its shape as well as in some details have gone back to II and III Edgar may perhaps be due to instructions given at the assembly mentioned in the D version.

Jost draws attention to the omission of VI Ethelred 37, which is used by II Cnut 57, from the D version. Yet the presence of this clause in Cnut's code, though lacking in the D version, looks less like an argument against the priority of the latter when one examines the context in which it occurs. The clause in question, VI Ethelred 37 (V Ethelred 30) is itself based on chapters 4-4.2 of Alfred's laws, and Cnut's laws include it in a section mainly drawn from Alfred, as is shown clearly by the obvious dependence of the clauses immediately following, II Cnut 58, 58.1, 58.2, 59 on Alfred 3 and 7. The compiler of the D version omitted the whole section VI Ethelred 33–39, and therefore these chapters do not appear in Cnut's full code in the portion dependent on the D version; but some way farther on, after the compiler of the full code had ceased to use D,[1] and was drawing on the laws of Alfred, he preferred to give chapters 4-4.2 of these in a more modern wording, and turned to the form in which it occurs in VI Ethelred 37. We can thus add another instance to many previously demonstrated [2] which show that the compiler of Cnut's code was not only well acquainted with Wulfstan's writings, but knew also what sources these used. Thus the absence of VI Ethelred 37 from the D version does not prove that this version could not have been one of the sources of the long code.

Finally, Jost claims that Cnut's letter of 1020 is not written in Wulfstan's style, and implies that this lessens the probability of the archbishop's participation in Cnut's law-giving. I am prepared to admit that Wulfstan's influence on this letter is not direct, but I do not draw from this the conclusion that Cnut did not include the northern archbishop in his counsels. For it seems to me that the letter has every appearance of being addressed to a regent, and so was presumably written from Denmark. Already its address, which singles out Earl Thurkil from the other earls, leaving these unnamed, would suggest this, but more cogent is chapter 9, where in the event of disobedience to ecclesiastical and secular law and of refusal to make amends, Cnut asks Earl Thurkil to deal with the wrong-doers. If Cnut himself had been in England, Thurkil's responsibility would have been confined to his own earldom, and

[1] Except for II Cnut 73, which is from VI Ethelred 26.1, as given in the D version, the dependence of the full code on this version ceases with II Cnut 15.3. VI Ethelred 26.1, which concerns widows, was obviously moved to its position in the long code because it fits better in this context, following clauses concerning heriot and inheritance after a man's death.

[2] See *ante*, lxiii. 445 f.

it would have been for the other earls to establish order in their own provinces. It is surely in the capacity of regent in Cnut's absence that Thurkil alone is mentioned here.[1] Hence this letter cannot be taken as a sign that Wulfstan's influence was waning.

As Jost rejects the view that the D version is prior to Cnut's code, he rejects 'with still greater determination' the attribution of this code to Wulfstan. But, in fact, the two things do not stand and fall together. The use of the D version by the longer code was only one of many reasons that led me to postulate Wulfstan's authorship and to re-examine the evidence for the date. Jost does not bring any evidence for the date of Cnut's laws. What led me, before I had even noticed the peculiarities of the D version, to suspect Wulfstan's authorship, was first, the author's extraordinarily close familiarity with the Wulfstan writings and with the sources on which these were based; secondly, his tendency to go back to the source of a passage he is copying and to introduce some modification or addition from the original, a method frequently employed by Wulfstan; thirdly, the addition of Wulfstan phrases to those passages drawn from legal texts not of his composition; fourthly, the inclusion of passages undoubtedly in the Wulfstan style for which no source exists among his extant works; fifthly, the change of the law in accordance with a known tendency of Wulfstan's, namely, the avoidance of the death penalty; and finally, the absence of influence from other writers. The use of the D version, a text preserved in a manuscript with much Wulfstan matter, is only a supporting piece of evidence; it affords strong support, but the hypothesis could stand without it.

I should be interested to know how scholars who date Cnut's laws later than Wulfstan's death envisage the process of their compilation. It must surely be universally admitted that the compiler had access to an amazingly full set of Wulfstan writings, to such a collection as can hardly have been available outside the two sees which Wulfstan held, York and Worcester.[2] If the laws are after his death, are we to assume that it had now become traditional to apply to one of these places when laws were wanted, rather than to obtain the collaboration of influential prelates, such, for example,

[1] Liebermann nowhere makes it clear why he should so confidently date this letter after Cnut's return in 1020. Sir Frank Stenton has communicated to me that he also regards this letter as sent from Denmark. In that case we must date it 1019–20.

[2] Wulfstan held York until his death in 1023, whereas Leofsige was appointed to Worcester in 1016. But it seems likely that Wulfstan regarded him merely as his suffragan, for we find Wulfstan still disposing of Worcester estates in 1017. A somewhat similar position arose after Ealdred was forced by the pope in 1061, when he became archbishop of York, to relinquish Worcester to St. Wulfstan. It is a pity that Jost refers to this Wulfstan, the second of that name at Worcester, as Wulfstan III of York, a see which he did not hold, for this slip will encourage a confusion of the two Wulfstans which is already too common.

as Æthelnoth of Canterbury?[1] Such a proceeding cannot be shown to be impossible, but unless stronger evidence than any hitherto produced is forthcoming to necessite a late date for Cnut's laws, I hold to my opinion that the more natural explanation is that the laws were drawn up in Wulfstan's lifetime under his direction. Has any good reason ever been offered as to why Cnut should have reigned for ten years or more before promulgating any laws?

[1] The relation between Cnut's laws and VIII Ethelred is also suggestive, for I Cnut 2.3–3.2 seems based, not directly on VIII Ethelred 1.1–5.1, but on an extract from this code which survives as a separate text with the title *Be cyricgriðe* in the Wulfstan manuscript Nero A. I, in a hand which Mr. N. R. Ker dates early eleventh century. This little text includes a passage omitted in Cnut's laws, so it cannot have been extracted from them; on the other hand, it has a phrase which is in I Cnut 2.3 but missing from VIII Ethelred 1.1; in minor matters it agrees now with one and now with the other of these codes. It looks as if we have here another instance of a Worcester extract from one of Ethelred's codes being then used by the compiler of Cnut's laws. But this is not the only possible explanation of the facts: VIII Ethelred has come down to us only in the D manuscript, and its variations from the text of *Be cyricgriðe* could be ascribed to later alterations by the careless D scribe; or *Be cyricgriðe* might be a source used for VIII Ethelred rather than an excerpt from it. In that case we should have another example of the tendency of the compiler of Cnut's laws to go behind the codes he is using to their sources.

XIV

INTRODUCTION TO

SERMO LUPI AD ANGLOS

ABBREVIATIONS

Anglo-Saxon laws are quoted with Roman numerals for the codes and Arabic for the chapters, and the kings' names are abbreviated as follows:

Af	Alfred
As	Athelstan
Atr	Ethelred
Cn	Cnut
Edg	Edgar

AGu stands for the Treaty of Alfred and Guthrum, EGu for the Treaty of Edward and Guthrum, Hn for the *Leges Henrici Primi*.

Archiv	(*Herrigs*) *Archiv für das Studium der neueren Sprachen und Litteraturen*
ASC	*Anglo-Saxon Chronicle*
BCS	W. de G. Birch, *Cartularium Saxonicum*, 1885–93, quoted by number of document
Bethurum	D. Bethurum, *The Homilies of Wulfstan*, 1957
BT	J. Bosworth and T. N. Toller, *An Anglo-Saxon Dictionary*, 1882–98 (Suppl. 1908–21)
Campbell	A. Campbell, *Old English Grammar*, 1959
CCCC	Corpus Christi College, Cambridge
CH	*Catholic Homilies* (Ælfric's *Homilies of the Anglo-Saxon Church*, ed. B. Thorpe), 1844–6
EETS	Early English Text Society
EHR	*English Historical Review*
FlWig	*Florence of Worcester*, ed. B. Thorpe, 1848–9
Hickes, *Thesaurus*	G. Hickes, *Linguarum Veterum Septentrionalium Thesaurus*, 1705
JEGP	*Journal of English and Germanic Philology*
KCD	J. M. Kemble, *Codex Diplomaticus Aevi Saxonici*, 1839–48, quoted by number of document
Ker, *Catalogue*	N. R. Ker, *Catalogue of Manuscripts containing Anglo-Saxon*, 1957
Liebermann	*Die Gesetze der Angelsachsen*, ed. F. Liebermann, 1898–1916
Luick	K. Luick, *Historische Grammatik der englischen Sprache*, 1914–29
MGH	*Monumenta Germaniae Historica*, ed. G. H. Pertz, 1826–
ME	Middle English
MLN	*Modern Language Notes*
MLR	*Modern Language Review*

ABBREVIATIONS

Napier . . .	A. (S.) Napier, *Wulfstan: Sammlung der ihm zugeschriebenen Homilien*, 1883 (Roman numerals refer to homilies)
NED . . .	*New English Dictionary*
OE . . .	Old English
ON . . .	Old Norse
Phil Qu . .	*Philological Quarterly*
PMLA . . .	*Publications of the Modern Language Association*
Polity . . .	*Institutes of Polity, Civil and Ecclesiastical*, ed. K. Jost, 1959
Proc. Brit. Acad. .	*Proceedings of the British Academy*
Robertson . .	A. J. Robertson, *Anglo-Saxon Charters*, 1939 (Roman numerals refer to documents)
RS . . .	Rolls Series
SB . . .	F. H. Stratmann, *A Middle English Dictionary*, re-edited by H. Bradley, 1891
S.C. . . .	*A Summary Catalogue of Western Manuscripts in the Bodleian Library at Oxford*, 1895–1953
Trans. R. Hist. Soc.	*Transactions of the Royal Historical Society*
Wanley, *Catalogus* .	H. Wanley, *Librorum Veterum Septentrionalium Catalogus*, in Hickes, *Thesaurus* II, 1705

TABLE

of the corresponding numeration of Wulfstan's Homilies in Napier and Bethurum

Napier	*Bethurum*
II	VI
III	VII
IV	VIIIa
V	VIIIc
VI	XI
VII	IX
IX	Xb
X	Xc
XI	Ia
XII	Ib
XIII	V
XIV	II
XV	III
XVI	IV
XVII	XIV
XVIII	XII
XIX–XXII	XIII
XXVI	VIIa
XXVIII	XIX
XXXII	XV
XXXIII	XX
XXXIV	XXI
XXXVII	XVII
XLI	XVIb
LIV	XVIII

Bethurum VIIIb, Xa and XVIa are not in Napier.

I. MANUSCRIPTS

Versions of this text occur in five manuscripts,[1] as follows:

I.[2] British Museum, Cotton Nero A i, fols 110–15. Mr N. R. Ker dates the handwriting of this part of the manuscript early eleventh century, and considers that the hand of certain additions is probably that of Wulfstan himself.[3] This manuscript contains also laws, both the earlier and later versions of *Polity*, the Wulfstan homilies X, XXVIII and XXXIV, and texts assigned to Wulfstan by Jost and printed in his edition of *Polity* (167–9, 210–16, 262–7). It has a Latin collection by Wulfstan of passages from Ezechiel, printed by Bethurum as XVIa. Though Liebermann[4] thought a Canterbury origin possible, the manuscript must have been written at one of Wulfstan's sees, Worcester or York.[5] Though carelessly written, it sometimes has more original readings than other manuscripts of Wulfstan's homilies.

E.[6] Bodleian MS Hatton 113 (formerly Junius 99), fols

[1] Excluding Junius 102, a transcript by Junius of six 'Wulfstan' homilies. There are also passages from the *Sermo ad Anglos* embedded in other homilies, and these are referred to in the notes. Napier XXVII is mainly made up of extracts from it, in a different order.

In my descriptions of the MSS I am much indebted to N. R. Ker, *Catalogue of Manuscripts containing Anglo-Saxon.*

[2] I use the same sigla as Napier. Thorpe, Liebermann, Fehr and Jost call this MS G.

[3] See below, pp. 29 f. Marginal additions in this hand to Napier X, V Atr and II Polity 36 (ed Jost 56) occur in the text of later manuscripts: cf also textual note to l. 81 *infra.*

[4] *Die Gesetze der Angelsachsen* I. xxv.

[5] On p. 90 (*Polity* ed Jost 112) a statement enjoining celibacy on priests has been erased, and replaced by an outspoken comment in favour of clerical marriage: *Riht is þæt preost him lufie clænlicne wimman to gebeddan.* This seems to fit York, where married priests were common in the eleventh century, better than monastic establishments such as Worcester and Canterbury. Ker, *Catalogue* 214 f, points out that certain scribbles of s. xiii/xiv suggest that by this date the manuscript was not in a monastic house.

[6] Sweet's *Anglo-Saxon Reader* (14th edit. 82–9) cites it as H, though Napier and others denote by this letter Bodley 343, cited as D in Sweet.

84v–90v. With Hatton MS 114 (Napier's F) this manuscript forms a collection of homilies, which Mr Ker suggests was intended as a continuation of Junius 121,[1] a manuscript of ecclesiastical institutes, &c, including the second version of *Polity* and other Wulfstan texts. Much of these three manuscripts is in the same hand, dated by Ker as third quarter of the eleventh century. They used to be regarded as the work of *Wulfgeatus scriptor wigornensis*, but Ker considers that the colophon which gives this information was probably copied from the exemplar. The Worcester origin seems certain. E has notes by Coleman[2] and glosses in the well-known 'tremulous hand' which occurs in many Worcester manuscripts.[3] E is the principal manuscript of Wulfstan's homilies.

C.[4] Corpus Christi College, Cambridge, MS 201 (formerly S. 18), pp. 82–6. This is a mid-eleventh-century manuscript containing laws and several Wulfstan texts. Its compiler had access to some Wulfstan material not found elsewhere, including the first draft of Cnut's laws. Though it has been assigned to Worcester,[5] it has none of the glosses or other marks which would support this provenance. York cannot be outruled. The Wulfstan material which it contains is as likely to have been available there as at Worcester, and it includes the only surviving copy of the *Law of the Northumbrian Priests*, a text relating to the province of York.[6]

[1] Called G by Napier, X by Thorpe, Liebermann, Fehr, and Jost.

[2] Probably the author of a lost vernacular *Life* of St Wulfstan, Bishop of Worcester (1062–95). *v.* N. R. Ker, 'Old English Notes signed "Coleman" ', *Medium Ævum* xviii.

[3] See Ker, *Catalogue* p. lvii; and 'The Date of the "Tremulous" Worcester Hand', *Leeds Studies in English* vi; also S. J. Crawford, 'The Worcester Marks and Glosses of the Old English Manuscripts in the Bodleian', *Anglia* lii.

[4] Cited by Thorpe, Liebermann, Fehr, Jost, and myself, when writing on laws, as D.

[5] E.g. by Wanley, *Catalogus* 141, and by Feiler, *Das Benediktiner-Offizium* 8.

[6] L. Whitbread, *Phil. Qu.* xxxviii. 106–12, arguing that the material was collected at Worcester, says York 'can hardly be considered inviting', since only one item is specifically connected with it. But

MANUSCRIPTS

B. Corpus Christi College, Cambridge, MS 419 (formerly S. 14), pp. 95–112. This manuscript is of the first half of the eleventh century and is a companion volume to MS 421. Both contain homilies by various authors. B has, besides the *Sermo Lupi ad Anglos*, the Wulfstan homilies Napier II, III, V, X, XIX–XXII, and part of VII. MS 421 has additions written at Exeter.

H.[1] Bodley MS 343 (formerly NE. F. iv. 12), fols 143v–144v. This is a collection of homilies, probably written in the West Midlands, in the second half of the twelfth century. Besides our *sermo* it includes the Wulfstan homilies Napier II, V, XII, XIII and XVI. Most of its homilies are by Ælfric.[2]

These five versions form three groups, which differ considerably, especially in length. The shortest version is in B and H, and there is a close connexion between them, though neither is derived from the other.[3] Though they omit several passages, they include a few clauses not in other manuscripts,[4] of which the most important is the phrase *and Æþelred man dræfde ut of his earde* (ll. 79 f) which must have been in the original text of the homily. The longest version is represented by I and E, and here also

not a single item is specifically connected with Worcester, for Wulfstan's writings may have been produced at either place. Whitbread would attribute the manuscript to Canterbury, but not on strong evidence. Linguistic features which have been claimed as eastern occur in manuscripts from other areas (*v.* pp. 40–3 *infra*). Among related MSS which he claims for Canterbury, Claudius A iii and Nero A i have the 'Wulfstan' hand (*v.* pp. 29 f *infra*). He dates the collection to Cnut's reign because the law-codes 'only go as far as II Cnut': there were no later Anglo-Saxon laws. In any case, the manuscript does not contain the full version of Cnut's code, but only the first draft, which was probably no later than 1018.

[1] Confusingly cited as D in Sweet's *Anglo-Saxon Reader*.

[2] For other texts from this manuscript, *v.* A. S. Napier, *History of the Holy Rood Tree*, EETS, 1894, and A. O. Belfour, *Twelfth-century Homilies in MS. Bodley 343*, EETS, 1909.

[3] B cannot of course be derived from the later MS H. For its better readings, see textual notes to ll. 9, 14, 17, 23, 33, 40, &c. H agrees with the other versions against B in ll. 74 f and 211.

[4] See textual notes to ll. 32, 44.

the textual variants show that these manuscripts, though closely connected, have independent copies of a common exemplar.[1] In length midway between these groups comes C, sharing with I and E some, but not all, of the passages missing from B and H, and having a little additional matter of its own. C is more closely related to I and E than to B and H.[2] It agrees with I and E in omitting the reference to Ethelred which is necessary for the balance of the sentence; C and I have essentially the same rubric, and E has a modified version of it; in C, I and E the same homily (Napier XXXIV) follows our text, whereas it does not occur in B and H; there is a close connexion between the C and E versions of other homilies, over against B versions,[3] and C and E have groups of Wulfstan's homilies in the same order, when B and H have them scattered, if they contain them at all. The following scheme seems therefore justified:[4]

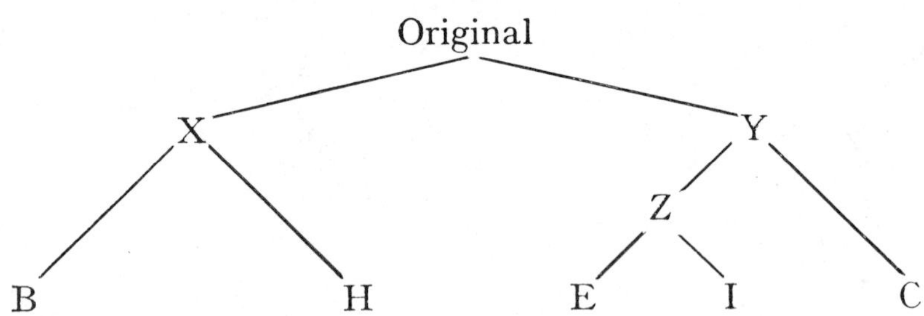

with X, Y and Z representing lost archetypes of the extant versions. There may, of course, have been intermediate versions.

Sweet regarded the varying length of the three types of text as due to a process of repeated cutting, and the text in Sweet's *Reader* is conflated from them all. Napier, on the other hand, relegated to the footnotes passages which are

[1] For I's independence, see e.g. textual notes to ll. 38 and 41. E has preserved the better reading in ll. 59, 65.

[2] This was assumed by Becher in his scheme (*Wulfstans Homilien*, p. 71) and by Napier in his reconstruction of the text. Dr Bethurum supports this conclusion.

[3] See Bethurum 11–21.

[4] It does not differ in essentials from that given in Becher, *op.cit.*, or by Bethurum 22.

in one group of manuscripts only. It is probable, as Dr Bethurum suggests,[1] that the short version of B and H is the oldest. This would not necessarily be proved by its retaining the reference to Ethelred's exile, which was certainly in the original; but since there seems a strong likelihood that I, one of the manuscripts which omit this clause, is connected with Wulfstan himself, one would not expect the short version to retain it if this were a later curtailment by Wulfstan. It is, therefore, probable that Y expanded the original with the material common to C, E and I,[2] and that further additions were made in Z.[3] Even some of the additions in E alone may be Wulfstan's own, for some words which are in the text in E alone are added in the margin of I in a hand which may be Wulfstan's.[4] One of the longer additions in C (*v.* textual note to l. 48) may be his, but another, at l. 7, looks like the incorporation of a later marginal note into the text.[5] It would not be alien to Wulfstan's practice of using his writings again and again if he produced two versions of Y, namely, Z and C.

The text chosen here is that of I, for, in view of the close connexion of this manuscript with Wulfstan, one cannot doubt that it had his approval. That it is closer than E to what he originally wrote is shown by the passage translated from one of Alcuin's letters, for the I text corresponds better with this Latin source than does that in E.[6] In most places where I differs from E, it has the support of other manuscripts. Dr Bethurum has shown that in some other homilies the text in I was probably revised by Wulfstan.[7]

[1] Bethurum 22 f.

[2] The sentence at ll. 86–93, which is missing from B, H and C, may first have been added in the margin of Z, for I at first went on for a few words without it, and then inserted it.

[3] It is obvious that the passage only in C, E and I at ll. 102–32 was written before Cnut's accession in 1016; it does not fit later conditions.

[4] See textual note to l. 81.

[5] But cf p. 6 *infra*. I see no reason for denying Wulfstan's authorship of the C readings given in the textual notes to ll. 48, 70, 117, 129 f, 157, 177 f, 179 and 201.

[6] *v.* note to ll. 184–99, and D. Whitelock, MLR xxxviii. 125 f.

[7] Bethurum 11, 18 f, 331.

SERMO LUPI AD ANGLOS

II. DATE

There is strong evidence for 1014 as the date of the first composition of this homily. In B and H occur the words *and Æþelred man dræfde ut of his earde*, and their omission from the other manuscripts leaves an incomplete sentence. Policy may have dictated this omission, if made in Cnut's reign, for the expulsion of Ethelred, which Wulfstan calls 'a very great treachery', was in favour of Cnut's father.[1] Swegn was accepted as king in 1013, and Ethelred fled to Normandy after Christmas, which would be reckoned as 1014, since the year normally began on 25 December. He returned in 1014. The rubric of I, a manuscript closely connected with Wulfstan, gives the date as 1014. This rubric must have been in Y, for C has it exactly except for the date 1009. As this is too early for Ethelred's expulsion, it is simplest to assume that the scribe misread or miswrote MVIIII for MXIIII, an easy error. In the text of C, however, occur the words: 'This was composed in the days of King Ethelred, a space of four years before he died.' They are awkwardly entered, and perhaps were taken from a marginal note. As Ethelred died on 23 April 1016, this disagrees with the indications for 1014; it seems probable that *feower geara* is an error for *feaw(e)ra geara* 'of a few years'.[2] If one wished to accept a date of 1009 or 1012, one would have to postulate an original version lacking the sentence which contains or requires a reference to Ethelred. There is not the slightest evidence for such a version. E replaces the precise date of the rubric with the vague *in dies Æþelredi regis*; possibly the note incorporated into C was in the margin of Y, and the E scribe recognized a discrepancy; alternatively, if the homily was revised later in Ethelred's reign, the scribe may have preferred a vaguer date than that of the original composition.

[1] Ethelred's name is similarly omitted from V and VIII Atr, which survive only in manuscripts connected with Wulfstan.

[2] I had reached this conclusion independently of the same suggestion by J. C. Pope, in his review of Bethurum, *The Homilies of Wulfstan*, MLN lxxiv. 338. The gen.pl. of *fea* 'few' is recorded as *feawra, feawera*.

III. WULFSTAN'S CAREER

The credit for the identification of Lupus with Wulfstan, Bishop of Worcester and Archbishop of York, belongs to Wanley,[1] and, if 1014 is the date of this homily, this alone rules out any claim for other bishops with the element *wulf* in their names. The identification is supported by the connexion of manuscripts of his work with Worcester, by the version of the Pastoral Letter in MS C, beginning *Wulfstan arcebisceop greteð* . . . , by the close parallels between the *sermones Lupi* and a code of Ethelred, the Latin version of which mentions Wulfstan's instigation, and by the use of the name *Lupus* by Wulfstan, Bishop of London, in some penitential letters,[2] since there are strong reasons for identifying Wulfstan, Bishop of London from 996, with the future archbishop (*v.* EHR lii. 460–5).

We have no definite evidence for Wulfstan's career before he became a bishop. Though Florence of Worcester[3] is wrong in giving him the title of abbot in 1002, it may have been correct at an earlier date in his life; but he signs no charters with this title and his name occurs in no monastery's list of abbots. Some early connexion with the east of England is suggested by the fact that, though he died at York, he was buried at Ely, which is not in any of the dioceses he had governed. This house never claimed him as a former member, and the twelfth-century Ely chronicler[4] can explain this choice of burial-place only by a tale of a miracle which befell him there on a visit. He was held in great esteem at Ely; it was claimed that miracles were performed at his tomb, and as late as the reign of Edward III an effigy was placed over his remains when, along with those of six other early benefactors, including Ealdorman Brihtnoth, they

[1] *Catalogus* 140 f.

[2] On these letters, which survive in CCCC MS 265, Copenhagen MS Gl. kgl. S. 1595, Bodleian MS Barlow 37 (S.C. 6464), see M. Bateson in EHR x. 728 f, Jost, *Wulfstanstudien* 16–21, Bethurum 374–6.

[3] Ed. B. Thorpe, I. 156.

[4] *Historia Eliensis* II. c. 87.

were built into the north wall of the choir.[1] His obit (28 May) is entered in an Ely calendar.[2]

The abbey of Peterborough also claimed Wulfstan as a benefactor; Hugo Candidus[3] states that he had 'given himself and all his possessions' to Peterborough, but fell ill at Ely, when visiting the tombs of the saints, and died and was buried there. Though the statement that he died at Ely is wrong, the entry shows that his memory was honoured at Peterborough. It may have been family connexions which made him a benefactor of at least two Fenland monasteries. There is no room for him in the lists of abbots of Ely, Peterborough, Thorney, or Ramsey; the succession at Crowland is not fully known, but this house preserved no memory of him. He could have been a monk at any of these places except Ely,[4] but their records make no claim to him.

In contrast to the esteem in which he was held in the east of England, he had a bad reputation in some twelfth-century writers in the diocese of Worcester. A list of Bishops of Worcester in an Evesham manuscript (Harley MS 229, fol.

[1] Before the removal of the choir wall in 1770 drawings of these effigies were made and can be seen in the supplement to J. Bentham, *A History and Antiquities of the Conventual and Cathedral Church of Ely*, ed. by W. Stevenson in 1817, plate facing 69, or in R. Gough, *Sepulchral Monuments in Great Britain* I, plate facing cxlvi instead of clvi. An account of this removal is given in Bentham, *op.cit.*, Addenda 23, and in C. W. Stubbs, *Historical Memorials of Ely Cathedral* 92. The bones were placed in Bishop West's chapel, where they still remain.

[2] Trinity College, Cambridge, MS O.2.1. Professor Dickins has examined this manuscript for me. Wulfstan's obit is entered also in Hatton 113 (Worcester) and in Cotton MS Titus D. xxvii (Winchester, before 1035).

[3] W. T. Mellows, *The Chronicle of Hugh Candidus* 73.

[4] Neither the *Historia Eliensis* nor the Ely Calendar calls him a brother of the house. No importance can be attached to the spurious Ramsey foundation charter dated 974 (BCS 1311) which includes six priests among its witnesses, one being Wulfstan, for it is unusual to have priests' signatures, and four of the names, Wulfstan among them, occur in other texts of this time among the *ministri*.

15) calls him *impius*, and another in a Worcester register[1] gives him the epithet *reprobus* and adds: *Nam nimis erravit dum nos rebus spoliavit.* The reason for this accusation is unknown, but probably it had its origin in the conflicting interests of the sees of Worcester and York which Wulfstan held in plurality.[2] Seeing that he issued two leases of Worcester lands in 1017,[3] although Abbot Leofsige of Thorney had been appointed Bishop of Worcester in 1016 and issues a lease in that year (KCD 724), it is probable that he regarded Leofsige merely as his suffragan,[4] whereas later Worcester writers may have considered his dealings with their lands after 1016 as unjustifiable interference. William of Malmesbury blames Wulfstan for holding in plurality, though he has excused his predecessors Oswald and Ealdulf; Wulfstan, he says, *sanctitate discrepabat et habitu* from them.[5] This is possibly the source of statements that he was not a Benedictine monk. But Dr Bethurum points out[6] that *habitus* need not mean profession, and suggests that William meant that he differed in both saintliness and attitude. He is called a monk in the *Historia Eliensis*, was claimed as a benefactor by the Benedictine houses of Ely and Peterborough, is said to have re-founded the monastery of St Peter at Gloucester,[7] and can be seen in his works to share the ideals of the Benedictine reformed party, and to be very familiar with the Benedictine Rule.

[1] Register 1 (now A iv) belonging to the Dean and Chapter, fol. 2b. Hearne, *Hemingi Chartularium Ecclesiæ Wigorniensis* II. 516, prints the passage in question from an epitome by Patrick Young.

[2] See Bethurum 65–8. She points out that the silence of Hemming regarding any misdealings by Wulfstan makes it unnecessary to take seriously the accusations by other Worcester writers.

[3] KCD 1313 and a lost lease of Wolverton, mentioned in a list by Dugdale, printed in Hickes, *Thesaurus* II. 299 f, item 8.

[4] The first of the attestations in KCD 724 is that of Archbishop Wulfstan, which confirms the impression that he retained his interest in the see of Worcester, and so does the fact that both he and Bishop Leofsige witness an Evesham agreement, Robertson LXXXI.

[5] *Gesta Pontificum* 250.

[6] Bethurum 57, note 4.

[7] *Historia Monasterii S. Petri Gloucestriæ*, ed. W. H. Hart, RS I. 8.

From 996, when he became Bishop of London (ASC 996 F), until his death in 1023, Wulfstan's signatures on charters are common. While Bishop of London he was left the estate of Barling, Essex, by Leofwine, Wulfstan's son, in 998.[1] Probably he left it to St Paul's, for they were holding land there in 1066.[2] As Bishop of London he issued some penitential letters (*v.* p. 7 *supra*) and an anonymous letter[3] written to him at this time shows that already he had acquired a reputation as a writer or preacher in the vernacular. The writer has been asked by Wulfstan to translate some documents from English into Latin, and in his refusal speaks with high praise of the bishop's own eloquence.

After Archbishop Ealdulf's death in June 1002, Wulfstan was translated from London to Worcester and York, probably before the end of the year.[4] It seems to have been the policy of the English kings, after the death in 956 of Archbishop Wulfstan I, who had been suspected of supporting the Northumbrian rebels, to appoint to the northern archiepiscopate a man with connexions with the eastern Danelaw, presumably because such would be familiar with a mixed English and Scandinavian population, but would not be likely to support Northumbrian independence. Probably from the same time, and certainly from 972, it was the practice to let the northern archbishop hold a southern see as well, partly because of the impoverishment of the diocese of York, but perhaps also to keep a better hold on him.[5] Wulfstan, like his two predecessors, Oswald and Ealdulf,

[1] A. S. Napier and W. H. Stevenson, *The Crawford Charters*, 22. Leofwine refers to Wulfstan as 'his lord'.

[2] KCD 913 which claims that Edward the Confessor confirmed an ancient *libertas* of 8 hides there to St Paul's is spurious. In Domesday Book, St Paul's had nearly 2½ hides at Barling in 1066.

[3] W. Stubbs, *Memorials of St Dunstan* 404 f, BCS 897, and Bethurum 376 f. See D. Whitelock, EHR lii. 463. On Vespasian A xiv, which contains this letter, *v.* pp. 32 f *infra*.

[4] I have discussed this date in EHR lii. 461 f.

[5] *v.* D. Whitelock, 'The Dealings of the Kings of England with Northumbria in the Tenth and Eleventh Centuries' in *The Anglo-Saxons. Studies in some Aspects of their History and Culture presented to Bruce Dickins*, 72–6.

has some connexion with the eastern counties, and, like them, was allowed to hold Worcester and York in plurality. In 1016 Leofsige was appointed to Worcester, but probably only as an assistant bishop (*v.* p. 9 *supra*). There are several references to Wulfstan's activities relating to the Worcester estates. Three documents about them issued by him survive, a lease of Perry to a *matrona* Wulfgyfu,[1] a lease of Bentley to his brother Ælfwig in 1017 (KCD 1313), and an agreement made with a certain Brihtric when he married Wulfstan's sister.[2] Three other Worcester charters of Wulfstan once existed, dealing with estates at Wolverton, Throckmorton, and Tidmington, respectively, the first being issued in 1017.[3] In another charter we find him taking a different part; he had been asked by the king to set down in writing the agreement reached between the Bishop of Hereford and a certain Leofric about estates in Worcestershire, not later than 1011.[4] If a hand which Mr Ker has found in marginalia and other additions to many manuscripts connected with Wulfstan is,

[1] *British Museum Facsimiles* IV. 13.

[2] KCD 738: Robertson LXXVI. It is not earlier than 1014, and is witnessed by Brihtheah the monk, probably the later Bishop of Worcester, 1033–8, who was Wulfstan's sister's son. Brihtheah had a brother Ægelric, who received from him many Worcester estates, and a kinsman Atsere (*v.* Robertson 458 f). Dr Bethurum (p. 55) tentatively suggests that a Wulfmær who witnesses a grant of Potton, Bedfordshire, by Ælfhelm Polga as 'the bishop's brother' (Robertson LXXI) and may perhaps be the Wulfmær to whom Ælfhelm Polga bequeathed Barnham, Suffolk, is another brother of Wulfstan's. This would be welcome confirmation of a family connexion with the eastern counties, but the bishop referred to in the grant, which survives on a leaf from an Ely gospel-book, could have been Bishop of Dorchester or of Elmham.

[3] They are items 8, 15 and 23 in Dugdale's list in Hickes, *Thesaurus* II. 299 f. Note also that the bounds of Bengeworth in KCD 1358 include the words: 'Within these boundaries are the five hides which Archbishop Wulfstan gave to Ælfric.'

[4] KCD 898: Robertson LXXXIII. It cannot be later than 1011 if Archbishop Ælfheah was present, for he was taken prisoner by the Danes before Michaelmas in that year. The name of the bishop concerned, Æthelstan of Hereford, must be a mistake for that of his predecessor, Athulf, if KCD 719 with the latter's attestation is correctly dated 1012.

as seems certain, either his own, or that of someone closely connected with him,[1] we get a glimpse of him as an administrator of the lands of both of his sees; for it makes entries of the names of estates in the margin of the older portion of the Worcester cartulary in Tiberius A xiii[2] and interlineations in the memoranda drawn up by Archbishop Oswald about the estates of York.[3] In this context we should note that both Professor Bethurum and Professor McIntosh have called attention to the similarity between his style and that of the documents on the management of a great estate, i.e. *Rectitudines Singularum Personarum* and *Gerefa*.[4] Worcester possessed many estates that would require the sort of administration here envisaged. That we know nothing of his dealings with the lands of his northern see is to be ascribed to the lack of records from this area. He was present when Styr's gift of Darlington to St Cuthbert's at Durham was confirmed at York some time in Ethelred's reign.[5]

The administration of church lands was only one part of his duties. In a later section we shall consider his writing of pastoral letters and other injunctions which concern his clergy. According to the *Historia* of St Peter's at Gloucester he reformed this house in 1022.[6]

[1] *v.* pp. 29 f *infra*.

[2] This whole cartulary used to be assigned to Hemming, but Ker, 'Hemming's Cartulary', *Studies in Medieval History presented to F. M. Powicke* 49–75, shows that it consists of two parts, of which the first belongs to the early eleventh century, and only the second is by Hemming.

[3] Robertson LIV: Whitelock, *English Historical Documents c. 500–1042*, No. 114.

[4] See Bethurum, JEGP xlix. 456 note; A. McIntosh, 'Wulfstan's Prose', *Proc. Brit. Acad.* xxxv. 126.

[5] Symeon of Durham, RS. I. 83. The *Historia de S. Cuthberto* (*ibid.* 212 f) names the archbishop Ælfric, Wulfstan's successor, but gives the king as Ethelred, who died before Wulfstan.

[6] Hart, *op.cit.* I. 8. The date could have been taken from the following document, which purports to be an agreement made at Gloucester in 1022 and includes both Archbishop Wulfstan and Bishop Leofsige among its witnesses. The historian of this house is ill-informed, for he says that Wulfstan was Bishop of Worcester in 1022 and afterwards became Archbishop of York. He says the foundation

WULFSTAN'S CAREER

Wulfstan's influence extended outside his own diocese and province. He was in constant attendance at meetings of the witan. Only three times do we hear of him in York, i.e. on the undated occasion when he witnessed Styr's grant, on 16 February 1014 when he consecrated there Ælfwig to the see of London (ASC 1014 D), and at the time of his death in 1023. This does not imply neglect of his province; our records for the North are scanty.[1] He was in the South in 1020, when he consecrated the church which Cnut had built at Ashingdon, Essex, for the souls of those killed in battle there.[2] On 13 November of that year he consecrated Æthelnoth as Lyfing's successor as Archbishop of Canterbury, probably at Canterbury, and his letter informing Cnut and Emma that he has done so is extant.[3] It may have been in the same year that he consecrated Edmund to the see of Durham at Winchester.[4] According to the *Historia* of St Peter's, Gloucester, he was there in 1022.

of Gloucester was with Cnut's consent. If Leofsige was only Wulfstan's suffragan, the latter may well have reformed Gloucester in Cnut's reign.

[1] The compilation of a set of regulations for the priests of the diocese of York, known as the *Law of the Northumbrian Priests*, very probably belongs to Wulfstan's archiepiscopate. See D. Whitelock, *English Historical Documents, c. 500–1042*, 434–9, and for an argument for its date additional to those given there, note that the text in the Brussels MS, mentioned on p. 29, note *infra*, uses one of its sentences along with others from Wulfstan's work.

[2] ASC, FlWig, and chronicles based on him, *s.a.* 1020; *Historia Eliensis* II. c. 87.

[3] KCD 1314: Harmer, *Anglo-Saxon Writs* No. 27.

[4] Edmund's consecration is dated 1020 in a marginal addition in the C MS of FlWig. Both this and Symeon of Durham (*Historia Dunelmensis Ecclesiæ* 85) say there had been almost a three-year vacancy after the death of Aldhun, and Symeon dates this 1018, though allowing him a twenty-nine-year episcopate after his accession in 990. But he calls 1040 the twentieth year of Edmund's episcopate, and says he died in the twenty-third year, was succeeded by Eadred, who died within ten months in 1042, to be followed by Æthelric (*ibid.* 90 f). The ASC (D) dates the latter's consecration 11 January 1041, and as this was a Sunday in 1041, this is probably correct. Discrepancies may have arisen through the inclusion of the years of the vacancy in Edmund's episcopate.

His writings show him in contact with Ælfric, Abbot of Eynsham. Relations with Archbishop Ælfric (994–1005) can be seen from his appearing as executor and legatee in his will[1] and by the inclusion of a letter addressed to this archbishop in the collection of penitential letters mentioned above.[2] When in 1012 the Ætheling Edmund wished to obtain an estate from the monks of Sherborne it was Wulfstan whom they chose to act as their spokesman before the king.[3] But the strongest evidence for his influence and power outside his own dioceses is shown by his drafting several codes for King Ethelred and the laws of Cnut.[4]

Wulfstan's career coincides with a stormy period of English history. Danish raids had recommenced in 980 and were a serious menace by 996 when Wulfstan became Bishop of London. The king, who had come to the throne as a child after the murder of his brother Edward in 978, showed himself incapable and untrustworthy when he came of age. Desultory efforts to resist the invaders were unsuccessful, except for the defence of London in 994, and in 991 and 994 the Danes had been bought off at a heavy price. During Wulfstan's episcopate in London there were heavy raids in the west in 997 and 998, when Hampshire and Sussex were also affected. In 999 Kent was seriously ravaged and a resistance planned on a large scale came to nothing. In 1001 the forces of Hampshire, Devon, and Somerset were all defeated, and 1002, the year of Wulfstan's translation to York and Worcester, saw another expensive treaty, followed by the massacre of Danes resident in England on St Brice's day. For the next few years the Chronicle is a gloomy record of harrying and defeat, relieved only by the heroism of the East Angles in 1004 and of the men of Cambridge in 1010, and the steady resistance of London. Archbishop Ælfheah was captured at Canterbury in 1011, and his martyrdom the following year shocked Christendom. Finally, in 1013, Swegn was accepted as king, first by the people of the Five Boroughs

[1] D. Whitelock, *Anglo-Saxon Wills* XVIII.
[2] See p. 7 *supra*.
[3] KCD 1302; Robertson LXXIV.
[4] *v.* pp. 23–5 *infra*.

and of Northumbria, later by the western thegns and last of all by the people of London. Ethelred was for a time with the fleet in the Thames, spent Christmas in the Isle of Wight, and then fled to Normandy. It is to this exile that Wulfstan refers in this homily, written in 1014, the year in which Ethelred's return was made possible by Swegn's death at Candlemas.

It is only the detailed study of Wulfstan's writings in comparatively recent years that has revealed him as an important political figure.[1] The first datable code of laws which he drafted is that of 1008, though this does not prove that his influence was not exercised earlier. As the northern archbishop, he must have had a very difficult task, for Northumbria was an unruly area, which had received a large influx of Scandinavian settlers in the ninth and early tenth centuries, and had retained Scandinavian customs. Even by the eleventh century heathen practices had not entirely been eradicated.[2] Up to 954 it had had during intervals independent Scandinavian kings, and probably even in Wulfstan's time it felt little loyalty for the West Saxon royal house. Unfortunately we do not know what lay behind the slaying of Ælfhelm, ealdorman of southern Northumbria, and the blinding of his two sons, with the king's connivance, in 1006, or what Wulfstan's attitude to this affair was. It is not surprising that Northumbria led the way in accepting Swegn as king in 1013. We do not know where Wulfstan was at the time of the submission, but he was at York within a fortnight of Swegn's death and we can hardly be wrong in assuming that he used his influence to win back the province to the English king.[3]

Ethelred's return did not bring peace, least of all to Northumbria. Wulfstan is likely to have attended the 'great

[1] On the neglect of Wulfstan by historians, see D. Whitelock, *Trans. R. Hist. Soc.* 4th Series, xxiv. 25 f.

[2] *v.* note to l. 140.

[3] On the position in Northumbria *v.* D. Whitelock, in *The Anglo-Saxons. Studies in some Aspects of their History and Culture presented to Bruce Dickins* 70–88, and on the events of the reign in general *v.* F. M. Stenton, *Anglo-Saxon England* 368–87.

assembly' at Oxford in 1015, at which Ealdorman Eadric engineered the murder of two prominent northern thegns, Sigeferth and Morcar, thegns of the Seven Boroughs,[1] after which the king seized all their property. This led to a breach between the king and his son Edmund, who seized and married Sigeferth's widow, went north to the Five Boroughs, took possession of both thegns' estates, and received the submission of the people. One may suspect that Wulfstan remained loyal to Ethelred in this crisis, for he constantly harps on the theme 'let us all loyally support one royal lord' in his writings. We know nothing of his movements in 1016, in the earlier months of which year the Ætheling Edmund was acting in concert with Ealdorman Uhtred of Northumbria, until the latter submitted to Cnut and was killed. Cnut then placed the Norwegian Eric as earl of Northumbria. After Ethelred had died on 23 April, and Edmund's heroic resistance came to an end at the battle of Ashingdon on 18 October, Northumbria remained part of Cnut's kingdom. Whether Wulfstan accepted Cnut as king at this time, or not until after Edmund's death on 30 November, there is no doubt that he worked with Cnut to re-establish peace and order. When in 1018 'the Danes and the English reached an agreement at Oxford according to Edgar's law' (ASC D), it appears to have been Wulfstan who composed the document which was accepted on this occasion, and later a full code of laws was drawn up by him for Cnut.[2] This suggests that his was an important influence among those which made a pious king and effective ruler out of a young Viking. In 1020 Wulfstan dedicated the church at Ashingdon which Cnut built on the site of his victory.[3]

The *Historia Eliensis* says of Wulfstan: 'by them (the

[1] This expression is unique. It presumably refers to the Five Boroughs, Lincoln, Stamford, Derby, Nottingham, and Leicester, with the addition of two others, probably York and perhaps Torksey.

[2] *v.* pp. 24 f *infra*.

[3] No weight should be attached to the fact that it was Wulfstan, and not Lyfing, Archbishop of Canterbury, who consecrated the church, for Lyfing died that year, and may have been too ill to participate.

kings, Ethelred, Edmund, and Cnut), he was loved as a brother and honoured as a father, and frequently summoned to the highest affairs of the realm, as being the most learned of counsellors, in whom spoke the very wisdom of God, as if in some spiritual temple'.[1] The evidence of law-codes shows that this claim regarding his political influence is not without basis.

IV. WULFSTAN'S WRITINGS

For a long time it was held that only four homilies, i.e. Napier II and III, which in four manuscripts immediately follow the rubric *Incipiunt sermones Lupi*, plus our present text and Napier XXXIV, both assigned to Lupus by their rubrics, could be accepted as unquestionably Wulfstan's work. Napier[2] then added the so-called Pastoral Letter (XIX–XXII), which in MS C begins *Wulfstan arcebisceop greteð*. But detailed studies have since made it possible to attribute to him a great number of other works.

Since the evidence for his authorship depends in the first place on stylistic features, though it may be supported by other considerations, it is desirable to mention the outstanding characteristics of his style.[3] He had pronounced preferences in vocabulary, using, for example, *lagu* and not *æ*, *beorgan*, not *arian*, *gesælig*, not *eadig*, *dryhten*, not *hælend*, *lac*, not *onsægdnes*, &c.[4] He uses some words frequently, e.g. *fadian*, *afyllan*, *forfaran*, *forrædan*, while others occur rarely, if at all, outside his writings, e.g. *sibleger*, *ægylde*, *fes(i)an*, *læw* 'injury' and its derivative *læwan*, *aweodian* 'to root out'. He is fond of compounds beginning with *worold*

[1] *Historia Eliensis* II. c. 87.

[2] *Über die Werke des altenglischen Erzbischofs Wulfstan*, 1882.

[3] For fuller treatment see Jost, *Wulfstanstudien*, especially 155–68; Bethurum 27–9, 87–98; D. Whitelock, EHR lvi. 6–11, lxiii. 438 f; R. J. Menner, MLN lxiii, 1–9.

[4] This criterion should not be too rigidly applied. Wulfstan may occasionally have used words not part of his normal vocabulary under the influence of his recent reading. One cannot safely reject a work on the evidence of one or two words.

or *þeod*, in an intensive sense, such as *woroldscamu, woroldstrudere, þeodscaða, þeodlicetere, þeodloga.* He has also peculiarities of syntax, e.g. *gebugan* with a direct object, *deofol* without a definite article, *ænig*, not *nænig*, in negative sentences,[1] *fela* (*manna*, &c) with a singular verb. More obvious is his excessive use of intensitives, like *mid ealle, georne, to wide, ealles to swyþe, ealles to gelome, oft 7 gelome,* and of other tags, *elles, nyde, mid rihte,* &c. Certain set phrases occur again and again in his work, as *gime se þe wille, swa hi betst mihton, us selfum to þearfe, gecnawe se þe cunne, swa hit þincan mæg, swa swa man scolde.* Such words and phrases are often added by Wulfstan when he revised the work of others, and the purpose was often to bring the passage into line with his own rhythmical patterns. For the same end he makes tautological additions, and he was fond of arranging words in pairs, sometimes linked by alliteration, or rhyme. This *sermo* affords instances of the long lists, piling up to a climax, which are another feature of his style. Alliteration and rhyme are not confined to these lists: great use is made of the former, e.g. *byrsta 7 bysmara gebiden, 7 gif we ænige bote gebidan scylen, þonne mote we þæs to Gode ernian bet* (ll. 15–17), and clauses like *healdan unwemme 7 a butan glemme,* or *gebugan mid rihte to bisceopa dihte* are not uncommon in Wulfstan's work. He expended much care on the balance of his sentences, often accentuating the parallelism of clauses by identity of rhythm, and then drawing attention to a conclusion by a subtle change. His repetitions are used deliberately, driving home a point as if with the blows of a hammer, and he is skilled in the use of the rhetorical question, which he often uses to sum up a paragraph. Dr Bethurum has pointed out how little he depends on metaphor or simile, and how he completely avoids poetical imagery. It is attention to sentence structure, and the strong and varied rhythms, which give his style its

[1] The fact that he never uses uncontracted forms of *ne* plus the verbs *habban, witan, willan, wesan* and *āgan*, discussed by Samuel R. Levin, JEGP lx. 451–9, serves only to distinguish him from writers with a dialect colouring, for the West Saxon literary language used the contracted forms.

lucidity and force. She also notes that he can vary his style for different purposes. He uses his rhetorical devices less in his expositions of the Christian doctrine than in his impassioned appeals for reform or his denunciations of contemporary abuses.

His rhythm has been fully considered in an article by Professor McIntosh,[1] which shows that Wulfstan's prose can be differentiated from other forms of rhythmical writing, including that of Ælfric, and that it consists 'of a continuous series of two-stress phrases related in structure to the classical half-line, and severely restricted in somewhat the same fashion to certain rhythmical patterns'.[2] This is a valuable study, for it gives a criterion by which to reject claims that texts are the work of 'Wulfstan imitators'. Professor Jost doubted the existence of such. While one can conceive that other men might have copied some of his obvious peculiarities, as his use of tags and intensitives, it passes belief that any other writer would adopt his minor syntactical mannerisms or consistently avoid vocabulary alien to his practice, or could reproduce the rhythmical patterns of his work. In the following discussion of the canon of his writings, it is assumed that works with all these features come from his pen.

Besides the works mentioned on p. 17, the following homilies in Napier's edition can be accepted as genuine:[3]

[1] In *Proc. Brit. Acad.* xxxv. 109–42.

[2] *Op.cit.* 114. I do not, however, agree with Jost in his edition of *Polity* that this makes it desirable to print Wulfstan's prose as if it were verse. This over-accentuates the rhythm, and tends to obscure the sentence construction and the subtler underlying rhythms.

[3] Napier included all attributed to Wulfstan, not merely those which he thought genuine. Several are in styles different from Wulfstan's, though passages from his works have sometimes been interpolated into them. XXIX is based on the poem *Be Domesdæge*, XXX and XL are compilations using homilies also in the Vercelli MS, and XLIX is found there and its beginning (the rest is lost) in the Blickling Homilies. Wulfstan was not responsible for the homilies on Sunday observance, XLIII, XLIV, XLV and LVII, though the last has a passage influenced by him, nor for XLII, a translation of Adso's *Libellus Anticristi*, nor for XLVI, a translation of a *Visio S. Pauli.*

V and X, with their Latin sources IV and IX; VI, a series of denunciatory passages from Isaiah and Jeremiah, with free translation; XXVIII, a similar treatment of extracts from Leviticus xxvi, and XLI, which deals in the same way with some Latin excerpts from Ezechiel and Isaiah which occur in MS I and were first published by Bethurum (No. XVIa); the eschatological homilies XII to XVI, probably with the exception of that part of XVI (Napier 98.13–101.5) which tells the legend of St Peter and St Paul, and, along with these, XI, a collection of excerpts from Latin authors which is the basis of XII; XVII and XXXII, both concerned with penance enjoined during Lent, and depending, XVII in part and XXXII entirely, on a sermon of Abbo of St Germain; XXIII and XXIV, probably connected, as Dr Bethurum (p. 36 f) suggests, with the Pastoral Letter with which some manuscripts associate them; XXV, a short text on baptism, and XXVI, on the paternoster and creed; that portion of XXXVII, a sermon preached at the consecration of a bishop, which is contained in MS E; the first part of XLVII (the second being from Byrhtferth), believed by Jost[1] to be derived from a lost Wulfstan homily, though it has similarities with the *Sermo ad Anglos*; LI, which Jost thinks may be connected with a meeting of the witan; LIX, LX and LXI, all contained in the York Gospels, the first with the title *Sermo Lupi*, and the others 'made up of combinations of Wulfstan's phrases so astutely put together as to make unlikely the probability that anyone else was responsible for them' (Bethurum 39).[2]

VIII is Ælfric's *De septiformi spiritu* and XXXI is an extract in Ælfric's style from a lost work. Also to be rejected are LVI, from the introduction to the *Confessionale Ps.-Ecgberti*, the second part of XLVII, which occurs at the end of Byrhtferth's *Manual*, XLVIII, the *Ammonitio amici* which follows it, and LXII, an account of the Ages of the World. In XXXVIII a few Wulfstan phrases have been added to a short admonition on confession, and LVIII is called by Dr Bethurum (42), 'a rather disorganized pastiche of passages from several sources'; among these are some from Wulfstan's works.

[1] *Wulfstanstudien*, 240 f.

[2] Mr Ker has noted that corrections to LXI are in a hand which is probably that of Wulfstan himself; *v*. pp. 29 f *infra*.

WULFSTAN'S WRITINGS

To the undoubtedly genuine homilies must also be added two not in Napier, printed by Dr Bethurum: one, which is number VIIIb in her edition, is from CCCC MS 302, and is Wulfstan's first reworking of the Latin excerpts on baptism given as IV in Napier; the other, numbered Xa, is a translation of c. 45 of Amalarius's *De regula canonicorum*. It is printed also in the Appendix to Jost's edition of *Polity* (pp. 248–55).[1] As item *k* in this Appendix, Jost prints part of a text from CCCC 201 which he regards as a compilation of *Polity*, legal texts and some lost work of Wulfstan, but which I believe to have been from a homily by him, drawn on later for *Polity* and for the legal texts which share its readings.[2] It deals with the respect and rights due to the clergy, drawing interesting comparisons with the rights of different orders of laymen.

Some texts in Napier call for further discussion. XXXIX (printed by Liebermann as VIIa Atr) is the Old English version of a code imposing a fast on the whole nation 'when the great army came to the country' and is in Wulfstan's style; XXXV and XXXVI are variant versions of a text based on this, but made to fit any calamity, and adding Old Testament parallels. XXXVI begins: 'If it should happen that serious disaster befall the nation on account of men's sins, ravaging or famine, pestilence or murrain, burning or bloodshed or disastrous storms, or sudden disease or sudden death . . .' and XXXV has a similar list. XXXV is in Wulfstan's style, while XXXVI has a few alien usages.[3] L, which combines sentences and passages from a number of Wulfstan works, was rejected by Jost because some are from Cnut's laws, which he believed later than Wulfstan's time;[4] but I doubt whether anyone else could have moved

[1] For other Wulfstan writings, not homilies, in this Appendix, *v.* pp. 26 f *infra*.

[2] It is printed in M. Ångström, *Studies in Old English Manuscripts*, Uppsala, 1937, 125 f, whereas Jost gives the first part, which agrees with *II Polity* cc. 130–4, on pp. 104 f and the rest pp. 256–61.

[3] Jost discusses the connexion between these three texts in *Wulfstanstudien* 213–16. Cf also Bethurum 38.

[4] Jost *op.cit.* 249–61. On the date of Cnut's laws *v.* pp. 24 f *infra*.

so easily among so many of his writings, and Dr Bethurum (pp. 39 f) also is inclined to accept it as genuine. LII and LIII are extracts from Wulfstan's *Polity*, and XXVII is apparently a collection of sentences from the *Sermo ad Anglos*.

In some homilies Wulfstan has worked over texts by others; I survives in two versions, both of which begin with a translation by an unknown writer of a passage in Book IV, c. 1 of Gregory's *Dialogues*; in E this is followed by a homiletic conclusion which Wulfstan often used, but in the other version (in C and Tiberius A xiii) passages from Book IV, c. 6 of the *Dialogues* have been translated in Wulfstan style.[1] VII is a revision of Ælfric's *De septiformi spiritu*, XVIII of his *De falsis deis*, and LIV is based on his *In dedicatione ecclesiæ* (CH II. 574–94).[2] LV on the other hand is only a combination of two of Ælfric's homilies with an introduction from Napier II, with no sign of Wulfstan's re-writing.[3]

There seems, however, to be traces of the re-working by Wulfstan of another Ælfric homily, as well as of passages from a lost Wulfstan text, in a compilation in Hatton MS 114. fol 97v–102v entitled *De letania maiore*. This begins with the first ten lines of Ælfric's homily on this subject in volume I of the Catholic Homilies (p. 244) and later uses a passage from his treatment of the same theme in volume II (p. 330). Wulfstan alterations occur in both extracts, but expecially in the first: *gecweden* is replaced by the favourite Wulfstan word *genamod*, *abiton* becomes *tosliton 7 abiton*, and the Wulfstan phrases *ealles to fela þurh godes yrre* and *fela ungelimpa geweard for folces synnan* are added. Moreover, the intervening passage, giving details of a three-day

[1] *v.* Jost, *Wulfstanstudien* 184–7, Bethurum 41 f.

[2] Bethurum 35.

[3] The above statements on the authenticity of the texts in Napier are in essential agreement with the views of Jost and Bethurum, except that Jost's belief that the laws of Cnut were later than Wulfstan's lifetime make him reject XXIII, XXIV, L, LX and LXI, and he does not accept XXXV and XXXVI. Dr Bethurum excludes from her edition the texts Napier XXIII, XXIV, XXV, XXXV, XXXVI, L, LX–LXI, not because she thinks them spurious, but because they are not homilies.

fast, has Wulfstan's expressions, *georne god gladian* (cf Napier 169.10, 112.12), *unsceodum fotum* (170.16, 173.12) and the common *ealle to criste geornlice clipian*. There are other Wulfstan passages, such as one on fol. 99r which uses phrases in II, V and XII, or a passage on fol. 99v–100r dealing with the approaching end of the world and the coming of Antichrist, many phrases and sentiments of which can be paralleled in several Wulfstan homilies, though the passage is not identical with any other treatment of the theme. The homily uses other sources and is the work of a compiler. It ends with a passage from Wulfstan XV. But the sources seem to have included a lost Wulfstan homily which expanded passages from Ælfric on the origin of the Rogation Day observances, a subject of interest to him, since similar practices in time of calamity are advocated in VII Atr, and in homilies XXXV and XXXVI.

Wulfstan was not only a preacher. He drew up several law-codes. The Latin paraphrase of Ethelred's sixth code, issued at Enham, speaks of *archipresulumque Ælfeahi et Wulfstani hortatu instigante*, while the conclusion has: *idcircoque ego N* (*Wulfstanus*), *gratia Domini disponente Eboracensium archiepiscopus, eadem* (i.e. the previous statutes) *ad sequentium memoriam, necnon et ad praesentium uel futurorum salutem, litteris infixi* . . .[1] There are two Old English versions of these statutes, known as V Atr and VI Atr, and both are written in Wulfstan's style. V Atr is dated 1008 in one manuscript. Jost has shown that it uses Latin sources, and that the Latin account of the council at Enham makes use not only of it, but also of the Latin excerpts which it used, and that VI Atr is based on the Latin version. The most probable account of the relationship between the three texts is that given by Dr Sisam,[2] who suggests that V Atr gives the statutes which were promulgated at Enham, and

[1] Liebermann, I. 247, 257. Jost, *Wulfstanstudien* 16–35, has strengthened the attribution of this text to Wulfstan by a comparison between it and the penitential letters issued by Wulfstan. He has also pointed out the influence of Aldhelm, the use made of the Benedictine rule, and the reliance on Frankish sources.

[2] *Studies in the History of Old English Literature* 278–87.

that Wulfstan was authorized to issue for his Danelaw province a version with modifications. His Latin version would then be meant to guide his higher clergy and the English version known as VI Atr drawn up for wider circulation, so that the clergy of his province could make its provisions known.[1] If we accept this, we should note that this was not the only occasion when Wulfstan drew up a code primarily intended for the Danelaw, for my claim made in 1941[2] that he composed the code known as the *Laws of Edward and Guthrum* has been generally accepted, and this is a set of regulations on the observance of ecclesiastical laws, especially in the Danelaw, with a preface explaining that these had been agreed on in the earliest days of Danish settlement.[3]

The style of Ethelred's later codes shows that Wulfstan drafted these also, i.e. VII Atr, on the three-day fast to be observed 'when the great army came to the country',[4] VIII Atr, a code issued in 1014, of which only the ecclesiastical section has survived, and the fragments IX and X Atr. Of even greater interest is his connexion with the legislation of Cnut. There is a text in CCCC 201 which was regarded by Liebermann as a late combination of parts of Ethelred's laws and those of Cnut, but which is, I am convinced, what its rubric claims it to be, the agreement that 'took place as soon as King Cnut with the advice of his councillors completely established peace and friendship between the Danes and the English', presumably referring to the Oxford gathering of 1018. This rubric is in Wulfstan's

[1] This seems preferable to Jost's view that the Latin text is a record of the proceedings at Enham voluntarily drawn up by Wulfstan, and VI Atr merely a private work, based on V Atr and the Latin account, giving a code 'not as it had actually been decided at Enham, but as he subsequently would have wished it' (*op.cit.* 36). So busy and practical-minded a prelate would be unlikely to draw up a set of statutes without at least an intention of using it later.

[2] EHR lvi. 1–21.

[3] The rubric does not claim that the agreement was reached only in the reign of Edward; it attributes it first to King Alfred and King Guthrum.

[4] *v.* p. 21 *supra*.

style, and there is no conceivable motive for forgery. This text, therefore, is earlier than Cnut's code, for which it was one of the sources. The style, sources and method of work both of this document and of Cnut's full code show that the compiler was Wulfstan. Liebermann's dating of Cnut's laws as after 1027 is not based on strong evidence.[1]

Other codes have been convincingly attributed to Wulfstan by Professor Bethurum,[2] namely *Grið*, which deals with penalties for violating the peace of the Church, and a series of five short texts, known as *Geþyncðo, Norþleoda laga, Mircna laga, Að* and *Hadbot*, which all deal with rank and status, secular or ecclesiastical. They betray Wulfstan's style, though he incorporated earlier legal texts. They all fit in with Wulfstan's general preoccupation, as seen in his other legal writings and in *Polity*, with 'an orderly arrangement of society'.[3] The recent edition by Jost of this last-named Wulfstan work sheds considerable light on the author. It allows us to distinguish a first version, *I Polity*, a work with a sense of form uncommon in the eleventh century, which, while showing the author's familiarity with canonical writings, has no single main source, but appears to be the outcome of the archbishop's own meditations on the conditions of his time. It deals with the duties of the king, taking over from Ælfric the doctrine of the three supports of the throne, *Oratores, Laboratores* and *Bellatores*, and next with the duties of those in authority, first treating of the behaviour of bishops, and then with secular government by both ecclesiastical and lay magnates. Chapters follow on priests, men in orders (with stress on the requirement of celibacy), abbots, monks, nuns, (secular) priests and women

[1] For these views *v.* D. Whitelock, EHR lxiii. 433–52. They have been accepted by D. Bethurum, p. 64 (*v.* also *Philologica: The Malone Anniversary Studies* 102 and JEGP xlix. 449) and by A. McIntosh in *Proc. Brit. Acad.* xxxv. 142. Jost opposed them in *Wulfstanstudien* 94–103 and he did not reply to my answer to his objections in EHR lxx. 72–85.

[2] JEGP xlix. 449–63.

[3] The text in CCCC 201 which I have discussed on p. 21 fits well into this group.

living under religious vows. The section on laymen is concerned only with their religious duties. A later version, *II Polity*, has interesting additions which, however, sometimes upset the balance of the work. These include a warning to the laity against using the bishop's sins as an excuse for disobeying his teaching, with a personal note 'I know very well myself to be guilty in word and deed all too greatly, yet dare not for the fear of God keep entirely silent on many of the things which are harming this people';[1] also accounts of a bishop's 'daily work', of the corruption of reeves 'since Edgar died', of the misuse of church funds by some priests to adorn their wives, and of misbehaviour of monks. Thus *II Polity* affords many glimpses into contemporary conditions when *I Polity* was content to speak of duties only. The Appendix gives the text of interpolations into one or other of the manuscripts which were not an original part of the work. The first, *Be godes þeowum*, may be by Wulfstan or be made up from his homilies; the second is an address to priests and may be by Wulfstan, working over someone else's work; the third also is addressed to priests, and in it Wulfstan appeals for their help and prayers and expresses a wish for an annual assembly henceforward; the fourth is the so-called *Canons of Edgar*, long ago assigned by Jost to Wulfstan; the fifth a collection by him of synodal decisions on the duties of bishops; the sixth is of particular interest, for in it concern is expressed at the ordination of unfit persons to the priesthood, and practical instructions are given for the examination of candidates in future. The tone is authoritative, and the style is Wulfstan's.[2] It admits that it may sometimes be necessary to ordain those of inadequate education, but enjoins that such must give surety to continue their studies. The seventh shows how Christ in his life had symbolically represented the seven orders of priesthood, and is probably a Wulfstan revision of the work of an un-

[1] Ed. Jost 66.

[2] It is preceded (pp. 217 f) by a passage from a lost work of Ælfric, but it is uncertain whether the combination was made by Wulfstan or later.

known author. The eighth is not by Wulfstan, and the ninth is his *De regula canonicorum.*[1] The tenth is the text discussed on p. 21 above; finally, there is an admonition, probably by Wulfstan, to bishops, complaining of their various misdemeanours. In this work Jost also attributes to Wulfstan the text *Episcopus,*[2] on the duties of bishops.

It will be seen that this collection of texts adds greatly to our knowledge of Wulfstan's activities to reform the clergy in his province and diocese. This concern is seen also in his obtaining from Ælfric pastoral letters,[3] one of which he rewrote in his own style. There is extant also an answer by Ælfric to a lost letter from Wulfstan, which had asked queries on canonical practices.[4] Wulfstan's authorship of the prose parts of a text known as the *Benedictine Office* has long been recognized;[5] its latest editor points out that it is not an office, but 'a commentary upon, or exposition of, a Latin ritual in English prose and verse', and gives good reasons for considering it an adaptation for the use of the secular clergy.[6]

Among the most interesting of Wulfstan's minor works is the addition of two passages by him to the northern recension of the Anglo-Saxon Chronicle, pointed out by Jost in 1923, for one, at annal 959, is a panegyric on King Edgar,[7]

[1] Also printed by Bethurum, as Xa. [2] Liebermann I. 477–9.

[3] Edited by B. Fehr, *Die Hirtenbriefe Ælfrics* 35–221. Two are in Latin, two in Old English. Wulfstan's revision of the first of the Old English letters is in MS CCCC 201. It must be distinguished from the so-called Pastoral Letter of Wulfstan, i.e. Napier, XIX–XXII (= Bethurum XIII) which gets this name from its beginning in C: *Wulfstan arcebisceop greteð freondlice þegnas on ðeode, gehadode 7 læwede, ealle gemænelice, þa ðe him betæhte sindon for gode to wissianne.* This shows that it was not intended for the clergy only.

[4] Fehr, *op.cit.* 222–7. On this *v.* D. Whitelock, *Trans. R. Hist. Soc.* 4th Series xxiv. 34 f.

[5] First edited by E. Feiler, *Das Benediktiner-Offizium*, 1901.

[6] *The Benedictine Office. An Old English Text*, ed. J. M. Ure, 63. His claim that Wulfstan was rewriting an already existing vernacular text, probably by Ælfric, has been disputed; *v.* review by Jost, RES, N.S. x. 75–7 and P. Clemoes in *Anglia* lxxviii. 265–83.

[7] It makes use of Ælfric's *Judges* (ed. S. O. Crawford, *The Heptateuch* 416 f).

of whose government Wulfstan speaks frequently elsewhere with nostalgic regret, and whose laws he made the basis of his drafts for Ethelred and Cnut. The second, in annal 975, speaks of the anti-monastic reaction and the lawlessness after Edgar's death. It is of interest that Wulfstan should have had access to a manuscript of the Chronicle. Familiarity with other English writers, i.e. with Bede's *Ecclesiastical History* and with a letter of Alcuin, is shown by a Latin letter sent by the English bishops to the pope to protest against the insistence that archbishops should fetch the pallium from Rome, the authorship of which has been claimed for Wulfstan by Dr Bethurum.[1] The attribution to him of *Rectitudines Singularum Personarum* and *Gerefa* has been mentioned above.[2]

V. WULFSTAN'S LEARNING

The increased number of works that can now be assigned to Wulfstan, and studies on their sources, have added to our knowledge of his range of reading. But this is not our only source of evidence on this matter. In addition to manuscripts consisting mainly of his works, we can use the evidence of manuscripts compiled for his use, and may reasonably assume his familiarity with the texts in them, even with those which have not been identified among his sources. Vespasian A xiv,[3] Nero A i, fols. 70–177, and the Copenhagen MS Gl. kgl. S. 1595, belong in this category,[4] and there must also once have existed what Dr Bethurum has called 'Archbishop Wulfstan's Commonplace Book', i.e. a collection of texts and excerpts of use to him in 'his attempt to regulate the practices of both bishops and lesser clergy under his supervision'. This survives in greater or less measure in the CCCC MSS 265 and 190, Bodley MS 718 (S.C. 2632), Junius 121 (S.C. 5232), Nero A i, Bibl. Nat.

[1] *Philologica: The Malone Anniversary Studies* 97–104.

[2] *v.* p. 12 *supra*.

[3] Only fols 114–70 form the MS in question.

[4] *v.* D. Whitelock, *Trans. R. Hist. Soc.* 4th Series xxiv. 30–4 and D. Bethurum, PMLA lvii. 916–29.

Paris Fonds 3182, Bodleian MS Barlow 37 and the Copenhagen MS mentioned above.[1] CCCC MS 201 is another which had access to material used by him, mainly of a legal nature, and laws which he used for the codes he drafted, or these codes themselves, are to be found in Nero A i, CCCC 190 and 265, and in another Worcester manuscript, Nero E i; the part of Claudius A iii which contains VI Atr and its Latin version has corrections and interlineations probably by Wulfstan, and similar entries are made in some memoranda on York estates[2] in Harley 55, which has also, in this pre-Conquest section, II and III Edgar. Cnut's letter of 1019/1020 was added, along with some Wulfstan pieces,[3] into the York Gospels.[4] Wulfstan is expressly mentioned in two manuscripts: Vespasian A xiv has a poem addressed to him,[5] and there are three lines of Latin verse which make a pun on his name in that part of the Worcester cartulary, Tiberius A xiii, which Mr Ker assigns to the early eleventh century.

The connexion of several of these manuscripts with Wulfstan has been confirmed by Mr Ker's recognition that they

[1] Bethurum, *op.cit.* Brussels MS Bibliothèque Royale 8558–63 (Ker, *Catalogue* 8 f) should also be reckoned with. It includes in an early-eleventh-century hand a group of penitential texts found in CCCC 265 and CCCC 201, and others found in Bodleian MS Laud Misc. 482, a mid-eleventh-century penitential which was at Worcester by the thirteenth century; an early-twelfth-century hand has added a short Old English set of canons which in places agrees verbally with the *Canons of Edgar* 2, 13, with another Wulfstan work (printed as an appendix to *Polity*, Jost 169) and with the *Law of the Northumbrian Priests* 25. Dr Bethurum suggests (p. 281) that a manuscript of the late eleventh or early twelfth century, Vespasian D ii, is also to be connected with Wulfstan; it is a Latin manuscript containing penitentials, canons, homilies, &c., including Napier XI and Adso's *Libellus Anticristi*.

[2] *v.* p. 12 *supra.* [3] *v.* p. 20 *supra.*

[4] But for the interest taken in legislation at Worcester, we should have had no copy of IV Edgar, and three of the four versions of II and III Edgar come from manuscripts connected with Wulfstan. The copy of Cnut's letter in the York Gospels is unique.

[5] BCS 896; W. Stubbs, *Memorials of St Dunstan* p. liv note; Bethurum 375 f. The poem is in the hand discussed in the next paragraph.

contain passages, corrections, interlineations and marginalia in a single handwriting, 'not so much a professional as a scholar's hand'.[1] This enters a passage, apparently written at different times, in the Copenhagen manuscript,[2] and it makes corrections and additions elsewhere in this manuscript, as well as in Claudius A iii, Harley 55, Tiberius A xiii, and Nero A i, where it also writes in four places a few lines of the text. It is probably the same hand which makes entries in homily LXI in the York Gospels and writes the poem in Vespasian A xiv. A fragment, British Museum Additional MS 38651, fol. 57v, has what appears to be notes for a sermon in this same hand. Some of the additions are in line with Wulfstan's practice: they add his favourite words and pay the attention to rhythmical considerations shown in his writings;[3] some marginalia are related to his other works.[4] In Hatton 42, a ninth-century collection of canons,[5] this hand makes marginal entries by works which Wulfstan can be shown to have known. It seems almost certain that it can belong to no one but Wulfstan himself. It is very interesting that it also annotates Alfred's preface to his translation of the *Cura Pastoralis* in Hatton 20, the manuscript which was sent to Werferth, Bishop of Worcester.[6] While these two manuscripts, and some others mentioned above, were at Worcester, the York Gospels were at York, and so probably

[1] N. R. Ker, *Studies in Medieval History presented to F. M. Powicke* 71; *v.* also his *Catalogue* p. lvi and comments on the individual manuscripts.

[2] Jost, *Wulfstanstudien* 268–70, rejects the authenticity of this passage because it contains words and usages not paralleled in Wulfstan's writings; but he was depending on a faulty version. Mr Ker informs me that the true reading in the first line is *þyses lytlan*, not *þyses lyden*, to which Jost took objection.

[3] See also McIntosh, *Proc. Brit. Acad.* xxxv. 138.

[4] See p. 1 n. 3 *supra*.

[5] The editors, Ivor Atkins and N. R. Ker, of Patrick Young's *Catalogus Librorum Manuscriptorum Bibliothecae Wigorniensis* show that this is to be identified with item 221. It used to be attributed to Glastonbury, but was probably brought to Worcester by Dunstan.

[6] These annotations are discussed in Ker, *The Pastoral Care* (*Early English Manuscripts in Facsimile* VI, Copenhagen, 1956) 24 f.

was Claudius A iii, if we accept Mr Ker's attractive identification of *þureð*, who paid for the binding of the benedictional to which the additional leaves containing VI Atr and its Latin version were attached, with Thored, Earl of Northumbria from about 975 until 992. Much of the material in Vespasian A xiv is of northern interest and was probably collected at York.[1]

If we pool all types of evidence—the sources he used, the works copied or excerpted in manuscripts probably compiled under his direction, the evidence for his reading of older works afforded by entries in his hand or by interpolations in his style—we find Wulfstan a learned man. Naturally he was very familiar with the Vulgate, and he knew some of the works of the Fathers, Augustine and Gregory and at least one sermon of Caesarius of Arles. He also used Isidore, Sulpicius Severus, the seventh-century *Liber scintillarum* of Defensor, and works of the eighth-century writers Pirmin of Reichenau and Eligius of Noyon. He was versed in the Rule of St Benedict. His debt to later continental authors is heavy, especially to the Carolingian writers Jesse of Amiens, Theodulf of Orleans, Amalarius of Metz, and Atto of Vercelli; he knew the *De institutione clericorum* of Hrabanus Maurus and the *De rectoribus Christianis* of Sedulius Scottus. His manuscripts include and his works use the Frankish *Capitulare episcoporum* and other Frankish capitularies and canons of councils. His knowledge of penitential literature was wide, for he used the genuine penitentials of Theodore and Ecgberht, as well as the ninth-century penitential falsely attributed to the former, and the translation of the work of Halitgar of Cambrai attributed to the latter. Hatton 42, which is annotated in the 'Wulfstan' hand, includes the *Collectio Canonum Hibernensis*, and the influence of this Irish collection is seen in *Polity*. The Copenhagen manuscript includes several of the sermons of Abbo of St Germain, one of which Wulfstan translated in Napier

[1] *v.* note 2, p. 32 *infra*. On the possible York provenance of manuscripts connected with Wulfstan *v.* my article 'Wulfstan at York' in a forthcoming volume of studies in honour of F. P. Magoun, Jr.

XXXII; he used one continental work written as late as 954, Adso's *Libellus Anticristi*.

Of even greater interest to Anglo-Saxon historians is his knowledge of earlier works produced in England, or by Englishmen abroad. Besides the penitentials of Theodore and Ecgberht, he knew Bede's *Ecclesiastical History*, and his Latin style was influenced by Aldhelm. He used Alcuin's *Liber de virtutibus et vitiis*, his outline of the baptismal rite,[1] and some of his letters. Vespasian A xiv, which is undoubtedly connected with him, includes twenty-seven letters of Alcuin, only two of which are addressed to continental recipients, and one of these was written from England. It has also a letter from Arno, Archbishop of Salzburg, to Cuculus, who was probably in England, and another from Eanbald, later Archbishop of York, to his namesake and predecessor.[2] Wulfstan used also a letter from Alcuin to King Offa not in this or any other collection of Alcuin's letters, but which was found in a manuscript at The Hague by Lehmann in 1920.[3] Vespasian A xiv includes other letters of northern interest, one from Alchfrith the anchorite to Higbald,[4] and the very interesting letter of Pope Paul I to Eadberht of Northumbria and Archbishop Ecgberht complaining of their giving monastic lands to a layman.[5] It has also the letter of Leo III to Cenwulf of Mercia on the aboli-

[1] D. Bethurum, *Philologica: Malone Anniversary Studies* 98.

[2] One should note that Harley MS 208, a ninth-century continental manuscript of Alcuin's letters, was at York in the Middle Ages. This does not prove it to have been there in Wulfstan's time, but it is remarkable how little overlap there is with the collection in Vespasian A xiv; only two of the 91 letters in Harley are found in Vespasian, and the latter is without 26 letters addressed to English correspondents which are in Harley. The difference between the two collections may be accidental, but one cannot help wondering if the collection in Vespasian was meant to supplement that in Harley. In that case, the repetition of two letters was presumably by inadvertence. One had lost its beginning in the Harley MS.

[3] W. Levison, *England and the Continent in the Eighth Century* 244 f.

[4] See Levison, *op.cit.* 295–302.

[5] BCS 184; translated in D. Whitelock, *English Historical Documents c. 500–1042*, 764 f.

tion of the archbishopric of Lichfield,[1] decrees of the synods of Hertford (672)[2] and of Chelsea (816),[3] and the canons issued by Oda, Archbishop of Canterbury (941–58).[4] This last may have reached Wulfstan from a southern source, which also provided a set of tenth-century letters written to archbishops of Canterbury from the Continent, and a letter from Lantfrith to the brothers of the Old Monastery of Winchester concerning the miracles of St Swithun.[5] Wulfstan knew some other English records not preserved in Vespasian A xiv; he uses a letter of Boniface to Cuthbert, Archbishop of Canterbury,[6] and the report of the legates of 786, a document which has not come down in English sources.[7] His collection of penitential letters includes one to Ælfric, Archbishop of Canterbury (994–1005), and one of his own has identical wording with one written by Bishop Wulfsige of Sherborne.[8] We saw above that he added passages to the northern version of the Anglo-Saxon Chronicle, and that he read in Hatton MS 20 Alfred's letter prefixed to his *Cura Pastoralis* and made modifications. He had a thorough knowledge of previous Anglo-Saxon laws, and draws on them, especially those of Edgar, when drafting codes for Ethelred and Cnut. Many codes, though not those of Kent, which he used, are contained in manuscripts connected with him.

He was in contact with the homilist Ælfric, and familiar

[1] BCS 288; translated in D. Whitelock, *op.cit.* 793.

[2] Bede, HE iv. 5.

[3] *Councils and Ecclesiastical Documents*, ed. A. W. Haddan and W. Stubbs, III. 579–85.

[4] *Concilia Magnae Britanniae et Hiberniae*, ed. D. Wilkins, I. 212–14.

[5] These letters are printed in *Memorials of St Dunstan*, ed. W. Stubbs, 369 f, 380 f, 383–9.

[6] Haddan and Stubbs, *op.cit.* III. 376–83; M. Tangl, *Die Briefe des heiligen Bonifatius und Lullus*, No. 78. This letter is one of two which have survived in the form in which they reached England, whereas most letters of Boniface are preserved only in collections made at Mainz.

[7] The only complete text, from a Wolfenbüttel MS, is in E. Dümmler, MGH *Epist.* IV, No. 3; translation of part by D. Whitelock, *op.cit.* 770–4.

[8] *Memorials of St Dunstan* 409. The use of the same formula-book might account for this agreement.

with the pastoral letter which the latter wrote for Bishop Wulfsige, as well as with those he himself commissioned. We have seen that he re-wrote some pieces of Ælfric in his own style,[1] and he can be shown also to have known parts of both volumes of the Catholic Homilies, the letter to Sigeweard *On the Old and New Testament*, and *Judges*, as well as the letter Ælfric wrote for his monks at Eynsham, abridging the *Regularis Concordia*.[2] Sometimes Wulfstan also worked over other vernacular writings by anonymous writers.[3]

Wulfstan's range of reading may have been wider than our evidence proves. His selection of works to be copied and passages to be excerpted shows the same preoccupations as do his writings: with the nearness of the end of the world and the necessity to recall men to repentance; with the evils and corruptions of his time, which had in his opinion brought down the vengeance of God in the shape of the Viking invasions; with the proper ordering of all ranks of society, ecclesiastical and lay; with the securing for the ecclesiastical orders all the respect and rights to which they were entitled, emphasizing the high importance of the priestly functions; and, in connexion with this, with making the ecclesiastics worthy of their calling, especially those under his own charge. As has been well shown by others,[4] many matters of interest to his contemporary ecclesiastics are not touched on: he does not discuss problems of theology, nor concern himself with the allegorical exposition of the scriptures; he makes no attempt to hold his hearers' or readers' interest by poetical description, by miracle tales or incidents from saints' lives. The care he took with his writing was directed towards making it memorable, forcible and effective. In his responsible position, he could not indulge any personal interests; he must have spent long hours in his study, but all to a practical end—the reform of church and society in the

[1] See p. 22 *supra*.

[2] On Wulfstan's relations with Ælfric see P. Clemoes, in *Anglia* lxxviii. 265–83.

[3] See p. 26 *supra*.

[4] Especially by Bethurum 86, 96 f. See also the review by J. C. Pope in MLN lxxiv. 336.

troubled days in which he lived. And nowhere does the urgency of his message come out more strongly than in the *Sermo ad Anglos.*

This *sermo* owes little to other men's work. A passage which occurs only in I and E is based on a letter of Alcuin.[1] There is a Latin text on the theme that the calamities and invasions afflicting the English are God's punishment for sins in CCCC MS 190,[2] a manuscript connected with Wulfstan, and though such sermons were not uncommon, this is close enough to the *Sermo ad Anglos* in its contents as to suggest a connexion between them.[3] Wulfstan may possibly have known Ælfric's Mid-Lent Sunday homily in his *Lives of Saints,* which has a few similar passages,[4] and uses, like our *sermo,* Matthew x. 21, but the resemblances may be accidental, called forth by similarity of theme.[5] The end of the anonymous *Life of St Neot*[6] affords a closer parallel, for

[1] See note to ll. 184–99.

[2] Printed by Mary Bateson, EHR x. 731. She heads it, with a query, Alcuin. It sounds more like a work of Ethelred's reign, for it refers to the payment of *infinitam pecuniam* by the people *pro libertate regni* which recalls the great tributes to the Danes in this reign, while the reference to the slaying of thousands of the people seems to imply far bigger invasions than those known to Alcuin.

[3] Cf *bello videlicet, fame, igni cædibusque* with *here 7 hunger, bryne 7 blodgyte* (l. 56); *legem & precepta domini omni modo neglexerat & monita doctorum contempserat* with *naþor ne heoldan ne lare ne lage Godes ne manna* (l. 67): *diversis criminibus pene omnis ordo gentis anglorum maculatus* with *wearð þes þeodscipe . . . swyþe forsyngod þurh mænigfealde synna 7 þurh fela misdæda* (ll. 135 ff); cf ll. 166 f.

[4] Ed. W. W. Skeat, I. 282–306, especially ll. 139–55, 281–308. Wulfstan shows no knowledge of the *Lives of Saints* elsewhere, but this is inconclusive, for it mainly deals with topics which were not his concern.

[5] Professor Dickins suggests comparison with stanza 45 of the Edda poem, *Vǫluspá*:

> *Brǿþr munu berjask ok at bǫnum verþask,*
> *munu systrungar sifjum spilla;*
> *hart's í heimi, hórdómr mikill;*
> [*skeggjǫld, skalmǫld, skildir 'u klofnir,*
> *vindǫld, vargǫld, áþr verǫld steypisk;*]
> *mun engi maþr ǫþrum þyrma.*

[6] Ed. R. P. Wülcker in *Anglia* iii. 102 ff.

it refers to pestilence, bad crops, loosening of the ties of kinship, strife between father and son, and the imminence of doomsday; the passage in question has Wulfstan phrases lacking from the rest of the *Life*,[1] and, though the date of this is uncertain, it seems probable that its author has drawn on some homily by Wulfstan on this theme.

On the other hand, the *sermo* contains many reminiscences of Wulfstan's earlier writings. It has in its introductory passage phrases from his eschatological sermons[2] and from one of these, Napier XIII, it drew the remarks on the decay of the ties of kinship (ll. 62–4) which are eventually based on Matthew x. 21. Napier XXVIII, called by Dr Bethurum 'God's Threat to Sinning Israel', has influenced the list of calamities (ll. 56–60) and the lament for the defeat of the English (ll. 108–16). Lists of sinners, like that in I and E at ll. 166–73, occur in many of Wulfstan's works, homiletic and legal,[3] and the wording of another passage in this version only, at ll. 185 f, is closely paralleled in Napier II. The conclusion, ll. 199–211, is very similar to that in many of Wulfstan's homilies[4] and is used also in *Polity*. There are other similarities with the last named work, apart from those where both texts are drawing on a common, legal, source. Though it is not possible to give a precise date to *Polity*, it seems to me likely that a passage in this on the spoliation of churches and lack of respect for the clergy,[5] which shares several expressions with the *sermo* (ll. 31–3, 40 f) and is in a good context, may be the earlier.

There are also many phrases which are almost or exactly identical with some in the statutes of Enham, a code drafted by Wulfstan for King Ethelred in 1008;[6] it survives in two

[1] e.g. *for folces synnen; wide on eorðe; Godes lage ne gemeð swa swa men scolde*. Use of Wulfstan is shown also by the sentence *7 se þincð nu wærrest 7 geapest þe oðerne mæig beswican*, with which compare *ac nu þincð ðe wærra 7 micele þe snotera, se ðe can mid leasungan wæwerdlice werian* (Napier 168, 20 f), from the homily which follows the *Sermo ad Anglos* in three MSS.

[2] Napier XII–XVI.

[3] See note to ll. 166–73.

[4] See Bethurum 96.

[5] Ed. Jost 146–8.

[6] See notes to ll. 25, 44 f, 86–93, 107, 137–48.

Old English versions, V and VI Atr, and one Latin one, and the *sermo* agrees in one place with V and in another with VI, while one of its phrases has a correspondence only in the Latin version.[1] Wulfstan may have been drawing on a repetition of this code promulgated in 1014, but we cannot be certain as only the ecclesiastical part of the legislation of this year has survived.

For much of this homily, however, Wulfstan seems to have drawn on his own experience of conditions in England, and few men could have had such opportunities of knowing what these were. In the notes I have assembled evidence to show how his statements on the prevalence of treason, traffic in slaves, heathenism, &c, can be corroborated from contemporary evidence. Even where he appears to be using his own earlier writings, I suspect that he did so from memory, rather than from deliberate consultation of manuscripts. No work smells less of the study; and in the urgency of his message he has made a more intensive use than anywhere else in his work of the rhetorical devices which lend such vehemence and fervour to his oratory.

VI. WULFSTAN'S LANGUAGE[2]

The entries in various manuscripts in a hand probably Wulfstan's own[3] are in the normal West Saxon standard of his day. Thus it writes *y* for the i-mutation of *ŭ̄* (*gebyreð*,

[1] At l. 107, *ealre his mægðe* corresponds to *eallan his freondan* in V Atr 31. 1, missing from VI Atr 38; in the list of criminals in ll. 137–148, only VI Atr 28. 2 f has anything to correspond with *þurh mistlice forligru* and *freolsbricas 7 fæstenbrycas*; as pointed out by Jost, *Wulfstanstudien* 24, the phrase *fremdum to gewealde* (ll. 45 f) corresponds to *paganorum dominio* in the Latin version of VI Atr 9.

[2] In this section the following abbreviations are used, in addition to the sigla for the MSS of Wulfstan's homilies: Cop = Copenhagan MS Gl. kgl. S. 1595; Claud = Claudius A iii (VI Atr); Cleo = Cleopatra B xiii (some homilies); CP = corrections in the 'Wulfstan' hand in Hatton MS 20 of *Cura Pastoralis*; Harl = Harley 55, fols 1–4 (York memoranda and II and III Eg); Jun = Junius 121 (*Polity*, &c); and Tib = Tiberius A xiii (the early-eleventh-century portion, a Worcester cartulary, with entries in the 'Wulfstan' hand).

[3] See pp. 29 f *supra*.

fyrðrige, unscyld . . . I, *spyrian, cyððe* Cop); it has *y* as the i-mutation of *ēa* and *io* (*gehyrað, gyman, -að* Cop, *gehyrað* I, *gelyf, gelyfað* Tib; *hyrde* I), and it alters the spelling of words in the Hatton MS of the *Cura Pastoralis* from *ie* to *y*; it has only broken forms of *æ* before *l* plus consonant (*healde, -an, eal*, &c, I); it never writes *e* for *æ*, or for *ǣ* of either origin (*gebæran, dædan, dæd-* I, *gesællice* Cop; *rære, clænsie* I, *lære* Cop). On certain minor possibilities of variation in late West Saxon texts, it shows that the writer used *æghwar* (I), *ægþor* (I), *mænige* (CP), *-bryce* (I) (not *-brece*), *worolde* (Cop), *swutelige* (Harl), the contracted form *biscpas*[1] (I), and *opþon* (I) for *opþe*. Among features which are sometimes considered not pure West Saxon we get only *scolde* (Cop), *scoldon* (I), with no cases of diphthongization of a back vowel after *sc*; and some instances of uncontracted forms of the third person present (*gehyreð, gymeð* I, Cop, *gebyreð* Cop) beside contracted forms (*lið, gefærð* Cop). As examples of late inflectional endings there are both in I and Cop dative plurals in *-an*, while the corrections in CP reveal a preference for *-on* instead of *-en* as subjunctive ending, and for *-e* instead of *-a* as the feminine plural of the adjective. The corrections in CP show that the writer set store by linguistic minutiae; he corrects *feawe* (masculine plural) to *feawa, swæ* to *swa, mengeo* to *menigeo, reccelease* to *recelease, ebrisc* to *ebreisc*, and *creacas* to *greccas*.

Except for the unsyncopated presents, for *scolde, scoldon* and for *e* in the only word, *wencle* I, to show the i-mutation of *a/o* before a nasal, the entries in this hand have provided no evidence of its writer's practice on certain features common in manuscripts of his work, which have been regarded as not 'pure' West Saxon. Three manuscripts contemporary with Wulfstan, I, Claud and the York Gospels[2] are in close agreement on these matters. They all have almost consis-

[1] Contracted forms of this word occur in Wulfstan's works as follows: 9 times in I (6 in *Polity* and 3 in laws); twice in E, in one case in the Cleo text as well; 4 times in C (3 in *Polity*, once in laws); once in Claud; and once in the CCCC 383 version of EGu.

[2] That is, the entries made in the early eleventh century to this volume.

tently a single back vowel after *sc* (e.g. *scandlic, scamu, gescad, gescot, scolde,* &c); they use *biscop*(-) or *biscp-*, with the exception of a few cases of *bisceop*(-) in I; but only I ever has *sculon,* and then rarely, its normal form being *scylan, -on,* which is the only form in the York Gospels.[1] In all three, *weor-* before a consonant is almost constant, with hardly a trace of *wur-*. I and Claud afford instances of a sporadic *æ* instead of *e* before nasal (e.g. *mæn, Ængla, ænde, stænt, græmede,* &c). Both syncopated and unsyncopated presents occur, the latter sometimes (e.g. *geweorþeð, gefeohteð, healdeð, steleð*) without i-mutation.[2] Both I and the York Gospels supply each one instance of *waldend,* a form occasionally found in later Wulfstan manuscripts.[3]

The frequent retention of these features in later Wulfstan manuscripts supports the impression that they were in his drafts or those of his secretaries. Thus a single vowel after *sc* is normal in C,[4] more common than the diphthong in E, not uncommon in B (perhaps from Exeter) and occasional even in the Canterbury MS Tiberius A iii which has some of his homilies. That E took over this feature from its copy, against the scribe's own practice, is suggested by its absence from the Pseudo-Wulfstan homilies in the same manuscript; when the same scribe wrote Jun, he almost always uses the diphthong after *sc,* even in the Wulfstan work *Polity*.[5] Cleo uses only the forms with diphthongs. There is great variation in the spelling of *biscop,* &c: C has chiefly *biscop*(-) or *biscp-*; E has forms with or without *e* in about equal pro-

[1] The word does not occur in Claud.

[2] The York Gospels have also the contracted *healt* without mutation, and this, and *gehealt,* crop up occasionally in later MSS of Wulfstan's works, in B, E and Jun, in Cnut's laws both in Harley 55 (not originally part of the same MS as what I cite as Harl) and CCCC 383, and in the latter MS 3 times in *Rectitudines*; *wealt* occurs at one place in *Polity* in all MSS, I, C and Jun.

[3] i.e. 3 times in C, twice in E. E once has *haldan* which occurs in *Rectitudines* in CCCC 383. *Waldan* (vb.) occurs in *Episcopus* in Jun.

[4] C in this section = the main mid-eleventh-century hand.

[5] The difference in the treatment of *Polity* as regards this and other features (see *infra*) may indicate that *Polity* had had a different manuscript tradition before it reached the scribe of Jun.

portion, with occasional *biscp-*; Jun has a strong preference for *bisceop*(-); B prefers *biscop*(-) in its Wulfstan homilies, whereas Cleo has only *bisceop*(-), except for *biscpum* once. In C, the *scylon* form has been completely ousted by *sculon*, and so also in E except for rare exceptions; Jun also prefers *sculon*, but *scylon* and *sceolon* both occur occasionally. In B *scylon* is almost constant, and varies only with *sceolon* in *Cleo*.

Most later Wulfstan manuscripts retain *weor-* before consonants. Thus it preponderates in E (though the scribe uses *wur-* when copying non-Wulfstan material)[1] and in Jun, B, and Cleo; in C, however, it is very commonly replaced by *wur-*, with the result that the latter spelling occurs about five times as often as *weor-*. On the other hand, C very greatly extends the use of *æ* instead of *e* before a nasal, and has this also in its version of *Apollonius of Tyre*, which shows that it was part of the scribe's practice, or at least not confined to Wulfstan texts. In most other manuscripts, this *æ* occurs sporadically, i.e. in E and Jun, in Cleo, in CCCC 383, in EGu and *Rectitudines*,[2] and in that part of Nero A i which was originally distinct from what we cite as I, where it occurs in Cnut's laws. Both syncopated and unsyncopated presents occur in all the later manuscripts, as in the contemporary ones.

It seems likely that these features belonged, if not to Wulfstan himself, at least to his amanuenses. But it is less easy to decide whether they represent the practice of either the Worcester or the York scriptorium, and perhaps it is a waste of time to attempt to decide between them, for surely the Archbishop's secretaries would travel from place to place

[1] Napier XXX is particularly instructive as regards E's habits, for in the Wulfstan passage with which it begins it uses *sculon* and *weorðian*, but when drawing from a non-Wulfstan source it has almost consistently a diphthong after *sc-* (e.g. *sceolon, sceolde, forsceapene, tosceacen, sceort, besceofene*) and only one instance of a simple vowel, *gescop*. Napier XXIX, which is not Wulfstan, agrees in having a diphthong after *sc-* and has always *wur-* before consonants.

[2] The fact that there are no traces of this feature in this manuscript's version of Af-Ine shows that it cannot safely be assigned to the scribe of the manuscript.

with him. There is also the possibility that it is that of some other place where he or some secretary was trained. There is a shortage of comparative material for the scribal practice of Worcester and York in his lifetime. The retention of single back vowels after *sc*, and of *weor-* before consonants in copies of Gregory's *Dialogues*[1] and the *Cura Pastoralis*[2] is hardly relevant, for they may represent what was in the ninth-century exemplars. The same difficulty is present in copies of earlier charters. The Tiberius B iv manuscript of the Anglo-Saxon Chronicle, known as D, is a later manuscript, and is as likely to be from York as from Worcester; but the part referring to Wulfstan's time and earlier was certainly based on a northern exemplar.[3]

The few original charters which survived until modern times[4] show that in the time of Wulfstan's predecessor, Archbishop Oswald, though already a mainly West Saxon language was written at Worcester, more dialect forms, e.g. unbroken *a* before *l* plus consonant, *e* for the mutation of *ĕa* and *ĭo*, *o* for *a* before nasals, were tolerated than in the early Wulfstan manuscripts; *weor-* plus consonant is normal, *biscop*, *biscup* and *bisceop* all occur. In Wulfstan's time,[5] *bisceop* becomes more frequent and *gewurðe* occurs, and after his time,[6] *bisceop* and *wur-* plus consonant are constant. *Scolde* is retained. But *æ* for *e* before a nasal is extremely rare throughout.[7] Part of the Worcester cartulary,

[1] CCCC MS 322 (Hecht's C) is of uncertain provenance, but part, at least, of the early-eleventh-century MS Otho C i (Hecht's O) was probably written at Worcester, and Hatton 76 (Hecht's H), of about the same date, was at Worcester in the thirteenth century.

[2] The late-tenth-century CCCC MS 12 was at Worcester in the thirteenth century. Hatton 20 was not written at Worcester.

[3] On this matter *v.* D. Whitelock, *The Peterborough Chronicle* (Early English Manuscripts in Facsimile IV, Copenhagen 1954) 29 f.

[4] I include those lost charters published by Hickes and in the Appendix to J. Smith's edition of Bede's *Historia Ecclesiastica*, Cambridge, 1722.

[5] See Robertson LXXVI, LXXIX, LXXXIII, and cf LXXXI, an Evesham lease; also KCD 724.

[6] See Robertson LXXXVII, XCIV, CXI, CXII.

[7] It occurs only in BCS 1229 (dated 969) where *wændlesdune* occurs

Tiberius A xiii, was written in Wulfstan's time.[1] Where it can be compared with older charters, it shows that usually the scribe retained their forms, but did on occasion alter them, and usually to get rid of dialect features. He has a preference for *bisceop*. There is almost no trace of *æ* before nasals.[2] A rather later scribe who added the homily Napier I into this manuscript supplies *geweorðan* (*bis*) and avoids *æ* before nasals.

The evidence available for York practice is even scantier. Yet the short memoranda,[3] drawn up in Oswald's time, in Harley 55, and the entries on the estates of York in the York Gospels[4] are in West Saxon standard. Neither has *æ* before nasals; both use *biscop*; the later document uses *-weorð* and the earlier provides no evidence on this feature. Much later copies of York documents suggest that their exemplars had *biscop* and *weorðscipe*, and in the very corrupt boundaries to Cnut's Patrington charter[5] *aird* and *fannes* imply an original with *ænde* and *fænnes*. It is interesting to note that the first two scribes of the D manuscript of the Anglo-Saxon Chronicle, writing in the mid-eleventh century, use *æ* before nasals very frequently, but the last three scribes never. Scribe 2 ends in the middle of 1016, and the last instance of *æ* is *Cænt* a few lines before the change. The last scribe, not writing until almost the end of the century, has a decided preference for *weor-* before consonants and for *biscop*.[6] There are several features about this manuscript which make it difficult to believe that it was produced at Worcester[7] and

beside several forms with *e*, and in Robertson LXXXIII, a text of 1023, in *længast*. BCS 1229 is a royal diploma, so it need not have been written at Worcester.

[1] See N. R. Ker, in *Studies in Medieval History presented to F. M. Powicke* 49–75.

[2] I have only found *fæn* twice, in BCS 1299, dated 977.

[3] Robertson LIV.

[4] *ibid.* LXXXIV.

[5] W. Farrer, *Early Yorkshire Charters* I. No. 8, from the *Registrum Album* of the Dean and Chapter of York.

[6] As late as annal 1076 one gets *weorðscype*. Annal 1079 has *-scoten* (*bis*).

[7] The study by A. Flohrschütz, *Die Sprache der Handschrift D der*

one wonders if it represents the tradition established in the York scriptorium.

While these features which we have been discussing seem alien to some of the well-established West Saxon scriptoria in Wulfstan's time, further study on manuscripts which can be securely located is required before they are pronounced to be regional variations. *Weor-* and simple vowels after *sc* may merely represent conservatism, though the latter feature is characteristic of Mercian texts. As for *æ* before nasals, Dr and Miss Sisam have shown that it was widespread in many areas in southern England round about Wulfstan's time, and that manuscripts which contain it cannot be allotted to south-eastern England merely because here it lies behind the conditions in Middle English.[1] Yet its extreme rarity in Worcester is noteworthy, and leads one to think that its presence in Wulfstan manuscripts may indicate that it derives from his own practice or that of secretaries not trained at Worcester. He might have brought some with him from London when he was translated to York and Worcester. The presence of unsyncopated presents is not now regarded as a certain sign of non-West Saxon origin.[2]

The forms of the *Sermo ad Anglos* in MS I call for little further comment. In common with most texts of this period, *-an* can represent earlier *-on*, *-en* and *-um*; the neuter plural is *-a* in *gerihta*, the plural of i-stems is *-a* in *dæda*; the nom.acc.pl. of the adjective is *-e* for all genders; there is a tendency to reduce the back vowel of weak verbs of class 2, giving *lehtreð*, *þeowede* and, probably, *gelewede*; *syn* for the present indicative plural of the verb 'to be' is common in

angelsächsischen Annalen is of little use, for it fails fully to consider the changes in hand or the complicated history of the text.

[1] See *The Salisbury Psalter*, ed. Celia Sisam and Kenneth Sisam, EETS 1959, 13 f. The scribe in C who wrote only an extract from *Genesis* has *æ* before nasals (as has the Otho B x version of this). He also writes *u* for initial *f-*, a southern characteristic.

[2] See Campbell § 734; E. Vogel, *Zur Flexion des englischen Verbums im XI. and XII. Jahrhundert* § 3; J. Hedberg, *The Syncope of the Old English Present Endings* (Lund Studies in English XII).

Wulfstan's works, and is certainly not confined to the subjunctive.[1] The only dialect forms are: *e* instead of *y*, *i* as mutation of *ea* in *gewelede*, l. 125, where E has *gewylede* and C *gewilede*; *e* or *æ* for the mutation of *īo* in *gesene*, l. 53 in I, C, B (*isene* H, *gesyne* E), and *gesæne*, l. 132 in I (*gesene* C, *gesyne* E), beside *gesyne*, l. 100 (*isæne* H), and l. 175 in I and E; *e* for *ǣ* as mutation of *ā* occurs only in *lewe*, l. 164, beside the late West Saxon form *-leawa*, l. 166, and *gelewede*, l. 167. If *feseð*, l. 115, is from an Old Norse **feysa*, the only examples of *e* for *y* as mutation of *ŭ* are the *wælcerian* of E (a Worcester MS) and *berst*(*a*) of C. This is no proof of Kentish provenance, for *e* is widespread before *r*.[2] The form *lifiendne*, l. 77, is an occasional West Saxon variant.[3]

A few words should be said on Wulfstan's vocabulary. An article by Menner[4] in 1948 was only concerned to show that certain authors who claimed that Anglian vocabulary was used by Wulfstan had failed to distinguish between genuine and spurious texts. He concluded that as far as this evidence went, Wulfstan's vocabulary was West Saxon.[5] It was not within his theme to discuss the rather large Scandinavian element in Wulfstan's vocabulary. In this text we have *grið*, *griðian*, *griðleas*, *þræl*, *lagu*, probably *fesian*, &c; and the compounds *þegengild*, *nydgyld* and perhaps *nydmage* look like translations from Old Norse;[6] moreover, the expression *of life forrǣde* should be compared with ON *ráða af lífi*. It is natural enough that an archbishop of York should adopt some of the vocabulary of the Scandinavianized North, and this is clear in his adoption of their terminology. He uses words like *bonda* and *þræl* to denote the social classes and,

[1] See note to l. 72.

[2] L. Morsbach, *Mittelenglische Grammatik* § 127.

[3] See Campbell § 762.

[4] 'Anglian and Saxon Elements in Wulfstan's Vocabulary', MLN lxiii. 1–9.

[5] It is interesting that there is one instance, *Hadbot* 9. 1, of the Anglian *wibede* (*sic* C and CCCC MS 190; *wigbede* Textus Roffensis) whereas the West Saxon *weofod* occurs frequently in Wulfstan's works.

[6] See notes to these words.

most significantly, *eorl* at a time when *ealdorman* was still the current term in the south of England, including the diocese of Worcester.[1]

[1] Wulfstan uses *ealdormen,* in its technical sense, only when he is quoting earlier legislation, such as that of Edgar; otherwise he uses *eorl,* although in the South in his time this was confined to holders of the office in Northumbria, or, after Cnut's accession, to men of Danish nationality. Even Ælfhelm, ealdorman of southern Northumbria (993–1006), a Mercian by birth, is called *ealdorman* as late as 1036 (ASC E) in a southern chronicle.

XV

Wulfstan at York[1]

WULFSTAN WAS bishop of London from 996 to 1002, when he was translated to the sees of York and Worcester. He was the third successive archbishop of York to hold this see in plurality with that of Worcester. In 1016, Leofsige, abbot of Thorney, was made bishop of Worcester, but perhaps only as a suffragan to Wulfstan.[2] Wulfstan died at York in 1023, and was buried in Ely. As well as an important political personage, he was a prolific writer, and there have survived several manuscripts containing his work and collections of sources which he used. It is perhaps too readily assumed that any manuscript connected with him emanates from Worcester. The purpose of this paper is to consider the evidence for his activities in his see and province of York.

There is no reason to suppose that he spent most of his time in Worcester. The English kings chose their northern archbishops with care, for it was a difficult province. After the death in 956 of Archbishop Wulfstan I, who had been suspected of disloyalty to the English kings, the choice fell on men of southern origin who had had some experience of the eastern Danelaw.[3] Such men would be in a better position to understand the problems of the Anglo-Scandinavian north than would men of purely West Saxon or Kentish experience. This policy would have been defeated if the men appointed spent most of their time in Worcester, leaving their northern province mainly to its own devices. They were allowed to hold Worcester in plurality, partly because the see of York was so poor, partly no doubt in order to anchor their loyalty more firmly to the English king, but hardly as a permanent place of residence. It is reasonable to assume that after the appointment of Leofsige as bishop of Worcester the aging archbishop's visits to Worcester would be less frequent than before. The reason why we do not find many references to him in the north is that our sources of evidence from this area are scanty. He was at any rate there a fortnight after the death of Swegn Forkbeard at Gainsborough at Candelmas, 1014, for it was at York that he consecrated Ælfwig as bishop of London on 16 February.[4] He was there also on an undated occasion, when he witnessed King Ethelred's confirmation of a grant of Darlington by a York citizen, Styr, son of Ulf, to St. Cuthbert's at Durham.[5] Possibly this was in 1014, for after Easter in that year King Ethelred had come as far north as Lindsey,[6] so this may have been the occasion of a further journey north to York. It was at York that Wulfstan died.

On general grounds there is nothing against the view that Wulfstan did some of his reading and writing at York. He would have to produce sermons for specific occasions and draft laws by fixed dates, and could not have relied on doing all his work at one only of his sees. He must surely have had secretaries available at both places; probably some traveled with him. He puts *bocweorc, ræding oððon rihting, lar oððon leornung*[7] as part of every bishop's daily work; and he stresses the need for those in a bishop's following to be suitable persons with some special skill.[8]

It is obvious that a scribe's skill would be welcome both *æt ham* and *on siðe*. We may compare the glimpse we get of Bishop Ælfsige of Chester-le-Street, accompanied on a journey south by his scribe Aldred, who entered for him some prayers into the manuscript of the Durham Ritual in his tent at Oakley Down in Wessex.[9] A later bishop of Worcester, St. Wulfstan, is shown by William of Malmesbury's *Life* of him to have traveled with several clerks on his journeys, including Coleman, the author of the vernacular *Life*, which William was using.[10] Archbishop Wulfstan was no doubt similarly accompanied, and hence one should not expect to find linguistic differences between a work first written down at Worcester and one first written down at York.

Several manuscripts connected with Wulfstan are shown by glosses in them or by mention of them in catalogs to have been at one time at Worcester. More than that, we can see that Wulfstan used manuscripts in the possession of that church, if we agree with Mr. Ker that a hand which makes entries in several manuscripts is very probably his own.[11] This hand is found in Hatton 20, the copy of Alfred's translation of the *Cura Pastoralis* which he sent to Worcester; it also annotates the early-eleventh-century part of Tiberius A.xiii, a Worcester cartulary;[12] and it is found in Hatton 42, a book of canons which once belonged to Dunstan and presumably was brought to Worcester by him when he became bishop there.[13] Certain later manuscripts containing Wulfstan's works, Hatton 113, Hatton 114, and Junius 121, were written at Worcester in the second half of the eleventh century, and one manuscript of the collection of Latin texts and excerpts which Dr. Bethurum has named his "Commonplace Book,"[14] that is, C.C.C.C. MS. 265, of the mid-eleventh century, is assigned by Mr. Ker to Worcester on account of its script and its containing a reference to St. Wulfstan.[15] It does not follow that the exemplars of these manuscripts of the generation after Archbishop

Wulfstan were themselves written at Worcester, though they may have been.

Glosses in the "tremulous" hand[16] prove Harley 55, ff. 1–4, to have been at Worcester by about 1200. These four half-sheets contain some medical remedies for hemiplegia, the code known as II and III Edgar, and a set of memoranda relating to lands alienated from the York estates of Otley, Sherburn-in-Elmet, and Ripon, followed by a list of lands acquired for York and Beverley by Archbishop Oscytel, which has notes in the "Wulfstan" hand.[17] York would seem the most likely place where these memoranda would be added, and it may be that the manuscript reached Worcester because Wulfstan, who made a lot of use of II and III Edgar, found it convenient to carry round with him a little manuscript containing it.[18] Yet it is of course possible that he sometimes had copied for him at Worcester matter concerning only his northern see. One may note that the code called IV Edgar relates to the Danelaw,[19] and yet it has come down to us in two manuscripts only, C.C.C.C. MS. 265, from Worcester, and Nero E.i, probably from this same church; however, there is no evidence that the latter manuscript, of about 1000, was actually written at Worcester, and it could have been brought from the north.

There are, however, some manuscripts connected with Wulfstan which supply no evidence of a Worcester provenance. A reluctance to consider the claims of York may arise from a belief that the destruction of St. Peter's at York after the Norman Conquest makes the survival of any of its manuscripts unlikely. The D version of the Anglo-Saxon Chronicle, written in this section by a man of strong York sympathies, records that in 1068 King William "made St. Peter's minster an object of scorn" and that in 1069 the Frenchmen "had thoroughly ravaged and burnt the holy minster of St. Peter." Yet this cannot have been as completely stripped and destroyed as this suggests, for the same authority tells how in 1075 the Danes broke into St. Peter's minster and captured a large amount of property there. If the church had been completely denuded in 1069, it would hardly have recovered much wealth in the troubled years before 1075. One can admit that the chances of survival of York manuscripts and documents were not very good; but the York Gospels have been preserved, and some other books may have escaped. Moreover, some manuscripts produced at York in Wulfstan's time could have found a home elsewhere before the Conquest. One cannot dismiss out of hand a York origin for a Wulfstan manuscript.

The York Gospels[20] afford one clear example of a York manuscript connected with Wulfstan. This was probably written in England about 1000, and has Old English entries on its last six leaves. These are: surveys of lands attached to Sherburn-in-Elmet, Otley, and Ripon, belonging to the see of York;[21] three short Wulfstan sermons, Napier Nos. LIX, LX, and LXI, of which the first is headed *Sermo Lupi* and the last has interlineations in the "Wulfstan" hand; Cnut's Old English letter of 1019–20;[22] a list of service books and plate at Sherburn-in-Elmet;[23] some bidding prayers; and a list of the sureties for a certain Ælfric, many of the names being Scandinavian.[24] Mr. Ker assigns the Wulfstan homilies, the Cnut letter, and the prayers to a single hand of the first part of the eleventh century, and the survey of York lands to three hands of about this time. There is no reason to doubt that the manuscript was at York when the Wulfstan entries were made. It has remained there ever since.

The next manuscript to be considered is Claudius A.iii., ff. 31–86, 106–50,[25] that is, the part of this composite manuscript which consists of a pontifical written in caroline minuscule about 1000[26] preceded by eight preliminary leaves. On the verso of the first of these is a metrical inscription[27] recording that a certain Thureth had had this *halgungboc* beautifully bound; then follow one bifolium and five half-sheets (ff. 32–38) containing the Latin and Old English versions of the code called VI Ethelred. The Latin version is expressly said to be by Wulfstan, and the Old English version is in his style. There are interlineations in the "Wulfstan" hand in both versions of the code. A pontifical is part of the necessary equipment of a bishop or archbishop, and includes the order of several ceremonies, such as dedication of churches and confirmation, which often took place away from the cathedral church. If this pontifical was one which Wulfstan took about with him, Ethelred's sixth code may have been added because he wished to have it available. But it is also possible that a book provided, as this one once was, with a rich binding was meant for ceremonial use at the cathedral, and perhaps kept on the altar; in that case the insertion of leaves containing legal texts could be paralleled by many examples of the entry of documents in blank spaces in gospels and fine ritual books, for their safer preservation. We need go no further than the York Gospels for an instance of this practice.[28] The presence in this part of Claudius A.iii of the "Wulfstan" hand makes unlikely the identification of the Thureth mentioned in the poem with Thored, a landowner who gave an estate at Horsley, Surrey, to Christ Church, Canterbury;[29] it is more tempting to accept the suggestion that he was the earl of Northumbria of this name. He is last heard of in 992, when he was one of the leaders of a disastrous campaign.[30] His successor Ælfhelm signs in 993, but Thored may have lived some years longer and have been deposed from office. If the donor mentioned in Claudius A.iii is this earl, one would expect his generosity to have been directed toward York rather than Worcester; yet, even so, the book might have been removed to Worcester by one of the archbishops who held both York and Worcester. Thus one cannot establish for certain that it was York where the leaves with VI Ethelred were written, though this place has at least an equal claim to Worcester's.

Vespasian A.xiv, ff. 114 – 70, of the first half of the eleventh century, is another manuscript with Wulfstan connections which shows no sign of having been at Worcester. It has a set of verses which Mr. Ker thinks are written in the "Wulfstan" hand, and which show that he was responsible for having the texts in this manuscript compiled. All are in Latin. Among them is a letter written to Wulfstan when he was bishop of London.[31] Several items in this manuscript are of northern interest and likely to have been available at York. These include a letter from Pope Paul I to Eadberht of Northumbria and his brother, Archbishop Ecgberht,[32] a letter from a northern anchorite, Alchfrith, to Higlac,[33] and a letter from Eanbald, before he became archbishop of York, to his predecessor, Archbishop Eanbald I.[34] There is also a collection of twenty-seven of Alcuin's letters, mainly to recipients in England;[35] only two are to continental recipients, and of these, one was written in England.[36] There is also a letter from Arno, bishop of Salzburg, to Alcuin's pupil, Cuculus, who was probably in England at the time.[37] It is of interest to compare this collection with that contained in Harley MS. 208, a ninth-century Continental manuscript which was at York in the Middle Ages. One cannot prove that it was there already in Wulfstan's time, though it was certainly in England by about 1000.[38] What is remarkable is that there is so very little overlap between the collections in Harley and Vespasian. Only two letters occur in both, and one of these has in the Harley manuscript lost its beginning and been run on to the preceding letter, so that its presence in the manuscript has been concealed.[39] In neither case has the Harley manuscript served as the exemplar for the text in Vespasian A.xiv, for the latter sometimes gives superior readings.

This slightness of overlap is not to be explained on the assumption that each compiler is selecting on a different principle. The compiler of the Harley manuscript was not avoiding letters to England; he includes twenty-six letters to persons in England, some of them important letters to Northumbrian kings and prelates. His collection, which has ninety-one letters, seems to have been made abroad: Continental letters predominate, but it avoids the correspondence between Alcuin and Charles the Great, except for three letters, and seems, therefore, to have been drawn up at some house that possessed, or was in process of compiling, a separate collection of these.[40] The absence from the Vespasian manuscript of those letters in Harley which are of English interest is easiest to explain on the assumption that the Vespasian collection was made by someone who had access to the Harley collection, and wished to supplement it. In that case, the inclusion, from some other source, of two letters which are in Harley would be by inadvertence; and the fact that an error in the Harley manuscript has concealed the presence of one of these suggests that the Vespasian compiler used this very manuscript.[40a] The collection as it stands in the Vespasian manuscript need not first have been made by the writer of this; he could have drawn on one made at any time after the Harley manuscript was brought to England. Since we know that this manuscript was at York at a later date, and since York is a place most likely to be interested in the letters of Alcuin, it is a reasonable surmise that it was there that a supplementary collection was made. Whether this was done by the compiler of Vespasian A.xiv, or whether he had access to an existent collection, it seems probable that he was working at York.

Nevertheless, it must not be claimed that Vespasian A.xiv is entirely made up of documents of northern interest. It has several of more southern provenance, for example, Pope Leo III's letter to Coenwulf of Mercia on the abolition of the archbishopric of Lichfield,[41] the decrees of the synod of Chelsea of 816,[42] the canons of Oda, archbishop of Canterbury,[43] a set of letters written to archbishops of Canterbury in the tenth century,[44] and a letter from Lantfrith to the brothers of the Old Minster at Winchester concerning the miracles of St. Swithin.[45] With the exception of the last, this looks like a set of texts obtained from Canterbury, and it may be that the letters of Alcuin addressed to Canterbury have come from the same source. It would, however, have been easy for Wulfstan to obtain such a set of records, for he was in constant contact with his archiepiscopal colleague. He occurs as legatee and executor in the will of Ælfric, archbishop of Canterbury,[46] and a papal letter to this prelate is included in a set of penitential letters which is found in some manuscripts connected with Wulfstan.[47] Wulfstan's interest in the ecclesiastical history of his nation would cause him to cast his net widely. Yet nothing in this collection has any specific relation to Worcester. If there is anything in the suggestion that Harley 208 was available to the compiler of the collection of Alcuin's letters in Vespasian A.xiv, then York is the more likely place of origin of the latter manuscript.

Entries in the "Wulfstan" hand are prominent in Nero A.i, ff. 70–177, which contains Wulfstan homilies, parts of *Polity*, and several law codes drafted by Wulfstan or used by him. Mr. Ker has pointed out that it has no Worcester marks or glosses, and that scribbles made in s. xiii–xiv suggest that at that date it was not in a monastic house.[48] It contains also an alteration in an eleventh-century hand, which may have a bearing on the question of provenance. When, in a chapter of *Polity*, Wulfstan declares: *Nis nanum weofodþegne alifed þæt he wifian mote, ac is ælcum forboden*, this has been erased and replaced with the statement: *Riht is þæt preost him lufie clænlicne wimman to gebeddan.*[49] Such an outspoken utterance in favor of priests' marriage would be less remarkable in York, where we know from the *Northumbrian Priests' Law* that this was tolerated,[50] than in a monastic scriptorium like that at Worcester. Yet it would be unwise to build too much on this. A passage in the *Life* of the later Wulfstan, bishop of Worcester, while showing the saint's stern disapproval of married priests, shows also that they were not rare in his diocese;[51] and there is a marginal note by William of Malmesbury in Oriel MS. 42 which should warn us against assuming that all monastic writers shared the views of reformers like the two Wulfstans, for it says, referring to St. Paul: *Posse presbiterum, ait, potius debere, uxorem habere.*[52] By William's time, however, papal attempts to enforce rules against priests' marriage had called forth much opposition, including several treatises in its defense,[53] so that William's note is not as surprising as is the alteration in Nero A.i.

So far, we have considered only manuscripts written in Wulfstan's lifetime. Another compilation of Latin texts which has some entries in the "Wulfstan" hand, namely Copenhagen Gl. Kgl. S. 1595, has, as far as I know, no indications to help one decide between Worcester or York as its place of origin. To turn to manuscripts with Wulfstan connections, written after his time, we have already seen that some were written at Worcester in the middle and latter part of the eleventh century. His work was also known further afield. Exeter seems to have had a particular interest in it. Two manuscripts with Wulfstan homilies, C.C.C.C. 421 and 419 (Napier's A and B), are from Exeter, and some of the Wulfstan matter in A was written there;[54] Cleopatra B.xiii and Lambeth 489, which Mr. Ker suggests once formed a single manuscript, were probably written at Exeter, and the first contains Wulfstan's homily on the dedication of a church (Napier LIV, Bethurum XVIII) and that on the consecration of a bishop (Napier XXXVII, Bethurum XVII), while the second has a homily (Napier LVII) with several Wulfstan passages, as well as a catena of extracts from Napier V (Bethurum VIII c), XIX (Bethurum XIII), XXIV, XL, and LVII; C.C.C.C. 190, one manuscript of Wulfstan's *Commonplace Book*, is probably to be identified with the item *.i. canon on leden. 7 scriftboc on englisc* in the list of Bishop Leofric's gifts to Exeter.[55] Three added quires are written in an Exeter script, but if this is the book given by Leofric, it is not known where he obtained it. About the same period a section of Tiberius A.iii was written at Christ Church, Canterbury, in the mid-eleventh century, and this includes Napier XIX–XXII (Bethurum XIII), XXIII–XXV, XXVI (Bethurum VII a), XXVII, XXVI, LI–LIII, and the Latin text Napier IV (Bethurum VIII a). The detailed history of the spread of Wulfstan's influence remains to be written, but it is clear that one cannot safely assume that a manuscript in some way connected with him must necessarily come from one of the sees which he held, at any rate when it is later than his time.

Yet it may be worthwhile to examine one such manuscript, of the middle of the eleventh century, namely C.C.C.C. MS. 201, pp. 1–178, which is one of the chief manuscripts of Wulfstan's works.[56] This has been written at two periods about a generation apart. Its first and thirteenth quires are half-filled by a hand of the early eleventh century, and the intervening and following parts by hands of the middle of the century. The earlier hand writes on pages 1–7 a fragment of a translation of the *Regularis Concordia*, with some additions to make it suitable for women's houses as well as men's.[57] The rest of this quire, and most of the next ten, are in a single mid-eleventh-century hand, and contain a miscellany of Wulfstan writings and sources, including the *Northumbrian Priests' Law*. There follows in the same hand the Old English *Apollonius of Tyre*,[58] then a tract on the Kentish royal saints and the resting places of the English saints.[59] A different hand of about the same date then fills the last leaves of quire 11, and the whole of quire 12, with a section of the Old English translation of Genesis, dealing with the story of Joseph. This is the same extract as one which was in the almost entirely burnt manuscript, Otho B.x,[60] and it is interesting to note that there it followed immediately a homily made up of Wulfstan passages (Napier LVIII), and that another part of this manuscript has a set of penitential texts found in Wulfstan's *Commonplace Book*.[61] Hence the only two known copies of this extract from Genesis occur in Wulfstan surroundings. In C.C.C.C. 201 it is incomplete, for two folios have been lost at the end of quire 12. With quire 13, we return to the first hand, that of the early eleventh century. It fills the first half of the quire with an Old English poem based on Bede's *De die iudicii*, and with two other religious poems.[62] The Judgement Day poem was used by the writer of a homily preserved in the Worcester manuscript Hatton 113,[63] a manuscript which includes some Wulfstan homilies, but the author of this homily had a different, and in some respects better, text of the poem than that in C.C.C.C. 201.[64] After these poems, the main mid-eleventh-century hand takes on again, with metrical paraphrases of the Lord's Prayer and the Gloria, that of the latter being the same as the one in Junius 121, where it forms part of the Benedictine office attributed to Wulfstan.[65] Finally, a third mid-eleventh-century scribe has added a Latin text on confession, which had already been entered by the main scribe as part of the Wulfstan miscellany.

It would appear that in the middle of the eleventh century two quires already half-filled with writing of the early part of the century were filled up, with prose following the prose on quire 1, and verse the verse on quire 13, and assembled with other quires at some place where a collection of Wulfstan material was available. It was an important collection, for among other things this is the sole manuscript to preserve Wulfstan's so-called Pastoral Letter with the address: *Wulfstan arcebisceop greteð freondlice þegnas on ðeode gehadode and læwede ealle gemænelice, þa ðe him betæhte sindon for gode to wissianne*;[66] it alone has the version of Ælfric's pastoral letter for him which he revised in his own style;[67] it supplies our only text of the *Northumbrian Priests' Law*; and it contains what appears to be a first draft of Cnut's laws, with a preface explaining that it was drawn up "as soon as King Cnut with the advice of his councilors completely established peace and friendship between the Danes and the English," presumably for the meeting at Oxford in 1018.[68] This suggests that the collection of Wulfstan's writings and sources copied into the manuscript was one not completed until toward the end of his life, after Leofsige had been appointed to Worcester in 1016, with the probable result that Wulfstan could devote more time to his northern see. The *Northumbrian Priests' Law* is a York document, whereas no item is specifically connected with Worcester. York is certainly a possible place for this assembly of material.

Yet it does not necessarily follow that the manuscript was written there. It has no marks or glosses which would place it at Worcester, but the combination of the Wulfstan material with items not apparently connected with him, that is, the parts written in the early-eleventh-century hand, as well as the *Apollonius of Tyre* and the treatises about saints, could have been made at any place which had secured a manuscript of Wulfstan's works and sources. The inclusion of a treatise on Kentish saints is no safe evidence for Kentish origin, for this was a widely known text: the other main manuscript of it was written at Winchester, and the work was used by Florence of Worcester, William of Malmesbury, and Hugo Candidus of Peterborough.[69] The peculiar features in the version of the *Resting-Places of the English Saints* in C.C.C.C. 201 do not point clearly to any place of origin.[70]

It remains to consider whether the language of the manuscript helps to locate it. In the main, all scribes write late West Saxon literary language, but a few features may be noted. Both the main mid-eleventh-century scribe (B) and his contemporary who wrote the extract from Genesis (C) often write *æ* for *e* before nasals, whereas the early-eleventh-century scribe (A) has only two instances, *længra* in the *Regularis Concordia*, *stænt* in a poem. This feature occurs sporadically in most Wulfstan manuscripts, but it should be noted that scribe B uses this spelling also when copying non-Wulfstan texts, and that it is a pronounced feature in the extract from Genesis in the other manuscript of this, Otho B.x.[71] It has been claimed as a sign of southeastern origin, since Middle English evidence shows that it survived in that area; but

Dr. and Miss Sisam have demonstrated its unreliability as a locating feature of Old English manuscripts, concluding that "it was at least tolerated over a wide area of Southern England."[72] It does not seem, however, to have been favored in the Worcester scriptorium: it is very rare in charters from this area or in either the early or the late portions of "Hemming's cartulary." There is, however, no instance of it in the Old English additions to the York Gospels. It is not uncommon in the first two hands of the D version of the Anglo-Saxon Chronicle (Tiberius B.iv), but does not occur after the third scribe took over in the middle of annal 1016; it is, however, by no means certain where this manuscript was written.[73]

A pronounced feature of the B scribe of C.C.C.C. 201 is the writing of *i* for *y* of any origin, including the mutation of *u* even where the surrounding consonants are not favorable to unrounding. There are few instances of this in scribe C, who does, however, write *scridde* (beside *scrydde*) and *þillican*; scribe A preserves *y* as mutation of *u* except in the neighborhood of front consonants, as in *drihten*, *þince*, *filige*. Scribe B's strong preference for *i* does not seem to support a Worcester origin, but in the present state of our knowledge it would be rash to try to locate him closely on this feature.[74] The extreme southwest is included among areas with unrounded *y*, as well as large areas of eastern England. Our manuscript shows hardly a trace of the Kentish and southeastern *e* for *y* as mutation of *u*. The C scribe appears to have been a southerner, for he has a striking peculiarity in spelling *u* for initial *f*, for example, *uæder*, *uerende*, *uoran*, *auandod*, *uætte*,[75] and so on, and this feature seems to have been lacking in the version of the same text in Otho B.x, so is unlikely to have been in their common exemplar.

The C scribe consistently writes a single back vowel, not a diphthong, after *sc*, and this is the usual practice also in the B hand, whether copying Wulfstan texts or others, while the A scribe also affords many examples of a single back vowel in this position. Most Wulfstan manuscripts contain instances of this feature, yet it does not seem to have been normal at Worcester. The Worcester scribe who wrote Hatton 113–14 and Junius 121 prefers diphthongs, but occasionally writes a single vowel, presumably retaining the spelling of his exemplar.

It seems to me that a great deal more study into the practice of scribes of manuscripts which can be located with reasonable certainty is necessary before one can safely assign a manuscript to a definite area on linguistic criteria like the above. It seems reasonable to see scribe C, with his initial *u* for *f*, as a man from the south or from the southwest midlands, but can one assume that he was writing there? There was a lot of movement among Anglo-Saxon ecclesiastics, and it is, for example, very likely that when Aldred, bishop of Worcester, became archbishop of York in 1060, some members of his familia went with him. Bearing in mind such possibilities, and also the varying degree in which individual scribes were faithful to their exemplar, it would be wiser to refrain from an exact location of C.C.C.C. 201, though there can be no doubt that it had access to a collection of Wulfstan material made at one of his sees.

Finally, there are two passages in Wulfstan's style added to the northern recension of the Anglo-Saxon Chronicle.[76] It is unnecessary to enter into the controversial issue of where the D manuscript was written. It certainly kept up a close interest in York almost to the end. There is no doubt that until the northern version split up, soon after 1031, into its two branches D and E (F), it was in the north, and strong evidence speaks for York as its home. Into this common ancestor of D and E (F) a panegyric on King Edgar was inserted in annal 959, and it survives in both branches; it is in Wulfstan's style, and we have other evidence for his great admiration for this king.[77] Another Wulfstan passage was added in annal 975, describing the antimonastic reaction on Edgar's death; this survives only in D, having been replaced in E by a brief statement. The presence of these passages points to Wulfstan's activity in York.

Thus an examination of the manuscripts gives support to the view that Wulfstan was not a constant absentee from his archiepiscopal see. His concern with conditions in the Danelaw is shown by his composition of the so-called *Laws of Edward and Guthrum*, which has a preface claiming that these ecclesiastical injunctions are no recent innovation, but were agreed on by King Alfred and King Guthrum, and confirmed by King Edward.[78] It seems likely that it was Wulfstan's interest in the code IV Edgar, a Danelaw code, which has preserved it for us, since it survives only in manuscripts probably from Worcester. In several places in the codes which Wulfstan drafted, it is said or implied that different rules and penalties are in force in the Danelaw; in some places, as in Cnut's laws, it is stated what these are,[79] but elsewhere we merely get the reservation that a regulation is valid "in the law of the English." Thus in V Ethelred 30 a man who wishes to clear himself of the charge of plotting against the king's life must do so by the king's wergild or threefold ordeal *on Engla lage*,[80] but in the repetition of this clause in VI Ethelred 37 the words ⁊ *on Dena lage be þam þe heora lagu sy* are added. When some clauses from VIII Ethelred are used in one of the Wulfstan passages added into the York Gospels (Napier LXI), the words *on Engla lage* are attached to the statement that failure to pay *Romscot* makes one liable to a fine of 120 shillings to the king, and, similarly, this phrase is inserted in the clause *and cyricsceat gelæste man to Martines mæssan*. This implication of a different practice in the Danelaw suggests that the omission of the clause relating to *cyricsceat* from v Ethelred and from the version of Cnut's laws in C.C.C.C. 201 was not necessarily accidental. Another recognition of variety of local custom in the north is the substitution of Christmas for All Saints' Day as one of the terms for payment of *leohtscot* in the passage in the York Gospels.

Since so clearly Wulfstan was familiar with Danelaw legal practices, it is to be regretted that his surviving works do not tell us more about them. It is possible that some laws issued for the Danelaw have failed to survive. Though we are fortunate in possessing a number of manuscripts which can be connected with him, it must not be supposed that we have his whole library. He used some sources, legal and others, which are not contained in any of the surviving manuscripts used by him;[81] and his *Laws of Edward and Guthrum* and one or two of his homilies are not included in any surviving manuscript directly connected with him.[82]

Wulfstan includes Northumbrian wergilds in the collection of texts on status which Dr. Bethurum claims as his.[83] The *Northumbrian Priests' Law* probably dates from his archiepiscopate. As we saw above, it survives only among Wulfstan material in C.C.C.C. 201; it uses sources with which he was familiar, and also his own writings; and on one matter it agrees with an addition which he made to the pastoral letter written for him by Ælfric.[84] A set of canons in the Brussels MS. Bibl. Royale 8558–63, written in an early-twelfth-century hand, has clauses very close to some in this code, along with others from a Wulfstan work, the so-called *Canons of Edgar*.[85] Liebermann's late dating of at any rate the second part of the *Northumbrian Priests' Law* depends on his date for Cnut's laws, which may have been used, that is, later than Wulfstan's death.[86] If, as I believe, this date is wrong, and Wulfstan drafted Cnut's laws,[87] this argument has no validity. One interesting feature of the *Northumbrian Priests' Law* is its evidence that heathen practices were a reality in the diocese of York, for it graduates the fines for them in accordance with the ranks of society. These practices include the worship of heathen divinities (*idola wurðinge*). This code is later than the accession of Cnut, yet one cannot regard this worship as a new introduction by his followers, for Wulfstan has several references to it in works written before 1016, for example, the Latin version of vi Ethelred refers to *idolorum cultores* and *idolatrie* and his homily Napier x (Bethurum x c) says *Ne ænig man idola weorðie æfre*, while a Latin addition to this text in C and E mentions *idolatria*. Napier LIV (Bethurum XVIII), which enjoins . . . *þæt cristene men þæne egesan æfre ne dreogan þæt hy deofolgyld ahwar weorðian*, cannot be closely dated. It seems unlikely that there was worship of heathen gods in southern England before the conquest by Cnut, even though superstitious practices of heathen origin may have continued; but in Northumbria it is possible that the heathen cults introduced in the tenth century by the Norse invaders from Ireland had not been eradicated. Wulfstan may have been speaking from personal knowledge of conditions in the north when, in his *Sermo ad Anglos*, he speaks of the way *gedwolgoda* and sanctuaries are honored "among heathen people." Similarly, the easy divorce and the disregard of the Church's laws on marriage within the prohibited degrees which prevailed in his northern province may explain his vehement fulminations against adultery and incest in this *Sermo* and elsewhere.

The influence of his sojourns in the north is seen in his terminology. While in general he writes a variety of late West Saxon literary language, he uses in some texts words of Scandinavian origin, especially in speaking of the various social classes. He often uses the Scandinavian *þræl*, besides English *þeowa*, *þeowman*, or *þeowetling*; in the codes which he drafted he uses *bonda* in VI and VII Ethelred, and in Cnut's laws, both in the sense of free householder and of husband, though he also uses the English *ceorl*. What is most significant is his preference for *eorl*, which in Northumbria had begun, under Scandinavian influence, to supplant the native *ealdorman*. Wulfstan uses *ealdorman* only in quotation from older legislation; his own word, in homilies, *Polity*, and laws, is *eorl*. This was not the normal practice south of the Humber in Wulfstan's time, though it became so later; except for the poetic use of *eorl* in the poem on the battle of Maldon to apply to Brihtnoth, the holders of the office are consistently called *ealdormen* until one comes to the appointment of Cnut's Danish followers, Hakon, Eglaf, and so on. In the diocese of Worcester, the holders of the Mercian earldom are called *ealdorman* at this time: we get, for example, Leofwine *ealdorman* in the marriage agreement for Wulfstan's sister,[88] and in an Evesham lease which Wulfstan witnessed about 1023, Leofwine is given this title when the Danes, Hacon and Eglaf, are called *eorl*.[89] Wulfstan's consistent employment of *eorl* does not represent the practice of his southern diocese. In Northumbria from the tenth century *eorl* was often used of this official, especially when the holders of the office were of Danish extraction. Oslac of Northumbria is called *eorl* in IV Edgar, when Æthelwine of East Anglia and Ælfhere of Mercia are given the title *ealdorman*. The northern recension of the Anglo-Saxon Chronicle calls Oslac *eorl*, although it refers to his office as *ealdordom*, and both Thored (c. 975–92) and Uhtred (1006–1016) are always referred to as *eorl*. The intervening holder of the office (992–1006) is, however, referred to as *ealdorman*, perhaps because he was a member of an outstanding Mercian family; otherwise the term *eorl* holds the field in Northumbria, and Wulfstan seems to reflect this usage.

NOTES

1. I am indebted to Dr. Peter Clemoes for reading this article and making many useful suggestions.

The following abbreviated citations are used: Bethurum = Dorothy Bethurum, *The Homilies of Wulfstan* (Oxford, 1957); Ker = N. R. Ker, *Catalogue of Manuscripts containing Anglo-Saxon* (Oxford, 1957); Napier = A. Napier, *Wulfstan. Sammlung der ihm zugeschriebenen Homilien* (Berlin, 1883); *Polity* = *Institutes of Polity, Civil and Ecclesiastical*, best edited by K. Jost (Berne, 1959).

2. This supposition would explain Wulfstan's issuing of leases of Worcester lands in 1017, and his witnessing of documents concerning this diocese after Leofsige's accession. See Dorothy Whitelock, *Sermo Lupi ad Anglos*, 3d ed. (London, 1963), p. 9.

3. See D. Whitelock, "The Dealings of the Kings of England with Northumbria in the Tenth and Eleventh Centuries" in *The Anglo-Saxons. Studies in some Aspects of their History and Culture presented to Bruce Dickins*, ed. P. Clemoes (London, 1959).

4. Anglo-Saxon Chronicle, 1014 D.

5. *Symeonis Monachi Opera Omnia*, ed. T. Arnold, I, p. 83.

6. Anglo-Saxon Chronicle, 1014.

7. *Polity*, ed. Jost, p. 75.

8. *Polity*, ed. Jost, p. 77.

9. See colophon on p. 167 of Durham Cathedral MS. A. IV. 19; printed in A. Hamilton Thompson and U. Lindelöf, *Rituale Ecclesiae Dunelmensis* (Surtees Society, 1927), p. 185.

10. See R. R. Darlington, *The Vita Wulfstani of William of Malmesbury* (London, 1928), pp. xxxvi, 33, 36, 40, 48.

11. See Ker, p. lvi, and Whitelock, *Sermo Lupi ad Anglos*, pp. 29–31.

12. On this see N. R. Ker, "Hemming's Cartulary," in *Studies in Medieval History presented to F. M. Powicke* (Oxford, 1948).

13. It is entered in *Catalogus Librorum Manuscriptorum Bibliothecae Wigorniensis* of Patrick Young, edd. I. Atkins and N. R. Ker (Cambridge, 1944), pp. 48 f. It is No. 4117 in the *Summary Catalogue of Western Manuscripts in the Bodleian Library at Oxford*.

14. D. Bethurum, "Archbishop Wulfstan's Commonplace Book," *PMLA* LVII, 916–29.

15. Ker, p. 94.

16. Ker, p. lvii; *idem*, "The Date of the 'Tremulous' Worcester Hand," *Leeds Studies in English*, VI (1937); S. J. Crawford, "The Worcester Marks and Glosses of the Old English Manuscripts in the Bodleian," *Anglia*, LII (1928).

17. W. de G. Birch, *Cartularium Saxonicum*, Nos. 1278, 1279; A. J. Robertson, *Anglo-Saxon Charters*, No. LIV; trans. D. Whitelock, *English Historical Documents c. 500–1042*, No. 114.

18. For Wulfstan's use of Edgar's laws see Dorothy Whitelock, "Wulfstan and the Laws of Cnut," *EHR*, LXIII (1948). The insertion of the Latin and Old English versions of Ethelred's sixth code into the pontifical Claudius A.iii could also have been for the convenience of carrying it round with him. See p. 215 above.

19. It mentions as responsible for its circulation only the ealdormen in control of Danelaw areas, Oslac of Northumbria, Æthelwine of East Anglia, and Ælfhere of Mercia, whose territory included that of the Five Boroughs. Since one clause says that the king and his councilors have decided what the penalty for an offense is to be "among the English," without specifying the penalty, one suspects that a companion ordinance relating to the English areas once existed.

20. Ker, p. 468; J. P. Gilson, *Description of the Saxon Manuscript of the Four Gospels in the Library of York Minster* (York, 1925).

21. W. H. Stevenson, "Yorkshire Surveys and other Eleventh-Century Documents in the York Gospels," *EHR*, XXVII (1912); Robertson, No. LXXXIV.

22. F. Liebermann, *Die Gesetze der*

Angelsachsen, I, pp. 273–75; trans. D. Whitelock, *English Historical Documents c. 500–1042*, No. 48.

23. Stevenson; Robertson, p. 249.
24. Stevenson; W. Farrer, *Early Yorkshire Charters*, I, pp. 27 f.; E. Björkman, "Die 'Festermen' des Ælfric: eine Namenliste aus York," *Festschrift für L. Morsbach* (Halle, 1913), pp. 1–19.
25. Ker, pp. 177 f.
26. See H. A. Wilson, *The Benedictional of Archbishop Robert* (Henry Bradshaw Society, 24; London, 1903), p. xviii. The Rev. H. M. J. Banting has kindly informed me that the text in Claudius A.iii has many agreements with Sidney Sussex MS. 100, an early-eleventh-century pontifical from Durham, and that both have connections with the so-called *Pontifical of Archbishop Ecgberht* (Surtees Society Publications, 27).
27. Published by E. V. K. Dobbie, *The Anglo-Saxon Minor Poems* (New York, 1942), p. 97.
28. For other examples, see F. Wormald, "The Sherborne 'Chartulary,'" in *F. Saxl, 1890–1948* (London, 1957), p. 106 and n. 2.
29. Dobbie, p. xc, says that the Horsley charter is in the same manuscript as the Thureth poem, but in fact the charter is on one of a group of leaves which Mr. Ker has shown were once part of a different manuscript, the gospel-book, Tiberius A.ii. See N. R. Ker, "Membra Disiecta," *British Museum Quarterly*, XII (1938), 130 f. The Horsley charter is No. LXXXVIII in Robertson, where it is suggested that the donor is a thegn who attests Cnut's charters. Professor Dobbie would identify both the donor of Horsley and the Thureth of the poem with Earl Thored of Northumbria; Mr. Ker also suggests identifying Thureth with this earl.
30. According to the Anglo-Saxon Chronicle, it came to nothing because Ealdorman Ælfric warned the enemy and then deserted.
31. Both the verses and the letter are conveniently printed in Bethurum, pp. 376–78.
32. Birch, No. 184; trans. Whitelock, *English Historical Documents*, No. 184.
33. See W. Levison, *England and the Continent in the Eighth Century* (Oxford, 1946), pp. 297–302.
34. E. Dümmler, *Monumenta Germaniae Historica: Epistolae*, IV, No. 46.
35. Certainly fourteen, perhaps fifteen, were sent to Northumbria, and five to Canterbury. In addition, one (No. 292) is to an English archbishop, and another (No. 70) to an Abbot Wulfheard, who may possibly be a later bishop of Hereford. No. 45 has no address, but the bearer was Eanbald, later to be archbishop of York. Nos. 235 and 274 have no address and cannot be located. One should note that fourteen letters in this collection occur only here and in Tiberius A.xv, which had access to the material assembled in Vespasian A.xiv (apart from a few extracts in William of Malmesbury, who used the collection in Tiberius A.xv, and for extracts in manuscripts of Wulfstan's Commonplace Book, C.C.C.C. 190 and 265). The presence of so many letters not in any Continental collection suggests that the Vespasian collection was made in England. Of the fourteen letters in question, seven were to Northumbria, three to Canterbury, one to an English archbishop, one to Abbot Wulfheard, and two to unnamed recipients.
36. Dümmler, No. 10. The letter written abroad to a Continental recipient is No. 96, to Paulinus of Aquileia.
37. Dümmler, No. 66.
38. Ker, p. 304. A scribble, reminiscent, as Mr. Ker points out, of *Beowulf*, l. 869, was added in the margin about this time: *hwæt ic eall feala ealde sæge*.
39. This is Dümmler, No. 128, a letter from Alcuin to Æthelheard, archbishop of Canterbury, reproving him for leaving his see, and referring to the archbishopric of Lichfield, a matter in which the Vespasian manuscript shows interest elsewhere. The only other letter to occur in both collections is Dümmler, No. 209, addressed to Calvinus, priest and monk of St. Stephen's, on the use of external things and on the difficulties of Eanbald II, archbishop of York. An error in Dümmler's list

(p. 6), by which the 57th item in Harley is given as No. 235 instead of No. 236, makes it appear as if the two collections shared a third item.

40. A separate collection of letters to or from Charles was available to the Troyes MS. 1165, of the ninth century, and the Vatican MS. Reg. Christinae 272, of the tenth century; part of it was used by the ninth-century Lambeth MS. 218. The three letters to Charles which are in Harley are No. 41, which has lost its address, and two of the latest letters, No. 249, written 801–802, which is preserved in Harley alone, and No. 308, of 801–804.

40a. This same error is, however, also in the tenth-century Vatican manuscript mentioned in the previous note, whose last fifteen letters are all in the Harley manuscript, and in the same order.

41. Birch, No. 288; A. W. Haddan and W. Stubbs, *Councils and Ecclesiastical Documents*, III (Oxford, 1878), pp. 523–25; trans. Whitelock, *English Historical Documents*, No. 205.

42. Haddan and Stubbs, III, pp. 579–84.

43. D. Wilkins, *Concilia Magnae Britanniae et Hiberniae*, I (London, 1737), pp. 212–14.

44. W. Stubbs, *Memorials of St. Dunstan* (London, 1874), pp. 380 f., 383–89.

45. W. Stubbs, p. 369.

46. Whitelock, *Anglo-Saxon Wills*, No. XVIII.

47. See most recently K. Jost, *Wulfstanstudien* (Berne, 1950), pp. 16–21, and Bethurum, pp. 374–76.

48. Ker, pp. 211–15.

49. *Polity*, ed. Jost, p. 112.

50. This code in clause 35 merely stipulates: "If a priest leaves a woman (*cwene*) and takes another, let him be anathema." There is no mention of any penalty for a priest who remains faithful to one "woman."

51. Darlington, p. 53 f.

52. See Hugh Farmer, "William of Malmesbury," *Journal of Ecclesiastical History*, XIII (1960), 49. I am indebted to Dom Hugh for sending me the wording of the marginal note.

53. See C. N. L. Brooke, "Gregorian Reform in Action: Clerical Marriage in England 1050–1200," *Cambridge Historical Journal*, XII (1956), 1–21.

54. Dr. P. Clemoes informs me that items from Ælfric's first series of *Catholic Homilies* in the main hand in C.C.C.C. 421, pp. 227–354, are textually very close to the corresponding items in Trinity College, Cambridge, MS. B. 15. 34, a manuscript probably written at Christ Church, Canterbury, since Ker (p. 132) thinks it written by the scribe of Harley 2892 (ed. R. M. Woolley, *The Canterbury Benedictional* [Henry Bradshaw Soc., 1917], and F. Wormald, *English Drawings of the Tenth and Eleventh Centuries* (London, 1952), p. 63, says that the drawing it contains resembles that in the Christ Church manuscripts Royal MS. I E. VII and Arundel MS. 155. There is a good chance, therefore, that C.C.C.C. 419 and 421 were written at Canterbury, except pp. 3–96 and 209–24 in C.C.C.C. 421, which were added at Exeter.

55. This is the reading in the version in the Exeter Book, f. 1^v, and is preferable to that in the Bodleian MS., Auct. D. 2. 16, which inserts. *i.* before *scriftboc*.

56. It is called C by Napier, Bethurum, etc., D by Liebermann, Fehr, Jost, etc. Since the time of Wanley, it has often been assigned to Worcester, but solely on the ground of containing Wulfstan's works. L. Whitbread, "MS. C.C.C.C. 201: A Note on its Character and Provenance," *Philological Quarterly*, XXXVIII (1959), 106–12, would assign the collection of Wulfstan material to Worcester, but the manuscript to Canterbury. My account of the manuscript depends largely on that in Ker, pp. 82–90.

57. Printed by J. Zupitza in *Archiv für das Studium der neueren Sprachen und Literaturen*, LXXXIV (1890), 1–24.

58. Ed. J. Raith, *Die alt- und mittelenglischen Apollonius-Bruchstücke, mit dem Text der Historia Apollonii nach der englischen Handschriftengruppe* (Munich, 1956); P. Goolden, *The Old English Apollonius of Tyre* (Oxford, 1958).

59. Ed. F. Liebermann, *Die Heiligen Englands* (Hannover, 1889).
60. See S. J. Crawford, *The Heptateuch* (EETS, 1922), pp. 5 f., 10, 427; J. Raith, "Ælfric's Share in the Old English Pentateuch," *Review of English Studies*, N. S. III (1952), 305–14. Though the extract in C.C.C.C. 201 has lost its last portion, the original identity of this extract with that in the Otho manuscript is shown by many agreements in wording, which differ from that of the complete version of the translation of Genesis.
61. It is possible, however, that this section, which is now completely destroyed, was not an original part of the manuscript.
62. All three poems are edited by Dobbie, *The Anglo-Saxon Minor Poems*, pp. 58–70.
63. Napier XXIX. See Dobbie, p. lxxii.
64. The fact that the version of the poem in C.C.C.C. 201 is an inferior text weakens Whitbread's argument for a Canterbury origin of this manuscript on the grounds that St. Augustine's Abbey had several copies of Bede's Latin poem and hence the Old English poem may have been produced there.
65. Ed. Dobbie, pp. 70–77. See also J. M. Ure, *The Benedictine Office* (Edinburgh, 1957).
66. Napier XIX–XXII, Bethurum XIII.
67. B. Fehr, *Die Hirtenbriefe Ælfrics* (Hamburg, 1914), pp. 68–140.
68. See D. Whitelock, "Wulfstan and the Laws of Cnut," *EHR*, LXIII (1948), 433–44.
69. See B. Thorpe, *Florentii Wigorniensis Monachi Chronicon ex Chronicis*, I (London, 1848), p. 259; N. E. S. A. Hamilton, *Willelmi Malmesbiriensis Monachi de Gestis Pontificum Anglorum Libri Quinque* (London, 1870), pp. 318 f.; W. T. Mellows, *The Chronicle of Hugo Candidus* (Oxford, 1949), pp. 57 f.; W. D. Macray, *Chronicon Abbatiae Rameseiensis* (London, 1886), p. 55. The bodies of the martyred princes Ethelred and Ethelbert were claimed by Ramsey abbey to have been translated to this house in 974; this may have caused the text to spread through the Fenland abbeys, and it would be likely also to arouse interest in York and in Worcester, since Oswald, who held both sees, was a founder of Ramsey.
70. The version in C.C.C.C. 201 knows that Cuthbert lies at Durham, not at *Ubbanford* (Norham); it adds Osthryth to the saints buried at Bardney, Lincolnshire. She is not regarded as a saint in any other record, but as she was responsible for bringing St. Oswald's remains to Bardney, whence they were later translated to Gloucester, it is possible that her memory was revered in Gloucester. Our text supplies a longer list of saints in the Old Minster, Winchester, and adds Queen Balthild at Romsey, Cwenburg at Wimborne, and Samson at Milton Abbas. It omits Amesbury, probably by accident.
71. No other part of Otho B.x was written by this scribe. Dr. Clemoes informs me that three folios of the *Catholic Homilies* survive in this manuscript, in another hand, and have two instances with *æ* out of six possible occasions.
72. C. Sisam and K. Sisam, *The Salisbury Psalter* (EETS 1959), pp. 13 f.
73. On the possibility that it comes from York, rather than the diocese of Worcester, see D. Whitelock, *The Peterborough Chronicle* (Early English Manuscripts in Facsimile, IV, Copenhagen, 1954), pp. 29–31; *idem*, with D. C. Douglas and S. I. Tucker, *The Anglo-Saxon Chronicle: A Revised Translation* (London, 1961), pp. xiv–xvi.
74. This question has most recently been considered by P. Gradon, "Studies in Late West-Saxon Labialization and Delabialization," *English and Medieval Studies presented to J. R. R. Tolkien* (London, 1962), pp. 63–76. Her study confirms that Devon was an area of unrounding. She concludes with a plea for more detailed investigation.
75. Middle English evidence shows that this voicing of initial *f* took place in the south and in the southwest midlands. Apart from the C scribe of C.C.C.C. 201, it is only slightly evidenced in Old English manuscripts. Even as late as the

post-Conquest entries in the Leofric Missal and on leaves of a gospel now bound up with the Exeter Book initial *f* is normally retained, though the latter entries have two examples of *u*, *ureode* and *Quikeuot*.

76. This was first pointed out by K. Jost, "Wulfstan und die angelsächsische Chronik," *Anglia*, XLVII (1923), 105 ff.

77. See D. Whitelock, in *EHR*, LXIII (1948), 442 f.

78. *Idem*, "Wulfstan and the so-called Laws of Edward and Guthrum," *EHR*, LVI (1941), 1–21.

79. E.g., II Cnut, 15, 15.1a, 15.3, 45.3, 46, 48, 71.3 ff.

80. In the version of V Ethelred in C.C.C.C. 201, the clause 7 *gif he ladigan wille, do þæt be þæs cynges wyrgylde oððe mid þryfealdan ordale on Engla lage* is replaced by *buton he hine ladige be þam deopestan, þe witan gerædan*.

81. Among legal texts, he knew the laws of Kent, which survive only in the *Textus Roffensis*, and probably II Ethelred, which is only in the twelfth-century manuscript C.C.C.C. 383. He knew the report of the legates of 786 (Dümmler, No. 3), though no text of this has come down in Anglo-Saxon manuscripts, and a letter of Alcuin which is in none of the collections of his correspondence (see Levison, pp. 245 f.). The range of his reading shows that he had the use of an ample library. See Bethurum, p. 61.

82. *The Laws of Edward and Guthrum* are preserved only in the twelfth-century collections, C.C.C.C. 383 and the *Textus Roffensis*. Among his authentic homilies Bethurum VIII b is only in C.C.C.C. 302, which does not otherwise appear to be connected with Wulfstan, and Napier LIV (Bethurum XVIII) is complete only in Cleopatra B.xiii, an Exeter manuscript.

83. D. Bethurum, "Six Anonymous Old English Codes," *JEGP*, XLIX (1950), 449–63.

84. See Whitelock, *English Historical Documents*, pp. 434 f.

85. Ker, pp. 8–10.

86. Liebermann, *Die Gesetze der Angelsachsen*, III, pp. 220–22. There are agreements with Cnut's laws, but it is not easy to tell which was the borrower.

87. See article cited in n. 68 above.

88. Robertson, No. LXXVI.

89. Robertson, No. LXXXI.

XVI

The Numismatic Interest of an Old English Version of the Legend of the Seven Sleepers

The Legend of the Seven Sleepers of Ephesus, which is first recorded early in the sixth century, became very popular. It survives in many versions, in Greek, Latin, Syriac, Arabic, and other Oriental languages, and it was translated into many of the modern European languages. It tells how seven youths hid in a cave from the persecution of the Emperor Decius, and, after a miraculous sleep, woke up in the reign of Theodosius, which it declares to be 372 years later. On awaking, they sent one of their number to buy food in Ephesus, where he was suspected of having found ancient treasure because he offered coins of the reign of Decius. He was therefore dragged before the bishop and the magistrate, and threatened with torture to make him reveal his secret, but eventually the truth was discovered, and he led the way back to the cave. The Seven Sleepers lived long enough to be visited by the Emperor in person, and then died. Thus the story provides an early instance of Treasure Trove. It makes it clear that to be in secret possession of ancient treasure is an offence, though it is not specified whether the treasure ought to belong, in whole or in part, to the State or to the owner of the land where it was discovered. All that is shown for certain is that the finder was not allowed quietly to pocket it, but one may well wonder if the possession of ancient coin would have created such a commotion if it was only the rights of a private individual – the owner of the land where it was found – which were involved.

The Old English version of this story is contained in the principal manuscript of Ælfric's *Lives of Saints*, British Museum Cotton MS. Julius E. vii, which belongs to the beginning of the eleventh century.[1] It was also in British Museum Cotton MS. Otho B. x, but this was almost entirely burnt in the fire of 1731, and only fragments remain, which allow it to be assigned to the first half of the eleventh century.[2] The style shows that this piece is not the work of Ælfric. Dr P. Clemoes, who is engaged on a study of it, has kindly informed me that he would assign its composition to the last quarter of the tenth century.[3]

Since the account of the accusation brought against the possessor of ancient coins is taken over from the Latin source, it cannot be regarded as safe evidence for the attitude in Anglo-Saxon England to the finding of buried treasure. Yet one would have expected the translator to have offered some comment or words of explanation to his readers if this attitude had not seemed to him perfectly natural. He is not slavishly wedded to his original. He expands it considerably, making the whole tale much more vivid and the dialogue more natural. He makes several additions from contemporary English conditions. Thus, when describing the persecution of the Christians, he adds that anyone who sheltered them would be condemned to death.[4] This is the serious crime of *fliemanfeorm* in Anglo-Saxon law, the sheltering of fugitives and the king's enemies, one of the pleas of the Crown. Other additions are that the Emperor announced his orders by beadles, and that these expected payment for tracking down the delinquents, and that a reward was offered to informers.[5] When he takes from his source the statement that the heads of the executed Christians were set on stakes outside the walls, he adds 'like others [who were] thieves'.[6] The accused kinsmen merely reply to the Emperor in the Latin version; in the English they swear great oaths.[7] When the Latin says that Dalius's shepherds built huts on the Caelian Hill, the translator explains 'that they might lie there close to their master's cattle, and shield themselves against cold and heat'.[8] The incident of the examining of the money is greatly expanded. For example, the short sentence *tulerunt argenteos et mirabantur eos* becomes:

> they took his pennies and examined them before the people and wondered greatly, for they had never before seen with their eyes such money, which was struck in old days in the Emperor Decius's time, and his image [*anlicnys*] was engraved thereon, and his name written there all around.[9]

If the translator had felt that the incident of Treasure Trove required any elucidation he would not have been debarred from giving it by fidelity to his source. So we may assume from his lack of comment that in Anglo-Saxon England, as in Ephesus in the story, the concealment of the discovery of treasure was a crime. This does not in itself prove that Treasure Trove belonged already to the Crown. The first evidence that it did comes from the reign of Henry I.[10] Yet there is nothing to suggest that this is an innovation then, and it is probable that Anglo-Saxon law, like that of some other Germanic nations, regarded ancient treasure as belonging to the king.[11]

Among the passages in which the translator appears to go beyond his source is one more closely concerned with numismatics. It is the description of the coins taken by Malchus, the emissary, to the town after the saints have awakened. It is as follows:

nam þa mid him sumne dǽl feos. swá micel swá hit mihte béon. ðeah swilce hit wære sum twá 7 sixtig penega. 7 wæs þæs feos ofergewrit ðæs ylcan mynet-sleges þe man þæt feoh onslóh sona þæs forman geares þa Decius feng to ríce; Feower siðon man awende mynet-isena on his dagum. þe ðás halgan ðagyt wunodon onmang oþrum mannum. 7 on þam frum-mynet-slæge wæron twá 7 sixtig penega gewihte seolfres on ánum penege. 7 on þæm æftran em sixtig. 7 on þæm þryddan feower 7 feowertig. 7 on þam feorþan git læsse swa hí hit þær heoldon; Ða wæs þæt feoh þæt Malchus hæfde þæs forman mynet-slæges on Decies naman; Ðonne betweonan Decies frum-mynet-slæges dagum þa þas halgan into þam scræfe eodon. 7 betweonan Theodosius timan þe ða wæs casere[12] þa Malchus þæt feoh bær to porte. be ealdum[13] getele wæron þa agane ðreo hund geara. 7 twá 7 hundseofontig wintra of ðam dæge þe ða halgan slepon. to ðam dæge þe hí eft awócon;[14]

TRANSLATION

He then took with him a certain sum of money, as much as was available – as if it were some sixty-two pence, however. And the legend on that money was of that same minting with which the money had been struck immediately in the first year when Decius succeeded to the throne. Four times were the dies changed in his days, when those saints still lived among men; and in the first minting were sixty-two pennyweights of silver in one penny, and in the second exactly sixty, and in the third forty-four, and in the fourth even less, as they reckoned it there. Now the money which Malchus had was of the first minting in Decius's name. Then, between the days of Decius's first minting, when these saints went into the cave, and the time of Theodosius, who was emperor when Malchus took the money to the town, there had passed by the old reckoning[15] three hundred and seventy-two years from the day when the saints slept to the day when they woke up again.

One naturally wishes to compare this passage with its source, if only to find out what gave rise to the nonsensical statement that there were sixty-two penny-weights in a single penny. The Old English text is derived from that version of the story which Huber, the scholar who has studied this legend in great detail, calls Latin group I.[16] His text of this passage, taken from a ninth-century Munich manuscript, Cod. lat. 14540, is as follows:

Surrexit Malchus mane, ut habuit consuetudinem, et accepit argenteos LXII; et quidam quidem fuerant numero LX, quidam vero XLIV. Erat autem superscriptio argentorum primi anni imperii Decii. – Hi enim fuerunt in diebus Decii et sanctorum istorum martyrum. In tempore, quo manifestati sunt, invenerunt, quoniam habuerunt CCCLXXII annos a die, ex qua requieverunt usque in diem, qua expergefacti sunt sancti martyres.[17]

Among the manuscripts from which Huber prints variants is one, British Museum Harley MS. 3037, of the thirteenth century, which is closer than the others to the Latin text which must have lain before the Old English translator, and I am indebted to Dr Clemoes for calling my attention to the existence of an earlier manuscript, unknown to Huber, of this version of the Latin text. This is the British Museum Egerton MS. 2797, of the eleventh century. Its version of the passage with which we are concerned reads:

> Et surrexit malchus mane ut habuit consuetudinem. et accepit argenteos sexaginta duos et quidam quidæm [*sic*] fuerunt numero sexaginta. quidam
> or
> uero quadraginta IIII; Erat autem superscriptio argenteorum primi anni imperii decii. Quator enim fuerunt in diebus decii anni et sanctorum istorum martirum in tempore quo manifestati sunt. Inuenerunt quoniam habuerunt ccclxxii annos a die ex qua requieuerunt usque in diem quo [*sic*] expergefacti sunt sancti martires.;

The faulty punctuation of the latter part of this suggests that the scribe did not understand what he was copying.[18] The interest for us is that here *Quatuor* occurs at the very point where the English translator speaks of four issues. It would be unlikely that this was mere coincidence, and, as it happens, many other readings prove that the translator used a Latin text of the group represented by the Egerton and Harley manuscripts. When other manuscripts read *misit deus* (or *dominus*)[19] *in corde Dalii domini montis*, Egerton and Harley have the corrupt reading *misit dominus* (*deus* Harley) *talem dominum montis*,[20] which accounts for the English rendering: 'God Almighty provided a very prudent man, who had possession of all the plot on the Caelian Hill'[21]. Again, when the various manuscripts differ regarding an embassy sent to Theodosius, some saying that the bishop sent the proconsul to him, others that the bishop and proconsul sent to him, only these two manuscripts supply the text corresponding to the English, namely *Marinus vero episcopus misit ad Theodosium imperatorem scribens ei epistolam* . . . which is rendered: 'And the Bishop Marinus immediately after sent a letter to the good Emperor Theodosius.'[22] We are therefore justified in assuming that the Latin version used by the translator was similar to that in the Egerton and Harley manuscripts. But, as Dr Clemoes has pointed out to me, it avoided some of their errors,[23] and it seems likely that, though it had the word *Quatuor*, it had not got the word *anni* in the sentence we are examining. *Quatuor* is most easily explained as a misreading of *hi*, written without division between the letters and so misread as 'Iu',[24] while *anni* represents somebody's attempt to supply something to go with the *Quatuor.*[25] If, then, our translator found himself faced with a statement 'For there were four in the days of Decius', he would ask himself the question 'Four what?' He has taken the answer to be 'Four issues.'[26]

Thus, though one might have preferred to take the alteration of the two issues of the original into four as having a bearing on Anglo-Saxon numismatic history, it turns out on examination to be only an attempt to make sense of a corrupt text. Yet it may have been familiarity with an English coinage which changed at frequent regular intervals that led to this interpretation, and the translator may have welcomed an opportunity to depict a persecuting Emperor as issuing a steadily deteriorating coinage. His source supplied him with values for only two issues. He required two more. The sixty and forty-four in the Egerton and Harley texts occur in most manuscripts of the Latin group I, and in all of Greek group II. A Brussels manuscript of the Latin group has sixty-two instead of sixty, but this is probably an accidental replacement of the number sixty by the figure given just previously for the number of coins Malchus had with him.[27] Huber suggests that the sixty-two given in the Old English version, in addition to the normal sixty and forty-four, is a sign that the translator was collating two different texts, and took sixty-two from one like this Brussels manuscript. But this is improbable; he would hardly have gone to so much trouble, and he is more likely to have chosen sixty-two because that figure was in his text, though there with reference to the number of coins, and not to their value. He did not venture to invent a figure for the fourth issue, merely saying vaguely 'even less'.

If the extant manuscripts of the Old English version represent accurately what the translator wrote, his attempt to remedy the silence of his source regarding the units in which they were reckoning cannot be regarded as a success. I suppose that his words 'as if it were some sixty-two pence' express his knowledge that *argenteos* were not really pennies, though he wished to use a term familiar to his readers. But it is a pity that he chose pennyweight for the unexpressed unit of weight, instead of grains, which would not have given such nonsense. Or, if he had said 'sixty-two pennyweights in a single coin' (as Skeat translates it), using the general term *mynet*, instead of the specific *pening*,[28] they would have been enormous coins, but he would not have written such a contradiction in terms. Perhaps he did not pause to consider the size of the coins he is describing; the native poetry describes the works of the men of antiquity as 'the works of giants', but the rest of his version is so closely related to contemporary Anglo-Saxon conditions that gigantic pennies strike an odd and jarring note. Is it possible that his clause, 'as they reckoned it there', which has no counterpart in the Latin, implies an awareness that what he has written does not make good sense as applied to English currency?

The pennyweight, which is sometimes called simply 'penny', was presumably a fixed weight by this time, not varying with the actual weight of different issues of pennies. A small picture of its use as a weight is given in an Anglo-Saxon homily, attributed, though wrongly, to Archbishop Wulfstan. There we read:

> Then let each man consider how much the soul will be tormented on Doomsday when the sins and the soul will be placed on the scales and weighed as gold is weighed against pennies; and if the pennies weigh more than the gold, it soon turns out badly for the man. So will it be with the soul and the sin; if the sin weighs more than the soul, they will both go to destruction.[29]

Though the passage on the four issues in the Seven Sleepers' legend proves on examination to have less interest for numismatics than at first sight it promised, it nevertheless adds to our knowledge of contemporary terminology. The word *mynet-slege*, 'minting, issue', literally 'coin-striking', is unique, as is its compound, *frum-mynet-slege*, 'first issue'. Similarly, we are given the word used for a die, *mynet-isen*, 'coin-iron'. The word for a legend, *ofergewrit*, and that later used in the text for a portrait, *anlicnys*, are, however, recorded elsewhere. They both occur, for example, to translate *superscriptio* and *imago* in Matthew xxii. 20 in relation to the tribute-money to Caesar.

REFERENCES

1. W. W. SKEAT (ed.) *Aelfric's Lives of Saints* I pp. 488–541
2. See N. R. KER *Catalogue of Manuscripts containing Anglo-Saxon* pp. 224–9
3. Dr Clemoes has already published his views on the inclusion of this piece in Ælfric's *Lives of Saints*, and shown that there are reasons to believe that this was not done by Ælfric himself, but that it became associated with this set of *Lives* for the first time in Julius E. vii. See 'The Chronology of Ælfric's Works', P. CLEMOES (ed.) *The Anglo-Saxons. Studies in some Aspects of their History and Culture presented to Bruce Dickins* p. 219 n. 2
4. SKEAT op. cit. lines 49–51
5. Ibid. lines 47, 51–3
6. Ibid. lines 75f.
7. Ibid. line 299
8. Ibid. lines 418–20
9. Ibid. lines 656–60

10. See SIR GEORGE HILL *Treasure Trove in Law and Practice* Oxford 1936 pp. 187f., 225 and n. 6; but see above p. 15
11. Ibid. pp. 31, 52–73, 173–6; F. LIEBERMANN, *Die Gesetze der Angelsachsen* II *Glossar* s.v. *Schatzfund*
12. Omitted in the Otho text, interlined in Julius
13. Otho reads *be getealdan*
14. SKEAT op. cit. lines 473–88
15. Or, in the Otho text, 'by estimated reckoning'
16. MICHAEL HUBER, O.S.B. *Die Wanderlegende von den Siebenschläfern* Leipzig 1910
17. Idem, *Beitrag zur Visionsliteratur und Siebenschläferlegende* I Teil *Lateinische Texte* (Programm des. humanist. Gymn. Metten, 1902/1903) p. 61
18. As the Harley text agrees in having no stop after *istorum martirum*, and has an inverted semicolon before *Inuenerunt*, this corruption must belong to their common source
19. This reading is in the Munich manuscript
20. Egerton adds *nomine dailum*, but since neither the Harley nor the Old English versions give the name, this is unlikely to have been in their common source
21. SKEAT op. cit. lines 414–16
22. Ibid. lines 791–2
23. e.g. *geþwærlice* (line 210) is translating an *omnes* omitted in Egerton and Harley, and *he swiðe micelne truwan hæfde* (line 628) renders *fidens*, where Egerton and Harley have *uidens* (corrected later in Egerton to *conuidens*)
24. Father Paul Grosjean has suggested to me that the error could have arisen from a text which wrote XL *quatuor*, for XLIIII, but it comes too far from this figure for this to be probable
25. Dr Clemoes suggests that the peculiar position of *anni* in the sentence may point to its being originally a gloss, at the end of a line
26. It is possible that his Latin text had tried to supply the apparent gap with some word for issues; but in any case it is clear that the translator greatly expanded the source at this point
27. It is improbable that this single manuscript should have retained sixty-two from some older version, though Syrian manuscripts and some of Greek group I give the figures as sixty-two and forty-four
28. It is tempting to suggest that *penege* has replaced *mynete* by scribal error, owing to the preceding *penega*, but the reading of the Otho fragment supports that of the Julius text
29. A. NAPIER *Wulfstan: Sammlung der ihm zugeschriebenen Homilien* pp. 239f.

XVII

SCANDINAVIAN PERSONAL NAMES IN THE LIBER VITAE OF THORNEY ABBEY.[1]

IN 1920, at the sale of Lord Mostyn's library, the British Museum acquired a book of Vulgate Gospels that once belonged to Thorney Abbey, Cambridgeshire. On several folios at or near the beginning the monks of the abbey had kept a record of the men and women in confraternity with them, similar to that in the *Liber Vitae Ecclesiae Dunelmensis*[2] or in the *Liber Vitae* of Hyde Abbey.[3] The Thorney MS, now Additional MS 40,000, is described in the British Museum *Catalogue of Additional MSS* 1916-1920,[4] and by Miss E. Jørgensen in *Nordisk Tidskrift för Bok- och Biblioteksväsen* xx,[5] where some of the Scandinavian and Old English names from fol. 10r are given, but with several misreadings due to unfamiliarity with this type of hand. With this small exception, none of these lists of names are accessible to scholars, and they would, I think, be worth publishing in extenso, not only for the sake of the student of personal names, but also

[1] This article owes much to Dr. O. von Feilitzen's *Pre-Conquest Personal Names of Domesday Book* and he has kindly given consideration to some of the problematic names in this text. I am also indebted to Professor B. Dickins for general criticism and many valuable suggestions and references, and to Professor F. M. Stenton for supplying me with parallels from his own collection of Scandinavian names in English sources.

The following abbreviations are used: KCD = J. M. Kemble, *Codex Diplomaticus Aevi Saxonici*; DCh = *Documents Illustrative of the Social and Economic History of the Danelaw*, ed. F. M. Stenton (British Academy Records of the Social and Economic History of England and Wales 5); DB = Domesday Book.

[2] Ed. J. Stevenson, Surtees Society 13, and, in facsimile, *ibid.* 136. It is quoted as LVD.

[3] Ed. W. de G. Birch, *Liber Vitae: Register and Martyrology of the New Minster and Hyde Abbey, Winchester* (Hampshire Record Society).

[4] Pp. 276ff.

Pp. 186-8. I owe this reference to Dr. von Feilitzen.

because of their interest for the genealogist and the Anglo-Norman historian. Here, however, I propose to discuss only those names that are of certain, or probable, Scandinavian origin.

The BM Catalogue considers that the main portion of this MS, the gospels themselves, was written on the Continent in the tenth century, and that the marginal lectionary indications, which are in English, were added in the tenth or eleventh century. The lists of names occupy ten folios, 1v, 2r and 2v, 3r and 3v, 4r, 9v, 10r and 10v, and 12r. In addition, three names occur on fol. 11r, which is otherwise occupied by a list of abbots in a fifteenth-century hand, ending with John Ramsey, who was abbot from 1450 to 1457. Another addition to this gospel book is a late eleventh-century list of the relics belonging to Thorney, with a twelfth-century addition at the end, on fol. 11v. Though not without interest in itself, it does not concern the present paper.

The order of foliation of the *Liber Vitae* lists is not their chronological order. This can be ascertained by the identification of some of the persons mentioned, and I have checked the information thus obtained with the palaeographical evidence supplied by Dr. C. E. Wright of the British Museum. The oldest entry is the statement in Old English on fol. 4r that 'Ælfric and Wulfwine, the goldsmiths of Eadgifu, gave in return for confraternity two ores of weighed gold, which is wired on to the outside of this book.' The BM Catalogue suggests that this Eadgifu is the mysterious *Eddeva pulchra* of Domesday Book, but Dr. Wright thinks that the hand belongs to the first, rather than the second, half of the eleventh century. Eadgifu is a common name (there are seven instances in this text), so that any attempt at identification could only be very tentative. Nothing was added to this folio for a long time, the names that follow this statement being in a twelfth-century hand.

The lists proper begin on fol. 10r, a page ruled in five regular columns, of which the first is headed: *Hæc sunt nomina fratrum istius loci.* Except for some later additions to the second column and in the bottom margin this page is written in two hands of about 1100, the first hand writing column 1 and the beginning of column 2, the second the last three columns. This second hand also wrote the first column of fol. 10v, which appears to be the folio next filled. Though the hands are as late as about 1100, some of the matter on fol. 10r belongs to the time of Cnut and it is clear that the scribe has had earlier lists in front of him. This is the most interesting folio for our purpose and I shall return to it later. After 10v, three names were entered on 11r, but this was then left. Fol. 9v is roughly contemporary with 10v and then comes fol. 3r, followed by 3v, both of the first half of the twelfth century. In 3r the arrangement in columns has become very irregular, by 3v it is given up altogether. The few names on 12r are probably contemporary with 3v. By fol. 2r we have reached the third quarter of the twelfth century, and fol. 2v follows immediately. Finally, fol. 1v is half filled with names of the very late twelfth or early thirteenth century. Such is the chronological order of the folios in outline, but on most of them, in addition to the original matter, itself often in a multiplicity of hands, additions have been made in the margins, between the lines, or in any available space. Nothing but a facsimile could hope to give anything like a fair representation of this text.

In all, the number of entries in these lists is 2133, not counting surnames, and the number of different names about 660.[1] Ignoring names that can be of more than one origin, and those whose interpretation is doubtful, one has

[1] Exact figures cannot always be given, for some entries may merely be corruptions of names occurring elsewhere in the lists. This is especially likely in the marginalia, which are often in most illiterate handwriting.

about 272 names of Continental[1] origin, in 1221 entries, 185 Old English names in 548 entries, and 123 Scandinavian names in 236 entries, not including those names, originally Scandinavian, that occur in a form showing Continental influence. Though we may assume that in general each entry represents a separate individual, and therefore these statistics are free from one difficulty besetting the use of some types of records, I doubt whether general statistics of this sort are of much use. It is more interesting to watch the changing proportions as the period advances. In the lists which contain no Continental names, and are presumably pre-Conquest, there are 85 Scandinavian names to 58 Old English, i.e. approximately 60 per cent Scandinavian. As we shall see later, this preponderance may not fairly represent the nomenclature of the district, for it includes a list of 35 Scandinavian names for whose presence in our text I shall have another explanation to offer. Even ignoring these the proportion of Scandinavian names is considerable. From the point where Norman names begin to occur, the proportions are as follows: (a) early post-Conquest—10 per cent Scandinavian, 45 per cent OE, 45 per cent Continental, *i.e.* the native and naturalised element is still in excess of the Continental.

(b) early twelfth century—7 per cent Scandinavian, 26 per cent OE, 67 per cent Continental, *i.e.* two thirds are Continental.

(c) the second half of the twelfth century—3 per cent Scandinavian, 16 per cent OE, 81 per cent Continental.

(d) late twelfth century, or very early thirteenth—little more than 1 per cent Scandinavian, about 4 per cent OE, nearly 95 per cent Continental. These figures are necessarily approximate only, as names of uncertain origin are excluded, but they are sufficient to show the

[1] Using this term to cover all names first introduced from the Continent, no matter what their remote origin may be.

rapidly growing popularity of Continental names among the classes of society represented in these lists.

Here, I am concerned merely with the 123 Scandinavian names and some problematic names that may possibly have this origin. By far the most interesting set of names occurs on fol. 10r, and it will be well to examine this page more closely. It begins with the kings Cnut, Harold and Hardecnut, Queen *Imma, et Ælfʒifa,* whom the BM Catalogue assumes to be Cnut's concubine, the mother of his sons Sweyn and Harold; but I do not consider this identification certain, for Emma received the name Ælfgifu when she came to England on her marriage with Ethelred. The original list may have had *Ælfʒifa* as a gloss to *Imma,* and the copyist may have taken it as another name. Æthelnoth, Archbishop of Canterbury, 1020-1038, and Ætheric, either the Bishop of Dorchester, 1016-1034, or, less probably, the Bishop of Selsey, *circa* 1032-1038, follow, and then immediately we get four bishops from the very end of the century, Remigius of Dorchester (afterwards Lincoln), 1067-1092, Herbert of Thetford (afterwards Norwich), 1091-1119, Wulfstan of Worcester, 1062-1095, and Robert, who may be the Bishop of Hereford, 1079-1095, or Remigius's successor in Lincoln, 1094-1123, or the Bishop of Lichfield, 1086-1117. The most probable explanation of this jump from the ecclesiastics of Cnut's reign to those of the first Norman kings is that the compiler had some lists referring to the reigns of the Danish kings, but little from the years between these and his own day.[1] We get the same impression from his list of earls later on. After the bishops come the names of the abbots of Thorney from *Godemannus* to *Gunterius,* omitting Leofwine II, and placing *Fulcardus,* whom Lanfranc deposed in favour of Gunterius, after the latter and without the title of abbot. The BM

[1] Miss D. M. B. Ellis has suggested to me that the omission of the magnates of the Confessor's reign may have been deliberate, due to the monks' dislike of the abbey's subjection to the pluralist abbot, Leofric of Peterborough.

Catalogue is without doubt right in taking the forty-three[1] men's names that follow, without titles, to be those of the community of Thorney. Norman names occur among them, showing that the list is post-Conquest, probably contemporary with the writing. Next come four abbots, *Gosbertus* (of Battle, 1076-1095), *Æʒelsi* (of Ramsey, 1080-1087), *Balduuinus* (of Bury St. Edmunds, 1065-1097), and *Toroldus* (of Peterborough, 1069-1098), and this list originally ended, at the top of column 2, with some prelates of various periods, i.e. Archbishop *Leuinʒ* (of Canterbury, 1013-1020), Ægelric, perhaps the Bishop of Durham, 1042-1056, Randulf *passe flambardus*, (Bishop of Durham, 1099-1128), *Eziʒ* (i.e. Eadsige, Archbishop of Canterbury from 1038 to 1050, but suffragan bishop before this), and two Archbishops of York,[2] Ælfric (1023-1051), and *Kynsi* (1051-1060). The rest of the column was left blank, presumably for later ecclesiastics to be added, lay magnates being left to the third column. The blank space was later filled in with Norman names.

Column 3 originally began with a list of Cnut's earls, *Turkil, Hacun, Eoric, Eʒlaf, 7 his broðer Vlf,* all except the last with the title *comes*. Later, as an afterthought, the scribe added above the column *Walðef comes* and his wife, and *Siwardus comes*. The latter is the only earl between Cnut's reign and the earldom of Waltheof (1065-1076) to occur here, and he is mentioned only because he is Waltheof's father. There is therefore a similar gap to that in the lists of bishops; there is no other trace of the great magnates of the Confessor's reign; not only the house of Godwine, but also that of Leofric of Mercia, is entirely unrepresented.

Cnut's earls are all well known from Scandinavian sources,[3] and in English records they appear in the Chronicle

[1] Not thirty-three, as stated in the BM Catalogue.

[2] Both of these were buried at the neighbouring monastery of Peterborough.

[3] For accounts of them see A. S. Napier and W. H. Stevenson, *The Crawford Collection of Early Charters and Documents*, pp. 139ff, and L. M. Larson, *Canute the Great*, passim.

and as witnesses to charters, but I know of no other record of them in confraternity with a religious house. In view of what the sagas tell us of Eric it is particularly interesting to find him here. He helped his father, Earl Hakon the Bad, to defeat the *Jómsvíkingar* at Hjörunga Bay in 986, where the victory was won, according to Scandinavian tradition, by Hakon's sacrificing a younger son to the gods at the critical moment.[1] Eric himself is said to have vowed to accept Christianity if victorious at Svǫldr (1000),[2] and, though he does not appear as a strenuous advocate of the new faith in his rule in Norway,[3] the sagas say that he died, of an unsuccessful operation, either just before or just after a pilgrimage to Rome. Their dating of this occurrence (shortly after Cnut had won England) is contradicted by the evidence of charters, which Eric witnesses as late as 1023. He had been made Earl of Northumbria by Cnut in 1016. The form in which his name occurs in this manuscript is puzzling. He is called in other English records *Iric, Yric, Yrc, Eiric*, etc., which led the editors of the *Crawford Charters* to suggest an original **Ýríkr*, later displaced by the common name *Eiríkr*, but Dr. von Feilitzen[4] considers ON **Øyríkr*, **Eyríkr* (OSw. *Ø̄rīk*) more probable. This diphthong normally appears in ME as *ei*, but in OE *y* occurs and there appear to be several instances of *e* (see infra p. 137).[5] The *Eoric* of this list might support the second theory, for *eo* could represent ON *ø*, as it is thought that the OE diphthong *eo* had become monophthongised to *ö* by about 1000.[6] The matter is, however, complicated by the occurrence of *Eoric* in the D version of the Chronicle 905, where the

[1] See *Jómsvíkinga Saga, Flateyjarbók* I, 191f.

[2] *Saga Óláfs konungs Tryggvasonar* (*Fornmanna Sögur* II), cap. 253.

[3] *Heimskringla* ed. Finnur Jónsson (København 1911), p. 181.

[4] *Op. cit.* p. 299.

[5] On its representation as *oe* in Northumbrian *floege* see R. Jordan, *Handbuch der mittelenglischen Grammatik*, § 130. 2 and note, and a forthcoming article by A. S. C. Ross.

[6] K. Luick, *Historische Grammatik der englischen Sprache*, § 357, note 7.

A text has *Eohric*, as the name of a Danish king of East Anglia. Björkman[1] suggests as a possible explanation of this name an anglicising of an ON **Jóríkr*, and if this is correct the identity in form with the Thorney name is perhaps accidental. Björkman admits, however, that the king may have been called *Eiric*, but does not explain the connection between this and the forms in the Chronicle. Is it possible that there was current, at least in East Anglia and Cambridgeshire, an OE **Eo(h)rīc*[2] which was substituted in these cases for an unfamiliar ON name **Øyríkr* ?

The *Hacun* who precedes *Eoric* in this list is his son, who came to England about 1017, having been driven out of Norway by St. Olaf. He was made earl by Cnut, of Worcester according to a charter of doubtful authenticity (KCD 757), and his signatures occur in 1019 and from 1023-1026. KCD 744, which contains his signature, is dated 1031, but other witnesses show that it cannot be later than 1027. He was made viceroy of Norway in 1028, and was drowned in the Pentland Firth in 1030.

Turkil, who heads the list, is Thorkell the Tall, son of Strút-Haraldr and brother of Sigvaldi the chief of the *Jómsvíkingar*, and he played a prominent part in the events of Ethelred's reign. After Cnut's accession he was made earl of East Anglia. He was exiled in 1021, and, though he and Cnut were later reconciled, he was apparently not restored to his English office.

Eȝlaf comes 7 his broðer Vlf are prominent figures in the Old Norse records. They were sons of Thorgils Sprakkaleggr, and Eilaf was in charge of the *þingamannalið* in London, escaping the massacre after Sweyn's death because he was forewarned by a man called *Þórðr*.[3] As *dux* he witnesses charters from 1018-1024. A charter

[1] *Nordische Personennamen in England*, p. 36.

[2] Professor Dickins has pointed out that it would correspond to Greek *Hippocrates* and Gaulish *Epo(redo)rix*.

[3] *Flateyjarbók* I, 203f.

which connects him with Gloucester survives only in a very late form,[1] yet his interference in Wales[2] also suggests authority over some part of West Mercia. He may have been succeeded by Leofric, whose first appearance as ealdorman is in an undated charter whose other witnesses belong to 1023-1024.[3] Ulf is the earl who became viceroy of Denmark in 1025 or 1026, and was murdered in the church of Roskilde at Cnut's instigation about 1027. He had married Cnut's sister Ástríðr and their son Sven later became King of Denmark. He signs as *eorl, dux,* in English charters between 1020 and 1024, but I do not know what province, if any, he held in England. Neither brother appears in England after 1024. The sagas say that Eilaf went to Constantinople, and, though they are wrong in placing this immediately after Sweyn's death, it may be true of a later date.

After the earls comes another identifiable figure, Osgot Clapa, a prominent thegn of the eleventh century, who was exiled in 1046, tried to return with a fleet in 1049, and died in 1054.[4] He is connected with the eastern counties in Hermann's *De Miraculis S. Eadmundi.* The *Toui* who follows in the list may be Tofi the Proud,[5] who, rather late in life, married Osgot's daughter, Gytha, in 1042. It was at their marriage feast that Hardecnut was taken suddenly ill, and died soon afterwards. Tofi was the founder of the first church at Waltham Holy Cross, Essex.

The list of names that comes next is the most interesting in the manuscript. While the whole of this column has a preponderance of Scandinavian names that is really remarkable (68 ON: 10 OE), it is even more striking that thirty-one ON names follow those of the earls before one

[1] KCD 1317, from the *Historia Monasterii S. Petri Gloucestriæ.*

[2] *Crawford Charters, loc. cit.,* L. M. Larson, in *American Historical Review,* xv, 727; W. J. Rees, *Lives of the Cambro-British Saints,* p. 77, where, styled *vicecomes,* he invades Glamorgan.

[3] KCD 1324. See also A. J. Robertson, *Anglo-Saxon Charters* pp. 412f.

[4] Anglo-Saxon Chronicle CD. See also my *Anglo-Saxon Wills,* p. 196.

[5] *Ibid.,* p. 186.

has a single OE name.[1] Miss Jørgensen takes the preponderance of ON names on this folio to indicate close Scandinavian settlement of the area immediately surrounding Thorney, but, without quarrelling with this general thesis, I would suggest that this exclusively Scandinavian list is capable of another explanation. I certainly know no list like it in English sources.[2] It is unlikely that the monks of Thorney would deliberately have sorted their benefactors according to nationality. May we not have in this list the following of one or more of the Danish magnates who head the column—a list of something in the nature of a *þingamannalið*? There is a complete absence of women's names that supports this suggestion, and it is tempting to suppose that the list was originally drawn up on the visit of one, or some, of these Danish chiefs to the monastery. This would not be without parallel elsewhere in this manuscript, where entries such as *Simon comes et omnes qui cum eo uenerunt*, or *Emma mater Alani de Perci . . . et omnes qui cum illa fuerunt*, occur; and a group of names on fol. 2v can be shown by comparison with the Red Book of Thorney to consist of the relatives, living or dead, of *Adelizia* (of Clermont), followed by the names of the persons who witness her donation to Thorney in the Red Book, and in the same order, so that one can hardly doubt that the whole group was entered in the *Liber Vitae* on the occasion of this donation. Perhaps another argument in favour of taking this list of Scandinavian names to represent a retinue, rather than the local settlers, is that the less common names in it do not occur among the signatures to

[1] I include *Guðmund* as ON, for though it could be OE, the much greater frequency of this name in the Danelaw than elsewhere suggests that its chief source of origin is ON *Guðmundr*.

[2] One may, however, compare the short list of persons in confraternity with Christ Church, Canterbury, on fol. 43b of MS Royal I.D. ix, to which Professor Dickins has called my attention. This mentions King Cnut, his brother Harold and, after a gap of two and a half lines, *Đorð*, *Kartoca*, *Thuri*. The gap was perhaps meant to be filled with the names of Cnut's earls.

eleventh-century charters, suggesting that at any rate we have not the more important landowners.[1] Nothing, of course, can be argued from the occurrence of very common names in both types of source.

Such common names occurring in the list are *Ulf, Turkyl, Sweʒn, Toui, Đolf, Askyl, Toki, Asbern, Đorð* and *Manni*. Rather less common are *Guðmund, Steʒn, Barð,* and *Scul,*[2] while *Scum* (ON *Skúmr*) has hitherto been recorded in the LVD, (as *Skumar*), and *Epi* (ODan. *Ø̄pi*) only in Domesday Book. *Owði* (ON *Auði*) and *Illhuge* (ON *Ill(h)ugi*) do not occur in other English records, though the former is postulated for the place-names Oadby, Leics., and Oby, Norfolk, and familiarity with the latter seems implied in the existence of the name *Godhuge,*[3] which must surely be formed in contrast to it. *Einder* is another name that is very rare in England, if I interpret it correctly. It is, I believe, an East Scandinavian form of *Eyvindr,* which appears in later times as *Ø̄nder*. Already on runic monuments in Denmark and Sweden one gets forms with loss of *v* and syncopation.[4] The retention of the *-r* of the ON nominative has parallels elsewhere in this manuscript. In England the name has previously been recorded only in the LVD, in the unsyncopated form *Æiuind*. Another peculiar form in the list is *Fresti,* which I believe to be an error for *Frestin,* with omission of the nasal mark above the *i,* and this I would take to represent OWN *Freysteinn,* ODan. OSw. *Frøstēn*. The *i,* for *ei,* in the second element is parallel to that in *Justin* (ON *Jósteinn*), and there are a number of recorded instances in England of *e* as the representative of *øy*.[5] The

[1] Only *Osgot Clapa* can be identified with certainty.

[2] For the form without a final *e* see von Feilitzen, *op. cit.* pp. 71f. Another example occurs in DCh.

[3] In D. C. Douglas, *Feudal Documents from the Abbey of Bury St. Edmunds* (British Academy Records of the Social and Economic History of England and Wales 8), p. 36.

[4] E.g. L. F. A. Wimmer, *De danske Runemindesmærker* III. 127, IV. lxxviii.

[5] I.e. OE *fēsian, ēre* (ON *feysa, eyrir*; see Luick, § 384. 4), *Lesing* in DB

name is very common in East Scandinavian. If this interpretation be rejected, we should perhaps consider an ON **Freistingr*, which Lindkvist[1] suggests as the first element in Fraisthorpe, Yorks, but *i* instead of *ing* is difficult to account for.[2] *Blihswegn*, while obviously Scandinavian, is not recorded in Scandinavia nor in England. *Blih* occurs in the list of *festermen* of Archbishop Ælfric of York[3] and represents ON *Blígr*, 'the staring one,' and *Blihswegn* may be a compound from this similar to the *Arkilbar*, *Gamelbern* etc. of Domesday Book, perhaps with the same meaning. One may also compare the Old English habit of putting *cild* after a name e.g. *Ælfric cild*. Otherwise one must regard the first element as descriptive, added to the name *Sveinn*, as in *Rauðsveinn* etc.[4]

Finally there are two patronymics that require comment, *Asbern Haces sunu* and *Đorð clapes sunu*. *Haces* may be from ON *Hákr*, a byname that occurs in Haxby, Yorks,[5] or from ON *Háki*, for the strong declension was spreading at the expense of the weak, and *clapes* is probably the ON byname *Klápr*, though it too could be from a weak name like the *Clapa* above. It is not necessary

(ON *leysingr*; see von Feilitzen, *op. cit.* p. 319), *hernes*, (*Havelok*, l. 1917, from ON *heyrn*; see G. V. Smithers in RES xiii, pp. 458ff). Some of these have been explained as due to English analogies, but it is strange that there should be so many instances unless the umlaut of ON *au* can appear as *ē* in English. For its appearance as OE *oe* (which would give ME *ē*) see p.133 note and authorities there cited.

1 *Middle English Place-Names of Scandinavian Origin*, p. 45. See also A. H. Smith, *The Place-Names of the East Riding of Yorkshire* (English Place-Name Society xiv), p. 87.

2 In cases such as *Hunni* beside *Hunning* there is a dissimilatory loss of *n* for which there is no reason here.

3 Ed. by Dr. Jón Stefánsson in *Saga-Book* iv; by E. Björkman in *Festschrift für Lorenz Morsbach*; by W. H. Stevenson in EHR xxvii; and by W. Farrer in *Yorkshire Charters* I, No. 9.

4 There is the further possibility that the copyist read two names as one, but normally his word-division is accurate.

5 *The Place-Names of the North Riding of Yorkshire* (English Place-Name Society v), p. 14, where reference is made to a personal name *Haac* in Lincolnshire in the early thirteenth century.

to assume that these names were used as personal names and not bynames here, for patronymics can be instanced in which only the byname of the father is mentioned.[1]

There is a marked East Scandinavian character about this list. *Manni* and *Epi* are recorded in East Norse only, *Toui* and *Toki* are essentially East Norse names, *Eȝlaf* and, if correctly interpreted, *Fresti* and *Einder* are in East Norse form. No name in this list is specifically West Norse, though, of course, many could be either East or West.

If there is anything in my suggestion that these men are followers of the earls, rather than landowners round Thorney, it is tempting to try to identify them with persons known from Scandinavian records. Could *Đorð clapes sunu* be the man who warned Eilaf of the impending attack on the *þingamannalið* in London? Is Ulf the Swedish viking commemorated on the Orkestad stone who 'three times received *giald* in England; the first time Tosti paid him, then Thurkil, and finally Cnut'?[2] Is it the same Manni who is mentioned on the Valleberga stone in Denmark, which was raised by *Sven* and *Þorgøtr* in memory of *Manni* and *Sveni*, who were buried in London?[3] Is *Fresti* the *Fraystain* who raised the Sjælle stone in memory of his man *Gyrð*, who was slain in battle, perhaps in England?[4] But however tempting, such speculations are not very profitable, for they are incapable of proof. They could be multiplied. At least they indicate the close similarity between this list and the

[1] See O. Rygh in *Sproglige og historiske Afhandlinger viede Sophus Bugges Minde*, pp. 114f.

[2] O. von Friesen in *Fornvännen* 1909, pp. 58ff.

[3] L. F. A. Wimmer, *op. cit.* III, 167.

[4] *Ibid.* I, 146ff. The inscription is mutilated, but ends with a reference to the 'drengs on *Visepi*.' Wimmer suggests that this may refer to some battle in England and that the ending represents -(*h*)*æiði*. Perhaps it could refer to the heathlands north of Thetford, with reference to their nearness to the R. Wissey (OE *Wise*) and the battle might then be that against Ulfketel in 1004. *Gyrð*, who is called 'Sigvaldi's brother' may be a brother of Earl Thurkil.

nomenclature of the tenth- and eleventh-century runic monuments of Denmark and Sweden.

After *Đorð claþes sunu* comes the first mention of a woman and then follows the first English name. From this point the nature of the list changes; women occur frequently, English names soon predominate over Scandinavian, and some of the persons mentioned can be identified with people in other English sources, especially with landowners in the neighbourhood. Thus *Turkyl Hoȝe* is clearly the *Þurkyl hoga* who witnesses a charter of Cnut's in 1024,[1] and another *Turkil,* followed immediately by *Turgund,* has been plausibly identified by Miss Jørgensen with Turkil of Harringworth, Northants, whose wife Thurgunt gave an estate at Sawtry to Ramsey Abbey during Ælfwine's abbacy (1043-1080). The Red Book of Thorney has an account of his dealings with Thorney.[2] He had held six hides at Conington belonging to Thorney, at a *caritas* of one mark of gold per annum. Domesday Book[3] gives the additional information that he held it on condition that it should revert to the abbey on his death, and with it three hides that he himself possessed in the same place. Such agreements were common in the eleventh century. According to the Red Book, Turkil left his lands[4] in the unsettled years after Hastings and went over to 'the Danes who were his kinsmen,' presumably at the time of Sweyn Estrithson's invasion in September, 1069. The king gave his estates, including Thorney's six hides, to Earl Waltheof, who was willing to return them to the abbey when the position was explained to him, but the monks preferred that he should hold them

[1] KCD 741. It is a grant to the Danish thegn *Orc,* founder of Abbotsbury.

[2] Dugdale, *Monasticon* (London, 1817-1827), II, 604. [3] Fol. 208 a and b.

[4] He held Fotheringhay, Harringworth, Lilford and some smaller estates in Northants, Sawtry, Conington (now in Cambs.) and Leighton Bromswold (where he is called 'the Dane') in Hunts. See DB I, fol. 206b, 228a and b, 229, and *VCH. Hunts* I, 327, 330. According to the Sawtry foundation charter (Dugdale, V. 522) he had received Sawtry from Cnut.

on the same terms as Turkil, for they were afraid that Abbot Fulcard would otherwise hand them over to one of his own relations. After Waltheof's death, however, his widow paid no rent and the estate was lost to the abbey.

I suspect also that the *Vuah* in my lists is the same as a certain *Wach* who is a donor to Ramsey in the *Historia* of this abbey.[1] The name is OEN runic *Ufagʀ* corresponding to ON *Ófeigr*, and it occurs in Domesday Book as *Unfac*. The Ramsey scribe has assumed that *uu* equals *w*, whereas in this case it is for *uv*. On a later folio of the Thorney lists we get *Unfef*, which may perhaps be an error for *Unfeg*, which would be an anglicised form of *Ófeigr*.

Ramsey Abbey had a benefactor called *Jol*,[2] and a little later is mentioned a *Scheldwara*, though she is not connected with *Iol*. Yet, as neither name is common, one seems justified in comparing *Iol 7 his wif Scelduuere* on fol. 9v of my text. *Scelduuere* is ON *Skialdvǫr*, which has hitherto been known in England only from a Domesday instance, which may refer to the same person, as it relates to Lincolnshire. *Seldwar* in the Lincolnshire Assize Roll of 1206[3] and *Sieldeware* (of Belaugh near Norwich) in the *Life and Miracles of St. William of Norwich*[4] clearly represent the same name. *Iol*[5] could be a strong variant of ON *Ióli*, but the Ramsey benefactor occurs in the cartulary of the abbey as *Johol, Jool*, as well as *Jol*, of Lincoln. This looks like the Breton *Juhel*, but may possibly be a later scribe's substitution for an unfamiliar ON name. The Ramsey cartulary says he

[1] *Chronicon Abbatiæ Rameseiensis* (RS), ed. W. D. Macray, p. 199.

[2] *Ibid. loc. cit.*

[3] *The Earliest Lincolnshire Assize Rolls*, ed. D. M. Stenton (Lincoln Record Society 22), p. 277.

[4] Ed. A. Jessopp and M. R. James, p. 226.

[5] It occurs as *Yol, Jol*, on pp. 84, 86 of *Transcripts of Charters relating to Gilbertine Houses*, ed. F. M. Stenton (Lincoln Record Society 18), who has also supplied me with a Yorkshire instance, *Tomas filius Yol*, in Pipe Roll 36, p. 69.

died in 1051,[1] but as it dates the Ealdorman Brihtnoth's death 1029 one cannot place much reliance on its dates.

As there is no other group of names in the manuscript with a general interest of this kind, it will be enough to extract the Scandinavian names. My first list[2] consists of names that are dealt with in E. Björkman, *Nordische Personennamen in England*, and, unless otherwise stated, are fairly common in English sources.

Aȝamundus: ON Ǫgmundr
Aki: ODan. Āki
Anandus: ON Ǫnundr
Arketelus: ON Arnkell, ODan. Arnketil
Asa (2): ON Ása f.
Asæ, Ase: ON Ási m, or ON Ása f.[3]
Asbern (2):[4] ON Ásbiǫrn
Asȝær: ON Ásgeirr
Askyl, Askillus, Aschillus, Askitillus:[5] ON Áskell
Atsere:[6] ON Ǫzurr
Barð: ON Bárðr
Bounde: ON Bóndi
Broþter:[7] (?) ON Bróðir
Eȝlaf (2), Æȝlif: ODan. OSw. Ēlāf, (beside OWN Eileifr); OWN Eilífr, a variant of the preceding name.
Einder:[8] ODan. Ø̄nder (OWN Eyvindr)
Eoric: ON Eiríkr or *Øyríkr[9]

[1] *Cartularium Monasterii de Rameseia* (RS), ed. W. H. Hart and P. A. Lyons, III, 167.

[2] Scandinavian names are quoted in an Old West Scandinavian form, unless they are recorded only in East Scandinavian, or unless there is a significant difference between the dialects. The order is alphabetical except that *c* is entered with *k*, and *u* and *v* are put together. Figures in brackets signify the number of occurrences in this text. *Wynn* is replaced by *w*.

[3] The bearers of the name in the form *Asa* are shown to be women in the text.

[4] Besides *Osbernus* (20), which may be a Normanised form, or OG.

[5] Besides the Normanised forms *Ansketillus*, etc.

[6] The final *e*, which occurs elsewhere in versions of this name in England, is due to analogy with English names in -(*h*)*ere*.

[7] Probably an error for *Broþer*.

[8] See p. 137.

[9] See pp. 133 f.

Epi:[1] ODan. Ø̄pi
Erberni (gen.): ON Arnbiǫrn
Farman: ON Farmann
Faðer: ODan. Father, OSw. Fadhir
Gamel: ON Gamall
Gihta:[2] ON Gyða f.
Grimketelus, Grinkel: ON Grímkell (from -ketill)
Gudredus: ON Guðrøðr
Gudrun: ON Guðrún f.
Gunnar: ON Gunnarr
Gunni: ON Gunni
Gunnild(a) (7): ON Gunnhildr f.
Gunuwara, Gunuuere, Gunnor[3] (2): ON Gunnvǫr, ODan. Gunwor, Gunnur f.
Guðferð, Gudford: ON Guðfrøðr
Guþrum: ON Guðþormr
Hacun (2): ON Hákon
Halden, Alden: ON Halfdan, ODan. OSw. Hal(f)dan
Hamund: ON Hámundr
Hardecnut:[4] ODan. Harthaknūt
Harold(us) (5): ON Haraldr
Hauegrim: ON Hafgrímr
Helȝi: ON Helgi
Huscarl: ON Húskarl[5]
Ingerith, Iggeriða: ON Ingiríðr f.
Iware: ON Ívarr[6]
Ketel, Kitel: ON Ketill
Ketelbern: ON Ketilbiǫrn

[1] Previously recorded only in DB.
[2] For *Githa*.
[3] This form occurs in Normandy also
[4] Only as the king's name here.
[5] As a personal name recorded only in Sweden.
[6] With final *e* due to analogy with OE names in *-ere, -ware*. In this form it occurs also in the *Register of the Abbey of St. Benet at Holme*, ed. J. R. West (Norfolk Record Society), p. 90, and as *Yware* in the Anglo-Saxon Chronicle 1070E.

Ketelho:[1] ODan. Kætelǿgh, OSw. Kætillǿgh f.
Cnut:[2] ON Knútr
Colbeȝn: ON Kolbeinn
Langliue: ON Langlíf f.
Manni: ODan. Manni, OSw. Manne
Orm (3): ON Ormr
Osgodus (2), Osgot (2), Oseȝod: ON Ásgautr
Oþild:[3] ON Auðhildr f.
Oðin: ON Auðun, ODan. Ø̄thin, OSw. Ø̄dhin
Raganild, Ragenild(a) (2), Raganid: ON Ragnhildr f.
Raganoldus, Raunaldus: ON Rǫgnvaldr
Sæȝrim: ODan. Sēgrīm
Sarle:[4] ON Sǫrli
Sigerit:[5] ON Sigríðr f.
Sistricus: ON Sigtryggr
Siuad: ON Sighvatr
Siwarth:[6] ODan. Sigwarth
Scelduuere:[7] ON Skialdvǫr f.
Scul, Scule:[8] ON Skúli
Scum:[9] ON Skúmr
Steȝn: ON Steinn
Stiȝand: ON Stígandr
Suardebrant:[10] ON *Svartbrandr
Sumerlede: ON Sumarliði

[1] Probably for *Keteloh*; the name is only later borrowed into Norway, as *Ketillaug*. Another possibility is that it is *Ketel* with a nickname attached, in which case *ho* could be ON *hár*, whether as the noun 'dogfish' (cf. *Thurketel Heyng* 'salmon' in my *Anglo-Saxon Wills*, p. 180), or the adjective 'the tall.'

[2] Only as the king's name here.

[3] Björkman, *op. cit.* p. 182. He only knows one example, *Outhild* in a Lincoln obituary. Professor Stenton has called my attention to an *Outhilda* in *Catalogue of Ancient Deeds in the Public Record Office*, D 1137 (about 1215).

[4] Whereas *Serlo* (2) is more probably Continental.

[5] Unless an error for *Sigeric*.

[6] Beside *Siward(us)* (5), which could be OE.

[7] See p. 141. [8] See p. 137. [9] See p. 137.

[10] To the instances in Björkman can be added *Suartebrand* the priest in *Registrum Antiquissimum* (Lincoln Record Society 27), I, 286 and *Swartebrand Svortebrand* in *The Earliest Lincolnshire Assize Rolls*, pp. 165, 254, 273.

Swartinȝ:[1] ON Svertingr, ODan. OSw. Swærting, OSw. Swarting

Sweȝen (3), Sweȝn (3), Suein, Suuein, Suenus, Sweng, Swanus:[2] ON Sveinn, O Dan. Svēn

Ðolf: ON Þólfr

Ðorir (2), Thuri (2), Turi, Thurius:[3] ON Þórir

Ðorð, Thorð (2): ON Þórðr

Ðurȝær, Turȝær, Turgarus: ON Þorgeirr

Toki (2), Toky (3), Toke, Tochi: ODan. Tōki[4]

Toroldus (7), Toraldus, Turold:[5] ON Þóraldr

Toui (6), Touius: ODan. Tōfi[4]

Tura: ON Þóra f.

Turbærn: ON Þorbiǫrn

Turȝod(us)[5] (2): ON Þorgautr

Turȝysle: ON *Þorgisli

Turkil (2), Turkyl (5), Turkyll: ON Þorkell

Turstan(us) (8), Thurstanus:[6] ON Þorsteinn

Turuer: ON *Þorfrøðr

Ulf (9): ON Ulfr

Vlfketel (2), Wlketel(us) (5) Wfketelus, Vlfkil, Vlfkel: ON Ulfkell (from -ketill)

Vnspac: ON Óspakr

Vuah, Vnfef (?):[7] Runic ODan. OSw. Ufagʀ., ON Ófeigr

Vui: ON Úfi

Walðef: ON Valþiófr

Westmanus:[8] ON Vestmaðr

[1] On the *a* in this name see von Feilitzen, p. 381.

[2] This last form is anglicised and latinised like *Turgarus* and *Thurstanus*.

[3] Björkman takes *Thuri* as equivalent to *Þórir*, but it appears to have been used sometimes as a short name for compounds in *Thur-*, e.g. in *An Outline Itinerary of Henry I*, ed. W. Farrer, p. 79 (also EHR xxxiv, 381), where *Turi* refers to Archbishop Thurstan of York.

[4] Later taken into West Scandinavian.

[5] These names were common in Normandy, and some, at least, of the bearers of them here were Normans.

[6] This is partly anglicised. There is also the form *Turstin* (2), probably Norman, and two corrupt forms, *Thurthanus* and *Tursthana*.

[7] See p. 141. [8] Previously recorded only in DB.

The foregoing list does not include names which may be Old English or Scandinavian. *Alger* could be ON *Alfgeirr* or OE *Ælfgar*; *Æiulf*, ON *Eyiolfr* or OE *Æþelwulf*.[1] *Almoth* suggests ON *Qlmóðr*, but the archdeacon who bears the name appears in two other sources as *Almod*, which is probably OE *Æþelmōd*. *Botild* may be the OE name *Bōthild* occurring in the early names in the LVD, but it is not recorded later in OE, whereas the corresponding ON *Bóthildr* is common in Scandinavian, and in Middle English the name is common in the eastern counties.[2] *Duua*, *Duue*, can be derived either from OE **Dūfe* or ON *Dúfa*,[1] *Hereward* from OE **Hereweard* or ON *Hervarðr*, *Hilda* from OE *Hild* or ON *Hildr*, though it must be noted that there seems to be no record of the use of the English name after the seventh century. One cannot tell whether *Mannus* is latinised from OE *Mann*, *Manna*, or ODan. *Manni*. The locality of the recorded instances of *Milda*, apparently a latinised form of a feminine name, occurring twice in our text, would favour a derivation from ON *Mildr* rather than OE **Milde*.[1] Other ambiguous names are *Osmundus* (OE *Ōsmund* or ON *Ásmundr*),[1] *Sigar* (OE *Sigegār* or ON *Sigarr*), *Simund* (OE *Sigemund* or ON *Sigmundr*), *Siward* (OE *Sigeweard* or ODan. *Sigvarth*), and *Tummes* in *Ringolf Tummes sunu* (OE *Tumma* or ON *Tumi*). *Sælide* is brought by Dr. von Feilitzen from either an OE **Sǣlida* or an ON **Sæliði*.[3] The latter is the more probable, as the element *-liði* enters into several ON names.[4] On *Guðmund* see p. 136 note.

[1] These names are discussed by von Feilitzen, *op. cit.*

[2] In this text it occurs four times.

[3] P. 353. The name occurs twice in our text and Professor Dickins has supplied another unrecorded instance in an unprinted Ely kalendar of the twelfth century (Trinity College Cambridge, MS O. 2.1).

[4] Note especially *Hafliði* with the same meaning as **Sæliði*.

Similarly, the following have been excluded because they may be Continental: *Fulco*, which occurs nine times, is probably the OG name; derivation from ON *Fólki* is possible for *Folke*, *Folch*, each of which occurs once; *Germund* can be OG or else ON *Geirmundr*; *Gunfridus* is more probably OG *Gunfrid* (< *Gundefrid*) than ON **Gunnfrøðr*; *Hunger* may be ON *Húngeirr* or OG *Hunger*, *Osbernus* either OG *Osbern* or an anglicised or normanised ON *Ásbiǫrn*,[1] *Rimild* either ON *Hrímhildr* or OG *Rimenhild*, *Rimhildis*, etc.

There remain to be considered some names whose Scandinavian origin is certain and which are not in Björkman;

Agga: ODan. *Aggi*. The replacing of the original ending by the *-a* of the OE weak declension is common. The name occurs also in the Lincs. Assize Roll of 1202[2] and in the Red Book of Thorney, where *Agge of Levering-ton* is probably the same man as the one in our list.

Anlef, (wife of *Turi welþ*), presumably represents an unrecorded ON **Óleif*, with the common anglicising of *Ó-* to *An-*. The element *-leif* occurs in the feminine names *Ingi-*, *Arn-*, *Ásleif*. The normal ON feminine name is *Ólǫf*, which corresponds to the masculine *Óláfr*, a variant of *Óleifr*.

Ape:[3] ODan. *Api*, OSw. *Ape*. This occurs in DB and probably in the *Oslacus filius Appen* of the *Historia Eliensis*.[4]

Batswegen: ON **Bátsveinn*. As a personal name this has only once been recorded in England, as *Batsuen* in DB.

[1] See von Feilitzen, pp. 338f.

[2] Pp. 141, 143, 151f. Professor Stenton tells me it is common in unprinted Lincolnshire records. Cf. also Aggbrigg Wapentake, in the West Riding of Yorkshire.

[3] See Björkman, *Zur englischen Namenkunde*, p. 13.

[4] Ed. D. J. Stewart, Book ii, cap. 15.

Blac:[1] ON *Blakkr.* This name is also in DB.

Blihsweȝn: see p. 138.

Erkelbern: this is clearly the same name as the *Archilbar* which occurs once in DB, and very probably the same person is meant, for the DB reference is to a Lincolnshire landowner, and the entry in the Thorney list is *Godgiue . . . filia erkelbern* and she is wife of Reiner of Bath, sheriff of Lincoln in the early twelfth century. No Scandinavian equivalent is recorded, and Dr. von Feilitzen[2] takes it to be the ON *Arnkell* plus the byname *barn,* as in *Siward barn, Askilbar,* etc. The initial *E-* of our form shows the anglicising of *Arn-* to *Earn-*.

Fegge: ODan. *Fæggi.* This does not occur in pre-Conquest records, but is fairly common in the eastern counties later, occurring in 1142 in a Northamptonshire charter,[3] in 1147 in the *Registrum Antiquissimum* of Lincoln,[4] as a sub-tenant in Leicestershire in DB (TRW), and, as a surname, in the Lincolnshire Assize Rolls.[5]

Fresti: see pp. 137 f.

Freðegyst, Freþegist: ODan. *Fredegæst*:[6]

Haces (gen): see p. 138.

Holfriþ, Holfriðe: OSw. *Holmfrīðr* f. The *e* of the second example is the ME analogical ending of the nominative of a feminine noun, taken from the oblique cases. The loss of the *m* between consonants is normal. The name has hitherto not been recorded in England. It is worth noting that Earl Eilaf's wife bore it, and this may be the reason for its introduction into England.

Illhuȝe: see p. 137.

[1] See H. Kökeritz, " Notes on the Pre-Conquest Personal Names of Domesday Book," (*Namn och Bygd*, xxvi), p. 39.

[2] *Op. cit.*, p. 163.

[3] *Facsimiles of Early Charters from Northamptonshire Collections*, ed. F. M. Stenton (Northants Record Society 4), p. 3.

[4] III, 263.

[5] Pp. 116, 173.

[6] See von Feilitzen, *op. cit.*, p. 255.

Inger:[1] ON *Yngvarr.*

Ingoldus:[2] ON *Ingialdr.*

Inȝolf, Ingulfus:[3] ON *Ingolfr*, ODan. OSw. *Ingulf.*

Iol: see p. 141.

Clapes (gen.): see p. 138.

Osmoth (wife of Roger): ODan. Āsmōth f., hitherto recorded in England in DB only, as *Esmoda, Amod.*[4] It occurs also in the Red Book of Thorney, where an *Osmod*, wife of *Gobio*, is mentioned.

Owði: see p. 137.

Sæbern, Sebern: ON *Sæbiǫrn.* This was known to Björkman only as a surname in England. It occurs as *Sabern* in the *Historia Ramesiensis*, pp. 258, 265.

Sywate:[5] ON. **Sighvati. Siwate* occurs in the Gilbertine Charters[6] and in the *Life and Miracles of St. William of Norwich.*[7]

Sunhiue: ON *Sunnifa* f. This is recorded in DB, LVD, DCh. It was originally borrowed into ON from OE. See von Feilitzen, p. 378 and authorities there cited.

Sweȝninȝ: ON *Sveinungr.* It occurs once in DB and in the Lincs. Assize Roll of 1206.[8]

Tole: ODan. *Tōla* f. The wife of *Orc*, founder of Abbotsbury, bore this name and gave it to Tolpuddle, Dorset. It appears also in the Lincs. Assize Roll for 1208-1209.[9]

Turȝund: ON *Þorgunnr* f. On the ending *-nd* see A. Noreen, *Altschwedische Grammatik* § 340. 2b. A *Thurgunt* occurs in the *Historia Ramesiensis* and is probably the

[1] Björkman, *Zur englischen Namenkunde*, p. 49. It occurs in Normandy.

[2] See von Feilitzen, p. 297.

[3] Ibid. p. 298.

[4] Ibid., p. 168.

[5] Ibid., p. 363.

[6] *Transcripts of Charters relating to Gilbertine Houses*, ed. F. M. Stenton (Lincoln Record Society 18), p. 51.

[7] P. 181.

[8] P. 265.

[9] P. 283.

same person.[1] A *Thurgunda* in Derby is mentioned in Cotton Titus C ix, and another in Norfolk in the Feet of Fines, Norfolk.[2]

Yrr: This looks like the ON woman's name *Ýrr*, but in this list it is almost next to *Turkyl* and *Turgund* who were landowners in Sawtry, and we should perhaps compare the reference in the *Historia Ramesiensis*[3] to a *Tostius, frater Yri*, who gave land at Sawtry to Ramsey. In DB fol. 208b, the brother of this *Tosti* is called *Erik*. Is it possible that in *Yrr* we have a short form of the name *Iric, Yric*, which may represent an ON **Øyríkr* ?[4] Dr. von Feilitzen has suggested to me that *Yrr* is an error for *Yric*, and that *Yri* represents *Yric* with loss of *c* by scribal error or Anglo-Norman influence.

Yðun: ON *Iðunn* f. This name has not hitherto been recorded in England.

Finally, there are some more problematic names, for which ON origin is probable:

Ærli: if this is for ON *Erlingr*, the *-i* instead of *-ing* is difficult to account for.[5] Perhaps it is a short form.

Den, which occurs three times, may possibly be for *Dene*.

Elmi must surely be ON *Hialmi*. Loss of initial *h* is not uncommon, and *e* instead of the breaking diphthong is regular in ON loan-words into English.

Gussenib is probably ON *Gusir* with a nickname attached, perhaps 'nib,' 'beak.' See NED *s.v. nib* (earliest reference 1585), where MDan. *nibbe* is compared. See also S. Blöndal, *Islandsk-Dansk Ordbog s.v. nibba*.

Hamel, suspended by a stroke through the *l*, in *Turȝysle Hamel sune*, is most probably ON *Hamall*, not

[1] See p. 140.
[2] I owe these last two references to Professor Stenton.
[3] P. 175.
[4] See p. 133.
[5] See p. 138, note.

previously recorded in England, though the OE byname *hamel,* ' mutilated,'[1] or OE **Hamela,* presupposed in place-names,[2] are possibilities.

Lithewar could perhaps be ON *Liðvarðr,* with loss of dental after *r*[3] as in *Turver,* or an unrecorded ON **Liðvǫr* f.

Ostmud, corrected from *Osmud,* is perhaps ON *Austmundr,* which, however, occurs only as the name of a fictitious character in the *Sörla saga sterka.*[4]

Saforus may be a latinisation of ON *Sæfari,* which occurs in LVD, and in the Lincolnshire Assize Rolls.[5] In that case *o* is error for *a.*

Seforþ has a second element that looks like ON *-frøðr* (cf. *Gudford* and see von Feilitzen p. 256). No ON **Sæfrøðr* is recorded.[6] Possibly we have ON *Sigfrøðr,* with *e* instead of *i* as in DB *Seuuard,* etc.

Semild: the second element is *-mild,* which has not been noted as second element before, but which occurs also in *Meremild* in the Ramsey cartulary,[7] and in *Demilde* (dat) in the Lincolnshire Assize Roll of 1206.[8] Does the name represent *Sæmild* and is it formed in contrast to ON **Sægrímr* after *-grím* had been shortened to *-grim* and come to be interpreted as ' fierce ' ?

Siron could be ON *Sigrún,* f.

Siuerh is probably an error for *Siuerth, i.e.* OE *Sigefrið* or ON *Sigfrøðr,* which appears in DB as *Siuert*(*us*), *Siuerd.*

Sliki in *Willelmus filius Sliki,* a person also in the Red Book of Thorney, may represent the ON byname *Slíka.*

Swana is probably an anglicised form of ON *Sveini.*

[1] G. Tengvik, *English Bynames,* p. 317.
[2] *Place-Names of Bucks* (English Place-Name Society ii), *s.v. Hambleden.*
[3] See von Feilitzen, p. 99.
[4] *Fornaldar Sögur* III.
[5] Ed. D. M. Stenton, p. 135. See Björkman, *op. cit.* p. 115.
[6] Cf. OE. *Sǣfrið.*
[7] III, 310.
[8] *Op. cit.* p. 256.

Ðorcwer must be ON, with this first element, but what its second represents is very uncertain. If *c* is scribal error for *e*,[1] perhaps the whole is ON *Þorvǫrðr* (cf. *Þurwerd* in Björkman[2]), with loss of the dental through Anglo-Norman influence, or an unrecorded ON **Þorvér* (cf. ON *Guðvér*), though it is thought that *Þór-* plus this element gives *Þórir*.[3]

A disappointing feature of these Thorney lists is the rarity of nicknames. Though there are twenty-two Ælfrics, twenty-three Ælfgifus, twelve Thurstans and so on, the monks obviously felt that divine omniscience needed no bynames to distinguish individuals. So apart from patronymics, and Norman surnames, we have few bynames in this manuscript, and only a very small number have any claim to Scandinavian origin. *Turi welp'* might be called ' whelp ' in OE or ON, but if the suspension represents *er* here, as usual, it must be for the *r* of the ON nominative *hvelpr*.[4] There is also *Atsere hofð, i.e.* ON *hǫfuð*, and *Osgot clape,* whose nickname is generally compared with the ON byname *Klápr*, ' a coarse and rough fellow.'[5] *Tobbe,* added to the name *Vuluuine* might be a pet form of *Þorbiǫrn*.[6] *Duua,* the byname of a Leofric, could be either the OE or the ON for ' dove.'

With regard to the dialect provenance of some of these names, the East Scandinavian character of *Manni, Epi, Toki, Toui,* and of *Eȝlaf, Einder* and *Fresti,* has been

[1] A redundant *e* is often written after this element in English documents, e.g. *Þureferð* (Björkman, p. 155).

[2] P. 163.

[3] C. J. S. Marstrander, *Bidrag til det norske sprogs historie i Irland* p. 156; A. Noreen, *Altisländische und altnorwegische Grammatik*, § 235, 1(f).

[4] *Welp* occurs both as personal name and byname in DB. See von Feilitzen, p. 297.

[5] This name is discussed by Björkman, *op. cit.* pp. 81f, 212, by Finnur Jónsson in *Aarbøger for nordisk Oldkyndighed og Historie*, 1907, p. 334, by G. Tengvik, *Old English Bynames*, p. 303f.

[6] It still survives in Modern Icelandic.

pointed out above.[1] To these must be added *Agga*, *Aki*, *Api*, *Fađer*, *Fegge*, *Holfriđ(e)*, *Osmoth*, *Sæȝrim* and *Tola*. *Huskarl*, as a personal name, has been recorded in Sweden only. *Siward* is Danish in as far as it is not OE *Sigeweard*, and *Ketelho*, if for *Kætillǿgh*, represents an East Scandinavian name only later recorded in the West. *Cnut* and *Hardecnut* are of course Danish names, but they are used only of the kings here. Names that are on the other hand found in West Norse sources only are *Hauegrim*, *Scelduuere*, *Sumarlide*, *Sunhiue*, *Walđef*, *Yđun*, but, as Dr. von Feilitzen has pointed out, in view of the much richer records of West Scandinavian, one is hardly justified in assuming that names recorded only in these were never used in the East Scandinavian countries.

In conclusion, I should like to call attention to the way in which the Thorney lists support some general conclusions drawn by Professor Stenton from the nomenclature of the Danelaw Charters;[2] they prove the vitality of the ON system of naming shown by the large proportion of different names to the total number of instances, when compared with the OE names in this respect. If I may repeat the figures, the Thorney lists have only 185 OE names in 548 entries, whereas the 235 entries of ON names contain some 122 separate names. It would, however, be a mistake to consider the Old English system moribund. It is the tremendous popularity of names like *Godwine*, *Leofric*, etc. for men, and of names ending in *-gifu* for women, that lessens the proportion of names to entries to this extent. The less common names are by no means all of a conventional, stereotyped kind; many have considerable interest, and show that new names were being compounded even in this late period.

[1] P. 139.
[2] *Op. cit.* p. cxiii ff.

ADDENDA

Page references to the first edition of *English Historical Documents* can be altered to those of the new edition, as follows:

I 31 n.64: pp. 281, 284; II 8 n.4: pp. 479, 484, 486; 21 n.6: p. 906; 23 n.5: p. 905; III 71 n.4: pp. 128 and 281-4; 72 n.1: pp. 548-51; 79 n.6: p. 565; 80 n.1: p. 58; 85 n.2: p. 344, n.5; 87 n.2: p. 555; IV 247, n.94: pp. 431 f.; VII 129 n.20: p. 906; XL 57 n.2: pp. 471 f.; XIV 13 n.2: pp. 471-6; 32 n.5: pp. 830 f.; 33 n.1: pp. 861 f.; XV 231 n.84: pp. 471 f.

I P. 11 ll.25-7, and XII 438 n.4 Jost's edition, *Die "Institutes of Polity, Civil and Ecclesiastical"*, was published in Berne, 1959.

III P. 78 ll.4-15 As Oslac is mentioned as earl in Edgar's fourth law-code, and this was probably issued in 964, the Chronicle's date 966 for his accession cannot be accepted.

III P.79, n.6 In the second edition of my *English Historical Documents c. 500-1042*, p. 565, I withdrew my suggestion 'until Æthelred . . . '.

VI P.41 The plates referred to here have not been reproduced in this present volume. They showed the following works: Plate 1. 'Christ in Majesty', fol.11 from MS Cotton Tiberius C vi, in the British Library; Plate 2a. The Godwine Seal, c. 1000, in the British Museum. Illustrated in P. D. Kendrick, *Late Saxon and Viking Art*, London, 1949; Plate 2b. Triangular ivory panel with angels, c. 1000, in Winchester Museum. Illustrated in Kendrick, *op. cit.*; Plate 3. 'Christ in Majesty', Barnack, Northants. Illustrated in D. Talbot Rice, *English Art, 871-1100*, Oxford, 1952.

VIII P. 460 n.1 For this edition, see No. XIV.

XVII P. 138 ll. 7-8 It is not certain that the Ælfric whose *festermen* are listed was the archbishop of York of this name.

INDEX